Windows™ 3.1 Programming
for Mere Mortals

WOODY LEONHARD

Series Editor:

Andrew Schulman

Addison-Wesley Publishing Company

Reading, Massachusetts   Menlo Park, California
New York   Don Mills, Ontario   Wokingham, England
Amsterdam   Bonn   Sydney   Singapore   Tokyo   Madrid
San Juan   Paris   Seoul   Milan   Mexico City   Taipei

ISBN 0-201-60832-4

Series Editor: Andrew Schulman
Managing Editor: Amorette Pedersen
Production Editor: Andrew Williams
Set in 11-point ITC Galliard by Benchmark Productions

1 2 3 4 5 6 7 8 9 MW-9695949392
First Printing, April 1992

Dedicated to the Word for Windows Gadflies, Gadflits, and the denizens of CompuServe's MSAPP/12 and MSBASIC/5.

With a tip o' this Hacker's Hat to Andrew Schulman, Claudette Moore, Chris Williams and Amy Pedersen, who made it happen.

Special thanks to Linda, Justin and Sass, for giving me the time.

Contents

Acknowledgments

I'd like to thank all those who have contributed ideas, time, effort, code, solutions, and inspiration, to the enlightenment of this Mere Mortal.

Among those who have helped the most:

Vince Chen, Kate Edson, Nelson Ford, Keith Funk, Paul Friedman, Guy Gallo, James Gleick, Dennis Harrington, Lee Hudspeth, Laurel Lammers, T.J. Lee, George Mair, Taylor Maxwell, Mark Meyers, Hans Michna, Ellen Nagler, Sal Neuman, Mark Novisoff, Keith Pleas, Eileen Wharmby, Ted Young, Jonathan Zuck, and several more who must (regrettably) remain nameless.

If I've forgotten anyone, my sincere apologies!

Introduction

Do You Need This Book?

You finally figured out DOS, at least well enough to get some work done.

Maybe you can write .BAT files. Or you dug deep enough into 1-2-3 to get macros working. Perhaps you knock off dBASE or FoxPro programs with great relish. Or you might know how to make WordPerfect stand on its head with those {up 1} {down 2} custom macros.

No doubt you've seen a BASIC program—might have even written a couple of them, even if it was back in the days when all BASIC statements had those

```
00100 funky
00200 line
00300 numbers
```

and all the variable names looked like "X1" or "A$".

Now, all of a sudden, Windows has fallen into your lap; plop!, and you're wondering what in the blue-blazes to do with it. You spent a day or two playing with icons; that got real old, real fast. Maybe you wrote a couple of .BAT files and figured out how to get 'em attached to icons. They do their thing every time you double-click. Not exactly a customized system.

But still, in the back of your mind, you know you could do a whole lot more with Windows, if you could just get pointed in the right direction.

Windows programming? Sounds like a big pain. New language. New terminology. You know how it is. You get a great idea for this fancy new system—how the whiz-bang screens should pop up and around; with color and pictures and sparks flying from the tube; how the boss will like the printout so much she'll give you a raise on the spot; how the data should be mangled, to and fro—and it all looks great . . . until you have to sit down and program the lousy thing. Ugh! How does a Windows program handle a mouse click? A Scroll Bar? What in the Sam Hill is "the SDK"? And why does "the SDK" cost more than a week in Cabo San Lucas?

That's where *Windows Programming for Mere Mortals* comes in. We're going to introduce you to the big, wonderful world of Windows 3.1 programming, one step at a time, and we aren't going to bog you down in a bunch of technical mumbo-jumbo about Heaps and Global Allocs and Instantiations. Instead, we're going to concentrate on how to put together programs that work, with fancy screens and legible printouts, just the way you like 'em. You're going to see how easy it can be to program Windows: it's so easy you may not think you're programming at all. Really.

We'll get you started with two relatively simple—and very powerful—languages: Visual Basic and WordBasic. You'll see why all those magazine writers are raving about "Event Driven Programming." You'll learn this stuff not by sitting through a boring lecture, watching a tape of a guy clicking like a cricket in heat, or wading through an inscrutable manual, but by actually building Event-Driven programs, one step at a time, pushing and poking and stomping on the heart of things until you understand what's happening.

By the time you're through the first few chapters of *WinMortals*, you'll be able to put together Windows programs—real Windows programs—that do something worthwhile. By the time you're through with the whole book, you'll have a very broad exposure to a dozen or so Windows tools that you can use every day.

Along the way, we're going to keep things light and fun—some would say just a bit off-the-wall—and kick you every once in a while to make sure you're still breathing. We'll let you in on hundreds of tips and tricks, and warn you about bugs (uh . . . sorry . . . there's that "B" word again, would you believe undocumented design features?) and show you the places where products just plain fall short.

Most of all, you're going to get the straight scoop. We won't pull any punches or make any apologies. What you see is, most assuredly, what you're gonna get.

Read This First!

Before diving into *WinMortals*, make sure you have the following:

- Windows 3.1—should be alive and well and living on your computer.

- Visual Basic 1.0 or later—follow the easy installation procedures. Don't worry about taking the tutorial. We'll show you everything you need to know, and then some!
- The *WinMortals* Companion Disks—including a Working Model of Word for Windows 2.0, with a fully functional copy of WordBasic. You don't have to buy Word for Windows. Everything you'll need to take WordBasic through its paces is here, free, in the Working Model, compliments of Microsoft.

  The Companion Disk also contains all of the program snippets you'll find in this book—including a complete copy of CoolCons, the customizable tool bar for all your Windows applications—already typed, ready to plug into your computer.

There are lots of other goodies on the Companion Disk: listings of Windows API calls, customized for WordBasic and Visual Basic; some of the Shareware products you'll find mentioned in the book; stuff the editors tossed in at the last minute; old shopping lists; who-knows-what-all.

Check Appendix 3 for instructions on decompressing and using the disk.

Poke around a bit. You might be pleasantly surprised.

"Software is easy. Comedy is hard."

Woody Leonhard

CHAPTER ■ 1

Welcome to Windows

Come da Revolution . . . .

There's a revolution brewing in the computer business.

Thanks to Windows, macro languages are taking on a new life.

If you think a macro language looks like this:

```
{Shift}{F7}{Up}{Down}{Back}{Forth}
```

or like this:

```
/fr{myfile.dat}/tloops
```

you're in for a big surprise.

Microsoft's Word for Windows (WinWord) led the way with WordBasic. In 1990, when WordBasic sprang forth on an unsuspecting public, the response proved underwhelming. Another macro language, the cynics mumbled. Who cares?

But then came Visual Basic. Interest in the WinWord macro language blossomed. People started kicking WordBasic's tires, jumping in the driver's seat, taking a hand at the wheel, peering through its . . . windows.

WordBasic Power to the People

Guess what? Buried within Word for Windows—a *word processor*—lurks a full-blown programming language! It isn't a little toy macro language cobbled together by two hackers over a long weekend, but a real **language**. Variables. Functions. Subroutines. The whole nine yards.

Not only that, but the WinWord macro language can talk to Visual Basic. It can talk to Windows. Using something called "Dynamic Data Exchange" (DDE), it can talk to almost *any* well-designed Windows program or application.

1

WordBasic can work with "Dynamic Link Libraries" (DLL's), which are the basic building blocks of windows, to call practically any function in Windows.

Suddenly every Windows application started doing it. Macro languages slowly emerged from the closet, gaining function and form and capability. The few big software vendors that didn't have DDE and a fully functional macro language behind their Windows applications started announcing plans to incorporate DDE and macro languages in their new versions.

The developers who already had DDE started flirting with its uptown cousin, Object Linking and Embedding.

Macro languages grew up, or at least took their first few fleeting steps. That's the revolution.

In just a few years, probably sooner, almost every major Windows application will contain a macro language worthy of the name. A macro language that will talk to other applications and other macro languages, using DDE. A macro language that looks and acts like a computer language, not a string of ersatz keyboard entries. A macro language that works with and for Windows.

That simple fact is going to change the way we all work. Real people—normal people—can start using those macro languages to get some work done.

And that's what this book is all about.

One World, One Windows, One (BASIC) Glue

How can we be so sure that the future of Windows macro programming will be based on BASIC? Quite simply: Microsoft says so.

Bill Gates started Microsoft with a vision and with BASIC. The vision persists to this day. As does BASIC. *Only the tax bracket has changed.*

Top Microsoft brass have stated, repeatedly, implicitly and explicitly, that their objective is to tie all of the major Windows applications together with a BASIC glue. And why not? As the *de facto lingua franca* of the personal computer community, taking BASIC into every Windows nook and cranny just makes sense.

The BASIC Path to Enlightenment

Most of the new Windows macro languages draw their inspiration, if not their syntax, from BASIC. Not all industry pundits believe that's a good trend. Many people figure you must program in PASCAL or Modula-2 or C++ to be writing a "real" program. The same mindless, macho approach to defining programming castes was applied to the assembly language versus higher-level language debate a decade ago. The arguments were as bogus then as they are now.

It depends on what you mean by a "real" program, of course. BASIC *does* insulate you from much of the low-level complexity "real" programmers encounter. Macro languages, in general, do the same thing—so much so that many Windows BASIC and macro programming fans will agree, absolutely, that their way isn't really programming at all. It's too easy!

The BASIC Controversy
To say that BASIC has its detractors in the PC community would be to understate the case.

> "BASIC is to programming what crack is to your brain."
>
> —Philippe Kahn, Borland International
> *Infoworld*, August 5, 1991

> "...BASIC is destined to remain a toy language."
>
> —Steve Gibson, Spinrite Corp.
> *Infoworld*, July 8, 1991

Hold it right there, guys.

Yes, BASIC has its shortcomings. No doubt about it. But so do all the other languages, including the fancy new ones.

If you're concerned about strong data typing, rabidly goto-less structured strictures, run-time definable overloaded polymorphic operators, or dynamic inheritance of complex object classes, you're in the wrong place. You should be looking at Smalltalk, Turbo Pascal for Windows, Actor, or C++. You should also plan on spending the next six to twelve months in a classroom, hunched over a keyboard, trying to translate the instructor's jargon into something you can understand. Just leave your wallet at the door, thank you.

And if you think *any* existing language covers the entire Object-Oriented/Event-Driven schtick, you're in for a rude—and expensive—awakening!

On the other hand, if you want to get a job done, BASIC or one of the neo-BASIC Windows macro languages may be just the ticket. No, you won't be able to build a Nuclear Power Plant Command and Control System with Visual Basic. But you could sure give it one hell of a user interface!

The very first BASIC, foisted on unsuspecting college students some twenty years ago, bears little resemblance to the modern language. Its inventors created

BASIC as a vehicle for teaching programming; that's probably why it's easy to learn and use. It was never intended to be the ultimate programming language.

BASIC's Redeeming Qualities

BASIC is a simple language—or rather, like most spoken languages, a collection of dialects that loosely resemble one another. Tons and tons of learned tomes will tell you how BASIC should do this or can't do that; why feature "X" must be changed to act as it does in language "Y"; how some part of BASIC has poisoned the minds of a generation of programmers.

Hogwash.

BASIC isn't perfect, but it hardly ranks as the devil incarnate. It has its good and bad points. For example, misspelling variable names will drive you nuts.

Here are some of the good points:

If you have *any* exposure to computers, programming, macros, or customizing applications, you have probably seen some variant of BASIC. At the very least you can pick up the fundamentals quite easily. Good, bad, or indifferent, BASIC is the closest thing we have to a universal PC language. In other words, you probably already know BASIC. Perhaps humans are *born* knowing it.

You won't find too many := weird looking {@symbol{s%}} or utterly inscrutable statements in :=: most &BASIC &&programs. *Whew!* BASIC is reasonably easy to write, read, and understand. Especially now that line numbers are gone!

Perhaps most importantly, BASIC is and will be the "language behind the programs" in Windows. Like it or not (and many of Microsoft's competitors don't!), BASIC is the language that Microsoft will use to tie all its products together. Other manufacturers may have little choice but to follow suit.

WordBasic lives behind WinWord. Visual Basic straps onto Windows itself. As of this writing, EXCELBasic is in the works; it may even be available by the time you read this. The new Microsoft database, code-named "Cirrus" (and also possibly available by the time you read this), will have its roots in BASIC. There's a BASIC being grafted onto Project for Windows right now, and another variant of the mother tongue in the works for Microsoft PowerPoint. The Dynacomm macro language resembles BASIC. (Remember the Windows "Terminal" application? That's from the same folks who make Dynacomm.) And on and on. Even Amí Pro's macro language looks a lot like BASIC, and there's no love lost between Lotus, the purveyors of Amí Pro, and Microsoft, the progenitor of Windows BASICs.

Simply put, BASIC and the BASIC-like macro languages are the way of the future and (unless you're already a Smalltalk or Modula-2 guru) the best, fastest, and most versatile way to start making Windows work for you.

Method to the Madness

We're going to take an unusual path to Windows BASIC enlightenment. Instead of diving into one language and bleeding it to death, we're going to jump back and forth between two languages, WordBasic and Visual Basic. That's a weird way to learn a macro language or a programming language. But it's a great way to learn how to mangle Windows, to get it working the way you want it.

Why ping-pong between WordBasic and Visual Basic? Because the two languages have much in common. The syntax (always one of the largest hurdles to learning a new language) is remarkably similar, and in many cases identical. Most important, WordBasic is easier to use for simple input and output, and we can build on that foundation to learn the tougher parts of Visual Basic, in particular the Event-Driven way of looking at things.

Not coincidentally, it also helps to have two languages—two applications— under your belt when you try to make applications talk to each other, using Dynamic Data Exchange. As you're learning WordBasic and Visual Basic you'll also be learning the basics of DDE.

WordBasic has a small set of simple tools for talking with users and a large set of complex tools for constructing documents and printing them on paper. Visual Basic, on the other hand, has a small set of very simple tools for constructing documents and printouts, but it has a marvelously rich tool box for talking with users.

Once you're comfortable with the terminology we'll get a one-line "Hello, Word!" application going in WordBasic, and build it into something fun. Then we'll take those very same concepts, terminology, the whole enchilada, and apply them to Visual Basic. We'll dive into Visual Basic's toy box and see what's there, creating a few splashy displays. Then we'll tie the two together with Coolcons, an exciting DDE application that puts a fully customizeable icon bar into Word for Windows and any other Windows application that supports Dynamic Data Exchange.

You can do it. No sweat.

The Visual Basic/WordBasic Cookie Jar

Visual Basic may be the best cookie jar ever invented. Although its shortcomings are, frankly, legion, it's still very accessible to people who aren't professional programmers. When it comes to creating a user interface—you know, the important stuff, the part that working people have to play with and understand and use every day—Visual Basic gives you an incomparable level of support and help, with a minimum of futzing and fuming over the intricacies inherent in Windows. And it delivers all of that flashy neat stuff on a silver platter.

WordBasic, ever the plain-Jane little sister, packs a real wallop in one area where Visual Basic remains deficient: creating and printing documents.

To be sure, there are other places where Visual Basic falls short. For example, its support for data storage, retrieval, and manipulation qualify as rudimentary at best. (Actually they stink, but that's why you buy a database package, right?)

Visual Basic is built around the Windows user interface: call it a Graphical User Interface if you must, but it's a whole lot more than a garden-variety graphical interface. It's an entire world of conventions and methods and procedures, with pictures and clicks and drags.

If you want to get a flashy Windows application up and running—and working before you go home at night—Visual Basic is probably your best shot. Stick your hand inside the Visual Basic cookie jar, and here's what you'll find.

Tools for Putting Fancy Stuff on the Screen

With just a click or two you can plant custom pictures, buttons, boxes, almost anything you can imagine, in your application's screens. Take a look at Scroll Bars, for example, those funny little buggers that show up when you've got more stuff to stuff than room to stuff it.

Figure 1-1: Scroll Bars of Various Persuasions

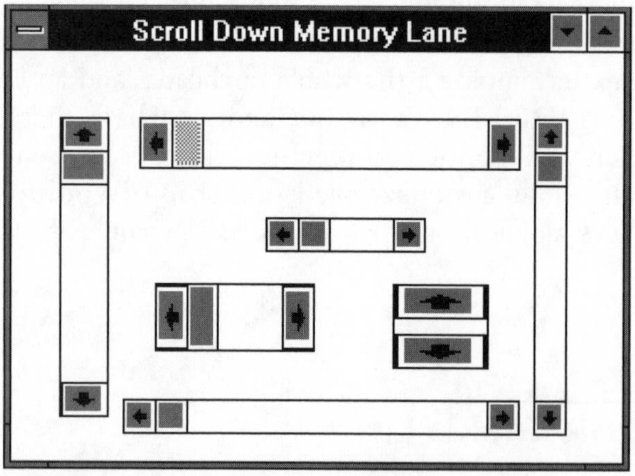

Think for a second and you'll probably come up with a zillion ideas for how you might use a Scroll Bar inside normal, everyday programs—they work great any time you want a user to input a value like "kinda big but not too big" or "sorta small but not as small as this other guy."

If you're writing a program that projects whether the world will end with a bang or a whimper, you might have one Scroll Bar labeled "Future Birth Rate," another labeled "Future Chlorofluorocarbon Emissions," and a third called "Rate of Third World Deforestation." The user could slide the values around and evaluate changes projected by your program visually, if not viscerally.

But, of course, you'd never be able to program one of those Scroll Bars into *your* programs. How do you figure out how tall the bar should be? Or where it shows up on the screen? And do you put an arrow on the end of the bar? Or make them move the box from side to side? Feed a value back to the program?

In Visual Basic it's a piece of cake. Scroll Bars come standard, a bone-stock part of the Visual Basic cookie jar. To create a Scroll Bar, you just click. (Well, it is not quite that easy—you have to **double**-click; still, you get the idea.)

Visual Basic's cookie jar lets you make as many Scroll Bars as you like, put them anywhere you like, with defined max and min values (corresponding to the Scroll Bar's box being all the way to the left or right), stretch them or scrunch them, turn them heads-to-tails, and on and on.

Tools for Shuffling Stuff on the Screen

Once you've got all those pretty pictures on the screen, Visual Basic lets you manipulate them in all sorts of ways. Do you want to make your pictures look different when the user clicks on 'em? Or highlight a negative number by showing it in red against a chartreuse background? Maybe you'd like to set things up so a click on a "Press Me" button pops up a bigger button that says "Go Ahead. Make My Day. Press Me Again!".

All of those manipulations are not only possible with Visual Basic—they're *easy!*

A Way to Talk to Other Windows Applications

It's called "Dynamic Data Exchange," but don't let the technospeak scare you off. Visual Basic, like most good Windows applications, supports DDE. That just means Visual Basic can talk to other Windows applications—or at least other Windows applications that, in turn, support DDE.

Think of DDE as if it were an internal Windows telephone exchange, set up to answer questions. When you get down to it, DDE is not much more complicated than picking up the telephone, dialing a number, and talking into the phone. If the connection is made and there's somebody at the other end, you might actually be able to ask your question. If you've made the appropriate arrangements in advance, the application on the other end of the phone line may even *answer* your question.

With a few minor technical details, that's DDE. And Visual Basic is good at both ends of the phone line: it can ask questions very well, and it can answer them, too. Perhaps surprisingly, that isn't true of WordBasic: in general, it's much easier to get WordBasic DDE to ask questions than to answer them.

Misconception the First: Windows Is Hard to Program

People have lots of reasons for not taking on the Windows challenge. We're going to disabuse you of some of those notions right now.

Yes, it's inarguable that, once upon a time, Windows really *was* tough to program. Only a hard-core masochist could warm up to the fact that it might take eighty lines of convoluted code to just paste up a Windows box that says "Hello, World." Fortunately, times have changed.

It's also absolutely correct that Windows 3.1 programmers have access to more than 700 different functions, different hooks into the operating system. In the DOS world that number is closer to 100 (if you equate DOS commands with Windows operating system calls; in fact, they're not all that comparable). This factor-of-seven explosion in available commands is often cited as proof-positive that Windows is enormously complicated.

Horsefeathers.

Perhaps the putative septupling of command complexity should make you worry, but you probably won't have any reason to call more than a handful of key Windows operating system functions—indeed, many people will write programs in Visual Basic or WordBasic for months before they have any reason to explore those Windows commands. Some of us who cut our teeth on WordBasic were shocked to discover that it was even *possible* to manipulate Windows from inside a WordBASIC macro!

You may have heard buzzy words like "Event-Driven" or "Object Oriented Programming" and how tough it is to work in that brave, new world. There's more than a nugget of truth in what you heard: the change to Event-Driven programming can be tough. Not to worry, though. We'll step you through it.

"Object Oriented" is a great marketing term that is only partially implemented in any widely available PC language, with the possible exception of Smalltalk and a handful of other languages few have ever explored. You would be completely justified in treating "Object Oriented" claims with skepticism. The early days of "Relational" databases exhibited the same characteristics. And unlike the Relational model—which has shown its usefulness in real-world situations—it remains to be seen if full Object Orientation, as currently envisioned, is more boon or bane!

Actually, once you get used to the funny terminology and the Event-Driven way of thinking, you'll probably find that it's easier to cook up a substantial—and useful—Windows system in one of the BASICs than in any other language. That's a rather broad statement, but it only hints at the enormous power of the tools available.

In fact, Windows programming with Visual Basic, WordBasic, and some of the other macro languages is so very different from other kinds of Windows programming that it's tempting to think that you really *aren't programming at all:* more than anything you're assembling bits and pieces that have already been made for you. Your primary job is to pick the right pieces, dress them up a bit, and provide a little glue to hold them together.

No matter what folks tell you, Windows programming is not that tough. You'll see.

Misconception the Second: No More Batch Files

Some people think that Windows makes all of those DOS batch files obsolete.

Wrong.

You'll use batch files; DOS batch files, Windows batch files. Windows batch files that call DOS batch files, and vice-versa.

As long as DOS is around there will be a need for good ol' .BAT. You just have to mold DOS batch files a bit to work the way Windows works. At the same time, not every Windows program needs to be Event Driven. You'll find many reasons for using simple, sequential Windows batch files—not as sexy as their Event Driven counterparts perhaps, but every bit as useful.

Often you'll want to make your old DOS programs work with Windows, and often the biggest trick is to make WinThings control DOS programs. The easiest way to accomplish this is through DOS Key Stuffers, tricky programs that fool DOS applications into believing that you're sitting at the keyboard typing away, while in fact the whole charade is orchestrated by Windows.

After you've got your feet wet with a real Windows application or two, we'll step through a little competition to see how various popular Windows programs handle DOS key stuffing duty. There are quite a few tricks; we'll see a few in action.

But don't throw away your .BAT files. Not yet anyway.

Misconception the Third: No More Macros

In some respects, the old macro languages are a dying breed. But that doesn't spell the end of macro languages. *Au contraire!*

Depending on how you look at it, much of the future of Windows will *be* macro languages. Some of this is a question of terminology: at what point does a macro language become less macro and more language? There's no definitive answer.

WordBasic is called a macro language simply because it's inextricably tied to Word for Windows. Along those lines, you could argue quite convincingly that Visual Basic is a macro language, too.

While it's certainly true that the old, ersatz-keyboard, one-F-key-at-a-time approach to programming will soon go the way of the dodo, those old macro languages will, of necessity, lead to new, powerful, and rich programming languages, buried within all of your favorite applications.

So don't get hung up by people who say, "Aww, you're just playing with a macro." You might not get much respect at the moment. At least until they see what "just" a macro can do.

The Monster BASIC from Hell

The vision of an all-encompassing BASIC—a *Monster BASIC from Hell,* for lack of a more descriptive term—with dialects in all of the major applications, communicating with each other, taking advantage of each host application's strengths, is one of the most exciting prospects for the future of Windows.

What a concept! You've already discovered how commonality in Windows applications makes it easier to use the applications, and use them well. If you learn how to cut and paste a cell in a spreadsheet, for example, then you automatically know most of what you need to cut and paste a sentence in a word processor or a picture in a paint program. Common user interfaces are old-hat in the Macintosh world, but in the IBM-compatible world they're truly revolutionary.

Make Mine a Macro

Just imagine what will happen when the same concept comes to macro languages: learn how to write macros in one language, and you'll know most of what you need to write macros for all the others. What you learn in WordBasic applies, by and large, to Visual Basic. And that in turn will apply (some day) to the EXCEL BASIC-like macro language, the PowerPoint macro language, the MS Project macro language, the Microsoft Cirrus database language . . . or a competitor's spreadsheet macro language, a communication program's macro language, a paint program's macro language. The mind boggles.

Sure, there are differences: each dialect reflects the biases and primitives and capabilities of its underlying application. But there are enough similarities that you can be up and running in a new macro language in days—maybe even hours—instead of spending weeks or months coming up to speed.

Equally important, applications will be able to *talk to each other*, using this common macro language. Microsoft estimates that by the end of the twentieth century, 85 percent of all computer users will be using languages—"macro" languages, if you must—to customize their own computers and systems.

Vox Populi Vox Dei

That's incredible. But if you think about it, it's also inevitable. Back in the early parts of this century, the automobile was a specialized instrument, considered to be beyond the ken of mere mortals. When you bought a car, you bought a chauffeur to go along with it: somebody who understood how to start and run and feed and maintain the inscrutable beast.

The first cameras required a detailed understanding of chemistry and control of chemical reactions. The first bicycles took daring, if not a significant death wish, and incredible coordination. Early telephones required extensive operator intervention, not to mention a strong wrist to crank the magneto. The first computer programs consisted of jumbled strings of 1s and 0s.

It took geniuses, the Fords and Eastmans of our century, to bring those technologies to mere mortals. Once the artificial technological shroud was lifted, we all learned to drive a car, shoot a picture, ride a bike, dial a phone, push the "Enter" key.

We aren't at that 85 percent mark. Not yet, not by a long shot. The Monster BASIC from Hell is still on the drawing boards. But we're headed in that direction. And *you* are at the vanguard of the wave!

If you learn WordBasic and Visual Basic now and pick up one or two other macro languages by the time you finish this book, you'll be in a good position to get going with EXCELBasic and CirrusBasic and who-knows-what-BASIC over the next year.

No More SDK

You don't need the SDK to program in Windows. No matter what people tell you.

The Microsoft Windows Software Development Kit (also known around these parts as the Sadist's Delightful Kludge) is an enormously powerful, enormously expensive support system for those who program Windows in the C language.

Save the money. Save the time. Save the frustration. Take the family to Florida or Mexico or Bermuda for a week.

You are going to learn a much better, faster, and easier way to get at the innards of Windows. Directly. Using BASIC, the language for mere mortals. And, although some parts of Windows don't readily yield to the BASIC approach, the parts that don't work with BASIC are parts that tend to be a bit abstruse, anyway.

A Note on Notation

We're going to use a different kind of notation from what you're used to seeing in computer books. A revolutionary, descriptive, depictive notation. It's called English.

Here's an example. In standard computer parlance the WordBasic MsgBox command looks like this:

```
MsgBox Message$ [,Title$ [,Type]]
```

and if you look up MsgBox in a reference book or manual, that's the kind of description you'll get.

Well, we're going to do things a little differently in *WinMortals*. We're going to show you a red-blooded example, explain things in English, take you through typing the example (or copying it in from the Companion Disk), and actually running it.

But we're going to leave all the gory details for the reference books. Convoluted syntax. Oddball options. Obscure switches and the like. You'll learn more by playing around with a language than by copying a reference book entry anyway.

We're also going to bypass detailed explanations of control syntax. You've seen an If-Then-Else statement before; we won't belabor the point or bore you with the details. If it's been a while since you wrote an If-statement, not to worry. You'll see quite a few of them—more than enough to trigger your memory.

WordBasic as a Stepping Stone

We'll start out with a peek behind the Windows curtain, something of a guided tour, using WordBasic.

I am the great Oz! Ignore that man behind the curtain!

There are several reasons for using WordBasic, aside from its position as the *pater familias* of the Monster BASICs from Hell: it's an easy way to get into the Windows swing of things; it's a fun way to poke around a bit; it's also a nice way to brush up on your BASIC, if you haven't played with the language for awhile.

And awayyyyyyy we go . . .

CHAPTER ■ 2

A Peek Behind the Windows Curtain

You've seen Windows' pretty face. You know how to click a mouse. Resize a window. Move an icon from one group to another.

Ah, but there's more to Windows, so much more. A lot of it is, unfortunately, couched in strange acronyms like "DLL" and "API" and the dread "DDE." But if you'll forgive those who stay up late concocting inscrutable TLAs (three-letter acronyms) and take a few minutes to see what they're talking about, you'll see that Windows is a rich programming environment, only occasionally marred by massive kludges.

So hang onto your hat. And keep the *WinMortals* glossary handy. Here's your chance to see what's going on behind the scenes.

The Weirding Windows Way

The world of DOS, the world you've known for so long, is based on character streams. Type at the keyboard and the keystrokes are fed into a buffer, which in turn disgorges its contents into a program. The program takes the input, wraps around a merry tune, and slaps characters on the screen. A fancy program might go out to a disk for another character string or ask the operating system about an inscrutable hex character string, but it's still basically the same: input-process-output; input-process-output; input-process-output.

That's the sequential view of the world. Nice and orderly. Start at point "A," and move to point "B," scramble things at point "C," and toss out the results at point "D."

This sequential view—or sequential *paradigm*, if you're into big words—drove PC processing through the 1970s and '80s. It drives most minicomputer and mainframe processing even today.

To be sure, there are many variations on the theme, and sequential processing can get mighty complicated at times. But it is still one-dimensional. Input. Process. Output.

Your nice, sequential program might call subroutines, which would then process whatever was proffered and send the results back to the calling routine. The subroutine might even inhabit a different computer or (seemingly) live in a different world; maybe you wrote it, or maybe you relied on somebody else to write it. But at the end of the day, the subroutines are still linear. Input. Process. Output.

Your sequential program might be a TSR that's smart enough to lurk in the background, examining character strings as they flow through the machine, jumping to life when the magical character combination appears. That's a half-step above real sequential processing, but it's still mighty linear.

Your program might handle character strings coming quickly from one source but moving slowly to another source. Or vice versa. Buffers have a dual linear quality to them, juggling input on one side and output on the other, but it's still the same old grind. Input. Process. Output.

Ah, the sequential games we've all played.

Windows will let you break out of that sequential treadmill!

SuperSequential Processing

It didn't happen overnight: programming languages based on non-sequential (or, more accurately, "SuperSequential") paradigms flourished two decades ago, but they were buried in labs and university experiments and had funny names like "Smalltalk" and "OOP."

(The term *SuperSequential* should convey one hard fact: even though Events may drive the Windows world, the snippets of programs that handle those Events remain, by and large, sequential. You might get ahead, but you'll never get out of the game!)

Several technological improvements in the past few years have made Super-Sequential processing possible on the PC; some would say inevitable. Two key developments brought SuperSequential processing to the hands of mere mortals.

Now You See It

First, we got screens capable of showing an enormous amount of information.

Variations on the character-based screen evolved rapidly as the technology allowed. For a long, long time, the state-of-the-art in PC screen presentations involved drawing boxes one line at a time and pasting characters into the blank spaces within the boxes.

Quick. What's the IBM ASCII code for an upper left box corner? Horizontal double-line? Buzz. You lose! They're characters 218 and 205. Now, confess. How many times have you looked up those numbers so you could draw pretty boxes in DOS .BAT files?

Boxes rapidly grew blasé as the fanciest programs and programmers learned about color, or at least shading. They played with the background and foreground, drawing in contrasting colors, and on and on.

Lucky PC owners with sufficient money and patience endowed their machines with CGA video adapters. They were treated to games where fuzzy bugs crawled around the screen, looking suspiciously like, uh, fuzzy bugs. Pictures displayed in CGA mode actually looked like pictures—even if it *was* a bit difficult figuring out if the picture more resembled George Washington or Martha. The pixels of progress.

Net result? We got screens that were only marginally easier to read or use but sure did look impressive when we showed them to the boss.

"Tab over to the blue box and type a negative number. Now push enter. See! It turns red!"

DOS shells flourished, and thousands of hours of heated debate among the top PC minds in the world revolved around whether file directory trees should be shown simply indented or with connecting lines in different colors.

Then came the VGA revolution. VGA and its variants finally gave computer jocks something to work with. Somebody discovered that a picture merely 32 dots wide and 32 dots tall—known today as an icon—could show a user something interesting, something worthwhile. The foundation of the graphical user interface was cast. Finally, information could be presented in a condensed form, a form most users could understand. Usually. Well, at least some of the time. With luck.

Click. Clickity-Click-Click

The second cornerstone of SuperSequential processing? Rodents!

Keyboard input—even simulated keyboard input from, say, a disk drive or a communications port—stagnated the industry's creative juices. We fell into a fetid pool of input-process-output, and it stuck to our shoes, our hands, our brains.

Enter the mouse. Or, if you prefer, the touch-screen, digitizer pad, joystick, trackball, football, whatever.

The appearance of *genus Mus* changed the industry forever. Why? Because we couldn't expect people to adhere to the confines of character streams! That unpredictable click-click-click of the left mouse button proved the death knell for blind sequential processing.

Although sequential programming isn't dead yet—and will never totally disappear—the writing's on the wall. Just about any computer user with a mouse, a VGA monitor, and a sufficiently fast computer will want a graphical interface sooner or later, and SuperSequential applications to go with it. It's inevitable.

Sequential Dinosaurs

Combine a mouse and a VGA display, and the sequential way of looking at things goes all to hell. Users get real lazy, real quick. They don't want to type:

```
c:\communic\tapcis\tapcis.exe g
```

any more. They want to click on a pretty icon with a picture of a telephone and let the computer do the work.

And therein lies the crux of the Event-Driven paradigm.

You see, we can't rely on typed-in character strings anymore. They don't rule the world. Don't control program execution. Don't pay the bills. One program, one string, input-process-output just doesn't cut it in an Event-Driven world.

Typed-in character strings are no longer the alpha and omega of computerdom. They're just . . . well, they're just typed-in character strings!

You'd be surprised how many gurus—real, living DOS gurus—are offended by the lack of a reliable character string. Hang around with some of these folks and you'll hear the moaning. They want an InKey$ function that swallows massive computer processing power looping—*doing nothing 33,000,000 times a second*—in anxious anticipation of the user pushing a single key. Or a macro recorder that remembers keystrokes but ignores mouse clicks. Or a way to send strings to parallel ports without considering the effect on other programs.

Not all of those ideas are bad ones, of course. But they tend to belie a way of looking at the world that's rapidly disappearing.

The Event-Driven Paradigm

Windows has finally brought Event-Driven processing to the masses. Double-click on an icon and crank up a program, say, a word processor. Type type type. Need to grab a graph? No sweat. Click the word processor's down-arrow (the one in the upper right-hand corner) and go find—or build—your graph. Copy it to the clipboard. Kill the graph program. Double-click on the word processor icon. Copy the clipboard to the document.

That's a pretty simple task if your word processor and graphing program are up to snuff. (It's downright trivial if you have OLE; more about that later.) But take a look at what's happening, how Windows has to handle what you're doing.

To crank up the word processor, some part of Windows had to understand that you were clicking—double-clicking, in fact—and had to somehow associate the icon receiving your clicks with the word processing program. It then had to understand that a double-click means "Oy! Get that program going!".

Once the word processor is in gear, something inside Windows has to be smart enough to realize that what you're typing is supposed to go to the word processor, not to a totally unrelated program sitting somewhere else in the Windows ether, and not to Windows itself.

When you minimize the word processor, Windows has to be smart enough to recognize that clicking on that down arrow means you don't want to watch that program right now; that it should be turned into an icon. And so on.

All of these actions are "Events." Push down the left mouse button, and that's an Event. Lift up the button, and it's another Event. Double-click on an icon, and that's yet another Event. Push down a key on a keyboard, and there's another Event. Lift your finger from the key, and that's another event. Move your mouse from one part of Windows to another, and there's another Event.

Windows, at its heart, is a massive Event processor.

When you write a real Windows program, an Event-Driven Windows program, you'll be concerned about all the things that can happen—all the possible Events— and how to deal with them.

That's an enormous shift in paradigm. No more input-process-output. With Event-Driven programming, you start wondering about how to handle mouse clicks over here, messages from other programs over there, and resizing the window in the middle of everything else crashing around your ears—all, potentially, *at the same time!*

You won't be comfortable with it for a while. Guaranteed.

It's like the first time you learned "*x*" could represent a number, and that the algebraic expression "$x + 3 = 1$" held some meaning. Mind-boggling.

Visual Basic is an Event-Driven language. You have to look at the world through Event-Driven glasses to get anywhere at all in Visual Basic. WordBasic, on the other hand, like most Windows macro languages, is mostly sequential. But it does have some Event-Driven bits and pieces.

Who's Got the DLL?

No doubt you're used to thinking of the DOS world as a nice, orderly collection of files and programs, stored away in their own subdirectories, invoked from the *big cheese*, the DOS command interpreter, COMMAND.COM (or 4DOS or NDOS).

The DOS world isn't anywhere near that orderly, of course, but in the simplest of cases, DOS programs come in nice, discrete, complete chunks. If a program needs a subroutine, the subroutine is usually compiled into the program. Once a program gets control, it usually completes its task, then exits back to DOS or the calling routine.

Some programs are smart enough to pull in an overlay, grabbing a hunk of subroutines from disk, transferring control to those subroutines, and then linking back to the controlling program again.

Some DOS programs are smart enough to die quietly, but leave vestiges of themselves still loaded in the computer. That's a neat trick; it's at the heart of every TSR (Terminate-and-Stay-Resident) program and the reason why you can pop up DOS programs with weird key combinations.

In Windows, *everything* is a TSR. Say goodbye to the neat and orderly.

The Windows Three-Ring Circus

Windows, in contrast to the mostly sequential operation of DOS, runs like a huge, chaotic three-ring circus.

Windows manages all the performances by keeping tight control over the screen, memory, and input/output. But other than that, by and large, pandemonium rules.

Programs can "talk" to other programs—start and end other programs, for that matter. The user can click on almost anything, and the underlying program has to handle the Event. Keyboard input has to be directed to the correct program.

Windows handles all of this enormous complexity by opening things up a bit, by letting programs in most cases control their own operational destiny. That's a major step forward in programming, and we're only beginning to see the impact.

Coping with that complexity led to one of Windows' most important artifices: the Dynamic Link Library.

DLL as Workhorse

Don't let the three-letter acronym put you off. A DLL is just a subroutine or bunch of subroutines. Of sorts. A very, very powerful bunch of subroutines that floats in the Windows ether.

Most subroutines in the DOS world are attached permanently to their programs, bound at the ankles and wrists, indentured to the calling program's whims. Not so Windows DLLs.

Windows Dynamic Link Libraries are not "connected" to their programs until they're actually needed. (Thus the "Dynamic Link," eh?) The DLL "subroutines" float in and out of memory, available quite literally at a moment's notice.

That wait-till-the-last-possible-moment method of linking things together opens up an entire new world of possibilities. One copy of a DLL can handle any number of "calling" programs. DLLs can be managed independently: change a DLL and you don't have to re-compile all the programs that use it. DLLs can call other DLLs. DLLs can be swapped in and out of memory using an omniscient handler independent of the local program. And on and on.

Windows itself is just a collection of DLLs. Windows routines bouncing around calling other Windows routines, the whole resembling nothing more than a daisy-chain of interlocking Dynamic Link Libraries!

And the nicest point of all: if Windows can call a DLL, then you can too. You can get your hands on all of that neat nitty-gritty inside stuff.

Imagine the power! Imagine the flexibility! Imagine the crashes!

Custom DLLs

You aren't limited to Windows' built-in DLLs. Home-grown DLLs, like home-grown subroutines in a kinder, gentler era, garner all the benefits of their commercial cousins. They can solve unique problems, attack deficiencies in the big-time packages, cater to your precise needs. Your program won't know a custom hot-shot DLL from a ho-hum built-in DLL. There is no hierarchy among DLLs: they all float around in the Windows primordial ooze; by and large they're all treated equally.

Building a custom DLL ranks as one highly nontrivial task. You won't be able to construct a custom DLL using the BASICs in this book; for that you'll have to master the C language and many of its nuances, or some equally obtuse language that will churn out custom DLLs. They're still that much of a black art. But you'll be able to use DLLs—custom, built-in, or otherwise—to your heart's content.

We'll look at some custom DLLs in the more advanced sections of *WinMortals*. For now, let's concentrate on the Windows DLLs.

Windows 3.1 DLLs

The three most frequently used Windows DLLs—called "KERNEL," "USER," and "GDI"—are augmented by less common ones, including "SOUND" the obscure. There is "TOOLHELP," which is supposed to . . . uh . . . help you with tools. And "OLESVR," "OLECLI" for OLE; "DDEML" for roll-your-own DDE; "COMMDLG" to give you a head start on common Windows dialogs like FileOpen; "SHELLAPI" for drag and drop functions; and on and on.

Kernel and User

What's the difference between "KERNEL" and "USER"? Good question. Unfortunately, there's no good answer. No doubt the creators of Windows had a clear idea of what kind of things belonged in each (some swear that "KERNEL" is connected more closely to the system than "USER") but in practice it's almost impossible to remember which routines are in which DLL.

■ **T I P**

Appendices 1 and 2 give you fairly detailed lists of some of the routines that can be called from "KERNEL" and "USER" and tell you which routine is in which DLL. Appendix 1 is geared to WordBasic; Appendix 2 covers the same ground from the Visual Basic point of view.

The Companion Disk gives a complete list of "KERNEL" and "USER" routines for Visual Basic. It's a mammoth collection, easily searched with any handy word processor.

If you find a reference book that tells you *"Try KERNEL first and if that doesn't work try USER"*—and that approach is without doubt the most common!—just remember that (almost) all is revealed in the WinMortals Appendices and Companion Disk.

GDI and Sound

The "GDI" (Graphic Device Interface) Dynamic Link Library concerns itself with drawing tools, the so-called . . . uh . . . graphic device interface. It's a flashy little hummer, full of ways to make circles and arcs and colored boxes fly around on your monitor or leap out to your printer. Good stuff.

B U G

Alas, the Windows 3.0-era "SOUND" Dynamic Link Library may be the buggiest DLL you'll ever find. There are alternate DLLs available for the AdLib and SoundBlaster cards. Mostly, though, the proper response to "Hey, let's use the Windows 3.0 Sound DLL" should be a loud "Over my dead body, turkey!"

Microsoft's multimedia extensions to Windows make the sound connection much more reliable. The new sound routines can be found in the Media Control Interface (MCI) DLL. At this writing, it's still too early to tell how reliable MCI will be, but at least it's a start. Don't bet the farm on Windows sound until you've had a chance to experiment!

What's an API and Why Should I Care?

DLLs are collections of "subroutines." You have to call the subroutines, right? If you can't call 'em, what's the use of having 'em . . .

"API" is another TLA that makes you sound knowledgeable and way-cool. It's also another fancy name for something very, very simple.

The API is the *Application Program Interface.* So far so good.

Imagine how silly you'd sound if you had to explain, "This is just the way you call all those subroutines. It's the names of the routines, see, and the stuff that you have to send the routines, and the stuff that you get back. You know, you send this critter the name of a program and he starts up the program, or you call this other guy and he tells you if there's a mouse around. That kind of thing." That's too easy. Decidedly nonprofessional.

Instead of saying something like that, or simply "It's just the subroutine calling conventions, that's all" you, too, can mimic the guru and say, "Harumph! API!"

So the next time you see an obtuse discussion of "The Windows API," just pause for a second and smile. They're talking about subroutine calls. That's all.

DDE and Me

Another fancy term: Dynamic Data Exchange. It's just a way for Windows programs to talk to each other. When it works.

At the risk of stretching a simile beyond recognition, DDE really behaves much like a telephone call between two Windows applications.

The Client

When you talk on the telephone, somebody has to dial the phone, right? The application doing the dialing—the one that starts a DDE conversation—is called a Client.

The DDE Client is in the driver's seat. Starts the ball rolling. Controls the conversation. Remember: the client is in control. Decides which topic will be discussed. Reaches out and touches the application on the other end of the phone.

The Server

The application that answers the phone is called a Server. Its sole purpose is to serve the Client.

The Server might rummage around in the attic and pick up a piece of data, then send it back to the Client. Or it could execute a command or a macro, if the Client so desires.

In general, the Server has absolutely no control over the conversation. Except it can refuse to talk. Or hang up the phone.

The Conversation

There's a set sequence for cranking up a DDE conversation. It goes like this, more or less:

- The Client looks up a phone number, picks a topic of conversation, and dials the phone.
- If the Server is home (i.e., if it's running), and it likes the topic of conversation, it answers the phone. Note how the server has to be prescient; it has to know the topic before it picks up the phone. Keeping Servers informed about the topics *before* they pick up the phone is a job for the DDE gods— we'll introduce you to them later. Also note how several Servers with the same phone number, all willing to talk about the Client's topic, could all pick up the phone at the same time! Oh yeah, it happens.
- The Client asks the Server to do its bidding. Usually this involves requesting a certain piece of information from the hapless Server or telling the Server to run a specific macro. Sometimes, though, the Client can just shove a bit of information at the Server and tell the Server where to put it.
- The Server acknowledges that it has completed the task.

For some reason many discussions of DDE overlook this vital step! If something holds up the Server's acknowledgment, many Clients will get confused. You'll see the confusion—and how to work around it—in Chapter 6.

- The Client may ask the Server to do its bidding again, over and over, and may issue as many commands (pertaining to the current topic of conversation) as it likes.
- Finally, if they're polite, either the Client or the Server hangs up the phone. If they're extraordinarily rude, one or the other may just walk away from the phone and leave the line open!

That, in a nutshell, is the whole story behind DDE. Truly, it is only a tad more complicated than picking up the phone. When it works.

Variations on the Theme

DDE, as you might imagine, can be very free-form. The few rules (like specifying a topic of conversation) exist primarily to keep you from bumping into yourself. And many of the rules can be bent or worked around, if you know the tricks.

The phone calls can twist all over the place. Application "A" might start a conversation with application "B," and then "B" might immediately respond by picking up another phone and calling "A" on another line! Application "C" might have five different conversations going on at the same time, all with different copies of application "D," or maybe have all five conversations going concurrently with a single copy of application "E." Any combination you can imagine is possible, although a program would not normally call itself.

DDE gives your program a chance to talk to other Windows applications, get data from them and make them dance like puppets on long-distance strings. With DDE you can make DynaComm dial up a stock quote database, bring the data back to EXCEL, perform sophisticated spreadsheet analyses to predict how far United Gizmos will fall today, alert you to pending disaster with a flashing red bar in Visual Basic, construct a Word for Windows memo to the Chairman of United Gizmos, print it on your letterhead, send a cc: Mail warning to your Comptroller, then have PackRat dial your stock broker and keep him on hold for ten minutes.

Enormous flexibility.

Along with the freedom, though, comes some responsibility. You have to control the details of the conversation: Windows only provides the DDE calling conventions, the phones and telephone wire as it were. If you mess up a DDE conversation, you can bring all of Windows crashing down. You have to know what can go wrong and set up your applications to handle all the problems.

Some Windows applications—EXCEL comes to mind—have a rich DDE history. People have been building EXCEL DDE applications ever since there *was* a DDE. Visual Basic works well with DDE, and in its short lifetime quite a few programmers have taken advantage of the almost-magical connecting force.

Other Windows applications, though, suffer from DDE neglect. WinWord is capable of working with DDE, both as a client and as a server, but until very recently nobody really had a handle on how to make WinWord *behave* as a server. None of the tricks had been documented. Until *WinMortals*, of course.

Hot, Warm, and Cold

There are three different kinds of DDE conversations, commonly called "hot," "cold," and "warm." We'll explore those in detail later, but the concept is pretty straightforward and has to do with whether the Server keeps track of changing data: in a "cold" link, the Server never notifies the Client when data changes; in a "warm" link, the Server notifies the Client once every time the requested data changes. In a "hot" link, the Server also sends along the updated data.

A *cold* link is like calling Pizz-a-Rama and asking for a Godzilla Double Cheese with Jalapeno, hold the anchovies. The guy on the other end of the phone takes your order, puts the phone on the counter, and only comes back if you start shouting loud enough. That's cold.

In a *warm* link, the guy on the other end of the phone takes your order, pauses, then mumbles, "Wait a sec, Bub. Hold the line? . . . Hey, Bub! We just gotta fresh truckload of anchovies! You want anchovies, too, doncha?" That's warm.

It could be worse. If you had a *hot* link to Pizz-a-Rama, the anchovies would end up on your doorstep before you had a chance to say, " *No!*"

Cranking up WordBasic

Time to get your fingers on the keyboard.

We're going to take you through a simple WordBasic exercise. If you've already discovered the wonders of WordBasic and tend to think intro stuff is pretty boring, stick around anyhow. Chances are pretty good you've never made WordBasic jump through these hoops.

If you have Word for Windows 2.0 or later installed on your computer, you're all set. We'll be working exclusively with WinWord 2.0 or later. If you are relying on the Working Model located with the WinMortals Companion Disk, you'll have to get it installed. Appendix 3 gives detailed instructions for installing the Working Model and getting WordBasic to respond to your every wish.

For the ultimate in no-hassle computing, we've put all the code you'll find in this book on the Companion Disk. At least in theory, you will never have to . . . *ugh!* . . . type any large pieces of actual code. Check Appendix 3 for details.

WordBasic Basics

This stuff is a whole lot easier to see when you're in front of a screen. So, crank up Windows. Double-click on the Word for Windows 2.0 icon. You should get something that looks a lot like this:

Figure 2-1: Word for Windows

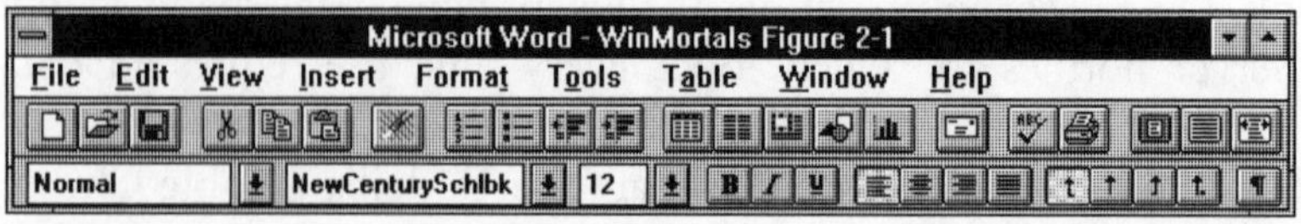

Great. Now click once on Tools. You should get the Tools pull-down menu, which looks like this:

Figure 2-2: Look at Them Tools!

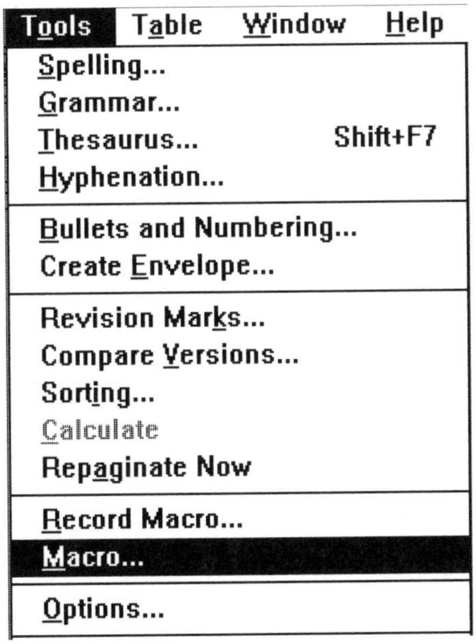

Tools	Table	Window	Help
Spelling...			
Grammar...			
Thesaurus...		Shift+F7	
Hyphenation...			
Bullets and Numbering...			
Create Envelope...			
Revision Marks...			
Compare Versions...			
Sorting...			
Calculate			
Repaginate Now			
Record Macro...			
Macro...			
Options...			

Most of our work will be with the Macro tool, which you can see down near the bottom of the list.

Click on "Macro." You should get a box that looks like Figure 2-3 on the following page.

(Your macro box won't look quite as full as this one, unless you've been collecting macros for quite a while.)

Next comes the toughest part of macro construction in Word for Windows. You have to choose a name for your macro. We'll pick something neat and original—"TEMP"—but you can pick any name you like, as long as it's under 256 characters. The name has to start with a letter and contain only letters and numbers (no underscores!): you'll know that your name is too weird if all of the boxes suddenly get grayed out and "Cancel" is your only remaining option. Subtle.

Down where the box asks for a description, type in something witty and concise, like "WinMortals Temporary Macro." You don't have to put in a description, but you'll probably find it's easier to keep track of things if you do.

The Macro Tool Box should look a lot like Figure 2-4 on the following page.

Figure 2-3: The Macro Tool Box

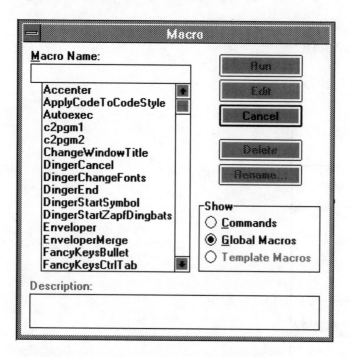

Figure 2-4: The Macro Tool Box, Stuffed

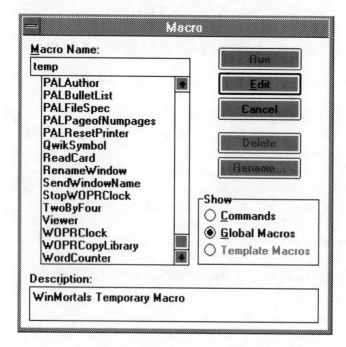

Click Edit.
Stand back.

Figure 2-5: WordBasic Central

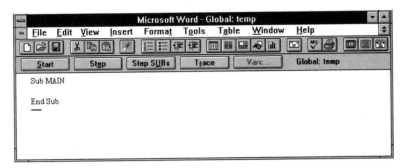

Whoa! Hey, we aren't in Kansas any more! Just look at that sucker.

As we said a bit earlier, buried inside Word for Windows is a fully functional programming language. You're looking at a reasonably sophisticated development package (might as well call it a macro writing environment), one that's going to save you a lot of time and hassle.

A Guided Tour of WordBasic Central

Let's start at the top.

The very first line tells you that you're editing a WordBasic macro. It's a global macro—one that will be available any time you're using Word for Windows. (There are other kinds of macros, but we'll concentrate on the global ones.) And the macro is called TEMP.

The second line is the WinWord command bar. In a flash of brilliance, the designers of WordBasic realized they didn't need a new editor for their macro language; WinWord itself would work just fine, thank you. If you play around with the commands on the second line—File, Edit, View, and so on—you'll soon discover that you have access to much of WinWord's powerful editing, right here *inside your macro.* That's a tremendous resource we're going to use a lot.

Next comes the WinWord Toolbar, the one with all the pictures on it. Those are just shortcuts, put there so you don't have to exert yourself and click on the menus.

The final line—the row of buttons—gives you the opportunity to run your macro while you watch it. We'll show you how in just a second. The important thing to note is that you have a fancy development environment right here in front of you, part and parcel of a word processor.

All the World's a Subroutine, and All the Code Merely Players

(Did you know that Guillaume de Salluste first claimed "the world's a stage" in 1578, twenty years before Shakespeare? Ah, well. Back to work.)

Get ready for a conceptual jump.

WordBasic has already set you up to write your first macro. It inserted two important lines of code and left your cursor in the middle, primed, ready to type away, thusly:

```
Sub MAIN
|
End Sub
```

Yes, it's a subroutine. *Every* WordBasic macro is a subroutine. In an Event-Driven world, though, that makes sense. You write subroutines that handle Events. Something happens to trigger the Event, and WinWord satisfies the Event by cranking up a subroutine.

Most people who use WordBasic don't quite "get" this subtlety. Actually, you can make WordBasic do all sorts of things without understanding the Event-Driven concept and how it applies. But we'll hit it later, especially in Visual Basic, so you may as well wrench your mind around now. Don't hurt your neck in the process.

Every WordBasic macro is a subroutine. And *every* WordBasic macro is called in response to an Event.

How Can I Use Thee / Let Me Count the Ways

Here are all of the Events that can trigger the execution of a WordBasic macro:

- A **Button Click** Event. Click on one of those buttons on the third line—Start, Step, StepSub, or Trace—while the macro is "active" on the screen, and the macro takes off.

- A **Keypress** Event. Press the right combination of keys. You have to teach WinWord which key-combination corresponds to which macro, by using the Tools Options Keyboard menu (i.e., click on "Tools," then "Options," then "Keyboard," and follow the instructions).

- A **Menu Click** Event. Click the right menu item. You have to tell WinWord what you want the menu to look like and teach WinWord to pick up the right macro, but that's easy. For example, if you built a File Delete macro, you might create a menu item called "Delete" under the "File" menu. A user would then click on "File," then the new item "Delete," and WinWord would run your macro. The Tools Options Menus combination (click "Tools," then "Options," then "Menus," and follow the instructions) controls the WinWord menu.

- A **Picture Click** Event. Click on the proper icon up on the Toolbar. Again, you have to tell WinWord which icon launches which macro. Piece of cake: take a look at Tools Options Toolbar.

- A different **Menu Click** Event. Run the macro manually. Click "Tools," then "Macro," then double-click on your macro's name.

- A **Queue** Event. Call the macro from inside another macro. Simplicity itself. To crank up a new macro called, oh, *SoLongAndThanksForAllThe Fish* from inside another macro, all it takes is one line:

```
SoLongAndThanksForAllTheFish
```

- A **DDE "Execute"** Event. Start up the macro as the result of a DDE conversation. When WinWord is the Server in a DDE link (i.e., the application that picks up the DDE phone, remember all of that?), it can be instructed by the Client to run a macro.

- A **Timer** Event. Using a WordBasic command called "OnTime," schedule the macro to be executed at any time in the future. We'll be taking a look at OnTime, in detail. Relax. It's another simple one.

BUG

Watch out! Most books on WinWord and WordBasic either fail to mention *any* of these methods for cranking up macros, or, worse, only get part of the list and miss the rest. Each of these methods can be crucial in the right situation. Microsoft's own publications seem to be as bad as all the others, so keep the list in mind.

"Hello, Word!"

With the WordBasic screen in front of you, staring you in the face, let's switch gears. That screen—and the language behind it—is a thing of beauty.

Here's your first lesson in WordBasic Appreciation.

Charles Petzold, in his pioneering work *Programming Windows* (Microsoft Press, 1990), starts with a remarkably simple Windows program: a little box that pops up and says "Hello, World." He modeled it after another classic, in Brian Kernighan and Dennis Ritchie's book *The C Programming Language* (Prentice Hall, 1988). Kernighan and Ritchie's "Hello, World" for DOS takes five lines of code.

Petzold's "Hello, World" for Windows takes eighty lines of code, three files, and thirty pages of dense explanation. Not to mention a spare day or two to wade through the example, see what's happening, and ultimately come away shaking your head.

No, Petzold isn't grandstanding; he isn't throwing in extra stuff; he isn't trying to make the problem more difficult than it really is. The plain truth: it takes *eighty lines of C code and three files* to slap a box up on the Windows screen that says "Hello, World"! It really is that complicated.

Now let's get back to WordBasic. We're going to duplicate Petzold, but instead of using C, we're going to use a much more civilized language. Yes, a "macro" language. Ready?

We're going to use a handy WordBasic Form called a "Message Box." Any window that pops up out of nowhere and requires a response from the user is called a Dialog Box: "dialog" because the program is communicating with the user and waiting for some sort of response; "box" because it's a . . . well . . . it's a box!

A Message Box is just one particularly useful kind of Dialog box.

Your cursor should be between "Sub MAIN" and "End Sub." Now type:

```
MsgBox "Hello, Word!"
```

Don't do anything else. Don't hit Enter. Don't move the cursor. Don't breathe.

OK. Run your macro by clicking on the Start button. What happens?

Figure 2-6: Hello, Word!

Now you know why some C programmers feel like crying when they see the Windows macro languages in action.

(Yes, it's true you can write something similar to this Message Box in C. But it's indisputable that interacting with the user in WordBasic and Visual Basic is enormously simpler than in C.)

Messy Message Boxes

A Message Box is one very simple kind of Dialog Box. It pops up, displays your message, waits for the user to click on a button, and then disappears. Not bad for eighty lines of C code.

As you may have guessed, we used the very simplest kind of Message Box in that example you just finished. Let's snaz it up a bit. You can add a title like this:

```
MsgBox "Hello, Word!", "My First Message Box"
```

And you can use various icons, buttons, mix and match, with the code in Program 2-1 shown below.

We've listed all of the options, so you can play with them. Various buttons and combinations, like the infamous "Abort, Retry, Ignore" and "Retry, Cancel," are readily available. You have four built-in icons. And you can choose whether the First, Second, or Third Button is the default—the button that's highlighted when the Message Box pops up. WordBasic deciphers which combination of buttons, icons, and default you want by adding together all the options.

Take a look. The working part of the program is a one-liner.

■ **TIP**

No need to type all of this in by yourself. It's on the Companion Disk. Easy to retrieve. Follow the instructions in Appendix 3 to decompress the file onto your hard disk. Select all of your old "TEMP" macro by clicking on "Edit," then "Select All." Hit the Delete key to get rid of it. Click on "File," then "Open," pick the directory (like C:\WINWORD\WMORTALS) containing the decompressed companion disk, wait a second while the drive responds, then double-click on C2PGM1.DOC (Chapter 2, Program 1, Document). Select all of the macro in C2PGM1.DOC with "Edit," "Select All." Copy it with "Edit," "Copy." Close the file with "File," "Close." Paste the macro into TEMP with "Edit," "Paste." You're ready. Finally. It'll get faster and easier as you get used to it.

So much for the preliminaries. Here's the program:

Program 2-1 (file C2PGM1.DOC): My First Message Box

```
Sub MAIN
REM Message Box options
mbButtonOK = 0
mbButtonOKCancel = 1
mbButtonAbortRetryIgnore = 2
mbButtonYesNoCancel = 3
mbButtonYesNo = 4
mbButtonRetryCancel = 5
```

```
mbIconStopSign = 16
mbIconQuestionMark = 32
mbIconExclamationPoint = 48
mbIconInfo = 64
mbDefaultFirstButton = 0
mbDefaultSecondButton = 256
mbDefaultThirdButton = 512
REM Here's the program
MsgBox "Hello, Word!", "My First Message Box", \
mbButtonOKCancel + mbIconInfo + mbDefaultSecondButton
End Sub
```

Now, click "Start." What happens?

Figure 2-7: My First Message Box

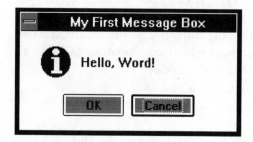

Pretty spiffy, no?

There's a WordBasic "Continue on next line" indicator down near the end of this macro. It's the backslash "\," and it tells WordBasic to treat the next line as a continuation of the current line. We used the backslash here to avoid confusion about where one line ends and another begins, but only because of limitations on the printed page.

■ **TIP**

When you're out in the real world typing away, you can forget about those pesky backslashes: WordBasic will put lines together just fine, even without the backslash, as long as you don't hit Enter at the end of the first line. Just type away. If you take a look at C2PGM1.DOC on the Companion Disk, you'll see how it works.

The abbreviation "mb" is just shorthand for Message Box; it's a decidedly non-standard use of the famed "Hungarian Standard" notation, where lowercase letters at the beginning of a variable name are supposed to give you a hint about the use of the variable.

Now that you've got all those weird button and icon options in your machine, play around with them a bit. Try long messages and short ones; take a look at all the icons; run the buttons every which way. You'll get the hang of it quickly.

B U G

Try to trigger an error or two; using a two-button option like mbButtonOKandCancel with a third-button default is interesting! Change the MsgBox statement to look like this:

```
MsgBox "Hello, Word!", "My First Message Box",\
mbButtonOKandCancel + mbDefaultThirdButton
```

The Error message you get may be completely bogus (unless Microsoft has caught and fixed it!). Fun out here on the edge, eh?

Your First API Call

When the critics claim that the Windows BASICs aren't real programming languages, they often argue that you can't "get to" Windows, that the baby macro languages shield you from all the fancy stuff inherent in Windows itself.

Pigpucky.

Yes, there are limitations, and we'll be discussing them throughout the rest of this book. But the simple fact is that the Windows BASICs give you nearly full access to the entire Windows API. That means you can call almost all the Windows subroutines, catch almost all the Windows hooks!

Said another way: with some limitations, WordBasic and Visual Basic programmers can do almost anything those fancy-schmancy C programmers do, and do it in minutes instead of hours. Your BASIC code won't run as fast, of course, but what's an extra tenth of a second running time when you're looking at development times measured in days instead of months?

Window Title Blaster

Let's build a little WordBasic program . . . er, macro . . . that picks up the title of the current window and lets you change it to anything you like. If you've ever taken a screen shot of a Windows window, you've probably wished you could change the Windows window's title.

You know the tune. The window says "Microsoft Word - HAVE.FUN," but the boss wants "Fussbudget Enterprises Outstanding Annual Report - WAYCOOL.YEP."

The Windows API Connection

The toughest part of this macro is the lousy terminology that's carried over from C-land. So put on your hip waders; it's going to get unnecessarily thick and mucky.

Before you can call Windows—or, in the parlance, "make a Windows API call"—you have to warn WordBasic. Here's what a typical warning looks like:

```
Declare Function GetActiveWindow Lib "User" As Integer
```

This command is reasonably comprehensible if you step through it slowly.

You're telling WordBasic that there is a function out there in the Windows primordial ooze that you'd like to use ("Declare Function"). The function's name is "GetActiveWindow." It's located in a DLL called "User." (Remember? A DLL is a Dynamic Link Library, something of a super collection of subroutines. USER is one of the Windows DLLs. And GetActiveWindow is but one of the subroutines in User; there are hundreds of others.) Functions in WordBasic—in most programming languages—return a value. The "As Integer" at the end warns WordBasic that this function, GetActiveWindow, will return an integer, as opposed to, say, a string of characters.

There. That's the hard part.

Gotcher Handle? 10-4, Good Buddy

GetActiveWindow returns an integer. A very special integer. It's called a "handle." Just like a good CB handle that uniquely identifies a CB nut, this integer uniquely identifies a window. It doesn't have any interesting characteristics all by itself, doesn't count how many windows are around, doesn't tell the time or shine your shoes. It's just a unique identifier, a handle.

We'll encounter window handles many times, so let's establish a naming convention right now. We're going to use a specific variable name for window handles: **hWnd**.

Every time you see hWnd, from now on, just think, "That's a nonsensical number that Windows uses to keep all its windows straight." No magic. Just a number.

Heeeeeeere's API

For the Window Title Blaster, we'll start with two Windows API calls. The first one returns the handle of the current window; the other one uses that handle to reset the title. Nothing to it.

Here are the two API declarations:

```
Declare Function GetActiveWindow Lib "User" As Integer
Declare Sub SetWindowText Lib "User" (hWnd As Integer, WindowText$)
```

We've already gone through the GetActiveWindow function; let's take a look at SetWindowText.

The Declare statement warns WordBasic that you'd like to hook up to a Subroutine (not a Function; Functions return values, whereas Subroutines just do stuff). The Subroutine is called SetWindowText, and it lives in the DLL called "User." SetWindowText needs two things passed to it—the handle of the window whose title you want to change and the new title's text itself.

(Note that WordBasic uses a dollar sign on the end of a variable name to indicate that the variable's a character string. Just about any BASIC you can mention uses the same strange notation.)

That's about what you would expect from a window text changing routine, no? Pretty easy.

Let's put it together. If you don't already have the "TEMP" macro in front of you, crank up WinWord, click on "Tools," then "Macro," then type in an interesting name. (Yes, "TEMP" will do.) Click "Edit." Select everything using "Edit," "Select." Delete it with the Del key. Now type, type, type:

```
Declare Function GetActiveWindow Lib "User" As Integer
Declare Sub SetWindowText Lib "User" (hWnd As Integer,\
NewWindowText$)
Sub MAIN
hWnd=GetActiveWindow
SetWindowText(hWnd,"So Far This Is Pretty Easy")
End Sub
```

Push the Start button. Look up at the top line of the window.

Take a look at Figure 2-8 on the following page.

Figure 2-8: So Far This Is Pretty Easy

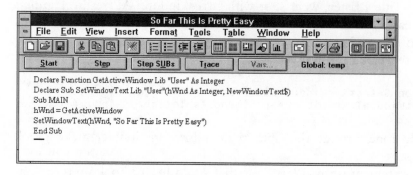

You just made your first two Windows API calls. That's about two more than most WordBasic programmers have ever tried. Pat yourself on the back.

Embellishment—the Mother of Insanity

Let's add a little pirouette to your virtuoso performance and make the Window Title Blaster a little more useful.

Just as WordBasic has a Message Box to tell the user what he or she needs to know, it also has an Input Box to let the user tell your program what *the program* needs to know.

The syntax sure does resemble MsgBox. It looks like this:

```
InputText$=InputBox$("Type In Something, Please","Title")
```

That InputBox$ function call slaps something like this up on the screen:

Figure 2-9: Type in Something, Please

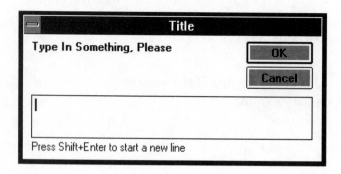

■ TIP

Yeah, that "Press Shift+Enter To Start a New Line" is really hokey. Like something out of the 1960s, for a Teletype machine or something. Unfortunately, if the user presses Enter while the InputBox$ is up on the screen, WordBasic interprets the action as a click on the OK button. Egregious, dude. Anyway, if you use InputBox$, you get that "Press Shift+Enter" message whether you want it or not.

In this example, after the user has typed in something and then either clicked OK or hit Enter, the typed-in text appears as the variable InputText$.

Programming a MessageBox like this in C might take several days if you were just starting out with Windows. It would take a hundred lines of code. *Your* main limitation, as a smart BASIC macro maven, is how fast you can type.

We'll need one more Windows API call to whip this program into shape. It's called GetWindowText$, and—like many Windows API calls—it's a little . . . uh . . . quirky when called from WordBasic.

This is what GetWindowText$ is supposed to look like:

```
LengthOfWindowText=GetWindowText$(hWnd, CurrWindowText$, MaxChars)
```

In theory, you should give GetWindowText$ a handle to a Window and state the maximum number of characters you want to see, and it's supposed to return the current Window title text and the length of that text. Simple enough. In theory.

B U G

In practice, WordBasic seems to have trouble with this API call if you use a MaxChars > 288. Why? Who knows? When MaxChars is set over 288, the API call sometimes fails and returns a zero for the length of the window text. You may have different results (see the note in Appendix 1), so poke around a bit and see what happens.

Note the bizarre syntax in GetWindowText$. Most BASIC groupies, if they thought about it for more than half a second, would probably put together a function call that looks like this instead:

```
CurrWindowTitle$=GetWindowTitle$(hWnd)
```

Windows likes to make things look complicated. Don't let it bother you. The folks who create Windows API calls have technical reasons for making you jump through the hoops; they mumble something about speed and integrity checking and interfaces. Bah humbug.

Add in GetWindowText$ and you have a rather sophisticated Windows application, in under a dozen lines:

Program 2-2 (file C2PGM2.DOC): The Window Title Blaster

```
Declare Function GetActiveWindow Lib "User" As Integer
Declare Sub SetWindowText Lib "User"(hWnd As Integer,\ NewWindowText$)
Declare Function GetWindowText$ Lib "User" (hWnd As Integer, \
CurrWindowText$, MaxChars As Integer) As Integer
Sub MAIN
hWnd = GetActiveWindow
LengthOfWindowName = GetWindowText$(hWnd, WindowText$, 288)
NewWindowText$ = InputBox$("Current window title is " + WindowText$ \
+ " Please enter a new title:", "Window Title Blaster")
SetWindowText(hWnd, NewWindowText$)
End Sub
```

Run the Window Title Blaster any time you want to change a Word for Windows' window's title text.

Figure 2-10: The Window Title Blaster in Action

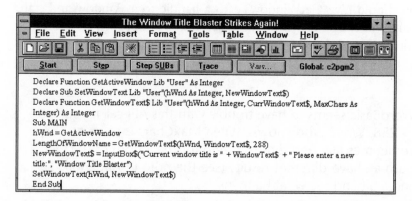

Word for Windows is smart enough to bring back the old window title whenever you shift windows: open a new file or use the "Window" menu command to move between windows, and the old name reappears. But if you need to change a window title for a screen shot, a change of scene, or to humor the boss, this should fit the bill.

CHAPTER ▪ 3

The Windows User Interface

Time for a bit of thinking and looking. We'll start coding again in the next chapter.

If you're in front of your computer, bring back the "Hello, Word!" Message Box (it's Program 2-1, file C2PGM1.DOC on the Companion Disk). We're going to dissect it here momentarily. If there's no computer handy, don't worry about it.

Sure it's a GUI, but . . .

Too many PC users equate the term "GUI" (Graphical User Interface) with "Windows" and a handful of Windows applications. Some like to think of Windows as "a Macintosh on the PC." Many think that Windows has the best user interface going. T'ain't necessarily so, folks.

A Short History Lesson, Class

Depending on how you define "Graphical," GUIs have existed for more than a decade; they run on all sorts of different computers; some look different as night and day; dozens of *different* GUIs are used by people all the time—thousands and thousands of people, all around the world. No matter what anybody says, there is no one "best" GUI.

Yes, the Mac did foster the first commercially successful GUI. No, it wasn't the first GUI—it wasn't even the first widely used GUI. First GUI rights legitimately go to Xerox's PARC, the Palo Alto Research Center.

Even PARC borrowed from other labs and others' work; they just never manufactured a commercial success on the order of the Mac. The mouse and Smalltalk grew up at PARC, as did the office worker's graphical display, our current concepts of clicking and dragging, and all sorts of other goodies we WinFans take as a given.

Intuitive? You Gotta Be Kidding!

People laud Windows' "intuitive" graphical interface.

Intuitive? Ha! Nothing could be further from the truth.

Windows is no more intuitive than the steering wheel, turn signal, or gas pedal. Like the atomic operations of running a car, the basic Windows moves—click, double-click, click and drag, grab and stretch, and all the rest—are easy to learn and potentially quite powerful. They're also extensible. Step on a gas pedal, and you know much of what you need to know to step on a clutch. Click on an icon, and you're halfway to learning about a double-click or a drag and drop.

But *intuitive*?

If you can recall your first few times behind the wheel of a car—or the first dozen times you tried to use a mouse—you'll realize that even though the operations are simple, they take some learning. They are most certainly *not* intuitive. Watch a three-year-old puzzle through the horizontal movement of a mouse on a desktop translating to the vertical movement of a cursor on a screen.

E Pluribus, Anything but Unum

That lack of intuitiveness has led to an enormous diversity in the types of GUIs people have implemented on all sorts of different computers.

For example, we WinFans take overlapping windows for granted: one window pops up on top of another, and they overlap like sheets of paper on a desktop. Yet other GUIs won't overlap their windows: each one is tiled on the screen, checkerboard fashion, so you can immediately get at all windows all the time. That's a big conceptual difference. Windows 1.0 looked like that.

Another favorite example: the Mac trash can. To delete a file on the Mac, you drag a picture representing the file to the trash can. If you want to retrieve a deleted file, well, it's time to rummage through the trash can. The can has to be "taken out" from time to time and once it's emptied, neither wailing nor an Act of Congress will bring it back. *(Norton will, but that's another story.)*

In Windows, there's no equivalent to the Mac trash can. Apple's lawyers make sure of it!

Several Windows add-ons give you trash can compatibility, but the original Windows approach—the Del key—is quite different. Highlight a file or (sometimes) an icon and press the Del key. Poof.

Now we could argue all day and well into the night—and some otherwise intelligent people have already done so—about the benefits of the trash can versus the superiority of the Del key. Such ramblings resemble nothing more than the old debates about how many angels can fit on the head of a pin, whether IBM SEs should be allowed to wear brown shoes, or if the original Star Trek is better than Next Generation.

The point is they're different. Not better. Not worse. Different.

Vive la Difference!

So, you see, there are things that make Windows unique.

■ T I P

Right, wrong, or otherwise, there is a Windows way of doing things, looking at things, presenting things. And you'll have to stay within many of those (admittedly subjective) constraints if you want to create your own programs with the Windows "look and feel."

The most important Windows constraint is in the user interface itself, and there are hundreds of conventions: windows usually have minimize/maximize buttons; Check Boxes, squares that can be "X"ed or blank, almost always are used for "on or off, yes or no" choices; buttons can have black circles inside and usually indicate a choice among several options; and on and on.

We're going to spend the rest of this chapter looking at parts of the predefined, standard Windows user interface. We'll start using some of the baffling jargon, so you don't get confused when you read the manuals later on. (When there's a conflict in jargon, we'll stick with the Visual Basic terminology but keep dropping WordBasic terms as reminders.)

Most of all, we're going to take apart and examine all the little pieces that go into making a user interface, so you'll be able to put all the pieces together and make them work the way *you* want them to work.

Forms/Dialog Boxes

In order to draw your mighty interface and present it in the Windows scheme of things, you must first have a canvas!

WordBasic calls them "Dialog Boxes." Visual Basic prefers the term "Form," and that's what we'll use. (If you want to get technical, Dialog Boxes are a certain type of Form, but they're the type of Form you'll use most often anyway.)

Whatever you call them, Forms are just regular old windows—but windows with a purpose.

The foundation of a graphical user interface is . . . uh . . . interfacing with the user! *(Never expected such profundity in a computer book, huh?)* When your program reaches out to the user, and the user responds with something for the program, the interaction is called a "dialog." And the thing that you stick out for the user to interact with is called a "Form" or a "Dialog Box."

We've already seen two simple examples of Forms: the WordBasic MsgBox, which looks like this:

Figure 3-1: The Message Box—Remember Me?

and the WordBasic InputBox$, which looks like this:

Figure 3-2: The Input Box

They correspond to two very simple kinds of dialogs: the MsgBox notifies the user about something and waits for a click on one of its buttons; the InputBox$ asks the user to type in something and delivers the typed-in stuff to your program.

We'll dive into the wonderful world of complex Forms in a minute, but for now let's start with these two simpletons. Beneath the plain-Jane appearance of the Message Box and the Input Box lie all sorts of choices, design decisions, human engineering work; stuff that makes those boxes easy to understand and easy to use.

Form Properties
These Forms have some characteristics—some Properties—that are quite distinctive. At the risk of belaboring the obvious, let's try to list all of the Properties that characterize these two simple Forms.

- They both have that hyphen thing in the upper left corner. Click on the hyphen and a little box drops down; you'll have a chance to move the Form or close it (i.e., zap it out). Double-clicking on the hyphen will also close it. Closing the Form is the same as clicking "Cancel." Usually.

- They both have a Caption. You saw how to change the Caption earlier, when we were building those API calls. *(Did you see how you just naturally slipped into that fancy techno-talk—"API calls." Didn't even blink.)*

- They have a specific size. That's a mighty boring observation until you realize that the Message Box actually resizes *itself*, on the fly, to fit the text and caption in the MsgBox "Text","Caption" command. You don't have to touch a thing. Pretty smart.

- They have a location on top of the current window. Both MsgBox and InputBox$ automatically center themselves in the current window, as best they can. By clicking and dragging on the title, users can pick up the box and move it anywhere they like—although users can't resize the box by clicking on an edge or corner and dragging.

Modal and Modeless

- They take over the window. As long as a MsgBox or InputBox$ is showing, you can't do a bloody thing with WinWord. You can shift to another application, but once you come back to WinWord, those boxes simply freeze out everything else, waiting for your response. Forms like that—Forms that take control of everything and won't let loose until you feed them what they want are called "modal."

*Why would anybody in their right mind pick a name like "modal" to describe "Takes Over and Won't Let Go"? Jeez. They could have called it "sempiternal" and it would have made some sense. Instead we get **modal** and its reverse, **modeless**. Sounds like competing theories of auto muffler repair. Folks who pick names like that should lift their sights, draw inspiration from the classics: Rheingold Rings . . . Dante's Cerberus . . . Kirk's Tribbles . . . Dr. Demento's Shaving Cream . . . Pee-Wee Herman's Conkey.*

Form Borders

- Now here's a weird detail you might not have noticed. Both the MsgBox and InputBox$ have a specific kind of border, a thick solid line. If you think about the windows you've encountered in Windows, they have four different kinds of borders, and each signifies something different.

The thick solid border, a la MsgBox and InputBox$, and shown in Figure 3-3, says that you can't resize the window by grabbing an edge or a corner, you can't use the little up-and-down arrows to maximize it or turn it into an icon, but you can move the box around.

Figure 3-3: Thick Solid Border

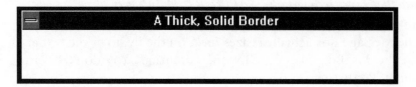

The thin solid border in Figure 3-4 signifies that you can't resize by grabbing an edge or a corner of the Form, but the up-and-down arrows are working.

Figure 3-4: Thin Solid Border

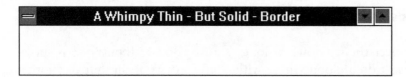

The normal border in Figure 3-5, a pair of railroad tracks with crossbars in the corners, indicates that the window can be stretched and moved and resized to your heart's content.

Figure 3-5: The Normal Border

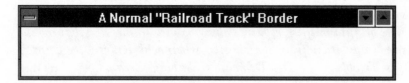

Finally, the hairless, borderless beast in Figure 3-6 can do nothing. This Form has a border only in the sense that *no* border *is* a border.

Figure 3-6: The SOL Borderless Form

No Border A-Tall

Border styles on Forms are a little bit of visual cue that you've no doubt seen a million times but may not have understood. They're almost subliminal. And, in Visual Basic at least, they're quite important.

That's a quick rundown of the obvious Properties for two simple Forms, MsgBox and InputBox$. Quite a few not-so-obvious Properties are floating around: the background color, say, or the type style (font) and size used for the caption. We'll take a look at many of those Properties later.

Controls

The Form is a blank canvas. Upon that canvas we carefully scatter . . . things. Pictures. Buttons. Bars. Boxes. Lines. Text. All sorts of things.

Those things, collectively, are known as Controls.

Visual Basic, bone stock, straight out of the box, has fourteen different Controls ready for you to use. WordBasic has eight. We'll take a look at all of them right now, concentrating on their physical appearance, how you might use them in a program, their more obvious Properties, and how they can interact.

Controls, the Great Communicators

The use of Controls is central to Windows programming. Your programs will live and die by how well they interact with the user; programs interact with the user via Controls. Simply put, Controls are crucial.

The Windows macro languages, the BASICs, have taken away much of the overhead in Windows programming. In doing so, they let you concentrate on the user interface, the most important part of almost any program. Take advantage of your new-found freedom by concentrating on Controls, on the way your program acts and reacts in response to what the user does, on how your program looks. A little effort in the Control department can pay off big-time in happier, more productive, less bewildered users.

Control Artistry

There's a real art to assembling Controls, to presenting information to the user in a way that can be understood. Like any art, "Painting with Controls" can't really be taught, and only rarely can be learned. We're going to try to show you examples of Controls that—while certainly not artistic—could be useful in designing your own applications. Take a look at how the Controls play off each other, and keep a mental note of the designs that appeal to you.

And, by all means, copy, copy! Mix and match. Take what you like, and leave the rest.

The Label Control

Let's start with the easiest Control, the Label. You can see an example in Figure 3-7:

Figure 3-7: Label Controls

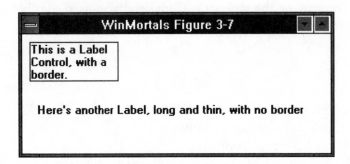

Befitting a Control so simple, Label (Visual Basic calls it a "Label," WordBasic calls it "Text") can't be changed by the user. It just sits there.

A Label Control can, however, be changed by your program. Every which way.

Label Control Properties

The Label Control has some obvious Properties: the text or Caption itself, of course. It also has a location on the Form and a size. In Visual Basic you can set up a Label to "AutoSize"; if the text laps outside of the Control area (for example, if you have a very long line but a narrow Label Control box), "AutoSizing" Label Controls will change the size of the box to fit the Label. In WordBasic, though, you're out of luck: AutoSizing is not a Label Control Property.

Label has a few Properties that aren't so obvious: the typeface (or font, if you will) and its size; the background color of the Control; alignment of text inside the box (left justified, centered, or right justified); a border. None of these Properties can be changed in WordBasic, but all of them are accessible in Visual Basic.

If you look at the InputBox$ example, shown in Figure 3-2, the line "I prompt for some sort of typed input. . ." is a Label Control.

Whenever you need to put text on your Form—and you want to keep the user's paws off—think Label Control.

The Text Box Control

A close relative to the Label Control, Text Boxes have the important distinction of being modifiable by the user. That's both blessing and curse!

We've already seen a Text Box Control. In Figure 3-2, the InputBox$ Form contained a box where the user is supposed to type in something. That box is a Text Box Control. Here's another example:

Figure 3-8: A Text Box

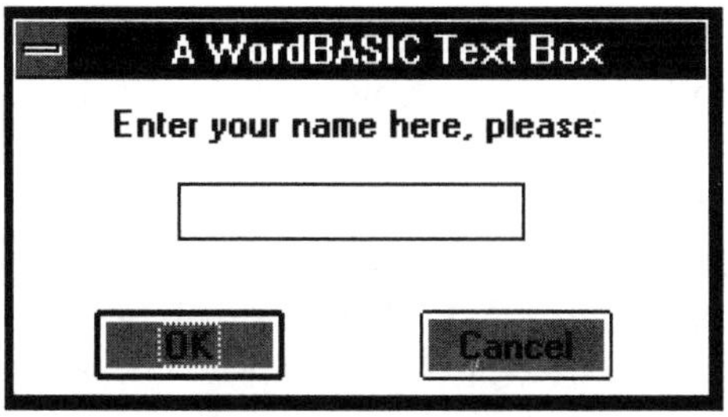

In Figure 3-8, we've used WordBasic to show you a possible use for the Text Box Control: a "fill-in-the-blanks" box where the user is supposed to type his or her name. The "Enter your name here, please:" is a Label Control, without a border. The box right below it is a Text Box Control.

The Text Box allows you to shove text out to the user (possibly "blank" or no text at all), and see if the user wants to change it. Simple enough.

Whenever you want to give your users a chance to type in anything—anything at all, free-form—the Text Box is generally the Control of choice.

Some people insist upon calling Text Box Controls by different names: "Edit Field" and "Edit Control" are popular. They're Text Boxes, pure and simple. You stick stuff in 'em, toss 'em out to the user, and bring back into your program whatever the user put in 'em. That's all.

Text Box Properties

Text Box Controls have Properties that generally parallel the Label Control, with a few important exceptions. They both have initial text.

Visual Basic draws a distinction between "Text,"which can be changed by the user—and "Caption," which cannot. Text Box Controls have Text.

The Text Box Control, unlike the Label Control, returns modified text to the program (else why have a Text Box, eh?).

Multiple-Line Text

B U G

There is a lack of consensus (now, how's that for being diplomatic?) on how Text Box Controls should behave. Some strange ways of handling multiple-line Text Boxes have emerged from the standardless early days of BASICdom. WordBasic itself has flip-flopped on how the Control behaves, from version 1.0 to 1.1.

You would expect multiple-line text (that is, text with embedded carriage returns) to show up as multiple-line text in a Text Box Control, no? Well . . . no. WordBasic only shows one line of text, no matter how large the Text Box Control, whether all the text would fit, whether the text contains carriage returns. Carriage returns in WordBasic appear as fat, ugly vertical bars—utterly inscrutable to most users, not to mention most programmers. And all the text is crammed into the very first line of the box: you can't move it around inside the box.

B U G

Worse, WordBasic disables certain types of input in Text Box Controls. The worst offender is none other than the carriage return! There is no way, for love nor money, to have a user type a carriage return into a WordBasic Text Box. Can't be done; don't even try.

To add a touch of historical perspective: WordBasic 1.0 (that is, the WordBasic in WinWord 1.0) handled the Text Box just fine. Carriage returns. Text automatically centered top-to-bottom inside the box. The works. Something got "improved" in version 1.1, and it hasn't been "unimproved" since then.

Visual Basic did it right. In the face of conflicting interpretation of Text Box Control rules, they left the multiple-line option in your hands. You, the programmer, get to decide whether you want carriage returns to act like carriage returns—or whether you want to show big fat, ugly vertical bars where carriage returns should be.

■ **T I P**

In fact, the multiline Property in Visual Basic Text Boxes controls two different but related behaviors: the appearance of carriage returns, as we just discussed; and also whether Visual Basic should wrap lines if they get too big for the box. Both characteristics are handled by the same Property setting. You can't have one without the other. But at least you have *some* choice.

Text Box the Versatile

Visual Basic extends the Text Box Control's repertoire in some worthwhile ways. You can specify Scroll Bars—horizontal, vertical, or both—to let the user take a look at all the text, whether it fits in your Control or not. And in a burst of insight, the designers of Visual Basic also let the user select (or highlight) text, then feed the selection and several of its characteristics back to the program. That's one high-powered capability.

Check Boxes

The Check Box Control comes in handy for simple yes-or-no choices. On or off. Binary. Bimodal. To be or not to be.

Let's start a running example here. Suppose you wanted to write a simple database program/roster for your local Basil Rathbone Fan Club.

A Check Box might look like this:

Figure 3-9: A Check Box Control

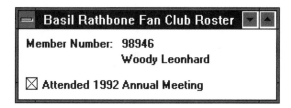

The Check Box, of course, is the last line in this Form.

Worth noting: you would probably set up the Member Number—in this case, "98946"—as a Text Box, so the user can pull up a member's information by typing in a new number. The rest of the Form, at this point, would probably consist of Label Controls, simply because you don't want the user to be able to muck with them.

The Three Check Box Settings

The Yes (checked; selected) and No (not checked; not selected; some people say "cleared") settings for a Check Box Control are obvious—but there's another setting that isn't obvious at all. A Check Box Control can be grayed-out or disabled. The grayed-out state of being is probably best described as a "don't know."

When a Check Box Control is disabled—in this case, if the information isn't in the database, say, and your program doesn't know whether the member attended the 1992 Annual Meeting—it looks something like this:

Figure 3-10: A Grayed Check Box Control

BUG

Visual Basic and WordBasic handle grayed-out Check Boxes differently. In WordBasic, the user can change a grayed-out Check Box to a "Yes" (checked) or a "No" (unchecked), as you might expect. In WordBasic, the user can also change a Check Box that was originally grayed-out *back to grayed-out.* In Visual Basic there is no such option: once the user clicks on the Check Box, there's no return to the grayed-out state. You can't go home any more.

That restriction in Visual Basic is a real pain. If a user accidentally clicks on a grayed-out "Don't Know" box, there is no way the user can turn it back to what it should be.

Beware! If your Visual Basic application includes any possibility for grayed-out Check Box Controls, you should put some hooks into your program allowing the user to return a box to its original grayed-out state.

Check Box Properties

Check Boxes have the usual list of Properties: a size and a location on the Form. They have a Caption. In Visual Basic you can change the Caption's font and color.

Check Boxes also have a Property that corresponds to the "checkedness" status of the box. You might expect that the check-off Property would be the same in Visual Basic and WordBasic, wouldn't you? No such luck.

In WordBasic, a zero says the box isn't checked; a one says it is checked; a minus one says it's gray. So far so good. In Visual Basic, a zero means not checked, a one means not checked, but it takes a two to turn the box gray.

Ah, uniformity!

Stop Making Sense

■ T I P

Let's pause for a second here. You've seen the BASICs' blank canvas—the *Form*—and three of the things—*Controls*—that can be placed on a Form. Those Controls each have strengths and weaknesses, and you should take their characteristics into account when using them. Misunderstanding the Controls at your fingertips can lead to no end of mayhem.

It's scary how often otherwise-sane people produce a Form like this:

Figure 3-11: All Wrong

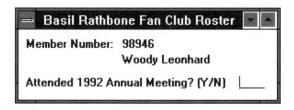

with a Text Box Control trying to do the work of a Check Box.

Horrors! This abomination of a program has to check for upper case and lower case ("YES" and "yes"; "Yes" and yES"), for misspellings ("YEP," "YO"), for one letter ("Y," "y") and full-word responses ("UH_HUH"), leading blanks ("_YES"), all sorts of strange garbage ("WUH?", "HELP," "?").

Why put yourself through the hassle? Why subject your users to such monstrosity?

If you have a yes-or-no choice, don't make the user type in "yes" or "no." That's what Check Boxes are for.

That's what *Controls* are for: to make your job easier—and the user's job, too.

Option Buttons

The Option Button Control, bless its pointed little head, comes in handy in all sorts of strange situations. Basically, you would use Option Buttons when you want the user to choose **ONE** option out of a group of possibilities. Like this:

Figure 3-12: The Option Button Control

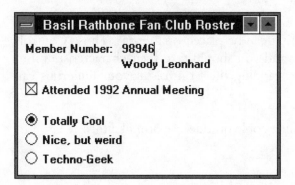

People seem to get confused about the Check Box and the Option Button. No reason for any confusion; they're very different animals. The Check Box is yes/no, on/off. The Option Button lets you choose one out of a group.

Option Button Groupies

Of course, you may have many groups of Option Buttons on a single Form. Here's an example that should make things a bit clearer:

Figure 3-13: Check Box and Option Buttons

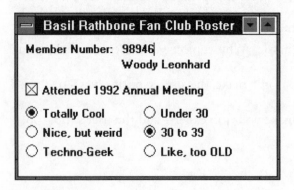

You have to be careful when assembling Option Buttons and sticking them into groups. Groupings that may be obvious to you might not be obvious at all to the user. Putting a box around the groups always helps. Like this:

Figure 3-14: Check Box and Grouped Option Buttons

Option Buttons are also called Radio Buttons, due to the fact that if you push one in, the others pop out—just like the radio buttons in a '58 Chevy.

Option Button Properties

Option Button Controls have their own Properties. They have Captions, of course (not "Text" in Visual Basic parlance, because the wording can't be changed by the user). And Height and Width and Location on the Form. Fonts and Color (which can be changed in Visual Basic but not WordBasic). The usual.

In addition, at most one Option Button in each group may be specified as the default. The default button is the one that pops up with its circle already clicked.

With WordBasic—and not Visual Basic—double-clicking on an Option Button Control is the same as clicking the Button, then pressing Enter. Visual Basic, being Event-Driven, doesn't need this kind of quasi-accelerator.

The Control Quad

These four Controls—Label, Text Box, Check Box, and Option Button—rate as the most-used tools you're bound to encounter when programming BASICs, macros or otherwise, for Windows. They're enormously powerful, and once you get used to them they'll become second nature.

Know thy Control, for it bears thee.

But wait! There's more!

List Boxes

List Box Controls are nothing more than condensed Option Buttons.

Instead of slapping options onto the Form, with a button in front of each one, the List Box lets you stick a whole bunch of options into a small piece of real estate. The condensation makes it easier for the user if there are more than, oh, five or six things to choose from.

Let's say you wanted to break down the age choices in the Basil Rathbone Fan Club Roster to ten age groups. You could make a Form that looks like this:

Figure 3-15: A Whole Lotta Buttons Goin' On

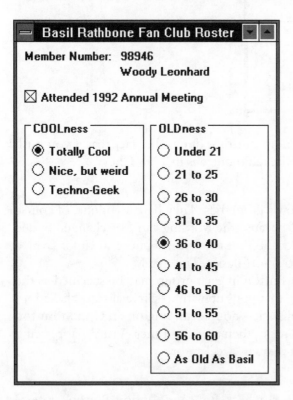

That's starting to get a bit ridiculous. Aside from the fact that a Form like this can take up the whole screen, it's a real pain to lock up so much of a Form's limited space with something so trivial.

Enter the List Box Control.

Like Option Buttons, List Boxes are a "Select **ONE** only" proposition. Here's an example that corresponds to all those Option Buttons:

Figure 3-16: The OLDness List Box

Pushing on the up and down arrows scrolls through the list of ages, just as you would expect.

List Box Differences

B U G

Here's another oddity you may bump into some day. Visual Basic and WordBasic handle List Boxes a tad differently: it's a cosmetic difference, but if you're trying to match Forms between the two languages, it can cause no end of grief.

When Visual Basic has enough room to display all the List Box choices in the allotted space (in Figure 3-16, say, if there were only five age choices), Visual Basic will not put that Scroll Bar on the right end of the box. WordBasic, contrariwise, puts on the Scroll Bar *but grays it out.*

A grayed-out Scroll Bar is about as useful as bristles on a boar.

With WordBasic—and not Visual Basic—double-clicking on a List Box Control item is the same as clicking the item, then pressing Enter. Again, Visual Basic, in its Event-Driven superiority, doesn't need this kind of quasi-accelerator.

List Box Properties

List Box Controls have all the usual Properties. They have Height and Width and Location on the Form, Fonts and Color (which can be changed in Visual Basic but not WordBasic).

List Box Controls also have a Property that lets you get at the selected item. It's called a List Index. The List Index runs from zero (not one!) to one less than the number of items in the List Box.

And therein lies a tale.

Base Zero

"Gain not base gains; base gains are the same as losses."

—Hesiod, *Works and Days*, ca. 720 B.C.

■ **T I P**

If you are accustomed to indices running from one to the number of items in an array—or List Box—you're in for a bit of frustration. While it's true that Visual Basic lets you change the lower bound on arrays, the vast majority of Visual Basic and WordBasic operations use a lower bound of zero. That's the way it is.

The first item in a list is item number zero. The second is item number one. And so on.

Combo Boxes

The Combo Box Control is an odd bird. Neither fish nor fowl. It's a List Box with a Text Box pasted on top, as shown in Figure 3-17 on the following page. At least that's the theory. In practice, there are all sorts of weird contortions.

Click on one of the Combo Box items, and violá! The user's choice appears in the box. Like Figure 3-18 on the following page.

The user is then empowered to edit the chosen item, pick a new one, wipe out everything and type in something completely different, whatever. In this example, should the member's COOLness fall outside the normal definitions, the user may type in something new. Click on "Totally Cool," put the cursor in front of the word "Totally" and type, and the user could make it "Almost Totally Cool" with just a few keystrokes.

Figure 3-17: Drop-Down Combo Box

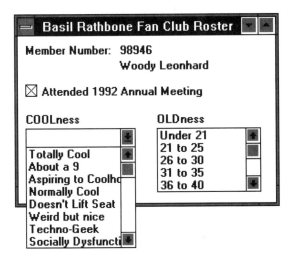

Figure 3-18: Pick an Item and It Appears

The intent with Combo Box Controls is to present some ideas, some options, but not restrict the user to anything in particular.

Combo Box Wannabes

Alas, implementation of the Combo Box Control runs all over the place. WordBasic has the most straightforward flavor of Combo Box, the "Combo Box Classic," as it were, as shown in Figure 3-19 on the following page.

Figure 3-19: This Is Only a Test!

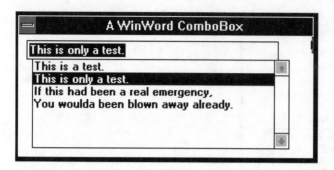

Note how WordBasic puts a neat rectangle, offset a bit to the left, on the top of the Combo Box. Nice touch.

But also note that if WordBasic doesn't have enough items to fill up the Combo Box, it sticks those grayed-out Scroll Bars on the end again. Utterly useless—and potentially confusing—clutter.

Visual Basic goes WordBasic one better. There are three different styles of Visual Basic Combo Box Controls. Or two, depending on how you count. More about that momentarily.

The Visual Basic Combo Box Classic

Visual Basic has a Classic Combo Box, not too unlike the WordBasic version. It looks like this:

Figure 3-20: Visual Basic Combo Box Classic

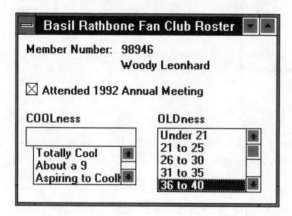

If the user chooses "Totally Cool" by clicking on it, the Combo Box Classic changes to look like this:

Figure 3-21: Totally Cool Classic

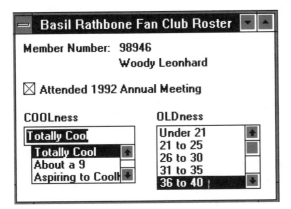

At this point, the user may modify "Totally Cool"; he or she can add characters, delete the selection entirely, or scroll down and find another entry more to the user's liking: the whole Combo Box Control *schtick*.

Not too surprisingly, Visual Basic is smart enough to can the Scroll Bars if they aren't needed.

The "New, Improved" Visual Basic Drop-Down Combo Box

Visual Basic has a variation on the Combo Box Control that approaches the clean simplicity of the Classic Combo Box but doesn't quite make it. Although this box is well-suited for densely populated Forms, in most cases you probably won't use it.

It's called a Drop-Down Combo Box and it looks like this:

Figure 3-22: Disembodied Drop-Down Arrow

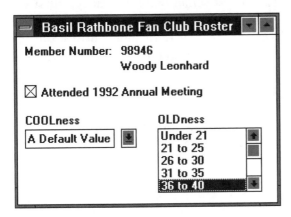

Click on that drop-down arrow, and here's what you'll find lurking underneath:

Figure 3-23: Visual Basic Almost-Classic Combo

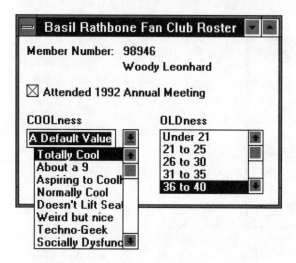

What's wrong with this picture? A couple of things.

First, this kind of Combo Box Control first appears to the user as a box with a disembodied down-arrow. Click the down-arrow and the list appears. That's not nearly as intuitive as the WordBasic approach—the *let it all hang out* approach to Combo Box design—but most users manage to figure it out sooner or later.

Second, though, that nice little drop-down box disappears! As soon as the user makes one selection, all the rest go away. Only another click of the down-button will bring the drop down box back. In some cases that might be the best way: it *does* conserve on Form real estate. But there are many situations where it would be better to leave the list up and available, so the user is reminded of the predefined alternatives.

It's a question of taste. *De gustibus non est disputandum,* usually, but we'll make an exception right here. Yes, this Drop-Down Combo Box looks a little less cluttered, particularly if your Form has six or eight or ten Combo Boxes. On the other hand, the Drop-Down Combo Box fails to remind the user—graphically—of all the choices you have set up. Kind of a waste.

When in doubt, and unless there are compelling reasons to the contrary, forget the Drop-Down Combo.

Visual Basic uses the Drop-Down Combo Box as a default; if you want a real Combo Box, you have to specify it by choosing the "Simple Combo" style. It's the

KISS principle, as always: Keep It Simple . . . even if you have to override the default to do it.

Liszts and Rhapsodies

■ **T I P**

This is a good time to take a look at how the Combo Box and List Box differ. In Figure 3-23, COOLness is chosen by Combo Box, while OLDness appears in a List Box Control.

Obviously, Combo Boxes offer more latitude: the user may pick a single entry and then modify it. List Boxes aren't nearly as flexible.

And, obviously, you should only use Combo Boxes when you really want to give the user the latitude to go off and dream up whatever he or she wants. Because of that, Combo Boxes are not nearly as widely used as List Boxes.

What's not so obvious: once the user has made a choice—any choice—from a List Box, there is no way to go back, no way to say "Oops! I shouldn't choose anything here!".

Like the grayed-out Check Box that (in Visual Basic) cannot be reset to gray, once the user lets the List Box genie out of the lamp, there's no way to stuff him back.

Combo Boxes aren't susceptible to that kind of trap. Users can set the Combo Box value to whatever they like: if all else fails, most users in the "Oops!" conundrum would just blank out the field. Which, most of the time, is precisely what should be done.

List Box TV

B U G

Visual Basic claims to have three Combo Box "styles," but one of the three (the one Visual Basic calls "Combo Box style 2," the Drop-Down List Box) isn't a Combo Box at all—it's a type of List Box, where the user has to click a down-arrow to get at the list items. There's no Text Box pasted on the top of the List Box—at least not a functioning one—and the user has no opportunity to type in anything: it's a plain List Box. In drag.

Figure 3-24 shows the Visual Basic Drop-Down List Box in Combo Box clothing, first before the user clicks on that down-pointing arrow.

(Continued)

Figure 3-24: Drop-Down List Box, Before Clicking the Down-Arrow

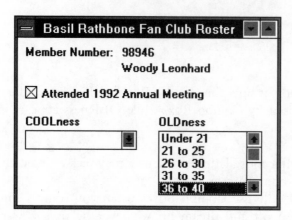

And here's what it looks like after the user clicks the arrow:

Figure 3-25: Drop-Down List Box, After Clicking the Down Arrow

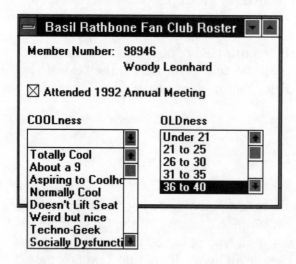

Note that box up at the top of the list, the one that looks like it should be a Text Box-style Control. It's totally bogus. You can't do anything with it: it just shows which list item you've chosen. Of course, a regular List Box Control does that—although it accomplishes the same thing by highlighting, not by stuffing a box.

You don't gain much by going to Drop-Down List Boxes. They look sexy, but they tend to be hard to live with.

B U G

There are other odd things about the Drop-Down List Box. Click on the down-arrow and nothing is selected. Immediately click on the Box itself, and it looks like there's a blank entry, but the user can't do anything with it. Push the down-arrow on the keyboard, and suddenly the first item comes up selected. Push the up-arrow on the keyboard, and the first item stays; the blank will not return. Odd.

Start again. Click the down-arrow. Now push keys on the keyboard, randomly. A sort of accelerated-lookup feature kicks in: if the letter you type matches the first letter of one of the items, it suddenly appears as the selection. This can be outrageously confounding behavior to a user who knows about Combo Boxes and couldn't care less about Drop-Down List Boxes.

T I P

Bottom Line: before using the Drop-Down List Box, play with it a bit. And if *you* find it frustrating, just imagine how your users will feel.

How, you might ask, can you be expected to keep Controls straight when Visual Basic calls them anything and everything, and puts them in such odd places—a List Box masquerading as a Combo Box, for example.

Good question. To which there is no good answer.

Combo Box Properties

Combo Box Controls have all the Properties of both Text Boxes and List Boxes. That means, in addition to location and size, font and color and all that, they also (in Visual Basic) have the nifty Text Box's "Selection" Properties and the List Box's "ListIndex" Property.

The "Selection" Property, as you may recall, lets the user select just a portion of the text in a Text Box and return just that part to your program. It's a very powerful, and rarely used, capability.

The "ListIndex" Property gives your program the index—starting at zero—of the item that was selected. For obvious reasons, if the user chooses an item and then modifies it, "ListIndex" is set to a nonsense value to warn you of the changes.

BUG

Because of the kludged-up misidentification of a Drop-Down List Box as a specific type of Combo Box, terminology in the manuals gets a bit confusing. You'll find references to Combo Box Properties that just don't make sense with Drop-Down List Box Controls—"Selection" comes to mind. When you find those references, ignore them.

In spite of what the books say, a Drop-Down List Box has all of the Properties of a List Box and none of the Properties of a Combo Box. It *is* a List Box. Not a Combo Box. Period.

BUG

Here's another little one that could jump up and bite you some day. In Visual Basic, the Combo Box color Property only changes the color of the Text Box-like top part of the Combo Box Control. For some reason, you can't change the color of the List-like bottom part of the Control.

BUG

The Combo Box shown in the Visual Basic manual (*Microsoft Visual Basic Language Reference*, pg. 52) isn't a Combo Box at all. It's two Check Boxes.

Command Buttons

Command Buttons stick out as something of an anomaly in the Event-Driven way of things.

If your computer were sufficiently prescient, it would know when you were done. When you'd typed the last number. When you were through inputting data. When you wanted to computer to "take it away." *In fact, if it were smart enough, it would tell* ***you*** *when you're done.*

Alas, the HAL 2000 is not yet a reality. Computers don't yet grok the situation.

Until computers get smart enough to read our minds, well, we just have to settle for some way of saying "Yo! 'Puter! Enough already. Go do your thing." That's precisely the function of a Command Button Control.

You might have noticed that in our ongoing Basil Rathbone example, there's no way for the user to tell the computer "Update the database with this stuff," or

"Let me work on another member," or even "Aw, jeez, I screwed it all up; let me start all over."

Your wish is Basil's . . . er . . . command. Button. Command Button.

Figure 3-26: I Command Thee!

While the visual effect is hardly Louvre material, the addition of Command Buttons to this Form makes it complete; the Form, as it stands, could certainly do the job.

■ **TIP**

All Command Buttons have an interesting characteristic: if you click on them, but slide the cursor off the face of the button before releasing the mouse, the click doesn't "take." This is described in some places as buggy behavior; it isn't. Command Buttons (and other Controls that behave like Command Buttons) are made to work that way.

WordBasic Command Button Funnies

WordBasic requires that every Form—every Dialog Box—have at least one Command Button Control, of some description. Without a Command Button, the logic goes, WordBasic would have no way of knowing when the user is finished using the Form.

■ T I P

Here's another WordBasic design feature worth keeping in the back of your head. It's confusing, but if you use WordBasic Command Buttons, it'll hit you sooner or later. And if you think the description is confusing, wait 'til you try to debug a program that's misbehaving because of this stuff!

WordBasic has three different kinds of Command Buttons. Two are predefined: "OK" and "Cancel." (They show up on the Form, as you might expect, saying "OK" and "Cancel." Ingenious. . . .) The third kind is just a regular Command Button: WordBasic calls them PushButtons, but you can call them anything you like.

Figure 3-27: WordBasic OK, Cancel, and "Other Command" Buttons

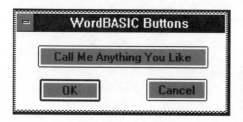

WordBasic has two ways of retrieving—identifying—the Command Button that the user pushed. The first way, the "Give Me That Button Number" approach looks like this:

```
ButtonThatWasPushed=Dialog(MyDialogBox)
```

The command buttons are numbered internally: the OK Button, if one exists, is numbered minus one; the Cancel Button, if it exists, is numbered zero; and each of the other Command Buttons is assigned a number, sequentially, starting at one.

When WordBasic runs this first way, it splashes your dialog box up on the screen and waits for the user to push a button. When the button is pushed, WordBasic sets the variable—in this case "ButtonThatWasPushed"—to the number of the button. If the user hits the Esc key, your program gets a zero.

B U G

Both the WordBasic Manual ("Using WordBasic," Microsoft Press, 1992) and the Word for Windows 2.0 on-line help say that clicking on "Cancel" will result in a minus one being returned to your program. Not so. It's a zero.

The second way of retrieving the Command Button has its roots in older versions of WordBasic. It looks like this:

```
Dialog MyDialogBox
```

Note how there's no direct way to retrieve the number of the Command Button that was pushed—no variable in the program, nothing to receive any indication of what the user has done.

In this second situation, pushing on a Cancel button, hitting the Esc key, or pushing Enter if the first button is a Cancel button will *trigger an Error condition!* If you don't have a routine set up specifically to handle Errors, everything goes quickly south in a handbasket; WinWord croaks, your carefully crafted macro grinds to a complete halt.

Save yourself a lot of headaches. Don't use the second method, the "I Don't Care Which Button Was Pushed" approach to WordBasic Command Buttons. Always retrieve the button number, even if you never use it. Above all else, don't change horses mid-stream; innocently switching your program between the first way and the second way can really make things go bump in the night.

Visual Basic Command Buttons
Visual Basic, as usual, is a touch smarter.

You needn't use a Command Button Control anywhere on your Visual Basic Forms. As the Event-Driven champ, it's entirely possible that your Visual Basic programs won't ever need to be told, explicitly, to take control. Instead of requiring the user to click on a Button, some Visual Basic programs can take their cues from the outside world: a timer goes off, a program is started, and the user types in a fixed-length I.D. number. Any of these Events could tell Visual Basic to "take it away" with no click of a button required.

Or—even better—you may find it easier for your users to click on pictures instead of those dull, drab, text-only Command Buttons. More about that and the Picture Box Control at the end of this chapter.

Command Button Control Properties
Command Buttons have all the Properties you would expect—Caption (not "Text" because it can't be changed by the user), size, location, font, and so on—plus a few unusual ones.

In Visual Basic, you can make one Command Button the "Default." That's the button that automatically gets pushed whenever the user hits Enter. You can also make one Command Button the "Cancel": it gets pushed whenever the user hits Esc.

■ **T I P**

Somewhat surprisingly, the Visual Basic Default and Cancel buttons can be the same button!—If you want to be absolutely, positively sure that a certain Button gets pushed, make it both Default and Cancel.

B U G

According to the manual, Visual Basic Command Buttons can also have a color Property. Close but no cigar, folks. The color you specify is plastered on the Form, but then Visual Basic draws a drab gray Command Button Control *on top of* the colored box! On some machines, some of the time, you can see a bit of your chosen color, very briefly when the button is pushed or occasionally surrounding the Button's Caption when you Tab over to the Button. But it's mighty fleeting, and not exactly what you would call a Property.

Changing Command Button Colors

■ **T I P**

If you want to change the color of a Command Button, your only choice is to change the color of all Command Buttons, everywhere throughout Windows. It turns out that changing the color of all Command Buttons is like falling off a log.

Use any character-based editor: the DOS 5 EDIT editor works fine; SYSEDIT is simpler if you know how to use it—and **don't** use Word for Windows; it isn't a character-based editor, unless you remember to save as text + breaks. Open up WIN.INI, a file in your Windows directory. Scroll on down until you find three lines in the [colors] section that look like this:

```
ButtonFace=192 192 192
ButtonShadow=128 128 127
ButtonText=0 0 0
```

Those three numbers specify the intensity of Red, Green, and Blue respectively: 0 for none, 255 for maximum intensity. Black is 0 0 0, and by default you get black text on your buttons. If you want to make all your Command Button Control faces white—all of them, throughout Windows—change that first line to:

```
ButtonFace = 255 255 255
```

Or you can make them red with:

```
ButtonFace = 255 0 0
```

Each time you'll have to close WIN.INI, then restart Windows.
Neat, huh?

Frames

Sometimes you have to draw boxes around things, to visually (or logically) group them. The simplest kind of box is called a Frame Control.

Let's go back to an earlier Basil example and take a look:

Figure 3-28: Frames

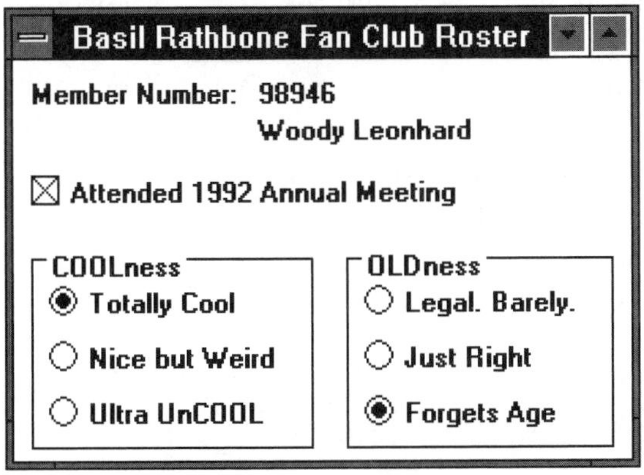

In this case, there are two groups of Option Button Controls. The user can pick exactly one COOLness and exactly one OLDness. The Form emphasizes that point by drawing Frame Controls around the groups of Option Buttons. More importantly, behind the scenes, Visual Basic has separated the two groups *logically*, by associating each set of Option Buttons with a Frame: the three Option Buttons on the left are part of the COOLness Frame, and the three on the right are part of the OLDness Frame.

Frames (called "Group Boxes" in WordBasic) are rather unassuming types. Can't do too much with them; don't have too many Properties to play around with. A Control Milquetoast.

Frames have a size and a location, of course. A background color, at least—in Visual Basic. A Caption (can't be changed by the user, so it isn't "Text"). But that's about it. Even the box border is pretty much fixed; no fancy Frames allowed. No bugs. No tips. No errors. No runs batted in.

Would that they were all this easy!

End of the Line for WordBasic

That exhausts WordBasic's Controls. Let's take a quick glance backward.

WordBasic uses a specific type of Form (or window, if you prefer) for interacting with users. It's called a Dialog Box.

Every WordBasic Form must have at least one Command Button Control. WordBasic needs that Control so the user can tell your program "Hey! I'm done!" Not being overly endowed in the Event-Driven department, WordBasic needs little tips like that from time to time.

WordBasic Forms may also include plain old text, which cannot be modified by the user: i.e., Label Controls. They may have places where the user can type away to the heart's content: those are Text Box Controls. There can be Check Boxes. And Option Buttons. Frames ("Group Boxes") can separate the Option Buttons.

Finally, WordBasic has List Boxes and Combo Boxes. They're a bit plain-vanilla compared to Visual Basic's flavors, but they'll do in a pinch.

Eight Controls. That's what you get in WordBasic.

Figure 3-29: That's All She Wrote

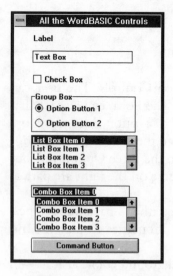

Visual Basic has six more Controls. Let's take a look.

Scroll Bars

Scroll Bar Controls rate as a giant leap forward in communicating with users. They aren't appropriate in most situations, but when you hit the right application, you'll wonder how you ever got along without them.

You know those survey Forms?—The kind that say "Rate Homer's Squirrelburgers on a Scale from One to Ten, Where Ten Is Perfect and One Is the Pits"? That's a Scroll Bar application.

Homer's Squirrelburgers
Take a look at this:

Figure 3-30: Homer's Squirrelburger Scroll Bars

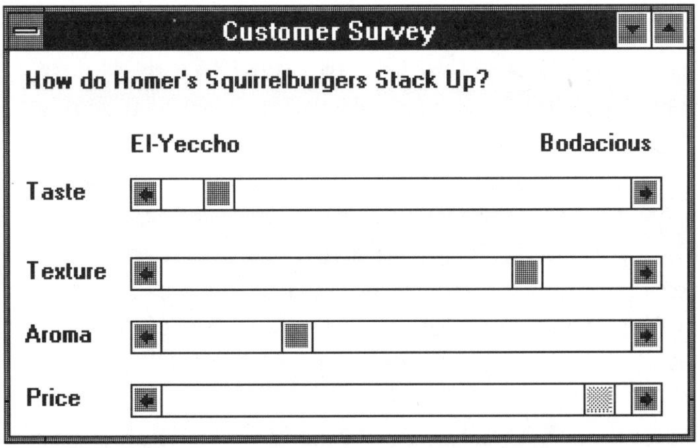

Instead of making the user think of numbers—when numbers don't really have any direct meaning—the Scroll Bar Control lets you capture subjective information, letting the user see how values interrelate. It's quite a step forward in user interfaces.

Even more powerful is the ability, in Visual Basic, to give immediate feedback. You don't have to wait for the user to click a button or hit the Enter key.

The Scroll Bar's great advantage is how intuitive it makes things. Show users how to use a Scroll Bar once, and you'll never have to show them again.

Scroll Bar Properties
Visual Basic gives you lots of flexibility in working with Scroll Bars. You can have horizontal or vertical Scroll Bars. You set the size and location, and the arrows and that little floating square are all drawn for you.

The Scroll Bar reports back to your program with a number that indicates how far the little square (it's called a "thumb") has been scrolled. Your program sets the minimum and maximum values, the numbers that correspond to "Square is all the way left" and "Square is all the way right," and Visual Basic takes care of the rest.

Your program has control over how far the little square moves when the arrow is clicked; that's called the "SmallChange" Property. You even have control over how far the square moves when the user clicks inside the Bar itself. That's called the "LargeChange" Property.

The user can always pick up the square and drag it, too.

All in all, this is a wonderfully powerful Control. Too bad you can't set the color!

BUG

For reasons known only to Microsoft, the default values for Scroll Bar Properties result in Scroll Bars that are ludicrously hard to use. Unless you change the numbers, a Scroll Bar has a minimum value of 0 and a maximum value of 32,767. That wouldn't be bad, except the "SmallChange" value, if you don't change it, is 1. *Small change, indeed.*

Using the default values, you can click on an arrow for about ten minutes before the little square moves all the way on a Scroll Bar Control. Lousy design decision. You'll have to reset at least one of those Property numbers (min, max, or SmallChange), if you want your users to really *use* Scroll Bars.

If that isn't an official bug, it should be.

Drive, Directory, and File List Box Controls

We'll group these three Controls together. They're all variations on List Boxes, executed with daring and verve!

Just to give you a glimpse of how powerful these Controls can be: the combination you see in Figure 3-31 on the following page can be made fully functional with just two—count 'em two—lines of Visual Basic code

```
DirectoryList.Path=DriveList.Drive
```

says that if the drive in the list of drives changes, Visual Basic should reset the path in the directory list, so it starts showing directories on the new dirve and

```
FileList.Path=DirectoryList.Path
```

says that if the user picks a new directory, change the list of files around so it starts showing files in the new path.

Figure 3-31: Drive, Directory, and File List Boxes

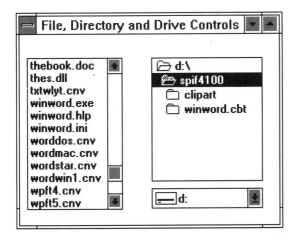

Of course, you sacrifice a bit of flexibility for that kind of power. Let's take a look at what these Controls do and how they may not do everything you want.

Drive List Box Control Properties

The Drive Control is a simple Drop-Down List Box. It lists all the drives available—including RAMdrives. Like this:

Figure 3-32: Drive List Box Exposed

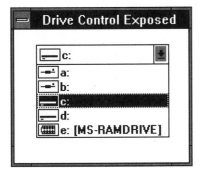

On the one hand, this is a sophisticated little Control. It finds all the outstanding drives, identifies them as floppy, hard drive, or RAMdrive (that little picture is supposed to look like a memory chip), and presents them to the user. The user can use the keyboard to select a drive: typing an "a" selects the "a:" drive.

On the other hand, it's a rather limited Control. It only comes in one flavor: Drop-Down List Box. If you want a regular List Box or a Combo Box of some sort, you're out of luck.

It doesn't let you override the choices presented—if, for some reason, Visual Basic failed to detect the presence of drive "f:" the user has no way to force this Control to give you an "f:".

■ TIP

And if you don't make the Control wide enough, the "[MS-RAMDRIVE]" shown in Figure 3-32 will be truncated to something inscrutable like "[MS-RAM...]" or, even worse, "[MS...]." Try explaining to a novice user that the weird picture (a 16-legged bug?) followed by "e:[MS...]" stands for a RAMdrive!

The Drive List Box Control shares all the Properties of a regular old List Box Control, with one exception. Instead of churning out a "Text," like the List Box, the Drive List creates a "Drive." The "Drive" Property isn't available when you are creating your Form, but your program can get at it when it's running.

Drive List Box Oddities

Another interesting design feature. Most "Drive" Property values—once you figure out that they're really the "Text" of a List Box—make sense. The Control generates things like "a:" and "b:" and "c:" in other words, the names of drives.

BUG

Alas and alack, when your user chooses a RAMdrive you get an abomination, something like "e: [MS-RAMDRIVE]"! Don't try to cobble together a DOS file name using the "Drive" Property. You'll get a sporadic error that only occurs when the user picks a RAMdrive.

A real killer.

Directory List Box Control Properties

One more powerful Control for your bag of Visual Basic tricks.

Feed the Directory List Box Control a DOS path, and it just takes off, like Figure 3-33 on the following page.

Figure 3-33: Pick a Directory, Any Directory

The beauty of this Control is that it is completely self-contained. If you start with a diskette drive path—say, "a:"—this Control goes out to the diskette drive and picks up all the directories on "a:". If you double-click on a subdirectory—say, "asp" in Figure 3-33—the Control is smart enough to bring "c:\winword\asp" to the top (showing a little open folder for "asp" below the open folder for "winword") and to look for the next lower level of subdirectories.

Mighty smart.

This Control has all the Properties you would expect from a List Box Control, plus one called "Path" that reflects the current path. The Path Property isn't available when you're designing your Form, but it's right there when the program is running.

Directory List Box Oddities

There are several Directory oddities. Not exactly bugs, perhaps, but not something you'd expect just by looking at the Control.

BUG

List Box Controls, as you may recall, have a ListIndex Property. The ListIndex is the number (starting at zero) of the item you've chosen; in the case of Directory List Boxes, it is the number of the subdirectory under the current directory that you've chosen. In Figure 3-33, if the user clicks on "asp," the ListIndex Property will be one, signifying the second choice in the list.

What if you click on a subdirectory above the current directory? For example, in Figure 3-33, what happens if you click on "c:\"? ListIndex goes negative!

Rule of thumb: click on the current directory, and ListIndex comes out minus one. Click one level above that and your program will get a minus two. Next level above comes out minus three. And so on.

Surprisingly, the array List—the one that contains all of the List Box items—is updated properly. In the Figure 3-33 example, ListBox(-2) will give you "c:\". Nice.

■ T I P

Be careful what you feed the Path Property. If you set it to "a:", the Directory List Box Control will work just fine, providing the a: drive exists. But if your program sends it an "a" with no colon, you'll trigger an error.

B U G

One of the idiosyncrasies of the Path Property can't really be considered a bug, but it's stupid enough that it should be: inconsistencies in the final backslash on the directory name. The final backslash on a string can make or break your program. Visual Basic should be consistent: when you ask for a directory, you should always get a string that either does or does not end in a backslash.

Not so the Path Property. The Path in Figure 3-33 will be reported as "c:\winword," which is just fine. But if you click on the "c:", the Path Property changes to "c:\". Note the trailing backslash.

That's a big-league pain in the neck because every time your program tries to put together a file name from the Path Property, you must check to see if there is a trailing "\" on the Path, and if there isn't you have to append one.

B U G

The Path Property ignores everything after a "[", that is, a left bracket. Set the Path to "a:ItWasTheBestOfTimes" and you'll get a runtime error. Set Path to "a:[LifeTheUniverseAndEverything" and Visual Basic won't even hiccup; it'll know you meant "a:".

■ **T I P**

The Directory List Box Control is mighty dumb in at least one way. If your user tries to access a drive that isn't ready—say, if he or she clicks on "a:" but there's no diskette in drive "a:"—the Control will not perform any checking. Not even a rudimentary "Abort, Retry, Fail?". Confronted with this situation, Visual Basic merely dies with a distinctly unfriendly message: "Device unavailable."

When you use Directory List Box Controls, be sure to include (and test!) rudimentary error handling routines. You'll see many examples of error handlers in Chapters 5, 6, and 7.

File List Box Control Properties

The File List Box Control rounds out the troika. Set the File Box's Path Property, and up pops a list of files:

Figure 3-34: The File List Box

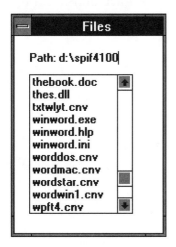

The File List Box has some interesting capabilities, buried away in its Properties.

There are several selection Properties. The Pattern, for example, lets your program restrict displayed files to those that meet a DOS file pattern; for example, a Pattern Property of "*.doc" will limit the File List Box Control to only show you files that end in ".doc."

You may also limit displayed files depending on the files' attributes: Archive, Hidden, ReadOnly, System. Neat stuff.

It would be nice if File List Boxes had a few additional options: the ability to display folders for subdirectories, much as File Manager does, comes to mind. It would also be nice if your users could select more than one file at a time, using the Windows Shift+ and Ctrl+ selection conventions; being a List Box, though, that seems out of the question.

All in all, this Control does yeoman work, with few if any bugs.

The Timer Control

Integral to the Event-Driven way of things, the Timer Control lets you fire off any series of commands at a predetermined time. Your program might use a Timer Control to say "Run this backup every night at midnight," or "Wait ten seconds before continuing with the next part of the program."

When the appointed time comes, your time-delayed instructions are executed, just like any other instructions.

Windows, as a giant message handler, merely queues up your Timer Control instructions. Come the time, Windows wakes up whatever needs to be woken and performs the tasks. When you design your program with a Timer Control, you'll see a little clock like this:

Figure 3-35: The Design-Time Timer

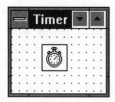

That clock disappears as soon as your program starts. Fades into the background, and keeps on ticking.

WordBasic OnTime

WordBasic has an OnTime capability, in the form of a WordBasic command. It isn't really a Control. At least, not exactly. The primary problems with WordBasic's OnTime are twofold:

- Only one WordBasic OnTime can be in effect at any given moment. If you try to do a second OnTime before the first one is done, the second one completely obliterates the first one.

- WordBasic OnTime is a "flaky function," with many known (and no doubt lots of unknown!) side effects.

B U G

A simple example: if you use WinWord's F8 key—the "Extend Selection" key—and an OnTime Event happens while you're in the middle of extending a selection, the whole operation is called off. Why? It's a bug, pure as can be.

Visual Basic Timer Control

Visual Basic, by contrast, can handle up to 16 different Timer Controls; 16 different clocks, as it were, can be ticking away simultaneously, each connected to a specific piece of code that will execute at the appointed time.

■ **T I P**

Note that Timer Controls (including WordBasic's OnTime) don't guarantee that your code will be run immediately when its appointed time is reached. Windows has no preemptive capability. The best Windows can do is wait until the time arrives, then stick your program's timed code in line, queuing it up with any other activities that may be pending.

In practice, on a normal system, that delay is insignificant. Usually. But if your whole system bogs down under some unforeseen gargantuan processing load—or if you're sitting in a DOS box while in standard mode—the difference between "time posted" and "time executed" can be significant.

■ **T I P**

Sometimes Timer Controls can interfere with the functioning of screen blankers. It seems to vary with the particular Control and the specific blanker. If it's important that your program execute at predetermined intervals, and if it's also important that a screen blanker kick in properly, you should test both the precise Timer Control and the exact screen blanker you'll be using and make sure they don't step on each other's feet.

Picture Boxes

Saving the best for last here.

Visual Basic Picture Box Controls have an enormous range of function and flexibility. There's a simple example in Figure 3-36 on the following page.

Those pictures of floppy disks are more than mere pictures: they're Picture Box Controls. As such, your program can use them for all sorts of things, including

Command-style Buttons! The user might select the size of diskette they want to format by *clicking on the diskette*.

Figure 3-36: Two Picture Box Controls

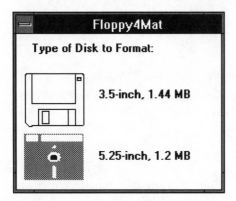

A Picture Box Control can be filled with any .BMP bitmap picture, .WMF Windows Metafile format picture, or .ICO icon. In fact, your program can swap pictures in and out of the Control at will. We'll take that capability to some strange extremes in the next few chapters.

Picture the Versatility

Behind the pretty face, Picture Box Controls have all sorts of capabilities.

For example, your program can "Print" text to a Picture Box, just as if it were printing to a printer. The printed text inside a Picture Box can be formatted with fonts, size, bold, italic, color, the works.

More than that, your program can "Draw" lines, circles, arcs, all sorts of things, in a Picture Box. You have control over the width and location of the pen, colors, shading, scale, direction, anything you can imagine.

You'll also find that you can use the Picture Box for any Windows GDI (Graphic Device Interface) API call: in short, anything you can draw in Windows, you can draw directly on a Picture Box.

A Picture Box Control can—at your option—be resizable by the user. If you take advantage of the AutoSize Property, the picture inside the Control is dynamically stretched to fit whatever size box the user constructs.

All in all, it's one powerful Control. We will use it often.

Back to the Keyboard

That's it for built-in Controls. They'll serve as the foundation of all that is to come.

We'll take a look at some custom Controls, home-grown Controls that solve specific problems, near the end of the book.

For now, brush off your keyboard. Time to get back into WordBasic and cook up a little code.

Working with WordBasic

Take out the Companion Disk. We're going to poke around Windows a bit and learn some WordBasic while we're at it.

We'll be building and running a program—a macro, if you must—called "Windows Explorer" that examines all sorts of Windows settings and prints out a report of what it finds.

There are nine programs in the WinExplorer series, and we'll spend the rest of this chapter going through them. On the Companion Disk they're numbered C4PGM1.DOC, C4PGM2.DOC, on up to C4PGM9.DOC. Each builds on the last: WinExplorer program 2 contains all of program 1, program 3 contains all of program 2, and so on, up to program 9, the final program, which contains all of programs 1 through 8.

WordBasic Variables

Let's start with a very, very brief discussion of variables. This is the extent of the textbook-style lecture. *(Hold the applause for the end, please.)* After we get variables out of the way, you'll learn everything else in this chapter by doing, hands-on, nitty-gritty.

WordBasic has two types of variables. That's it. Every variable is either a string of characters or a floating point "real" number.

String variables have names that end with a "$" dollar sign. Numbers don't. Here are a few examples:

```
MyName$="Woody Leonhard"
Pi=3.14159
Index=3
```

MyName$ is a string: the dollar sign is a dead giveaway. Pi is a real number. Perhaps not so obvious, Index is a real number, too. You might think it would be an integer or something, but it isn't. All WordBasic variables are either strings or reals. Period.

You can make variable arrays by using the Dim statement ("Dim" is derived from "Dimension"). Like this:

```
Dim Names$(10)
i=323
Dim ActiveWindowNumbers(i)
```

WordBasic subscripts start at zero, so in this example there are eleven Names$—from Names$(0) to Names$(1) up to Names$(10)—and 324 Active-WindowNumbers. You can put a Dim statement just about anywhere.

When WordBasic first encounters a variable or a Dim statement, it initializes the variable. Numbers start out at zero; strings start out empty.

And that's everything there is to know about variables! There are some nuances, especially when you have to work with Windows' API calls (some Windows subroutines need numbers fed to them in a certain form), but we'll worry about the variable gymnastics as we encounter them.

Just remember: all WordBasic variables are strings or reals. Period.

Okay. That's the end of the lecture. It's all hands-on from here.

WinExplorer 1—Creating and Printing a Document

Time to dig in and build a real application.

By the time you're through with Chapter 4, WinExplorer will be able to print a fancy report showing you all sorts of things about the Windows environment that engulfs you: which applications are active, how long Windows has been running, available memory, the nefarious Free System Resources, and much, much more.

Then we'll pick up WinExplorer again in Chapter 8. By the time you emerge from that chapter, WinExplorer will pop a Windows status summary up on your screen, and let you push a button that will print a detailed report, in a nice font. Fancy stuff. Light-years ahead of the good old days when you'd be lucky to write a routine that flashes numbers on the screen, and if it's very sophisticated dumps the screen to the printer.

WordBasic, as the brains behind Word for Windows' pretty face, will let you create, manipulate, mangle, and print any document you can imagine: that's WordBasic's *raison d'etre*, and not surprisingly WordBasic is mighty good at it.

What's surprising is how well WordBasic functions as a spelunker in Windows' innermost recesses: a simple, easy macro language most often used to record and play back repetitive Word for Windows keystrokes can actually dig into the belly of the Windows beast and return with valuable information.

If you tried to duplicate WinExplorer in a lower-level language like C or Pascal, it would take many hundreds—perhaps thousands—of lines of code, weeks of effort, and more than a few gray hairs.

By contrast, you will probably find the WordBasic way to WinExplorer a fun challenge, a way to brush up on your Basic code, a chance to say, "Oh, I remember how to do that!" . . . . simply a pleasant way to spend a rainy Saturday morning.

Loading WinExplorer from the Companion Disk

The program you want, the WinMortals Windows Explorer Program 1, is called C4PGM1.DOC. (Chapter 4, ProGraM 1, DOCument.) Crank up Word for Windows. Click on File, then Open. Click on the directory that contains the uncompressed Companion Disk (if you follow the Appendix 3 directions literally, that will be "C:\WINWORD\WMORTALS"). Double-click on C4PGM1.DOC.

You should see something that looks like this:

Figure 4-1: Arise, C4PGM1.DOC!

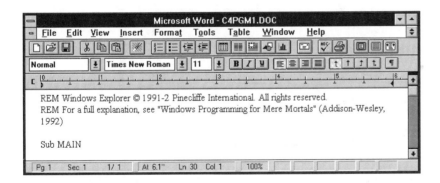

Yeah, it's big. But it's nice.

Click on Edit, then Select All. The whole thing should suddenly turn black. That's good. Click on Edit, then Copy. There. You've copied all of C4PGM1.DOC onto the Windows clipboard.

Now, you want to start a new WordBasic macro. Click on Tools, then Macro. Type in a good name—"WinExplorer" comes to mind. Click Edit. You'll see the WordBasic development environment, shown in Figure 4-2 on the following page.

Figure 4-2: WordBasic Home, Sweet Home

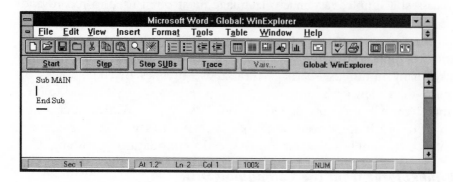

Select all of the stuff there, from Sub MAIN to End Sub (it's easiest to drag your mouse over all of it, or slide the cursor down the left side; if all else fails, click on Edit, then Select All). Hit the "Del" Delete key. Poof! It's gone.

Now, click on Edit, then Paste. WinExplorer is now in place.

Figure 4-3: WinExplorer, Ready to Rock 'n Roll

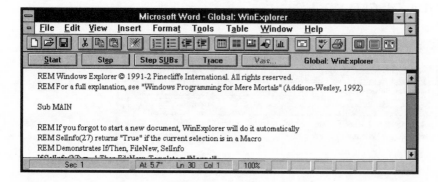

Don't get too excited if your screen looks a little different from this one. WinWord has all sorts of customizing capabilities, ways to move things around and make your copy unique. We'll play with some of them shortly.

If you have to take a break in the middle of things, click on File, then Close. Say "Yes" when asked if you want to "Save Changes to Global: WinExplorer." Click on File, then Exit. Say "Yes" when asked if you want to "Save global command and summary changes." Next time you fire up WinWord, click on Tools, then Macro, click once on WinExplorer, and click Edit. You'll be right back where you started.

(If you're impatient, you could go ahead and load up C4PGM9.DOC, and click on "Start." Neat stuff, huh? Now, don't get ahead of yourself—even if you've been programming WordBasic since the time of the pterodactyls, you'll learn quite a lot by stepping through this chapter. So go back to C4PGM1.DOC and follow along.)

When it comes time to look at program 2, you should select all of the macro WinExplorer, hit the "Del" key to delete it, then go through this procedure all over again, this time copying in C4PGM2.DOC. Same for program 3. And so on.

Typing WinExplorer

If you don't have the Companion Disk, there's a lot of typing in your future. Instead of repeating the same code over and over, we'll give you the "incremental" additions for each of the nine programs, and show you where to stick them.

If you get confused or something somehow doesn't work right, there's a complete listing of WinExplorer in Chapter 8.

Here's the Windows Explorer Program 1, verbatim:

Program 4-1 (file C4PGM1.DOC): WinExplorer Program 1

```
REM Windows Explorer © 1991-2 Pinecliffe International.
REM All rights reserved.
REM For a full explanation, see "Windows Programming for Mere
REM Mortals" (Addison-Wesley, 1992)

Sub MAIN

REM If you forgot to start a new document, WinExplorer will do it
REM automatically
REM SelInfo(27) returns "-1" if the current selection is in a
REM Macro
REM Demonstrates If/Then, FileNew, SelInfo
If SelInfo(27) = - 1 Then FileNew .Template = "Normal"

REM Start pouring in text
REM Demonstrates Insert, Time$(), Date$()
Insert "Windows Explorer -- a WinMortals Program"
InsertPara
Insert "Run at " + Time$() + " on " + Date$()
InsertPara

REM Wrap up
REM Demonstrates MsgBox() function, FilePrint
If MsgBox("Want To Print the Report?", "WinMortals Window" +\
" Explorer", 4 + 32 + 256) = - 1 Then FilePrint

REM Demonstrates File Save, and use of On Error to trap a
REM "Cancel" in the File Save dialog
On Error Goto Bye
If MsgBox("Want To Save the Report?", "WinMortals Window" +\
" Explorer", 4 + 32 + 256) = - 1 Then FileSave
Bye:
End Sub
```

You'll probably find that the Windows Explorer program is quite useful in its own right and well worth the time it'll take to type.

We'll tackle those commands one at a time.

REM

The program starts with a handful of REM statements. They're actually *called* that—"rem statements." Back in BASIC's dark, dim (pun intended) past, "REM" meant "REMINDER," or "REMARK." So much for history.

Any line of WordBasic code that starts with "REM" is ignored. It's there for human, not computer, consumption.

Similarly, WordBasic ignores anything on a line after a single-quote. Starting a line with REM is the same as starting it with a single-quote.

Blank Lines

They're ignored, too.

Sub MAIN

As a *WinMortals* cognoscenti, you already know that every WordBasic program is a subroutine. The MAIN subroutine is the . . . uh . . . main subroutine! Funny how that works.

If you called this macro "WinExplorer," then every time you tell WordBasic to run "WinExplorer," it'll go fishing for the MAIN subroutine within the "WinExplorer" macro.

Whenever you start writing a macro, WordBasic automatically types in "Sub MAIN" and "End Sub" for you, so it's hard to mess up this part, except when cutting and pasting in macros from elsewhere.

If / Then

We're going to see several variations on the If/Then statement. Somewhat appropriately, this first one is the simplest form.

WordBasic evaluates the expression between "If" and "Then." If the expression comes up true, the command after the "Then" is run. If the expression comes up false, WordBasic goes on to the next command.

Ah, but you already knew that, didn't you?

WinExplorer generates a report by stuffing stuff into a document. The last thing you want WinExplorer to do is pour that report into the middle of your macro. That's why there's this little hook, right here, to see if the report would be dumped into a macro. If the active window is a macro, this If/Then statement creates a "real" document. Quick.

Here's how the program figures out if it's in the middle of a macro:

Built-In Function: SelInfo(n)

Like almost every computer language ever devised, WordBasic has several built-in functions, functions that are ready for you to use at any time.

SelInfo(n) is a rather powerful function. It tells you all sorts of things about the current selection.

The Selection What's a "Selection"? Good question.

Back in the good old days computer jocks had something called a cursor; it was usually an underscore that followed along as we typed in text strings. Fancy cursors might've been big or small, or blink, or turn the video "reverse" so you saw different colors.

What with mice and the Windows revolution, cursors aren't as simple as they once were. When a cursor is acting like a cursor—when it follows along as the user types in text—it's usually called an "insertion point." Fair enough. That *is* the point at which text is inserted.

But if you drag your cursor over a bunch of stuff, highlighting it or "turning it black," suddenly the old cursor isn't following along any more. It becomes a selection. A handful of text or pictures or spreadsheet cells or whatever.

SelInfo(n) Info That little "n" in SelInfo(n) tells WordBasic what you want to know about the current selection. SelInfo(1), for example, returns the page number for the first character in the current selection.

You can look up SelInfo(n) in a manual if you want. But it's a lot easier to use WordBasic's extensive (and amazingly accurate) HELP facility.

WordBasic Help You're looking at WinExplorer program 1, up on the screen, right? Good. Click somewhere inside "SelInfo(27)". Doesn't matter where.

Now hit F1.

Figure 4-4: HELP!

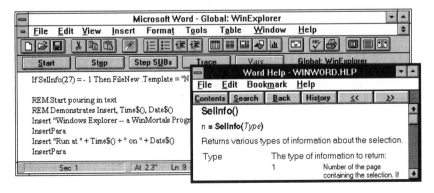

Any time you're uncertain about a WordBasic command, try to type something that you think might work, then hit F1. Help will suddenly appear. Want to insert text into a document? Type "insert" and hit F1. Like to change fonts? Type "font" and hit F1. It's that simple. When it works.

SelInfo(27) If you scroll down the help listing for SelInfo(n), you'll discover that SelInfo(27) returns a minus one if the "current selection is in a macro editing window." WordBasic calls its support system—the one you can see right now, with "Start" and "Step" and all that stuff—a macro editing window. So if you run this macro while you're editing a macro (and you're editing a macro right now!), the

```
If SelInfo(27)= -1 Then .....
```

statement will evaluate to "True."

■ TIP

You'll see something similar to this "If SelInfo(27) = -1 Then" phrase at the beginning of many macros, particularly those distributed with the commercial version of Word for Windows. They're there to keep casual weekend hackers from shooting themselves in the foot. You'd be surprised how many times people get to playing around in strange things, find themselves editing a macro, and decide to click "Start." Without the "If SelInfo(27)" test, many macros—being run *on themselves*—would self-destruct.

FileNew

If WinExplorer finds itself in a macro, it creates a new document, otherwise it already has a document.

FileNew is the WordBasic command that creates a new document. (It's kind of nit-picking, but the new document isn't really a *file* until you save it. Oh well, close enough for government work.)

WinWord always bases a new document on a template. A template is nothing more than a blueprint for how a document should look: margins, paper size, maybe a logo, boilerplate text, that kind of thing. WinWord ships with tons of templates, covering everything from in-house memos to Ph.D. dissertations to three-up labels.

Everybody has a "normal" template. It's stored away as a file called "NOR-MAL.DOT" (**DOT** = **DO**cument Template). The WordBasic command

```
FileNew .Template="normal"
```

merely tells WinWord to create a new document—or file, if you must—and base that document on the "normal" template.

Spelling counts, but capitalization doesn't. All of these are the same:

```
FileNew .Template="Normal"
FileNew .Template="normal"
FileNew .Template="nOrMaL"
```

But this isn't the same at all:

```
FileNew .Template="Normul"
```

FileNew, like many WordBasic commands, simply mimics a sequence of user mouse clicks. It's equivalent to— almost indistinguishable from—the user clicking on File, then New. (That's why they call it "FileNew", eh?)

Most Word for Windows dialogs have options: pick a file to open, choose how many copies to print, type in the characters you want to find, that kind of thing. WordBasic takes care of those options by sticking ".Field=Value" strings on the end of the command. Like this:

```
FileOpen .Name="Mydoc.doc"
FilePrint .NumCopies=22
EditFind .Find="Something"
```

A large part of mastering WordBasic consists of figuring out what those fields really mean, and how to take advantage of them in your programs.

If / Then Redux
So there you have the whole shebang.

```
If SelInfo(27) = -1 Then FileNew .Template = "Normal"
```

checks to see if the selection (cursor) is currently inside a macro. If so, WinExplorer starts up a new document. Otherwise, it has been invoked while there already was a document.

Insert
After a couple of (ignored) REM statements, you'll see the WordBasic command Insert. That command simply inserts text into the current document, at the current insertion point (or selection or cursor, if you prefer).

```
Insert "Windows Explorer -- a WinMortals Program"
```

simply inserts that text into the current document.

No brain surgery here.

InsertPara
Inserts a paragraph mark. It's the same thing as hitting "Enter."

String Concatenation

You can smash strings together—"concatenate" them, if you prefer—by using a "+" sign, just as you would expect.

```
MyName$="Woody " + "Leonhard"
```

is perfectly valid. Try doing that in C!

Built-In Functions Time$() and Date$()

These are two widely used built-in functions. See the "$" dollar sign on the end of them? That should tell you that they return strings. They do.

> ■ **TIP**
>
> There are lots of ways to print a time and a date: 24-hour format, month-day-year, and so on. When you use the WordBasic Time$( ) and Date$( ) functions, you'll get the format that's set in the Windows Control Panel and generally stored in a Windows system file called WIN.INI. More precisely, your program will receive a string that conforms to the Windows 3.1 time format or the short date format.
>
> The default format for the United States looks like this:

```
6:26 AM
1/15/92
```

> Other countries' versions of Windows will have different formats.

> ■ **TIP**
>
> The user may change the format of Date$( ) and Time$( ) by cranking up the Windows 3.1 Control Panel and clicking on "International"—*not* "Date and Time." Follow the instructions to change the time or short date format.

> ■ **TIP**
>
> Be cautious when using Time$( ) and Date$( ); your program shouldn't assume the format will always be the same. Your WordBasic program *can* control the format of the date and time, but doing so involves WinWord fields. You'll be happy to hear that we'll avoid fields for the time being. You're welcome.

If MsgBox()

Way back in Chapter 2 (in C2PGM1.DOC, to be precise) we played around with Message Boxes. You saw how to put a title on a Message Box, how to give one an icon, default button, that sort of thing.

The Chapter 2 Message Box looked like this:

```
MsgBox "Text", "Title", IconsButtonsAndDefaults
```

where "IconsButtonsAndDefaults" is the sum of:

```
mbButtonOK = 0
mbButtonOKCancel = 1
mbButtonAbortRetryIgnore = 2
mbButtonYesNoCancel = 3
mbButtonYesNo = 4
mbButtonRetryCancel = 5
mbIconStopSign = 16
mbIconQuestionMark = 32
mbIconExclamationPoint = 48
mbIconInfo = 64
mbDefaultFirstButton = 0
mbDefaultSecondButton = 256
mbDefaultThirdButton = 512
```

Remember that MsgBox?

This MsgBox(), by virtue of the parenthesis, is only slightly more complex: it returns a number to your program. The number tells you which button has been pushed. If the leftmost button is clicked, your program receives a −1. If the next button is clicked (assuming there *is* a next button!), your program gets a zero. And if the next button is clicked (assuming there are three of them), your program gets a +1.

Yeah, it's hard to remember all those icon numbers. That's why you can type "MsgBox," click F1, and you'll see all the numbers and what they mean.

The two MsgBox() commands we're looking at here in WinExplorer both follow this form:

```
If MsgBox("Huh?","WinExplorer",4+32+256) = −1 Then.....
```

The first MsgBox() string—"Huh?"—appears inside the box; the second string is the box's title. The 4 + 32 + 256 translates into "Yes and No Buttons" + "Put in a Question Mark" + "The Second Button—No—Is the Default." Thusly:

Figure 4-5: The MsgBox()

If the user clicks Yes (the leftmost button), your program gets a –1 and the If statement goes True. If the user pushes Enter, or clicks No, this MsgBox() returns a value of zero and the If statement comes up False.

FilePrint

In the first MsgBox(), users are asked if they want to print the report. If they click YES, WinExplorer prints the current document, using a simple

```
FilePrint
```

As you might imagine, FilePrint uses all the existing settings (margins, paper bins, and on and on) and prints the current document—or file, again, if you must. That's all.

FileSave

In the second MsgBox(), the user is given the option of saving the document. If they click Yes, WinExplorer executes

```
FileSave
```

which, in turn, brings up the standard WordBasic "File Save As" Dialog Box. It looks like this:

Figure 4-6: File Save

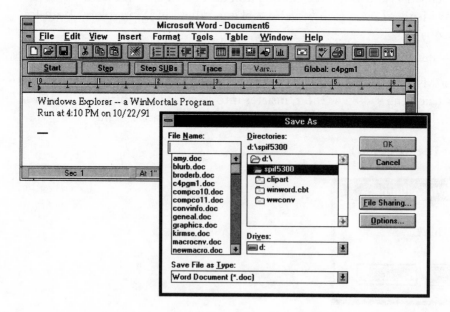

In the normal scheme of things, the user would just go ahead and save the file, giving it an appropriate name, sticking it in an appropriate subdirectory.

Sometimes, though, stuff happens.

In this particular case, the user could click "Cancel" during the FileSave. WordBasic, not knowing exactly how to warn the WinExplorer program, raises an Error condition.

Which leads us, appropriately, to the most complicated—and final—part of WinExplorer program 1.

On Error Goto

> What can we know? or what can we discern,
> When error chokes the windows of the mind?
>
> —Sir John Davies, *The Vanity of Human Learning,* 1596

Unless you take specific steps to change things, an Error condition causes WordBasic to pop up a Dialog Box with a particularly inscrutable message like:

Figure 4-7: WordBasic Explains "Cancel" in File Save

No kidding. That's the message a user will get if they click "Cancel" in the middle of a File Save, unless your program has something set up to handle the Error condition.

WordBasic has just three ways of handling Error conditions.

On Error Resume Next This particularly dangerous command should be called "Ignore All Errors." Once your macro executes an On Error Resume Next command, all error processing stops.

Be very, very careful using On Error Resume Next.

On Error Goto Label This is the most common way of handling errors. Instead of an inscrutable message and a grinding halt, WordBasic, upon encountering an Error condition, jumps to the "Label," and keeps on truckin'.

The WinExplorer command

```
On Error Goto Bye
```

says that if WordBasic hits an error from that point forward, it should hop to the label "Bye:". In this particular case, if the user clicks on "Cancel" while in the FileSave dialog, WordBasic skips on down to "Bye:" and ends the program.

On Error Goto 0 This should've been called "Reset Error Processing." It just cancels out any earlier On Error Resume Next or On Error Goto Label commands and returns WordBasic to normal error handling.

Custom error handling is a very important (and particularly difficult) part of WordBasic and Visual Basic programming, in fact of any kind of programming, in any language. Often the greatest problem is simply figuring out what kind of errors can occur—and how best to break the news to the user.

Bye:

That's a label. A label has to start in the first or second column, and it always ends with a colon.

Your program can Goto a label, but the label has to be hard-coded (that is, you cannot compute the destination for a Goto). Both of these are valid Goto statements, and they'll both transfer control to the same label, "Bye:":

```
Goto Bye
Goto Bye:
```

But WordBasic will have apoplexy over this:

```
Goto "Bye"
```

BUG

Make sure you don't put a tab (or more than one space) in front of a label. If you do, WordBasic won't recognize it. Visual Basic, as usual, is smarter; tabs and leading spaces don't confuse Visual Basic at all.

End Sub

That's all she wrote.

Playtime

Okay. Go ahead. Click "Start." You've earned it!

Figure 4-8: WinExplorer 1 Speaks

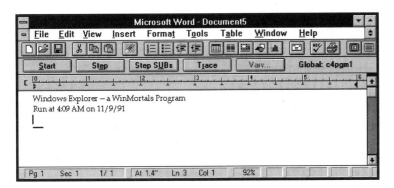

If you want to watch WordBasic struggle with each of your commands, one at a time, click Step. When WinExplorer creates a new document, simply click on Window, then Arrange All, and click Step again. You'll watch the whole thing run through, slo-mo.

When you're tired of looking at the report, just click File, then Close. You'll have another chance to save the report, if you haven't already. When the report file has been closed, your macro will reappear.

Congratulations. By any estimation, you've just written a "real" program in WordBasic.

Recap

So there you have it. Ten lines of WordBasic code, 20 if you count the comments. You've created a document, composed text to put into that document (nothing simple like "Hello, World", but something intelligent), inserted that text into the document, had it automatically formatted by Word for Windows, and given the user a chance to save or print it. Not bad, pilgrim.

You now know enough to write and run a WordBasic macro. Let's take a lingering glance at the commands you've used:

- **REM**—REMinder lines are ignored, as is anything after a single quote.
- **Sub MAIN / End Sub**—mark the beginning and end of the main subroutine. Declare Function and Declare Subroutine go outside the main routine.

- **If** *expression* **Then** *command*—evaluates the *expression*; if it's true, the *command* gets run.

- **SelInfo(n)** gives your program all sorts of interesting information about the current selection. Exactly what kind of information depends on the "n." When in doubt, hit F1.

- **FileNew**—creates a new document.

- **Insert "Stuff," InsertPara**—insert, respectively, "Stuff" and a paragraph mark (carriage return) into the current document, at the insertion point.

- **Time$()** and **Date$()**—return the time and date, in a format dictated by Windows Control Panel settings.

- **MsgBox()**—throws out a message box, waits for the user to click a button, and tells your program which button was pushed.

- **FilePrint**—prints the current document.

- **FileSave**—saves the current document.

- **On Error**—an all-purpose error trap; tells WordBasic where to go when an error condition is triggered. And all sorts of things trigger error conditions.

- **Label:**—something your program can Goto. WordBasic is very picky about labels: they have to butt up against the left margin (tabs are taboo), and they have to end in a colon.

That's a good start on WordBasic commands. Now let's try something a tad more difficult.

WinExplorer 2—Windows Version, Memory, Round(n,i)

On to WinExplorer program 2. This is the longest and most complicated of the bunch; you'll be tackling new stuff at breathtaking speed. Fasten your seat belt.

Loading WinExplorer Program 2

If you have the Companion Disk files, it's easy to copy in program 2. Make sure the old WinExplorer is in front of you. Select it all (click on Edit, then Select All) and delete it (hit the Del key). FileOpen C4PGM2.DOC (click on File, then Open, and go find the file C4PGM2.DOC, which is in C:\WINWORD\ WMORTALS, or wherever you put the decompressed Companion Disk). Copy the file to the clipboard (click Edit, then Select All—it'll turn black; click Edit, then Copy). Close C4PGM2.DOC (click on File, then Close). Copy it into WinExplorer (click Edit, Paste).

If you don't have the Companion Disk files, there are three blocks of code you'll have to type:

Program 4-2, Part 1: Type This Before "Sub MAIN"

```
REM Type this before "Sub MAIN"
Declare Function GetVersion Lib "Kernel"() As Integer
Declare Function GetWindowsDirectory Lib "Kernel"(DirPath$,\
 MaxChars As Integer) As Integer
Declare Function GetFreeSpace Lib "Kernel"(wFlags As Integer) As Long
```

Program 4-2, Part 2: Type This Before "REM Wrap Up"

```
REM Type this before "REM Wrap Up"
REM Get Windows version number, directory, free memory
REM Demonstrates simple arithmetic, Int, InsertPara, Str$
REM The version number is packed; unpack it thusly:
PackedVersionNumber = GetVersion
MinorVersionNumber = Int(PackedVersionNumber / 256)
MajorVersionNumber = PackedVersionNumber - 256 *\ MinorVersionNumber
InsertPara
Insert "Windows Version" + Str$(MajorVersionNumber) + "." +\
 Str$(MinorVersionNumber)
InsertPara
LengthOfDirectory = GetWindowsDirectory(DirectoryPath$, 200)
Insert "Windows loaded from: " + DirectoryPath$
InsertPara
AvailableMemory = GetFreeSpace(0) /(1024 * 1024)
Insert "Currently Available Memory (including virtual): " +\
 Str$(Round(AvailableMemory, 2)) + " MB"
InsertPara
```

Program 4-2, Part 3: Type This After "End Sub"

```
REM Type this at the end of the macro, AFTER "End Sub"
REM WinMortals Rounder © 1991 Pinecliffe International. All
REM rights reserved.
REM Rounds "Number" to "10 to the minus Int(DecimalPlaces)". Not
REM infallible, but usually reliable.
REM Round(1234.5,-2) returns 1200. Round(-4.5,0) returns -5.
REM Round(123.45,1.9) returns 123.5.
Function Round(Number, DecimalPlaces)
Base = 1
iDecimalPlaces = Int(DecimalPlaces)
Select Case iDecimalPlaces
Case Is > 0
    For i = 1 To DecimalPlaces
    Base = Base * 10
    Next i
Case Is < 0
    For i = - 1 To DecimalPlaces Step - 1
    Base = Base / 10
    Next i
```

```
Case Else
End Select
REM Strip out multiples of 32K to keep from blowing Int()'s
REM 32,768 overflow limit
On Error Goto Overflow
Over32KPart = Int((Number * Base) / 32767)
Under32KPart =(Number * Base) -(Over32KPart * 32767)
If Number >= 0 Then
     Round =(Over32KPart * 32767 + Int((Under32KPart) + 0.5)) / Base
Else
     Round =(Over32KPart * 32767 + Int((Under32KPart) - 0.5)) / Base
End If
Goto Bye
Overflow:
MsgBox "Calculation overflow in Roundoff routine. Returning a"+\
" value of" + Str$(Number) + ". Errors may result.", "WinMortals"+\
" Rounder", 16
Round = Number
Bye:
On Error Goto 0
End Function
```

That's the most typing you'll have to do at any single time.

Now follow the bouncing ball as we learn some new commands in WordBasic.

Declare Function/Sub

Back in Chapter 2 you made your first Windows API calls. In the process of writing those calls you used "Declare Function" twice. Let's now look at the "Declare" a little more closely.

Declare "Declare" statements usually appear at the beginning of a macro, before the "Sub MAIN."

Whenever WordBasic hits a "Declare" statement, it knows that it must find the subroutine or function somewhere outside of WordBasic, in other words, in a DLL. (Remember DLLs? We discussed them in Chapter 2). The "Declare" statement is nothing more than a warning to WordBasic.

Function vs. Sub Your program can "Declare Function" or "Declare Sub." There's only one difference: functions return values; subroutines don't.

Function/Sub Names and Libraries Your program must identify a function or subroutine by name and point WordBasic to a library that contains the particular function or subroutine. In the command

```
Declare Function GetFreeSpace Lib "Kernel"(wFlags As Integer) As Long
```

WordBasic had better find a function called "GetFreeSpace" in the (dynamic link) library called "KERNEL." If it doesn't, everything stops abruptly, and an Error condition is raised—assuming you even get to the point where the program will run. You know how much fun Error conditions can be.

This particular function harkens back to the Windows API—the subroutines and functions defined in the Windows Dynamic Link Libraries. Within the Windows DLL called "KERNEL" there is a function called "GetFreeSpace." All is right in the world.

Where Do I Find Out About Names and Libraries? The simple fact is this: it can be excruciatingly difficult finding out what functions and subroutines are available in which libraries. Once you know a particular function exists, it's easy to look up a C description: check the *Microsoft Windows Programmer's Reference* (Microsoft Press, 1990). But finding the right function in the first place is nothing but fun, fun, fun.

Remember that *WinMortals* Appendix 1 contains a list of many Windows functions and subroutines, set out in WordBasic form. Appendix 2 does the same for Visual Basic. And the WinMortals Companion Disk has a more detailed list for Visual Basic only. Unfortunately, there are few (if any!) other compilations geared to those not fluent in C and the Windows SDK—the mythical "Mere Mortal"—although that sad fact is bound to change as more and more of us mortals start working with Windows.

(Parameters) Most "Declare" functions and subroutines need parameters. Your program has to inform WordBasic about those parameters, inside parentheses, in the "Declare" statement.

The GetVersion function doesn't take any parameters, so your program shouldn't put anything between the parentheses. Like this:

```
Declare Function GetVersion Lib "Kernel"() As Integer
```

Contrariwise, the GetFreeSpace function requires one parameter, and it expects that parameter to be an integer. You inform WordBasic of that fact with a "Declare" like the one you've already seen:

```
Declare Function GetFreeSpace Lib "Kernel"(wFlags As Integer) As Long
```

Return Value Format If you've "Declare"d a function, the function returns a value. You have to tell WordBasic what kind of value is returned. GetVersion and GetWindowsDirectory return Integers. GetFreeSpace returns something called a "Long." And therein lies a tale. . . .

Declare Data Types
If you go out exploring, are you going to have headaches with this one!

■ **T I P**

The simplest way to avoid Data Type problems is the cookbook approach: copy, precisely, the "Declare"s in Appendices 1 and 2, and follow the examples there letter-by-letter.

If you're willing to follow that cookbook approach, you may safely skip the rest of this section (go on down to "**GetVersion**"), and forget that you ever heard about Longs and Doubles and Pointers and HiBytes and the like.

But if you're incorrigible—and you just gotta know—here's the scoop on WordBasic and data types. (If this stuff gets too thick for your tastes, just skip it. Use the cookbook approach. You won't be missing anything a good, stiff drink won't cure.)

Of Strings and Reals and Puppy-dog Teals . . . All WordBasic variables are either strings or reals. Period.

String variables have names that end with a "$" dollar sign. Individual characters within a string run from character #1 (which, in Windows, cannot be printed) to character #255 (which, in the USA version of Windows and the ANSI character set, is the "y with umlaut," or ÿ). WordBasic knows it has hit the end of a string, internally, in memory, when it finds a character #0. In techno-speak that's called a "null terminated" string.

Real variables have names that don't end with a "$" dollar sign. They're stored in memory as double-precision floating point numbers; on the PC that means they can run from about -1.7×10^{308} to $+1.7 \times 10^{308}$. It also means that numbers up to 14 or 15 digits long can be stored exactly, with no round-off error.

So much for the good news.

Unfortunately, WordBasic does not support other data types. And there are *lots* of other data types floating around in Windows; integers come to mind.

This causes no end of mayhem when interacting with a somewhat less restrictive outside world. When you take into account WordBasic's lack of reliable numeric functions, it gets downright infuriating.

Respite for the Weary Fortunately, there are a couple of hooks built into WordBasic that permit some communication with other Windows applications and Windows itself.

In a "Declare" statement—and nowhere else—your program may use two additional data types, "Integer" and "Long."

In the Windows world, an "Integer" is a signed 16-bit integer, i.e., an integer between -32,768 and +32,767. A "Long" (shorthand for "Long Integer") is a signed 32-bit integer.

Don't get carried away. "Integer" and "Long" data types aren't allowed in your program. No way. They are simply key words that warn WordBasic. They trigger conversions, to and from WordBasic variables. The API calls, indeed all of Windows, may deal in Integers and Longs, but by the time your program gets the data it's already been converted into a string or a real.

■ T I P

Don't get too excited when you find that WordBasic supports a "Double" data type in "Declare"d functions: the "Double" isn't a Windows-style double word, it's a plain, old boring WordBasic real. The term "Double" in this context is mighty confusing, but it simply refers to double-precision floating point—in other words, a regular old real, one of the two data types used in WordBasic.

The Politics of Conversion   Here's how it works. Take, for example, GetFreeSpace. It returns a Long value, like this:

```
Declare Function GetFreeSpace Lib "Kernel"(wFlags As Integer) As Long
```

When WordBasic hits a command that invokes GetFreeSpace, say,

```
MySpace=GetFreeSpace(0)
```

some serious shuffling takes place.

First—the easy part—WordBasic takes a look at the "Declare" and realizes that the parameter in parentheses has to be sent to GetFreeSpace as an *Integer*. So WordBasic converts the zero value in your program into an Integer zero and feeds that Integer zero to the GetFreeSpace routine.

This is good: if WordBasic sent GetFreeSpace a real (i.e., a floating point) zero, your whole system would crash, or at least set off a Fault of one sort or another. API calls are not very forgiving!

GetFreeSpace does its thing, then returns a value. WordBasic looks at your "Declare" statement again and realizes that the value coming back is a Long Integer. Alas and alack, WordBasic doesn't speak Long Integer. So it retrieves the value GetFreeSpace returns, and converts it immediately into a real, double-precision floating point number. *And there's nothing you can do about it!*

That wouldn't be so bad, except sometimes you really, really want to get at the value in the form returned by an API call. If Windows packs a bunch of information into a double-word, for example, the last thing you want is for WordBasic to summarily convert that double-word into some strange floating point number. Same for Longs.

There's nothing you can do about it.

Before You Think You Can Solve It, Read This!

B U G

Compounding the problem with using Integer and Long data types is one confounding factor: the integer arithmetic available in WordBasic is hopeless. We'll get into some specifics—the Int(n) function and the lack of a Round(n,d) function—momentarily. But the bottom line is that there are virtually no tools to reliably reconstruct Longs and double-words from the mangled double-precision real conversions WordBasic foists upon your hapless program.

As this book was going to press, work continued on finding ways around the WordBasic data type restrictions. Some of the BASICally best and brightest are banging their heads against the wall. So don't feel too bad if you can't make heads nor tails of it.

There are worse things than cookbooks.

GetVersion

Now that we have all those nefarious Declares out of the way, skip on down to the WinExplorer line that says:

```
PackedVersionNumber = GetVersion
```

GetVersion is a Windows API call that returns the Windows version number. Being a Windows API call, it doesn't return something nice and simple, like "Microsoft Windows Version 3.10." Instead, GetVersion returns a number that's calculated like this: take the "minor" version number—the number to the right of the decimal point, in this case "10" in "Windows 3.10"—and multiply it by 256. Then add the "major" version number, in this case "3." The resulting packed number is the one used by GetVersion to tell your program which version of Windows is running.

So, instead of returning "Microsoft Windows Version 3.10," or something people can understand, GetVersion when run under Windows 3.10 returns the number 2563. Run it under Windows 3.12 and it spits out 3075.

No, that isn't a joke. Well, it *is* a joke, but not one of ours. It's a little less amusing in hex (base 16).

You can trace through the unpacking logic yourself, if you like, or just take our word for it. If you ever need the Windows version number, take a look in Appendix 2 and you'll find the recipe, ready to copy into your program.

Built-In Function Int(n)

Int(n) is a deceptively simple built-in function. Feed it a number—say, 3.14159—and it returns the integer part of the number—in this case, 3. Try Int(-7.9) and your program gets a -7. Or, say, Int(3.5 * 3) returns a 10. Easy.

■ **TIP**

Now the deceptive part. Int(n) only works on relatively small numbers, between -32,767 and +32,767. Anything larger than 32,767 or smaller than -32,767 triggers an overflow Error condition that looks like this:

Figure 4-9: Int(32768) Overflow

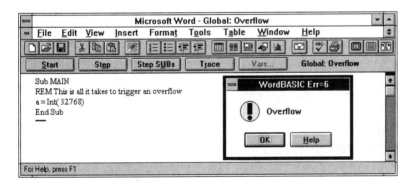

That makes it mighty hard to rely on Int(n) for anything more than predictably small numbers.

Fortunately, Windows version numbers are predictably small. For the foreseeable future, anyway.

Built-In Function Str$(n)

Want to turn a number into a string? This is the function that does it.

The Insert command only works with strings. Thus, WinExplorer uses Str$(n) to change MajorVersionNumber and MinorVersionNumber into strings.

```
Insert "Windows Version" + Str$(MajorVersionNumber) + "." +\
  Str$(MinorVersionNumber)
```

■ **T I P**

Str$(n) puts an extra space in front of a positive number (or zero). It does not put a space in front of a negative number. That can be a real pain at times. If you always want a space in front of your number, try using something like this:

```
If Number < 0 Then Insert " "
Insert Str$(Number)
```

GetWindowsDirectory

Not too surprisingly, this API call retrieves the directory containing Windows.

Here's another one of those Windows API calls with an amazingly convoluted syntax. Instead of something nice and simple like DirectoryPath$=GetWindows Directory, we have to live with C-speak:

```
LengthOfDirectory = GetWindowsDirectory(DirectoryPath$, 200)
```

That "200" on the end is the maximum number of characters your program wants to accept from GetWindowsDirectory. Microsoft recommends a minimum of 144 characters; theoretically, you can go as high as 32767 (the biggest Integer possible—this variable on the end is defined in the Declare statement as an Integer).

B U G

For some reason, though, in *any* API call, specifying a maximum number of characters larger than 255 gives the infamous "unpredictable results." Sometimes WordBasic picks up the correct answer, sometimes it doesn't. Stick to 200 and you should be safe.

B U G

Yeah, they call it a design feature. Sure. The DirectoryPath$ returned by this Windows API call may or may not have a trailing backslash ("\"). If the DirectoryPath$ consists of just a drive—say, "C:\"—your program gets the backslash. If it's more than just a drive—say, "C:\WINDOWS"— there's no backslash. So if your program wants to put together a file name using GetWindowsDirectory, it'll have to assemble it carefully.

GetFreeSpace

At last, an easy API call!

GetFreeSpace(0) returns the "number of bytes currently available in the global heap above the EMS bank line in large-frame and small-frame EMS systems."

Well, it sure *looks* like an easy API call. At least we all know what a bank line is, eh? You stand in one every payday to cash your paycheck.

The unfortunate fact is that there's no simple definition of "free memory" in the Windows world. Remember the first time you fired up Windows in extended mode, clicked on Program Manager's Help command, and found you had 16 megabytes of free memory on your 2 megabyte machine?

Well, this API call returns a number that bears some resemblance to the Program Manager Help's "Free Memory" number. Not identical, mind you, but close. It's a pretty good indication of how much virtual memory is ready for use.

WinExplorer divides the number by (1024*1024) to convert bytes into megabytes.

Combining Functions: Str$(Round(AvailableMemory,2))

WordBasic is very good at combining functions to almost any imaginable depth. The WordBasic command

```
Insert "Currently Available Memory (including virtual): " +\
  Str$(Round(AvailableMemory, 2)) + " MB"
```

takes advantage of the ability.

The function Round(n,i) takes in two numbers and returns another number. The function Str$(n) takes in a number and turns out a string. The two combine easily to produce Str$(Round(n,i)).

What is Round(n,i), you ask? Ah, such curiosity!

Round(Number, DecimalPlaces)

Round(n,i)—the function that rounds off the number "n" to "i" decimal places—should be a built-in WordBasic function. It isn't.

So we're going to build our own industrial-strength rounding function, right here, and learn a bit about WordBasic variables and control structures in the process.

(Visual Basic has a function called "CInt" that performs rounding, but it has two important drawbacks: it only rounds to integers—zero decimal places—and it dies if the integer is greater than 32,767 or less than -32,768. "CLng" will take on larger numbers, but still needs to be manipulated to round to arbitrary decimal places.)

Scroll on down to the WinExplorer line that says:

```
Function Round(Number, DecimalPlaces)
```

and brace yourself.

Defining "Round"

Although it seems like it should be easy to define what a Round(n,i) function should do—it just *rounds off the number,* right?—lack of standards and WordBasic idiosyncrasies conspire against us.

Just about everybody would expect the function Round(3.5, 0) to return a value of 4. So we'll start with that as a given.

Now, how about Round(-3.5, 0)? That's a judgment call; we're going to program Round(-3.5, 0) to return -4. If you want *your* Round to return a -3, all you have to do is change one "+" to a "-", and you're welcome to it. Our Round(-3.6, 0) gives -4 and Round(-3.4, 0) gives -3.

What about Round(3.51, 1.6)? Crazy stuff like that happens all the time! We could round off the decimal places before rounding off the number before rounding off the . . . too complicated. Let's just take the integer part of the decimal places and forget the rest. Round(3.51, 1.6) is the same as Round(3.51, 1). By management decision.

What about Round(12345, -2)? Does a negative "number of decimal places" make sense? Sure it does. A touch odd, perhaps, but why not? We'll make our function Round (12345, -2) return a value of 12300.

It Cain't Figger 'rithmetic Too Good

WordBasic has two limitations that'll drive Round(n,i) nuts.

First, there's no exponentiation. No "10 to the power of" command, no "10 ** 3" or "10 ^ 5." We'll have to do all the exponentiation in code.

Look on the bright side: it's a great excuse to learn the "For" command—and the whole purpose of all of this is to learn some WordBasic, right?

The next problem really cuts to the quick. The only WordBasic command that trims off fractions, Int(n), dies if it's fed a number larger than 32,767 or smaller than -32,767. We talked about that a little earlier, in the discussion about unpacking Windows version numbers. It wasn't such a big deal there—Windows would have to go up to "Version 3.127" before Int(n) started having problems. But when you're rounding off numbers, 32,767 is mighty puny!

We're going to work around that limitation a bit. The concept is pretty simple: before we feed a number into the Int(n) number-cruncher, our Round routine is going to lop off anything bigger than 32,767. The exact method for doing that is by using Int(n)! *(Hey, when your only tool's a hammer, every problem's a nail.)*

Net result: our Round(n,i) will work on intermediate values up to one less than (32,767 times 32,768), or 1,073,709,055. We'll leave it to the mathematicians in the crowd to figure out why. Anything larger than that will blow Int(n)'s mind and trigger an error that we'll handle in the rounding routine. Round(n,i) will deliver about ten digits of accuracy: not great, but not too bad for "just" a macro. Keep in mind, though, that requesting more than nine digits of accuracy may trigger an error: Round(123, 7), for example, goes bananas.

Now let's step through Round(n,i) and pick up all the neat new stuff.

Function

The "Function" statement tells WordBasic that a function follows. "Declare Function" tells WordBasic that it has to go find the function, out in the primordial WinOoze. Just plain old "Function" tells WordBasic that the function is right here; no hunting necessary.

Functions return values. Because the name of this function—Round—does not end in a "$" dollar sign, it must return a number.

This particular function takes two parameters, both of which are numbers. No problem.

Select Case/End Select

This may be the most powerful and most useful command in WordBasic. You've probably seen a similar syntax before. WordBasic evaluates the expression after "Select Case" and then chooses the first "Case" statement that matches the criteria.

The powerful part comes in what a "Case" statement can look like. There are five variations that look like this:

```
Case 7          'Any number or expression
Case 1,3,5      'A list of numbers or expressions
Case 2 to 4     'A range of numbers or expressions
Case Is > 2     'The word "IS" is necessary for comparisons
Case Else       'Matches anything
```

And you can mix and match a bit:

```
Case 1,3, 5 to 7, Is >10
```

■ T I P

You can use many different kinds of expressions—numbers, characters, whatever—in a Case statement. WordBasic just blithely jumps from Case to Case, evaluating and running the first bunch of code that matches the magic key.

If WordBasic gets through the entire list of Case conditions and doesn't find one that works—in particular, if there's no "Case Else"—an Error is triggered.

Moral of the story: always include a "Case Else" statement. As you can see in WinExplorer, there needn't be any statements *after* Case Else.

B U G

There's a very strange bug (or is it a design feature?) in WordBasic—and not in Visual Basic—that really gums things up if you have a Goto statement inside a Case statement. Be careful: don't Goto someplace outside the Case statement; your program will trigger an Error.

Try this:

```
n=1
Select Case n
Case 1
      Goto Bye
Case Else
End Select
Bye:
```

By skipping out of the Select statement (some people would say "by not executing the End Select statement," which is a mighty bizarre concept), WordBasic dies. Like so:

Figure 4-10: Select While You Can

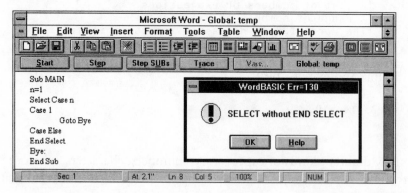

Proper Select Case etiquette demands that you put the destination of your Goto statement immediately before the End Select.

(Continued)

```
n=1
Select Case n
Case 1
     Goto Bye
Case Else
Bye:
End Select
```

For/Next

This part of Round(n,i) calculates the base multiplier used in rounding. If WordBasic had an exponentiation function, the whole Select Case/End Select and everything within could be replaced by a simple "Base=10**iDecimalPlaces".

Enter the For statement.

```
For i=start To stop Step increment
REM Do Stuff
Next i
```

In the above For statement, WordBasic evaluates the variables "start," "stop," and "increment" just once. If "increment" is positive, "i" starts with the value of "start"; if it's bigger than "stop," the program jumps on down to the next instruction; if not, the loop runs, "i" is incremented by "increment," and compared to "stop" again.

If "increment" is negative, "i" starts with the value of "start"; if it's smaller than "stop," the loop is bypassed; if not, the loop runs, "increment" (which is negative) gets added to "i," compared to "stop," and so on.

Just what you would expect in a smart For statement.

And you aren't confined to integers (WordBasic doesn't *have* integers anyway!): any or all of the numbers can be fractions, too.

B U G

This isn't a bug in WordBasic (or Visual Basic, which behaves similarly), but it could sure cause a bug in your programs! If "increment" is zero, you'll be stuck in that loop until something (like a Goto statement) makes your program jump out.

If you decide to jump out of the loop with a Goto statement, the value of "i" is at your disposal. In fact, you can jump out of the loop, reset "i," and jump back in! Not that anybody in their right mind would want to do such a thing.

■ **TIP**

The manual makes a big deal out of the fact that the "i" in

```
Next i
```

is optional. Leave it in, the books say, and you'll get extra error checking. That part is right. Take it out, the books say, and you'll speed up execution.

In a do-nothing For loop (where there are no commands at all between "For" and "Next") you might see a speed-up of 15%. Maybe. In any sort of normal loop, where your program is doing anything at all, the speed-up is more like 1 or 2%. Or less.

If you're concerned about wringing the last 2% of performance out of WordBasic, you're in the wrong ball game.

Round Logic

Back to the logic built into Round.

As mentioned before, Round strips off multiples of 32,767 to keep from triggering an overflow in the Int(n) function. You can step through the arithmetic if you like; it's really much simpler than it looks.

It's important to note, for a programming exercise, how Round uses the On Error statement to jump to a label called "Overflow:" whenever there's a problem in the last half of the routine.

We could've put that "On Error" way up at the beginning of Round, but that's not such a good idea. There are all sorts of things that can go wrong with WordBasic macros: if the "On Error" statement were way up at the beginning, then *any* error would make Round jump down to "Overflow:". That's not a good way to treat your users.

Rather, we're putting the "On Error" down at the last possible moment, just before the first Int(n) statement—the first statement that could trigger a relatively predictable overflow. And there's a very rudimentary error handling routine down at "Overflow:". Check it out.

■ **TIP**

Always, always, before exiting any WordBasic routine, turn error checking back on with "On Error Goto 0." It shouldn't make a difference: simply leaving the function should restore error checking. But maybe, just maybe, some day error checking won't go back to normal. If that ever happens to you, you'll be up a wide, deep creek with nary a paddle. *If you took it out, put it back. If you turned it off, turn it back on. Everything I need to know I learned in kindergarten. And grad school.*

If Then Else End If

One final note, and one last new function in Round(n,i).

We've already played with the simplest form of the If statement, way back at the beginning of this chapter, when WinExplorer's toughest task was to start a new file.

```
If SelInfo(27) = -1 Then FileNew .Template = "Normal"
```

Round(n,i) brings in a new flavor of the If statement, and it isn't as straightforward as you think!

```
If Number >= 0 Then
     Round =(Over32KPart * 32767 + Int((Under32KPart) + 0.5)) / Base
Else
     Round =(Over32KPart * 32767 + Int((Under32KPart) - 0.5)) /Base
End If
```

That's pretty simple. But take a look at this:

```
If Number >=0 Then
     MsgBox "Hi Scott, Laurel, Kate, Mark, Stu, Chase, Doug and crew!"
End If
```

Think you got it figured out? Try this one on for size:

```
If m=0 Then MsgBox "Zero" Else MsgBox "Not Zero"
```

The question is "When do I need an End If?"

■ **TIP**

Here's the rule of thumb: you need an "End If" statement if there is a carriage return (paragraph mark, if you prefer) after the "Then" statement.

■ **TIP**

And, just in case you stay up late at night wondering about such things, that "Else" statement is a bit touchy. You must have a carriage return after "Else" if and only if there is a carriage return after the "Then." It doesn't work any other way.

Not entirely straightforward, would you say?

Function's Return Value

The Round(n,i) function, like all good functions, needs to return a value.

The way you tell WordBasic "Hey, here's the value!" is to put the name of the function on the left side of an equal sign:

```
Round=Foo+Bar
```

would return the sum of "Foo" and "Bar" as the value of function Round.

Like so many other things, this isn't quite as simple as it looks.

■ **T I P**

Occasionally you can get away with putting the name of the function on the right side of the equal sign. Don't try it. You'll only tie your program up in knots.

■ **T I P**

If you don't assign a value to the function, your program will always return a zero. Should you write a function that mysteriously always returns a zero, take a look at the spelling of the function name. That's probably the culprit.

■ **T I P**

Your function can also change the value of the parameters passed to it.

If you're a programming language maven: WordBasic always passes variables By Reference when possible; there is no By Value or ByVal keyword, and thus no way to force passing By Value from inside the called routine.

English Translation: if you call a subroutine or function with a variable, that variable is fair game—the function or subroutine can change its value. Some languages don't let functions or subroutines mess with variables, or the language may put restrictions on which variables can be changed. *WordBasic rules are jungle rules: don't leave your variables unattended!*

Showtime for WinExplorer 2

Go ahead. Click Start.

Figure 4-11: WinExplorer 2 Lives!

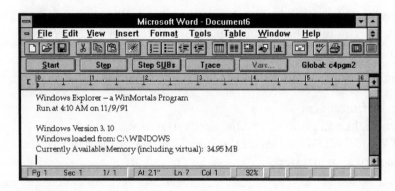

Neat, huh?

Click on File Close to get rid of the report. You've just completed the most difficult part of WinExplorer, this program 2. Take a breather.

Now wait 'til you see what's in WinExplorer 3!

Recap

Sorry for that long detour through Round(n,i) land. While the function has its . . . roots in some rather esoteric math, it provided a great chance to introduce (or re-introduce) you to a whole bunch of important Basic commands, and to show you how WordBasic interprets those commands.

Oh. Have you looked at your feet lately? Well, don't look down too fast. Wiggle your toes. In case you hadn't noticed, you're flying. You just put together several Windows API calls the hallmark of "real" Windows programs without C, without Pascal, without the big-bucks SDK.

Here are the WordBasic commands you've seen in WinExplorer 2:

- **Declare Function / Declare Sub**—tell WordBasic to venture out into the Windows ooze and find the indicated function or subroutine.

- **Int(n)**—returns the integer part of "n." Does *not* round.

- **Str$(n)**—turns the number "n" into a string, so you can insert it into a document.

- **Round(n,i)**—rounds the number "n" to "i" decimal places; a WinMortals routine on your Companion Disk.

- **Select Case / End Select**—branch to a specific bunch of code, depending on the value of a variable.

- **For / Next**—typical For loop, with all the bells and whistles.

- **If / Then / Else / End If**—lets you extend and nest If statements; watch out for situations where "**End If**" is required.

- **Function Return Value**—function tells WordBasic what value to return to the calling program by using the name of the function itself.

- **GetVersion**, **GetWindowsDirectory**, **GetFreeSpace**—three Windows API calls. See Appendix 1 for details.

WinExplorer 3—WIN.INI Settings

One of the most important files in all of Windowdom is WIN.INI (which stands for "WINdows INItialization file," pronounced "win innie"). Your WIN.INI file holds an enormous amount of information about your machine, its operating environment, and most importantly the choices you have made to tailor Windows and its applications to your whims. Windows gets a lot of its flexibility from these .INI files.

We're going to get our hands on it. Right now.

Loading WinExplorer Program 3

If you have the Companion Disk, select and delete the old WinExplorer. FileOpen C4PGM3.DOC, select it, EditCopy, FileClose. EditPaste. That's it.

If you're typing, there are two blocks of code:

Program 4-3, Part 1: Type This Before "Sub MAIN"

```
REM Type this before "Sub MAIN"
Declare Function GetProfileString Lib "Kernel"(AppName$,\
 KeyName$, Default$, ReturnedString$, MaxChars As Integer) As\
 Integer
Declare Function GetProfileInt Lib "Kernel"(AppName$, KeyName$,\
 nDefault As Integer) As Integer
```

Program 4-3, Part 2: Type This Before "REM Wrap Up"

```
REM Type this before "REM Wrap Up"
REM Settings from WIN.INI
REM Demonstrates GetProfileString, InStr()
InsertPara
Insert "Windows settings (from WIN.INI):"
InsertPara
LengthOfString = GetProfileString("windows", "load", " ",\
 LoadString$, 200)
Insert "Load= " + LoadString$
InsertPara
LengthOfString = GetProfileString("windows", "run", " ",\
 RunString$, 200)
Insert "Run= " + RunString$
InsertPara
LengthOfString = GetProfileString("windows", "device", " ",\
 DeviceString$, 200)
If LengthOfString = 0 Then
     Insert "No Default Printer"
Else
     FirstComma = InStr(1,DeviceString$, ",")
     Insert "Default Printer = " + Left$(DeviceString$, FirstComma -\
     1) + " on " + Right$(DeviceString$, 5)
End If
InsertPara
SSActive = GetProfileInt("windows", "ScreenSaveActive", 0)
If SSActive = 0 Then
     Insert "Windows Screen Save Is NOT Activated."
Else
     SSTimeOut = GetProfileInt("windows", "ScreenSaveTimeOut", 0)
     Insert "Windows Screen Save active;" + Str$(SSTimeOut) + \
```

```
    " seconds delay."
End If
InsertPara
```

You Got An Outie Or An .INI?

All Windows Initialization files—WIN.INI, SYSTEM.INI, and all the other .INIs—have a very specific format. They are set up that way so any program, especially the Windows "Profile" API routines, can take a look around and understand what it sees.

Break open an .INI file and you'll find a bunch of lines that look like this:

```
[Name That Disease]
Tool=Entrenching
AntelopeFreeway=256
Diseases=Jaundice,Plague
```

There's a madness to this method.

The first line in the group contains a name inside [square brackets]. This is often called an "Application Name"—and it often *is* an application name like "Word for Windows 2.0" or "EXCEL" or "Zotz"—but it's probably best to think of it as a category or group of settings. Windows 3.1 books often refer to it as a "section," and that's as good a term for it as any.

Following the first line can be a virtually unlimited number of settings. They all take the form

```
keyname=value
```

with the name of the setting on the left and its value on the right.

Here's the important part: if you follow a few simple steps, Windows will take care of the settings for you! There's an engine chugging away in the Windows API that will set, modify, and retrieve any .INI setting you want. Compared to normal BASIC file handling, that API engine runs like the wind. Slick.

We're going to take a look at one particularly flexible way to get at the WIN.INI settings. There are other ways; we'll discuss those at the end of this section. A complete description of WIN.INI ships with Windows in a Windows Write file called WININI.WRI, which should be available in your Windows directory. SYSTEM.INI is similarly documented in SYSINI.WRI. If you're curious about the details, take a look.

Settings We'll Need

WinExplorer takes a look at four different WIN.INI settings. Before going through *how* to get at the settings, let's touch briefly on *what* the settings mean.

Load= The WIN.INI Load= setting specifies all the programs that are loaded whenever you crank up Windows. Typically you would want to preload programs that are going to be used often.

It's a list of applications, separated by spaces, that are loaded one by one, in order, before the start-up group and the program manager get going.

Unless you've done something to change it, Load= is the very first line in [windows], the very first section of WIN.INI.

Run= Like Load=, the Run= programs are loaded before the program manager kicks in. Unlike Load=, all of the Run= programs are actually run, in order, one at a time.

Unless you change it, Run= is the second line in the [windows] section.

Device= Specifies your default printer. There are three items in the setting, separated by commas, like this:

```
device=printer-name,device-driver,port
```

Your program has to be smart enough to navigate the commas.

ScreenSaveActive= Indicates whether the Windows 3.1 screen saver is inactive (with a value of zero), or active (with a value other than zero).

GetProfileString

At last. Back to the program.

After a few REMs and Inserts, you'll see a line that looks like this:

```
LengthOfString = GetProfileString("windows", "load", " ",\
 LoadString$, 200)
```

That translates into English as something like: *Go out to WIN.INI, where the ProfileStrings are stored. Look for a section called [windows]. Then look for a line that says "load=." If there is no "load=" line, put one in there, and stick a " " space to the right of the equal sign. If there is a "load=" line, pick up the stuff to the right of the equals sign, stick it in a variable called "LoadString$," up to a maximum of 200 characters. If there is no "load=" line, return a " " space in "LoadString$."Finally, put the length of "LoadString$" in a variable called "LengthOfString."*

Whew.

There are all sorts of Profile String gotchas.

■ **TIP**

Do not ever, under any circumstances, ever use a null in a GetProfileString command. A null is formed by typing two quotation marks next to each other or omitting an argument entirely or using Character number zero. Playing with nulls is like playing with fire: you'll get burned sooner or later. Word for Windows 1.0, 1.1, and 1.1a would crash Windows if they passed a null; Word for Windows 2.0 is supposed to correct the problem. Supposed to.

B U G

For some unknown reason, WinWord has a hard time working with long character strings in GetProfileString and other Windows API calls that let you specify a maximum number of characters. In this particular case, we've limited the string to 200 characters. If you bump the max up to 300, WordBasic may completely blow the API call, return an empty LoadString$, and set LengthOfString to zero. And it won't tell you why.

Particularly frustrating: there appears to be no definitive "max max" that will always work. At this writing, 255 seems like a sure bet, but it's not absolutely guaranteed—and the number 255 is only magical because it seems to work. If you start getting strange results from ProfileString calls, cut the max characters in half and try again.

■ T I P

Upper- and lower-case don't matter when specifying the section or keyname for a setting. [Windows] is the same as [winDOWS]. The setting values themselves, however, do maintain their upper/lowercase characteristics.

InStr(Start, String$, Match$)

The "device" default printer setting has three values, separated by commas. Scanning a string for commas is quite simple in WordBasic. Welcome to InStr(), the InString function.

The command

```
FirstComma = InStr(1,DeviceString$, ",")
```

tells WordBasic to look at the string called "DeviceString$," starting with the first character (that's what the "1" means). If the substring "," is found anywhere in DeviceString$, the starting position of the substring is put into the variable "FirstComma."

If the substring isn't found, InStr() returns a zero.

Left$(), Right$(), Mid$()

Three WordBasic functions let you strip characters out of a string. They behave pretty much as you would expect.

```
Left$(Larry$,n)
```

returns the starting "n" characters of "Larry$." If "Larry$" is too short—if it has fewer than "n" characters—your program gets the whole "Larry$" string.

```
Right$(Moe$,m)
```

returns the final "m" characters of "Moe$," if the string is long enough. WinExplorer 3 uses

```
Right$(DeviceString$, 5)
```

simply because the last part of DeviceString$, the printer port, is always of the form "LPTn:" or "COMn:" or "FILE:" and is thus always five characters long. Cheap trick. ("FILE:" is used to print to a file, just as if it were a standard Windows port.)

The final WordBasic string manipulation function,

```
Mid$(Curly$,Start,Count)
```

returns "Count" characters from Curly$, starting at position "Start." If you leave out "Count", you get all of Curly$, starting at "Start."

B U G

If "n," "m," or "Count" in the above examples is negative, your program gets the whole string. Fair enough. But if "Start" is zero or negative it triggers a WordBasic error, "Illegal Function Call." Strange.

B U G

For a good time, try

```
A$=Mid$(Curly$,2,-1)
```

Unless Microsoft has fixed it, the combination of a "Start" greater than one and a "Count" less than zero produces a bizarre error message: "WordBasic Error 513, String Too Long." Totally bogus.

GetProfileInt

Windows will let you get at integer profile settings, explicitly, and your program doesn't have to go through any string-to-number-to-string conversion shenanigans.

The Windows API call

```
SSActive = GetProfileInt("windows", "ScreenSaveActive", 0)
```

can be translated thusly: *Go into WIN.INI, look for [windows], and the "ScreenSaveActive=" setting. If there is such a setting, evaluate it as an integer, and return that integer to the variable SSActive. If there is no such setting, return a value of zero (i.e., ScreenSaveActive=0).*

This API call is very strict in how it interprets settings. Which, by and large, is great—it'll save your program from all sorts of mickey-rodenting around.

If the value that GetProfileInt finds is zero, or if the value starts with nonnumeric characters, GetProfileInt returns a zero. If it finds a positive integer, possibly followed by nonnumeric characters, GetProfileInt returns the integer.

Nice and simple.

Playtime

Go ahead and click on Start.

Figure 4-12: WinExplorer 3

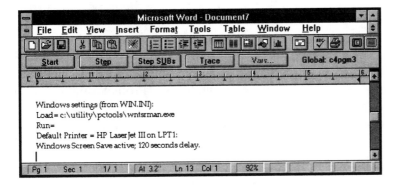

All sorts of things you never look at, huh?

WordBasic GetProfileString$(), SetProfileString

Strictly speaking, you needn't go out to the Windows API to get at WIN.INI profile strings. WordBasic has two built-in functions that replace the Windows calls. They look like this:

```
SettingValue$=GetProfileString$(SectionName$,Keyname$)
SetProfileString SectionName$, Keyname$, NewValue$
```

and, yes, they work. We avoided mentioning them until now for several reasons, most importantly that they only work on the WIN.INI file. The Windows API calls you see in WinExplorer 3, with a couple of small changes, will work on *any* .INI file.

■ **T I P**

Whenever possible, we strongly recommend that you avoid adding new Keynames and settings and stuff to WIN.INI. Why? Because every application you can name writes to WIN.INI; sometimes they screw it up; invariably they add dozens—even hundreds—of items to the file, bloating it beyond reason.

You don't need to write to WIN.INI. You can create your own .INI file, specific to your application, and your programs can mangle it to the nth degree. Nobody will ever think less of your application. And nobody will ever be able to accuse your application of trashing WIN.INI.

These "Private Profile Strings" and custom-built .INI files are discussed at length in Chapter 7.

Recap

Now you know how to get into the Windows *sanctum sanctorium*, WIN.INI and SYSTEM.INI, It wasn't that hard was it?

Here are the WordBasic commands you've hit in WinExplorer 3:

- **GetProfileString**—Windows API call retrieves a setting from the WIN.INI file.

- **GetProfileInt**—another Windows API call; like GetProfileString, except it forces the value to be a positive integer.

- **InStr(Start,String$,Match$)**—looks for Match$ in String$, starting at position Start. If it's there, returns the position where the match begins.

- **Left$(String$,n) / Right$(String$,m) / Mid$(String$,Start,Count)** —the primary WordBasic string manipulation functions. They do what you'd think they would do.

- **GetProfileString$() / SetProfileString**—WordBasic commands that mimic the Windows API calls to some extent.

On to WinExplorer 4.

WinExplorer 4—System Metrics: Size, Icon, Mouse

The System Metrics API can tell you all sorts of things you never wanted to know, like, say, the height of the arrow bitmap on a window's horizontal scroll bar (which, of course, is different from the height of the arrow bitmap on a window's *vertical* scroll bar).

Buried within the System Metrics API, though, are a handful of useful settings. We're going to pull out a few of them.

Loading WinExplorer Program 4

If you have the Companion Disk, delete the old WinExplorer and replace it with C4PGM4.DOC. (Hey, you're getting pretty good at that!)

If you're typing, here are the two blocks of code:

Program 4-4, Part 1: Type This Before "Sub MAIN"

```
REM Type this before "Sub MAIN"
Declare Function GetSystemMetrics Lib "user"(nIndex As Integer)\
 As Integer
```

Program 4-4, Part 2: Type This Before "REM Wrap Up"

```
REM Type this before "REM Wrap Up"
REM A bunch of miscellaneous info from the GetSystemMetrics API
REM Demonstrates nested If/Then/Else stuff
InsertPara
Insert "System Metrics Information:"
InsertPara
SM_CXSCREEN = 0
SM_CYSCREEN = 1
SM_CXICON = 11
SM_CYICON = 12
SM_MOUSEPRESENT = 19
SM_DEBUG = 22
SM_SWAPBUTTON = 23
Insert "Screen Width:" + Str$(GetSystemMetrics(SM_CXSCREEN)) + \
 ", Height:" + Str$(GetSystemMetrics(SM_CYSCREEN)) + " pixels."
InsertPara
Insert "Icon Width:" + Str$(GetSystemMetrics(SM_CXICON)) + \
 ", Height:" + Str$(GetSystemMetrics(SM_CYICON)) + " pixels."
InsertPara
If GetSystemMetrics(SM_MOUSEPRESENT) Then
    Insert "Mouse is present."
    If GetSystemMetrics(SM_SWAPBUTTON) Then Insert "Left and Right" +\
    " Mouse Buttons Swapped."
```

```
Else
     Insert "Mouse is NOT present."
End If
InsertPara
If GetSystemMetrics(SM_DEBUG) Then
     Insert "Running in DEBUG Mode. "
     InsertPara
EndIf
```

Windows Hungarian Notation

The first thing you'll see in this section of code is a bunch of variable assignments, where all the names start with "SM_." In later WinExplorers you'll see similar variables with names that start with "WM_" and "WF_"; the farther you dig into Windows documentation, the more often you'll see names like that. So we'll get you started here.

■ **T I P**

Word for Windows 1.0 and 1.1 get really cranky when you use an "_" underscore in a variable name. WinWord 2.0 has no problem with them. Since the "SM_SOMEVAR" kind of notation is so prevalent in the C world—you'll hit it sooner or later in your exploration through Windows—we will use it here. Keep in mind, though, that if you are using an earlier version of WinWord, you will have to drop the underscore.

Way back in Chapter 2 we talked briefly about the Hungarian Standard notation. The concept is simple enough: every variable name has a character or two tacked onto the front that tells you what kind of variable you're dealing with.

In WordBasic, the question of variable type is simple: if a variable name ends with a dollar sign, it's a string; if it doesn't, the variable is a double-precision floating point.

In Windows, though, life becomes a bit more complicated. Windows has quite a few variable types; we've seen a few already. More than that, though, each Windows API call can have dozens of variables or values of variables that affect the call.

To keep this all sorted out, WinFolks have standardized on a simple notation. Most of it has its roots in C, which means it's pretty convoluted. *(All capital letters, with an embedded underscore? Gimme a break!)* Still, a standard's a standard—most of the time, anyway—so we're going to follow the standard best we can.

Windows Data Types

Because WordBasic doesn't support any variable types beyond the two, we won't be using these prefixes in quite the manner they were intended. But for the sake of completeness, we'll toss them at you here.

These are the most common variable types you'll find in Windows and the prefixes that usually go along with them:

TABLE 4-1: WINDOWS VARIABLE TYPES

VARIABLE	TYPE
h	Handle (16 bits, unsigned); a handle is a number that has no meaning in and of itself; it's just used internally by Windows to keep track of windows and other things; e.g., *hWnd* is a handle to a Window, *hMod* is a handle to a Module.
n	Integer (16 bits, signed, goes from -32,768 to +32,767)
l	Long Integer (32 bits, signed, runs from -2,147,483,648 to +2,147,483,647)
lp	Long Pointer (32 bits); points to a location in memory
w	Word (16 bits)
dw	Double Word (32 bits)
b	Boolean (16 bits); usually zero=false, anything else=true
c	Character (ASCII character number or signed 8-bit integer)
rgb	Red/Green/Blue color combination
v	Void; no return value

There are a few others, but they're not very common.

Windows API Call Prefixes

To keep from going absolutely stir-crazy, prefixes will help us sort out values and API calls. Each prefix is unique to a small group of related API calls. These are the prefixes we'll be using; there are many others.

- GW_   Get Windows Flags
- SM_   System Metrics
- WM_   Windows Message
- WF_   Windows Flags

Some people get all flustered when they see prefixes and such. There's nothing to worry about. The code

```
SM_MOUSEPRESENT=19
Wuh=GetSystemMetrics(SM_MOUSEPRESENT)
```

is identical to

```
Wuh=GetSystemMetrics(19)
```

and you can use the two interchangeably. We'll be using the former method, just because if and/or when the time comes for you to look this stuff up in manuals—almost any manuals—or if you stumble on discussions in magazine articles, you'll see the funny naming conventions. May as well get used to it now.

It also helps your coding look waycool: this is the fancy naming convention the big-bucks C programmers use. IF_U_CN_RD_THIS_U_CN_PRGRM_IN_BASIC.

GetSystemMetrics

The Windows GetSystemMetrics API call delivers a hodgepodge of information. Mostly, it will tell you how tall and how wide for anything you can imagine: the screen, the caption, scroll bars, cursors, Kanji windows, and on and on.

Adding to the "kitchen sink" nature of the call are three interesting pieces of information that have nothing to do with metrics or sizes: whether a mouse is present, whether the left and right mouse buttons have been swapped, and whether the current version of Windows is a debugging version.

Calling GetSystemMetrics is like falling off a log.

For example, if your program says

```
Width=GetSystemMetrics(0)
Height=GetSystemMetrics(1)
MousePresent=GetSystemMetrics(19)
```

"Width" will contain the width of the screen in pixels, "Height" will have the height, and "MousePresent" will be 0 if no mouse is present. All pretty simple, really.

SM_Values

Here's a list of all the things GetSystemMetrics can tell you and the SM_ prefixed variable names (often called "indices" or "indexes") that C programmers use:

TABLE 4-2: THE SM_PREFIXED VARIABLE NAMES

SM_PREFIXED VARIABLE NAMES	INFORMATION GIVEN
SM_CXSCREEN=0	'Width of screen in pixels
SM_CYSCREEN=1	'Height of screen
SM_CXVSCROLL=2	'Width of arrow on vert scroll bar
SM_CYHSCROLL=3	'Height of arrow on horiz scroll bar
SM_CYCAPTION=4	'Height of caption
SM_CXBORDER=5	'Width of frame that cannot be sized
SM_CYBORDER=6	'Height of frame that cannot be sized
SM_CXDLGFRAME=7	'Width of frame in double-border style
SM_CYDLGFRAME=8	'Height of frame in double-border style
SM_CYVTHUMB=9	'Height of thumb on vert scroll bar
SM_CXHTHUMB=10	'Width of thumb on horiz scroll bar

TABLE 4-2: THE SM_PREFIXED VARIABLE NAMES (CONTINUED)

SM_PREFIXED VARIABLE NAMES	INFORMATION GIVEN
SM_CXICON=11	'Width of icon in pixels
SM_CYICON=12	'Height of icon
SM_CXCURSOR=13	'Width of cursor
SM_CYCURSOR=14	'Height of cursor
SM_CYMENU=15	'Height of single-line menu bar
SM_CXFULLSCREEN=16	'Width of client area, full screen
SM_CYFULLSCREEN=17	'Height of client area, full screen
SM_CYKANJIWINDOW=18	'Height of Kanji window
SM_MOUSEPRESENT=19	'Zero if no mouse
SM_CYVSCROLL=20	'Height of arrow on vert scroll bar
SM_CXHSCROLL=21	'Width of arrow on horiz scroll bar
SM_DEBUG=22	'Zero if not a debug version of Windows
SM_SWAPBUTTON=23	'Zero if left/right buttons not swapped
SM_RESERVED1=24	'For future use
SM_RESERVED2=25	'For future use
SM_RESERVED3=26	'For future use
SM_RESERVED4=27	'For future use
SM_CXMIN=28	'Min width of window
SM_CYMIN=29	'Min height of window
SM_CXSIZE=30	'Width of bitmaps in title bar
SM_CYSIZE=31	'Height of bitmaps in title bar
SM_CXFRAME=32	'Width of frame that can be sized
SM_CYFRAME=33	'Height of frame that can be sized
SM_CXMINTRACK=34	'Min tracking width of window
SM_CYMINTRACK=35	'Min tracking height of window
SM_CXDOUBLECLK=36	'Width of double-click "box"
SM_CYDOUBLECLK=37	'Height of double-click "box"
SM_CXICONSPACING=38	'Width between icons
SM_CYICONSPACING=39	'Height between icons
SM_MENUDROPALIGNMENT=40	'Zero if menus are left aligned
SM_PENWINDOWS=41	'Zero if not Pen Windows

Want to know how much room Windows leaves between icons? Just try a GetSystemMetrics(38). It's that easy.

WinExplorer 4 picks a handful of those SM_ indices and inserts them into the report.

Nested If Statements

Not unexpectedly, WordBasic allows you to put If statements inside of If statements.

The most common problem with nesting one If statement inside another is keeping the Else/End If parts straight. Indenting will help you eyeball the code, of course. But the toughest part for a lot of people is knowing when to "End If." The same old rule applies: you need an "End If" only when there is a carriage return after the "Then." Thus, the code snippet

```
If GetSystemMetrics(SM_MOUSEPRESENT) Then
    Insert "Mouse is present."
    If GetSystemMetrics(SM_SWAPBUTTON) Then Insert "Left and Right" +\
    " Mouse Buttons Swapped."
Else
    Insert "Mouse is NOT present."
End If
```

has two "If"s, two "Then"s, but only one "End If." *And it's perfectly valid*. Watch out. It'll catch you some day, guaranteed.

See how easy it is to find out if the mouse is present? It boils down to one line:

```
If GetSystemMetrics(SM_MOUSEPRESENT) Then ....
```

This is a fun time to see how C programmers approach the same problem. Here is the C code Microsoft uses as an example to replicate that one line:

```
HCURSOR hMyCursor;
POINT ptCursor;

case WM_ACTIVATE:
    if (!GetSystemMetrics(SM_MOUSEPRESENT)) {
        if (!HIWORD (lParam)) {
            if (wParam) {
                SetCursor(hMyCursor);
                ClientToScreen(hwnd, &ptCursor);
                SetCursorPos(ptCursor.x, ptCursor.y);
            }
            ShowCursor(wParam);
        }
    }
    break;
```

Just a teensy-tiny difference, no?

Playtime
Go ahead and click Start.

Figure 4-13: WinExplorer 4

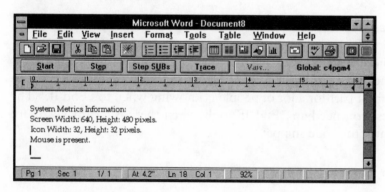

Now you know how many pixels are in your Windows icons! Yawn.

WinExplorer 5—Windows Flags, Booleans

This is a fun one. We get to kick around a rarely used WordBasic operator and do a little bit-twiddling with WordBasic commands. That's like eating rice with a baseball bat.

Loading WinExplorer 5

From the Companion Disk, delete the old WinExplorer and replace it with C4PGM5.DOC.

From the keyboard, here are the two blocks of code:

Program 4-5, Part 1: Type This Before "Sub MAIN"

```
REM Type this before "Sub MAIN"
Declare Function GetWinFlags Lib "Kernel" As Integer
```

Program 4-5, Part 2: Type This Before "REM Wrap Up"

```
REM Type this before "REM Wrap Up"
REM More System info, this time from GetWinFlags
REM Demonstrates ElseIf, and a (barely documented!) use of
REM And as a bitwise operator on
REM integers -- even though the integers are stored as reals. Go
REM figger.
WF_CPU086 = 64
WF_CPU186 = 128
WF_CPU286 = 2
WF_CPU386 = 4
WF_CPU486 = 8
WF_80x87 = 1024
WF_STANDARD = 16
WF_ENHANCED = 32
InsertPara
Flag = GetWinFlags
REM Find CPU type
Insert "Processor Type: "
If (Flag And WF_CPU086) = WF_CPU086 Then
     Insert "8086"
ElseIf(Flag And WF_CPU186) = WF_CPU186 Then
     Insert "80186"
ElseIf(Flag And WF_CPU286) = WF_CPU286 Then
     Insert "80286"
ElseIf(Flag And WF_CPU386) = WF_CPU386 Then
     Insert "80386"
ElseIf(Flag And WF_CPU486) = WF_CPU486 Then
     Insert "80486"
Else
```

```
        Insert "Unidentified"
End If
If(Flag And WF_80x87) = WF_80x87 Then Insert " -- With Math" +\
" Coprocessor"
Insert "."
InsertPara
If(Flag And WF_STANDARD) = WF_STANDARD Then
        Insert "Running in Standard Mode."
ElseIf(Flag And WF_ENHANCED) = WF_ENHANCED Then
        Insert "Running in Enhanced Mode."
Else
        Insert "Running in Real Mode." 'Not bloody likely in Win31
End If
InsertPara
```

Windows Flags

The Windows API call GetWinFlags returns a number that has all sorts of information encoded into it. We'll spend much of this section decoding what Redmond hath encoded.

The encoding method used here is probably the oldest (and most cumbersome) method known to computerdom: bits. This bit means something, that bit over there means something else.

Getting at all those bits would be tough, if it weren't for an amazing, rarely used, almost-undocumented (the *Technical Reference* devotes a whole sentence to it) feature of WordBasic: numeric-bitwise operators.

Boole's Basket: True, False, NOT, AND, OR

In WordBasic (and Visual Basic) the value "False" is stored as the number zero. If it ain't "False" it's "True"—in other words, anything other than a zero is evaluated as "True." If you have a choice in the matter, you should use the numeric value minus one for "True"—for reasons that will become clear sooner or later. Of course, sometimes you don't have any choice.

That's the whole story on Boolean variables!

WordBasic has three primitives for dealing with Boolean variables: AND, OR, and NOT. Visual Basic adds XOR, EQV, and IMP. In case you slept through the appropriate part of math class, here are the definitions:

- **A AND B**—evaluates True if both A and B are True.
- **A OR B**—evaluates True if either A or B is True.
- **NOT A**—evaluates True if A is False.
- **A XOR B**—evaluates True if either A or B, but not both, is True.
- **A EQV B**—evaluates True if both A and B are True, or both A and B are False.
- **A IMP B**—evaluates True unless A is True and B is False.

Once you translate that stuff into English it isn't so bad, is it?

Numeric Bitwise Operators

WordBasic and Visual Basic can treat numbers as if they were bunches of bits. (Which they are, but that's another story!) This is a perfectly valid snippet of WordBasic code:

```
Foo=3 'Binary 011
Bar=2 'Binary 010
FooNBar=Foo AND Bar
```

If you're accustomed to bits and bytes and that kind of thing, you'll realize immediately that the variable FooNBar should have a value of 2, which is "011" AND "010."

Not bad for a word processor, eh?

When WordBasic or Visual Basic encounters a number in the middle of a Boolean expression, it converts the number to a 16-bit signed integer and then performs the Boolean operation bit-by-bit.

And that is the key to unlocking bit-encoded stuff.

Decoding One Bit at a Time

Let's say you want to find out if the very first bit in a number—that bit way over on the *right*-hand side—is turned on. And you don't want to go back to algebra class to figure it out.

Easily done.

Reading backwards (an all-too-common problem for bit junkies), the very first bit position in a number—the one over on the right-hand side—has a value of 1. The next bit position has a value of 2. The next one is 4. Next one is 8, and so on, each double the one before.

Turning the tables, the number 1, when stuffed into a computer, is a bunch of zeros, ending in a 1. The number 2 is a string of zeros, then a 10. A 4 is zeros, then 100; 8 is all zeros then 1000, and so on.

So, starting at 1, and going up by powers of 2, we can figure out exactly which bits have been set. The trick is to use AND.

This little bit of WordBasic code will tell you if the very first, right-hand bit in the variable "EncodedNumber" is set to 1:

```
If EncodedNumber AND 1 = 1 Then ....
```

All of the zeros in the number 1, combined with the AND function, mask out everything except the very first, right-hand bit. That's all there is to it.

This will tell you if the next bit in "EncodedNumber" is set to 1:

```
If EncodedNumber AND 2 = 2 Then ....
```

the next bit:

```
If EncodedNumber AND 4 = 4 Then ......
```

and so on, with 8, then 16, then 32, doubling the number each time.

WF_ Values

Here's a list of all the things GetWinFlags can tell you, and the WF_ prefixed variable names that C programmers use:

TABLE 4-3: THE WF_PREFIXED VARIABLE NAMES

WF_ PREFIXED VARIABLE NAMES	INFORMATION GIVEN
WF_PMODE=1	'One if in protected mode
WF_CPU286=2	'One if CPU is 80286-class
WF_CPU386=4	'One if CPU is 80386-class
WF_CPU486=8	'One if CPU is 80486-class
WF_STANDARD=16	'One if running in Standard mode
WF_WIN286=16	'One if running in Standard mode
WF_ENHANCED=32	'One if running in Enhanced mode
WF_WIN386=32	'One if running in Enhanced mode
WF_CPU086=64	'One if CPU is 8086-class
WF_CPU186=128	'One if CPU is 80186-class
WF_LARGEFRAME=256	'One if running EMS large-frame config
WF_SMALLFRAME=512	'One if running EMS small-frame config
WF_80x87=1024	'One if 8087-class co-processor present

Note how these WF_ numbers are used differently from the SM_ numbers we kicked around in the last section. These WF_ numbers are so-called bit masks, used to flush out encoded numbers.

Not surprisingly, all of the WF_ values are multiples of 2; in bit-land that simply means that each bit of the GetWinFlags flag has a unique meaning; there is no overlap.

WinExplorer 5 jumps through each of the settings, using the AND Boolean operator, figuring out which bits have been set, plugging the appropriate text into the report.

ElseIf

This is the first time we've hit an ElseIf. It's a handy contraction of Else and If that lets you string along If statements without having dozens—or hundreds—of "End

If"s cluttering your program. Take a look at WinExplorer 5 and you'll see how they nest.

■ **T I P**

You'll find this maddeningly, stupifyingly infuriating. "ElseIf" is one word; "End If" is two. That's true in both WordBasic and Visual Basic. If you forget and spell "EndIf" as one word or "Else If" as two, you'll trigger an error. You'd think a language as sophisticated as Visual Basic would be smart enough to figure this out, but it isn't. There's nothing you can do about it.

■ **T I P**

Whenever you're tempted to use ElseIf in a program, pause for a second and see if "Select Case" won't work better. There are occasions when only an ElseIf will do—here in WinExplorer 5 is one of them—but if you can revert to Select Case, you'll find the result much easier to code and maintain.

B U G

With ElseIf, always use the "paragraph mark after Then" way of writing If statements. Stringing ElseIf after a Then—with no intervening paragraph mark/carriage return—will lead to the ElseIf not being recognized at all!

Playtime
Click Start.

Figure 4-14: WinExplorer 5

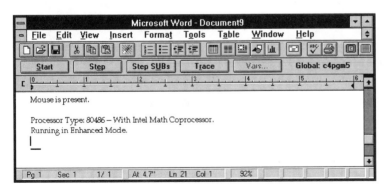

WinExplorer has your processor nailed!

Let's Crash the Sucker

Want to see what happens when you remove the paragraph mark after a "Then" that's involved with an ElseIf? Go ahead. Take the carriage return off the first "Then" in the Flag evaluation If statement. Put your cursor just after the "n," then hit Del once or twice—it'll look like this:

```
If (Flag And WF_CPU086) = WF_CPU086 Then Insert "8086"
ElseIf(Flag And WF_CPU186) = WF_CPU186 Then
```

Now click on Start. What do you get?

Figure 4-15: Carriage Return, or Else(If)

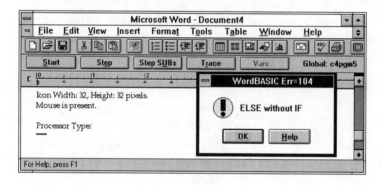

Scary, huh?

Recap

WinExplorer 5 has introduced you to:

- **GetWinFlags**—Windows API call pulls in a flag that, when decoded bit-by-bit, tells of the CPU type, operating mode, and a few other things.

- **Boolean Variables and Operators**—AND, OR, IF, NOT, Why not? Remember that numbers can be used in Boolean expressions.

- **ElseIf**—one word, not two (like "End If"); must always be used with the "carriage return after Then" type of If statement.

WinExplorer 6—Active Windows, Built-In Function Chr$(n)

Well, you've made it this far and haven't nodded off more than once or twice.

Now we're going to start exploring the innards of Windows, doing things that many people once thought couldn't be done from "just" a macro language.

Loading WinExplorer Program 6

From the Companion Disk, delete the current WinExplorer and copy over file C4PGM6.DOC.

Or, from the keyboard, type, type, type!

Program 4-5, Part 1: Type This Before "Sub MAIN"

```
REM Type this before "Sub MAIN"
Declare Function GetNumTasks Lib "Kernel" As Integer
Declare Function GetActiveWindow Lib "User" As Integer
Declare Function GetWindow Lib "User"(hWnd As Integer, wFlag As\
 Integer) As Integer
Declare Function GetNextWindow Lib "User"(hWnd As Integer, wFlag\
 As Integer) As Integer
Declare Function GetWindowText Lib "User"(hWnd As Integer,\
 CurrWindowText$, MaxChars As Integer) As Integer
```

Program 4-6, Part 1: Type This Before "REM Wrap Up"

```
REM Type this before "REM Wrap Up"
REM List open windows
REM Demonstrates While/Wend
GW_HWNDFIRST = 0
GW_HWNDNEXT = 2
InsertPara
n = GetNumTasks
Insert "Windows reports" + Str$(n) + " active tasks."
InsertPara
Dim WindowTitle$(50)
Dim Handle(50)
hWnd = GetActiveWindow
hWnd = GetWindow(hWnd, GW_HWNDFIRST)
While hWnd <> 0 And i < 50
    i = i + 1
    x = GetWindowText(hWnd, WindowText$, 200)
    WindowTitle$(i) = WindowText$
    Handle(i) = hWnd
    hWnd = GetWindow(hWnd, GW_HWNDNEXT)
Wend
If i = 50 Then MsgBox "Overflow. More than 50 open windows."
PrintWindows:
For j = 1 To i
    Insert "Window #" + Str$(j)
    InsertPara
    Insert Chr$(9) + "Window Title: " + WindowTitle$(j)
    InsertPara
    Insert Chr$(9) + "Window Handle (hWnd):" + Str$(Handle(j))
    InsertPara
Next j
```

GetNumTasks

To a first approximation, every program running in Windows is a "Task."

To a second approximation, every *copy* of every program (called an "instance" in WinSpeak) running in Windows is a "Task." If you're running two copies of EXCEL at the same time, for example, each copy is a "Task."

GetNumTasks is a very simple Windows API call that returns the number of active tasks in the system. If you want to think of it as the number of programs running, go right ahead. WinExplorer 6 goes out and picks up the number of tasks and slaps it on the report.

Dim

Way back in the Chapter 4 lecture on WordBasic variables, we talked about "Dim."

Well, here in WinExplorer 6 you can see Dim in action. It just sets up an array, with subscripts starting at zero. And it can appear anywhere in a program, subroutine, or function.

We're setting up arrays to stuff with window names and handles; the former are character strings, the latter numbers.

While/Wend

Let's skip ahead a few lines, just for a second. While/Wend is a very useful control structure that can save all sorts of contortions, generally cobbled together with If and Goto.

The expression after "While" is evaluated. If it comes up True, the following commands are executed until WordBasic hits a "Wend." At that point, control goes back up to the "While," the expression is evaluated again and the whole thing starts over.

With While/Wend, you've now worked with all of the WordBasic control structures: For/Next, Goto/Label, If/Then/Else/ElseIf/End If, Select Case/End Select, and While/Wend. That's all she wrote.

GetWindow

Windows come in many different flavors. You've already seen MessageBox windows and Input Box windows. There's a hierarchy of windows: higher-level windows spawn lower-level "child" windows, which in turn may generate other child windows at lower levels still.

The window manager is charged with keeping track of all of these windows. Your program can interrogate the window manager by using the Windows API call GetWindow:

```
hWnd = GetWindow(hWnd, GW_flag)
```

GW_ Values

Here's a list of all the things GetWindow can tell you, and the GW_ prefixed variable names that C programmers use:

TABLE 4-4: THE GW_PREFIXED VARIABLE NAMES

GW_ PREFIXED VARIABLE NAMES	NFORMATION GIVEN
GW_HWNDFIRST=0	'Get first sibling window
GW_HWNDLAST=1	'Get last sibling window
GW_HWNDNEXT=2	'Get next window on the list
GW_HWNDPREV=3	'Get previous window on the list
GW_OWNER=4	'Get owner of indicated window
GW_CHILD=5	'Get first child of indicated window

When the windows manager has fed you all the windows it can, it will send your program a "null" hWnd. Since we're working with numbers, that is converted into a zero.

The only real problem with all of this wonderful GetWindow stuff is that you have to start somewhere, have to pick up a handle to some window, some place, to get GetWindow kick-started.

GetActiveWindow

This Windows API call returns the handle to the currently active Window. You may recall that a handle is nothing but a number, with no meaning in and of itself, that helps Windows keep track of things.

Because WinExplorer is always run from inside WinWord, the GetActiveWindow call will always return a handle to WinWord. (Yes, other applications work differently and may return the handle for a document or a spreadsheet or some such. But whenever you're inside WinWord, the *only* active window is the WinWord window. If you're a Windows guru, keep in mind that WinWord does *not* conform to the Windows Multiple Document Interface specification.)

GetWindow Loop

WinExplorer 6 loops through all the windows by starting with the Active window, then using GW_HWNDFIRST to get the very first window that the window manager can find, looping through with GW_HWNDNEXT to keep pulling in subsequent window handles, and finally stopping when the window manager returns a null—zero—handle.

Any time you need a list of windows, remember this routine. There's a standalone version in Appendix 1.

IsAppLoaded?

One of the most common questions confounding a WordBasic Windows programmer is "How do I know whether Program X is running?". Most WordBasic references suggest using the Windows API call GetModuleHandle; the books often disguise it by renaming it "IsAppLoaded."

■ **T I P**

They can get away with that renaming sleight-of-hand because GetModuleHandle returns a zero if the module doesn't exist and a handle to a Module, hMod, if the Module does exist. The zero evaluates out as a False; the hMod, being nonzero, evaluates to True. Tricky, eh?

Unfortunately, GetModuleHandle (or IsAppLoaded) requires a very exacting variable, the module name, to work properly.

The module name for EXCEL is something you might guess, i.e., "excel"; that's why most examples you'll see in the books look like this:

```
If IsAppLoaded("excel") Then .....
```

■ **T I P**

What the books won't tell you: module names can be *very* strange! Programmers just love to play with things that don't show. The module name for WinWord 1.0 and 1.1 was "OpusApp" although in WinWord 2.0 it was changed to "msword." The module name for CorelDraw 2.0 is "waldo." Corel Trace is "toptrace." And on and on. We'll go through them in Chapter 6.

There may be times when you need the module name; but in many cases, you'll find it easier and better to pull in a list of window titles and work with them. Grabbing a full list of titles and dissecting it may be the only reasonable way to identify programs that are running multiple copies, for example.

GetWindowText

This Windows API call returns the text up in the title bar of each window. Many windows don't have a title bar or title text—aren't even visible for that matter—so don't be overly surprised when your WinExplorer report shows a bunch of "blank" window titles.

Where there's a window handle—an hWnd—there's a window. Whether the window has a name or not.

Built-In Function Chr$(n)

Here's something you'll use all the time. The line

```
Insert Chr$(9) + "Window Title: " + WindowTitle$(j)
```

tells WordBasic to insert character number 9 into the document, followed by some text.

What's a character number 9, you ask?

It's a tab. WinWord starts out new documents with tab stops set every half-inch (1 cm in some non-USA versions). By inserting a tab into a brand-spanking-new document, you're tabbing over a half inch. Makes the printed page much easier to read.

There's no magic to the character numbers between 32 (space) and 255 (y with umlaut). You can look them up in any chart of ANSI Windows characters, like the one in Appendix 4.

For example, the letter "A" is character number 65. Thus, these two WordBasic commands do precisely the same thing:

```
Insert "A"
Insert Chr$(65)
```

But there *is* a bit of magic in the character numbers *under* 32.

Useful Characters

Here are some Chr$(n) character numbers you might find useful, set up with variable names that you might use in a WordBasic program:

```
Tab$ = Chr$(9)
Quote$ = Chr$(34)
SingleQuote$ = Chr$(39)
Para$ = Chr$(13) + Chr$(10)
LineFeed$ = Chr$(11)
Esc$ = Chr$(27)
PageBreak$ = Chr$(12)
SectionBreak$ = Chr$(12)
ColumnBreak$ = Chr$(14)
```

■ T I P

Note that a paragraph mark is two characters—carriage return and then a new line—back-to-back. These two commands are identical:

```
InsertPara
Insert Chr$(13) + Chr$(10)
```

■ T I P

No, that Chr$(12) double-up isn't a typo. In WordBasic it is very difficult to differentiate between a page break and a section break. They're both stored as Chr$(12).

Playtime

Go ahead and click on Start. You'll get a long list of nameless windows, interspersed with some real nuggets.

Figure 4-16: WinExplorer 6

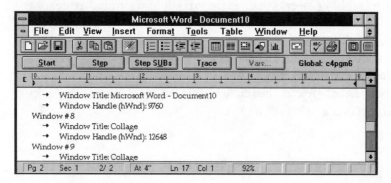

See if you can correlate the number of active tasks with the list of windows. Notice how the hWnd window handles have no apparent intrinsic meaning. They really *do* have a meaning, however, but to understand the inner workings, you need to read Chapter 6 of *Undocumented Windows* (Addison-Wesley, 1992).

Recap

In WinExplorer 6 we dug into the belly of the beast and polished off the last WordBasic/Visual Basic control structure:

- **GetWindow**—enumerates all windows.
- **GetWindowText**—retrieves the text in a window's title bar.
- **GetActiveWindow**—finds the handle for the active window; when run from inside WinWord, this is always the handle for WinWord.
- **GetNumTasks**—tells your program how many tasks (programs or copies of programs) are running.
- **Dim**—creates a subscripted "Dimensioned" variable; subscripts start at zero; the Dim statement can appear almost anywhere in a program.

- **While/Wend**—the final control structure: repeats the commands in a loop until the While expression evaluates False.
- **Chr$(n)**—allows your program to work with characters that may not be printable.

WinExplorer 7—Elapsed Windows Time, Free Resources

It isn't quite as easy to use up your Windows Free System Resources as it once was: Windows 3.1 makes much more intelligent use of the memory available to it. Windows 3.0 wasn't quite so smart.

We'll be using a Windows 3.1-specific API call to retrieve the Free System Resources, so if you're still stuck with Windows 3.0, *you're going to crash!*

Loading WinExplorer Program 7

From the Companion Disk, delete the current WinExplorer and copy in file C4PGM7.DOC.

And if you're plugging away at the keyboard, here are the commands:

Program 4-7, Part 1: Type This Before "Sub MAIN"

```
REM Type this before "Sub MAIN"
Declare Function GetCurrentTime Lib "User" As Long
REM Or, Declare Function GetTickCount Lib "User" As Long
Declare Function GetFreeSystemResources Lib "user"(wflags As\
 Integer) As Integer
```

Program 4-7, Part 2: Type This Before "REM Wrap Up"

```
REM Type this before "REM Wrap Up"
REM Get the Windows Time; the Windows API call returns milliseconds
REM Demonstrates more complex arithmetic
WinTime = GetCurrentTime
WinTimehr = Int(WinTime /(60 * 60 * 1000))
WinTimemin = Int((WinTime /(60 * 1000)) -(WinTimehr * 60))
InsertPara
Insert "Time since Windows was booted:" + Str$(WinTimehr) + \
 " Hours," + Str$(WinTimemin) + " Minutes (" + Str$(WinTime) + \
 " milliseconds)."
InsertPara
REM Use a Windows 3.1-specific call to retrieve pct Free System\
REM Resources
Insert "Free System Resources:" + Str$(GetFreeSystemResources(0))\
 + "%"
InsertPara
```

GetCurrentTime/GetTickCount

■ T I P

These are simply two different names for the same function. Surprisingly, some books make it sound like they're two different functions, but they aren't.

Both of these Windows API calls return the number of milliseconds that have elapsed since Windows was started. If you exit Windows and then start it back up again, these functions both reset to zero.

The time is accurate to +/- 55 milliseconds. And sooner or later (after roughly two months without exiting Windows; man, that's one long game of solitaire!) the time counter overflows, setting itself back to zero.

If you want to run Windows for two months straight to check it, go right ahead.

Built-In Function Int(n) Redux

This is one of those not-so-unusual situations where you want to truncate numbers, where rounding off just wouldn't give the right answer. We took a look at Int(n) back in WinExplorer 2, but let's knock it around again.

To pull the number of hours out of a millisecond-ticker, you'll have to divide by 1000 (milliseconds/sec) * 60 (sec/min) * 60 (min/hr), and then truncate the answer.

And then to pull the number of minutes out of that millisecond-ticker, calculate the total number of minutes and subtract the number of hours * 60 (min/hr).

Ah, arithmetic.

Any time you need to calculate elapsed time, remember this routine.

Free System Resources

"Free System Resources"—or just "FSR" to most WinMavens—is a euphemism for "available memory." The USER and GDI DLLs carve out a bit of memory for their internal use. FSR measures the percentage of memory left in those private enclaves. That's all.

Let's translate that into English. (It's a good opportunity to go back over some important Windows concepts anyway.)

As you've seen, Windows is composed of Dynamic Link Libraries. Two of those DLLs—called "USER" and "GDI"—need to glom onto some memory for their own internal use. Each time you crank up a new Windows application, USER and GDI may allocate some of that memory to take care of the new applications. (Exactly how and why and how much gets complicated.) If the Windows application is nice it releases all of that memory when it quits.

Unfortunately, not all Windows programs are nice. And even if they *were* all nice, starting more than a handful of programs can eat up a very significant percentage of the USER and GDI memory.

In theory, when Windows calculates the FSR number, it looks at the percentage of memory left for USER and the percentage left for GDI, and reports the smaller of the two numbers.

In practice, heaven only knows how Windows Program Manager calculates the percentage. An interesting exercise "left for the reader": use the Heap values returned by the undocumented GetHeapSpaces API call:

```
Declare Function GetHeapSpaces Lib "kernel"(hMod As Integer) As Long
Declare Function GetModuleHandle Lib "kernel"(Name$) As Integer
Sub MAIN
hModUser = GetModuleHandle("User")
hModGDI = GetModuleHandle("GDI")
UserHeapSpace = GetHeapSpaces(hModUser)
GDIHeapSpace = GetHeapSpaces(hModGDI)
End Sub
```

to replicate the Windows FSR figure. (UserHeapSpace and GDIHeapSpace have to be unpacked—and that won't be easy. Even tougher is getting numbers that match Windows' numbers.) More information is in Fran Finnegan's *Windows* column, *PC Magazine,* Vol. 10, No. 19, p. 449.

Fortunately, Windows 3.1 provides an API call that takes all the guesswork out of calculating FSR, the Windows Way.

```
x=GetFreeSystemResources(0)
```

returns the value used by Windows, right, wrong, or indifferent.

Playtime
Time to click Start.

Figure 4-17: WinExplorer 7

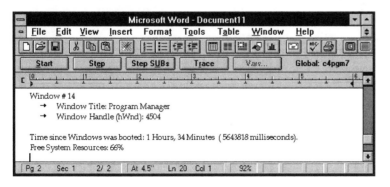

While Program Manager, File Manager, and many Windows programs will tell you how much FSR is left—all it usually takes is a click on Help, then About—Word for Windows is silent on the subject. There is no way within WinWord to see your FSR and monitor its (potentially devastating!) progress. You have to switch out of WinWord, then click away at Program Manager.

That's all changed now. Whenever you're unsure of your Free System Resources, just run WinExplorer and all will be told.

Recap

WinExplorer 7 gave one WordBasic command a workout and introduced a new Windows API call:

- **GetFreeSystemResources(0)**—returns the percentage of Free System Resources, calculated the Windows Way.
- **Int(n)**—hands your program the integer part of "n"; no rounding, it's truncated.

WinExplorer 8—Disk Drives

Windows can reach out and touch your disk drives. Sometimes in ways you never imagined . . . *or wanted, for that matter.*

Loading WinExplorer Program 8

From the Companion Disk files, get rid of the current WinExplorer, then copy in C4PGM8.DOC.

From the keyboard:

Program 4-8, Part 1: Type This Before "Sub MAIN"
```
REM Type this before "Sub MAIN"
Declare Function GetDriveType(nDrive As Integer) Lib "Kernel" As\
 Integer
```

Program 4-8, Part 2: Type This Before "REM Wrap Up"
```
REM Type this before "REM Wrap Up"
REM Sort out the drives
REM Demonstrates Case statement
InsertPara
Insert "Drives available to Windows (RAMdrives are Fixed, of"\
 + " course):"
InsertPara
REM Max 30 drives
For i = 0 To 30
```

```
type = GetDriveType(i)
Select Case type
    Case 0    'Function can't determine drive type; skip
    Case 1    'Drive does not exist; skip
    Case 2    'Removeable drive
        Insert "Drive " + Chr$(65 + i) + ": Removeable"
        InsertPara
    Case 3    'Fixed drive
        Insert "Drive " + Chr$(65 + i) + ": Fixed"
        InsertPara
    Case 4    'Remote/Network drive
        Insert "Drive " + Chr$(65 + i) + ": Remote/Network"
        InsertPara
    Case Else 'Skip
End Select
Next i
```

GetDriveType

The only strange part of this Windows API call is how it expects you to identify the drives. No, you don't use "a" or "A" or "a:" or "A:" for the first drive. You don't even use "1." You guessed it—GetDriveType wants a zero for the first drive. Drive "b:" must be identified as a one. And so on.

Anyway, GetDriveType returns one of five values:

- Zero if it can't figure out the kind of drive
- One if the drive does not exist
- Two if the disk media can be removed from the drive
- Three if the disk media cannot be removed from the drive
- Four if the drive is a remote, networked drive

Note the subtle distinction between "can be removed" and "cannot be removed." Good design decision: as the distinction between hard drives and floppy drives continues to blur—and as removable-cartridge drives become more common—it's comforting to know that Windows will be able to identify them properly.

If you have a RAMdrive set up, WinExplorer—and Windows itself—will identify it as a fixed drive. (A RAMdrive is something that looks like a disk drive to Windows, but is actually just a chunk of memory you've set aside to fake Windows out and speed up ersatz "disk" access.)

WinExplorer 8 loops through a maximum of 30 drives and uses a Select Case control structure to identify them.

Note how the individual "Case" statements don't have to have anything after them. No-command-at-all is equivalent to "Skip this case."

A Chr$(n) Trick

> In the places I go there are things that I see
> That I *never* could spell if I stopped with the Z.
>
> —Dr. Seuss, *On Beyond Zebra*, 1955

Did you see how WinExplorer 8 uses Chr$(i + 65)?

That's a common BASIC trick, but if you haven't seen it before it could be a bit mysterious.

Consider: character number 65 is "A." Drive number zero is "A:." Character number 66 is "B," which is drive number one. Character 67 is "C," drive number two. And so on. (Well, if you go beyond "Z," you should consult Dr. Seuss. The first letter beyond Z is, of course, YUZZ. A YUZZ drive is *not* removeable.)

By adding 65 to the number of the drive, you'll get the capital letter that corresponds to the drive.

You can use a similar trick for transforming the numbers zero through nine into the characters 0 through 9. Just use Chr$(number+48). Note that this doesn't work if the number is more than nine; Chr$(10 + 48) will give you a ":" colon.

Playtime

Go ahead and click Start.

Figure 4-18: WinExplorer 8

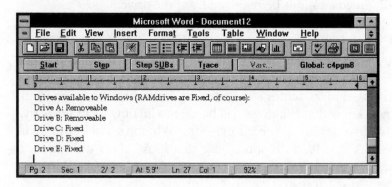

One more WinExplorer to go.

Recap

WinExplorer 8 used one Windows API call and a trick on one WordBasic Built-in Function:

- **GetDriveType**—tells your program which disk drives are available, and whether they're fixed, removeable or remote. *(To be absolutely correct, the word should be spelled "removable". Unfortunately, it's misspelled consistently in both the C books and the Windows books, and in the SDK, so we'll inflict you with some inherited lousy spelling. A standard's a standard, after all. Even when it's wrong.)*
- **Chr$(n+65)**—produces the letter "A" when n is zero, "B" when it's one, and so on. **Chr$(i+48)** takes a single digit from zero to nine and turns it into the character 0 through 9.

WinExplorer 9—DOS Environment String from Windows

Now for the trickiest part of WinExplorer: retrieving the DOS Environment string from Windows. Thanks and a tip o' the Hacker's Hat to Neil Rubenking for posing the question and to Hack Extraordinaire Jonathan Zuck for solving it. (Jonathan is author of *Visual Basic Techniques and Utilities* (Ziff-Davis, 1992), co-author of *Visual Basic How-to* (Waite Publications, 1992), a columnist for *Windows Tech Journal*, and one of the world's foremost authorities on Visual Basic.)

The DOS Environment string, if you didn't know, is a list of all DOS Environment variables and their current values. It's primarily the result of all the "SET" statements in your AUTOEXEC.BAT file, plus a few oddball machinations that may crop up in some DOS programs.

Loading WinExplorer 9

From the Companion Disk, zap out the current WinExplorer and replace it with file C4PGM9.DOC. Soon as you replace it, click on File, then Close, then click on Tools, Macro, WinExplorer, and finally Edit. This is the final version of WinExplorer; you may as well save it now.

From the keyboard, type:

Program 4-9, Part 1: Type This Before "Sub MAIN"

```
REM Type this before "Sub MAIN"
Declare Function GetDOSEnvironment Lib "kernel" As Long
Declare Function AnsiUpper$ Lib "user"(lpString As Long)
```

Program 4-9, Part 2: Type This Before "REM Wrap Up"

```
REM Type this before "REM Wrap Up"
REM Here's a tough one -- parsing the DOS Environment string
REM Thanks to Jonathan Zuck for ... er ... pointing the way
```

```
Dim EnvironmentString$(50)
InsertPara
Insert "DOS Environment String:"
InsertPara
lpEnvString = GetDOSEnvironment
StringLength = 1
i = 0
While StringLength > 0 And i < 50
     EnvironmentString$(i) = AnsiUpper$(lpEnvString)
     StringLength = Len(EnvironmentString$(i))
     i = i + 1
     lpEnvString = lpEnvString + StringLength + 1
Wend
For j = 0 To i - 1
     Insert EnvironmentString$(j)
     InsertPara
Next j
```

Who Cares About the Environment String?

Let's start with the basics. The DOS Environment string would seem to be pretty esoteric, but it has one very, very important use for WordBasic programmers. That use hinges on an important WordBasic Command: Shell.

```
Shell "c:\utility\myprog.exe"
```

for example, will crank up the program "myprog.exe," from the subdirectory "utility," and pass control to that program. The Shell command is WordBasic's main link to the outside world.

If you look in most books, they'll tell you that shelling out to DOS (that is, starting up a DOS window from inside WinWord and then transferring control to that window) is as easy as using the command:

```
Shell "command.com /c"
```

■ T I P

Not true. Won't work.

While, say, 90% of all Windows users do, indeed, rely on command.com as their DOS command interpreter, an increasing number of folks use competing command processors like the shareware 4DOS.EXE, and NDOS.EXE (which is 4DOS in Symantec/Norton commercial clothing).

In addition, some people don't keep COMMAND.COM in their root directory—or any directory on the DOS path. For these people, shelling to "command.com," with no directory information, can cause no end of headaches.

DOS to the rescue.

DOS itself maintains the name and path of the command interpreter, in *(surprise!)* the DOS Environment string, particularly in a DOS Environment variable called "COMSPEC."

The bottom line: if you want to "Shell out to DOS" from inside WinWord, you *must* shell to the command interpreter stored in the DOS Environment string as "COMSPEC." If you do it any other way, you're inviting sporadic disasters. "Shelling out" to Windows, i.e., running another Windows program from within WordBasic is of course simpler. COMMAND.COM is not needed.

Null Terminators

Further complicating matters: the DOS Environment string is not stored like a "normal" WordBasic string.

WordBasic strings are stored as sequences of characters; WordBasic knows it has hit the end of a string when it encounters a character number zero—the infamous Null *(apologies to Aaaarnold)* Terminator.

A WordBasic string might look like this:

```
Hasta la bye-bye, baby.§
```

The "§" is just our shorthand for Chr$(0), the null.

The DOS Environment string is stored differently. For example, a user might have the following lines in the AUTOEXEC.BAT:

```
Set COMSPEC=C:\DOS\command.com
Set PATH=C:\DOS;C:\WINDOWS
```

They would translate into a DOS Environment string that looks like this:

```
COMSPEC=C:\DOS\COMMAND.COM§PATH=C:\DOS;C:\WINDOWS§§
```

Did you notice the "§" null right in the middle of the string? WordBasic will take a look at that string and stop at the first "§" null, not knowing or caring that there are more pieces to the string!

Long Pointers to Strings

The first part of Jonathan Zuck's outstanding solution to the embedded-nulls problem relies on something we don't use very often in WordBasic: Long Pointers.

We've hit several Windows API calls that return strings: GetProfileString, you might recall, returns a string stored in WIN.INI; GetWindowText returns the window title as a text string. But here's the big lie: those Windows API calls don't really return strings. They return pointers—so-called Long Pointers—*to* strings.

A Long Pointer to a string is just the location in memory where that string begins. It's a number. A position. A starting place.

We've been sugar-coating things by ignoring the Long Pointer (which has very little use in WordBasic) and diving directly for the string. In spite of our extended deception, most Windows API calls are actually set up to return Long Pointers—not strings.

By telling WordBasic we want GetWindowText this way

```
Declare Function GetWindowText Lib "User"(hWnd As Integer,\
 CurrWindowText$, MaxChars As Integer) As Integer
```

we're telling WordBasic to forget the Long Pointer to CurrWindowText$, to go straight for the string itself. Had we set up the GetWindowText API call the way C programmers do, roughly translated into WordBasic as:

```
Declare Function GetWindowText Lib "User"(hWnd As Integer,\
 lpCurrWindowText As Long, MaxChars As Integer) As Integer
```

WordBasic would've received a Long Pointer to CurrWindowText$. Lot of good that would do: there's almost no way for WordBasic to translate a Long Pointer into the string itself.

Ah, but there's a trick!

GetDOSEnvironment

Instead of retrieving the DOS Environment string itself—the way we've handled every Windows API call involving strings—we're going to get tricky and retrieve a *Long Pointer to* the string.

Hang on. You'll see why in a second.

In normal circumstances, if there were any way within WordBasic to look at the whole DOS Environment string, the declaration

```
Declare Function GetDOSEnvironment$ Lib "kernel"
```

would work just fine. Note how you can dispense with the parenthesis if there are no parameters.

Unfortunately, though, those embedded Chr$(0) nulls, the markers inside the DOS Environment string, require drastic steps. The first step is to retrieve a *Long Pointer to* the DOS Environment string by telling WordBasic we want a Long Integer, not a string:

```
Declare Function GetDOSEnvironment ()Lib "kernel" As Long
```

Then the Long Pointer to the Environment string is just

```
lpEnvString = GetDOSEnvironment
```

The next drastic step involves marching through the DOS Environment string, using another Windows API call to hop over the Chr$(0) nulls. Yes, it can be done.

AnsiUpper$()

AnsiUpper$()—or AnsiLower$(), if you prefer—fit the bill. Both of these Windows API calls take a Long Pointer to the beginning of a string and return the string converted to upper (or lower) case.

If your program calls AnsiUpper$(), with the Long Pointer pointing to the first character in

```
COMSPEC=C:\DOS\COMMAND.COM§PATH=C:\DOS;C:\WINDOWS§§
```

the AnsiUpper$() routine takes everything up to the null—in this case "COMSPEC=C:\DOS\COMMAND.COM"—and returns it to your program in upper case, i.e., "COMSPEC=C:\DOS\COMMAND.COM". *Look familiar?*

If your program then changes the Long Pointer so it points to the "P" in "PATH," and calls AnsiUpper$() again, the AnsiUpper$() routine dutifully converts the "PATH=...." string to upper case and returns it.

The translation to upper case is entirely coincidental: what we're interested in is the way AnsiUpper$() takes a pointer, scans down to the next Chr$(0) null, and returns the string that it finds. Any equivalent string-handling function would do just as well.

■ **TIP**

You now know how to deal with Long Pointers to strings, should you encounter them, and embedded-null strings, too, from inside WordBasic. Many thought it couldn't be done!

Len() and the Loop

Tying it all together, here's how WinExplorer hops through the embedded-null DOS Environment string, skipping over the nasty nulls:

```
lpEnvString = GetDOSEnvironment
StringLength = 1
i = 0
While StringLength > 0 And i < 50
     EnvironmentString$(i) = AnsiUpper$(lpEnvString)
```

```
    StringLength = Len(EnvironmentString$(i))
    i = i + 1
    lpEnvString = lpEnvString + StringLength + 1
Wend
```

Len(String$) returns the length of the string. No big surprise there.

lpEnvString skips over the returned string, then skips over the null, in the line above "Wend."

When lpEnvString ultimately points to a null—the end of the DOS Environment strings is marked by two nulls back-to-back—WinExplorer gets a zero-length string.

At that point, the While statement turns False, and the array EnvironmentString$(i) has been stuffed with all of the pieces of the DOS Environment string, stripped out and ready to use.

That's all it takes.

Playtime

Click Start. You'll get the entire WinExplorer report, which ends with a listing of your DOS Environment string.

Figure 4-19: WinExplorer in Toto

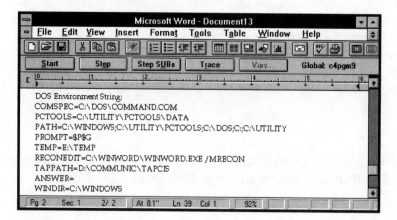

Recap

In this final installment of WinExplorer we've taken a look at:

- **GetDOSEnvironment**—a Windows API call that returns the DOS Environment string but has Chr$(0) nulls strung all through it.

- **lpStrings**—Long Pointers to strings that can be handled in WordBasic, providing you aren't concerned about upper/lowercase.

- **Len(String$)**—a built-in function that returns the length of the String$.
- **AnsiUpper$()**—the key to manipulating Long Pointers and to breaking down null-embedded strings.
- **Shell**—a WordBasic command that shells out to another program; be sure to use COMSPEC when shelling out to DOS.

Put Your App In Lights—On the Menu Bar

Now that you have WinExplorer stored away as a global macro, you might want to make it easier to get to.

Couldn't be simpler.

WinWord lets you assign any macro—built-in, home-grown, store-bought, or otherwise—to a menu. The key is Tools Options Menus.

Click on Tools, then Options. Scroll down those pretty pictures until you hit Menus, and click on that icon.

Figure 4-20: Assign to Menu

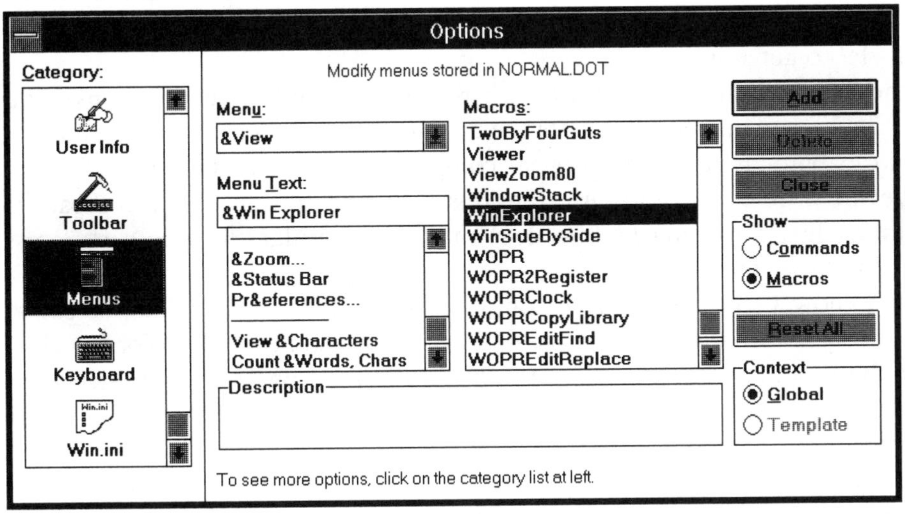

If you want to assign WinExplorer to, say, the "View" menu, scroll down the upper-left Drop-Down List Box Control—the one marked "Menu." Click on View.

Now scroll down the List Box on the right. Look for "WinExplorer" (or whatever you called the global macro). You may have to click the button that says "Macros," if it's set on "Commands." Click once on WinExplorer.

Finally, put your cursor over where it says "Menu Text" and type in something meaningful, like "Windows Explorer." If you want to have one of the letters underlined—so you can use an Alt+ key combination instead of the mouse—put an "&" ampersand in front of the letter.

Click Add. Then click Close.

Now look at your View menu. There it is! Click on View, then Windows Explorer, and the macro takes off.

Ah, macro immortality and accessibility. What more could you ask for?

Pause for a moment here and notice what you've been doing.

You've built a custom program—a Windows program—using WordBasic. The program dives into Windows, rummages around a bit, and extracts all sorts of useful information. It constructs a fancy document, and optionally saves or prints it. So far that's pretty impressive.

By putting that program on WinWord's menu, you've gone beyond writing a program; you've actually *extended WinWord's functionality*. Your program looks no different from any other WinWord command; users won't know that you stuck it on the menu, unless you tell them; your program looks and feels like it belongs there!

In the DOS world you might graft your program onto an application by creating a TSR and telling your users to push a strange key combination like Alt+Shift+F9 to get at it.

In the Windows world—at least with the major Windows applications—you can actually weave your program *into* the application itself. That's an enormously powerful capability: it opens the door for complete customizing, tailoring solutions to fit specific problems, in-house extensions that give you and your company a competitive edge, commercial add-ons, even building bridges for one-click access to other Windows applications.

Wanna know a secret; the real reason why you can tap into WinWord so easily, so "seamlessly", with your own macros? It's because some of WinWord itself— some of the product you pull out of the box and install on your computer—was written in WordBasic. You're taking advantage of the same hooks the developers themselves use.

Those guys aren't dummies. They know it's easier to write and maintain code in Basic. Their genius lies in opening up the same capability to mortals like you and me.

WinExplorer—Putting It All Together

Chapter 4 and the WinExplorer have exposed you to all sorts of things. Let's go back over the high points.

Subroutines and Functions

Every macro contains a Sub MAIN/End Sub pair. Several events can trigger macro execution, including clicking on "Start" in the macro edit pane; clicking on Tools, Macro, and double-clicking on the macro name; and assigning a macro to a menu and clicking on the menu item.

Macros may have their own Functions (which return values) and Subroutines (which do not).

Macros may also reach out to Windows Dynamic Link Libraries by using the Declare statement.

Windows API Calls

We've used many of the most common Windows API calls, including:

- **GetVersion**—returns the Windows version number.
- **GetWindowsDirectory**—the directory from which Windows was originally loaded.
- **GetFreeSpace**—how much memory (real and virtual) is currently available.
- **GetProfileString/Int**—retrieve and modify settings in WIN.INI.
- **GetSystemMetrics**—many of the sizes that define the Windows environment, especially the size of the display.
- **GetWinFlags**—processor type, running mode, and others.
- **GetActiveWindow**—returns a handle to the active window, the one that has focus; if you run this command from WordBasic, you will always get the handle for WinWord.
- **GetNumTasks**—how many programs (and copies of programs) are currently running in Windows.
- **GetNextWindow**—skips through all the windows' handles.
- **GetWindowText**—the title of the window.
- **GetCurrentTime/GetTickCount**—number of milliseconds since Windows was loaded.
- **GetFreeSystemResources**—percentage of available memory for USER and GDI Dynamic Link Libraries; new command for Windows 3.1; in 3.0, you can use the undocumented GetHeapSpaces explained in Fran Finnegan's column.
- **GetDriveType**—whether a drive is fixed, removeable, or remote.
- **GetDOSEnvironment/AnsiUpper$**—used to dissect the DOS Environment string.

There are cookbook examples of each of these API calls in Appendix 1.

Variables

All WordBasic variables are either strings or double-precision floating-point reals. String variables have names that end with a "$" dollar sign. Reals don't.

When declaring external functions, including Windows API and other Dynamic Link Library calls, you may also use variable types Integer (eight bits, signed) and Long (for Long Integer, 16 bits, signed), although WordBasic won't let you get at those data types directly: they're translated into Strings or Reals before you can get to them.

WordBasic numbers used in Boolean expressions are converted to eight-bit signed integers, then the Boolean operators are applied bit by bit. Zero evaluates False; everything else evaluates True. Whenever you can, use a value of minus one for "True."

Control Structures

You've used all of the WordBasic and Visual Basic control structures:

- **Goto / Label**—make sure you don't put a tab in front of labels.
- **If / Then / Else / ElseIf / End If**—use "End If" only when you have a carriage return after "Then"; note that "ElseIf" is one word, "End If" is two.
- **On Error**—event-driven commands that tell WordBasic what to do if an error occurs.
- **Select Case / Case / End Select**—versatile structure that lets you pick and choose values; beware the error raised if there are no matches (use "Case Else" to avoid it); don't Goto a label outside the Case construct.
- **For / To / Step / Next**—evaluates the "start," "stop," and "increment" values just once; can Step up or down; use the "Next i" form for added security; watch out for a Step of zero.
- **While/Wend**—as you would expect.

Built-In Functions

WordBasic has a number of functions ready for you to use:

- **MsgBox(), InputBox()**—communicate with the user, using pre-fabricated Controls/Dialog Boxes.
- **SelInfo()**—returns info about the current selection.

- **Time$() / Date$()**—gives the current time and date, in a format determined by the Windows Control Panel/WIN.INI settings.
- **Int(n)**—returns the integer part of "n"; watch out if "n" can exceed 32,768.
- **Chr$(n)**—character number "n"; beware of Chr$(0), which in WordBasic and Visual Basic is a null, a terminator for strings.
- **Str$(n)**—converts "n" to a string, and puts a space in front of positive numbers; to convert single digits and avoid the space, use Chr$(n+48).
- **Instr$(start,String$,Match$)**—returns the location of Match$ in String$; if start is > 1 the search begins at character position "start."
- **Left$(), Mid$(), Right$()**—return the beginning, middle, or ending characters of a string.
- **Len(String$)**—the length of the String$.

Word Processing-Style Commands

- **Insert / InsertPara**—puts characters in the document at the current insertion point. While you might think "Print" would do this, the WordBasic command "Print" is used to write records to a file, and display short notices on the status bar at the bottom of the WinWord screen.
- **FileNew**—creates a new document, based on the chosen template.
- **FilePrint**—prints the current document.
- **FileSave**—saves the current document.

Overloaded Operators

If one of your C++ programmer friends starts kicking sand in your face because WordBasic doesn't have any dynamically inheritable polymorphic overloaded operators, you can kick some sand back.

The "+" operator is valid for string concatenation.

And all of the Boolean operators—AND, OR, NOT—are valid on Boolean values and numbers.

That isn't exactly world-class object orientation, but it's a start. *At the very least, it'll evoke peals of laughter from your OO friend!*

What's Next?

We've gone through a very large percentage of the most useful WordBasic commands. The commands we've skipped are primarily related to the way WinWord does word processing: bookmarks, fields, headers and footers, tables, fonts, that kind of thing. We've also skipped custom-made Forms or Dialog Boxes (they're a lot more fun in Visual Basic).

We'll pick up on some of those topics in later chapters. But if you're interested in pursuing hard-core WordBasic, you'd be well-advised to learn the word processor itself next. It's tough slugging through a macro command for building tables, say, if you've never actually constructed and printed a table!

On the other hand, you should feel very secure in your exposure to WordBasic as it interacts with Windows 3.1. Some of the Windows API does not adapt to WordBasic smoothly; you've been through many of the roughest spots and are well-equipped to tackle whatever Windows and the great world of DLLs may have in store.

Dynamic Data Exchange with WordBasic is a topic unto itself; DDE has its own set of rules and caveats. We'll dig into DDE in Chapter Six.

In the meantime, let's take a shot at Visual Basic.

CHAPTER ▪ 5

Working with Visual Basic

Most Visual Basic books—most "Intro to Language X" books, for that matter— step you through little toy applications. A calculator. A mortgage amortization helper. A little database for your record collection or your friends' phone numbers. Stuff like that.

Nothing wrong with that, of course. But how many times do you need another calculator? How often do you analyze your mortgage? And do you really want to catalog your records? *When was the last time you bought a record anyway?*

We're going to take off the kid gloves.

You already know enough BASIC to do serious harm. Let's team that up with the Event-Driven approach you'll learn in this chapter and build an application you can use every day—a *commercial* application, something you might pay real money to buy.

You can do it. Visual Basic makes it easy!

The Why's and Wherefore's of WinLHA

> "Compression is the first grace of style."
>
> —Anonymous

If you've ever used a modem, you've probably encountered data compression software.

The concept is simple enough: take a file and squeeze out all the redundant stuff. What's left—a *compressed* version of the file—contains everything in the original; you just have to reconstitute it—*decompress* it—before your programs can use it.

Think of freeze-dried coffee. You can store many, many gallons of coffee in a little jar. Just add water. In theory.

Compression, Compression Everywhere

File compression has become a fact of life on-line. It's just too bloody expensive to store the full, uncompressed version of files on a bulletin board it: takes up too much room and folks don't want to pay for all the time it takes to move uncompressed files around.

File compression also has its place on *your* computer. When you have a file that won't be used all that often, you should compress it. You can save 30%—even 50%, or 70% in rare cases—of the original disk space by compressing those suckers and reconstituting them only when you need them. Suddenly your hard drive can hold almost twice as much data.

Some of the more enterprising compression programs can create self-extracting files. What's that? A self-extracting file is one you can run, just like a program, and *boom!* your files suddenly appear. It's a neat trick, one that we've used for the *WinMortals* Companion Disk.

The Compression Achilles' Heel

Surprisingly, few people compress their infrequently used files. Why? Because it's a pain. Crank up a DOS window. Try to remember the exact file names and the paths. Type in a series of inscrutable commands. Pray that the compressor understood what you were trying to do. If you guessed wrong, type, type, type again.

One solution is to go out and buy an on-the-fly data compressor—Stacker probably being the best-known of the breed. The latest compressors have overcome many of their earlier compatibility problems, they work well with Windows, and they require little care and feeding. On the other hand, they're fairly expensive, won't create individual compressed files (for, e.g., sending a file over the phone), and some folks still have a hard time trusting all their data to just one program.

Enter the Windows front-end. Several enterprising programmers have developed simple Windows applications that automate much of the compression headache: point and click at the files you want compressed, set options and modes, click a few more times, and voilá! there's your compressed file.

We're going to build a Windows front-end to the most efficient compression program available, LHArc. When we're done, you'll have a fully functional, commercial program *that you built yourself and understand and can change to your heart's content!*

We've chosen LHArc over the best-known compression program, PKZIP, for three important reasons: (1) LHArc creates smaller compressed files, (2) with LHArc it's easy to create self-extracting files, no additional software necessary, and

(3) the price is right: LHArc is free (there's a copy of LHArc Version 2.3 on the WinMortals Companion Disk).

Haruyasu Yoshizaki—better known as Yoshi—is the genius behind LHArc. He allows the program to be distributed freely, providing it is distributed in its entirety, unmodified, with the copyright intact. (LHArc is Copyright © by Haruyasu Yoshizaki.) While the documentation can be a bit inscrutable, the program itself is a tribute to Yoshi's skill and generosity.

Events—"Stuff Happens" and How to Deal with It

The WinLHA code is stuffed away on your Companion Disk. Simply follow the instructions in Appendix 3 to move that code into its own subdirectory under Visual Basic. If you follow the Appendix 3 instructions, you'll have a subdirectory called something like "C:\VB\WINLHA" that contains everything you'll need.

■ **TIP**

One tip for keeping Visual Basic both *visual* and *basic*: tell the Program Manager to minimize itself every time you start Visual Basic. It's easy: in Program Manager, click on Options, then Minimize On Use. Other desktop managers have similar options.

Visual Basic "design time"—that is, the part of Visual Basic you see when you're *writing* a program, as opposed to *running* one—has at least four independent windows, all of which float on the desktop. There's lots of blank space between and around those windows. If you let Program Manager stay full-size, the visual distraction from all the icons in the background will drive you batty. Try it once. You'll see.

So much for the preliminaries.

A Visual Orientation

Once more unto the breach, dear friends, once more...

—Shakespeare, *King Henry V*, 1598
(*pace* General Chang, *Star Trek VI*)

Visual Basic is unique in many ways, not least of which is how it forces you, the programmer, to think about your users. You can't just sit down and write code, hoping that everything will work out in the end. Rather, Visual Basic forces you to start with the user interface—the most important, and most often neglected, part of any computer program. It's almost impossible to write a Visual Basic program without first thinking through how the user will interact with the program.

That's going to be your first big conceptual jump.

The second big jump, of course, is the Event-Driven way of looking at things.

Crank up Visual Basic by double-clicking on its icon. Here's what you'll see:

Figure 5-1: Where Visual Basic Lives

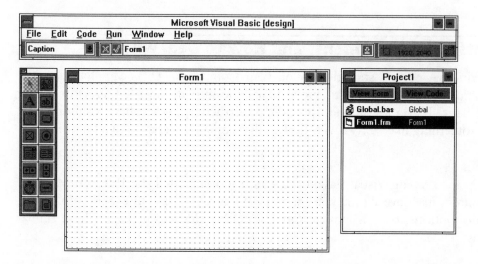

The first time you bring up Visual Basic you'll find a hodgepodge of overlapping Windows. Re-size them and move them around a bit, so you can see what's going on, and the result will be not unlike Figure 5-1.

Welcome to your new home. You'll be spending many enjoyable (and several not-so-enjoyable!) hours in front of this amazing screen.

Yes, there are names for all those windows, and those things inside the windows, and there are programming conventions, and confusing definitions, and arbitrary restrictions, and all the stuff you have to put up with in a programming language. But let's forget about all that for the moment and go have some fun!

Drive List Box Control

Double-click on that thing over there on the left that looks like a disk drive. You can see it; it's in the second column of pretty pictures, second from the bottom. Go ahead.

Figure 5-2: A Drive List Box

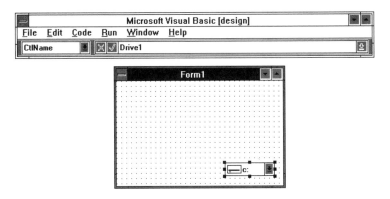

Believe it or not, you have just given your program access to all disk drives on the user's system. All it took was one double-click.

Note in passing that the Drive List Box Control has been selected (you can tell because of the sizing box and big black dots around the Control). And if you look up at the top, you'll see that the Control's name (abbreviated CtlName) is "Drive1." You can give this Control a new name by typing over the "Drive1."

To see how "Drive1" works, first grab that Drive List Box Control and move it to the lower right corner of the Form (we'll be using the rest of the form to play some more), then push F5.

Pushing F5 runs the "program" you've written—even though the program only consists of a Drive List Box.

Next, click on that down-arrow on the Drive List Box. Magic!

Figure 5-3: Drive List Box

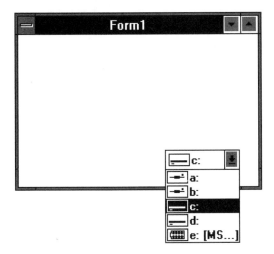

There, before your very eyes, is a list of *all* the disk drives available on your system—and all you did was double-click!

Stop your program by clicking on "Run," then "End."

Directory List Box Control

Now, add another Control—a Directory List Box—by double-clicking on the picture of a file folder. It's at the bottom left of the Toolbox. Stretch it out a bit and move it around, so it looks something like this:

Figure 5-4: A Directory List Box

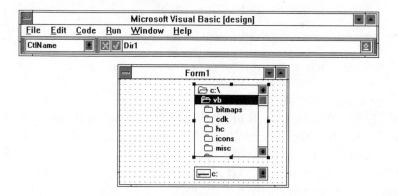

Let Visual Basic do the work for you!

See how the Directory List Box has a name—a CtlName? It's called "Dir1." Ingenuous, eh?

Here's the neat part: Visual Basic Directory Boxes have all sorts of capabilities built in; you don't need to do a thing. Play with it a bit. Press F5 (or click on "Run," then "Start"), and double-click around. See how the Control, automatically, all by itself, will let you hop through all of the directories on the disk? Most remarkable.

When you're through playing with this little puppy, click on "Run," then "End," and we'll build a program.

Your First Event-Driven Program

The Directory List Box and the Drive List Box work fine separately. Let's tie them together.

It would be very nice if changing the drive down in the Drive List Box would change the path up in the Directory List Box. That way you could jump around to *any* directory on *any* disk drive, even a floppy you put into drive a: or drive b:. Want to look at the subdirectories on drive a:? Just click on "a:" down in the Drive

List Box. Want to go back to drive c:? Click on "c:." Just like the File Open dialogs you've seen so many times.

In Visual Basic, that's an easy program. A one-liner. Watch. Double-click on the Drive List Box Control. Visual Basic takes a guess that you want to write a program that should be run whenever you change the drive. *Good guess!*

Figure 5-5: Ready to Write

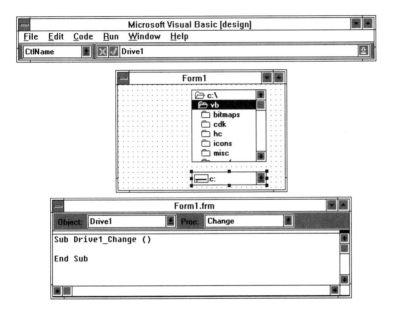

You'll get used to the "Sub Drive1_Change ()" gobbledygook before too long. For now—since we're just playing around—suffice it to say that this is a little subroutine Visual Basic will automatically run every time the drive in the "Drive1" List Box is changed.

Visual Basic has a funny Control variable name convention. Controls have properties, right? Things like color, location, size, different values. Control variables all look like this:

```
ControlName.PropertyName
```

It just so happens that all Drive List Box Controls have a "Drive" property that corresponds to the currently selected drive. *(A system designed by geniuses, no?)*

Directory List Box Controls have another property—the "Path" property—that corresponds to the currently selected path. It's the Path property of the Directory List Box that we want to change, every time the drive in the Drive List Box changes.

To accomplish that, just type the following on the line after "Sub Drive1_Change()":

```
Dir1.Path=Drive1.Drive
```

In plain English that says, *"Yo, Visual Basic! Every time the drive changes in that Control called "Drive1," I want you to automatically change the path in the Control called "Dir1" to the new "Drive1" drive."*

Imagine trying to write that in, say, C.

Now, push F5.

Figure 5-6: The Path-Drive Connection

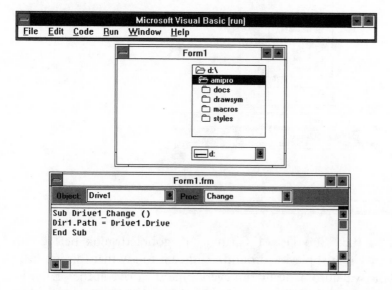

Take a few minutes to get the "feel" of it. See how changing the drive triggers a change in the directory box? You really can *feel* it. People can intellectualize and talk about it all they want, but that *feel* is at the heart of Event-Driven programming. A click—an Event—triggers a change somewhere else. There's no input, no process, no output. Just something that *happens*.

If you want to play around with your diskette drives, make sure you have a diskette in the drive before you click on it. (Clicking on a drive without a diskette raises an Error Condition—and you remember how much fun that can be until your error-handling code is in place, which isn't right now.) When you have the hang of it, click on "Run," then "End" to stop the program.

Congratulations. You've written your first Event-Driven program.

It's a real Event-Driven program, too. When you pick a new drive in the "Drive1" Control, an Event is triggered—a Drive1_Change() Event—and your program takes care of that Event by changing the path property in the "Dir1" Control. That's all there is to it.

Now, while we're still playing, let's turn this into a program that will thumb through all of your files. Hang in there. Your one-line directory changing program is about to turn into a three-line behemoth.

Your Second Event-Driven Program

Next we'll add a File List Box Control to the soup. Double-click on the picture that looks like a sheet of paper with the corner folded over—the picture down at the bottom right of the Toolbox.

Make it a little bigger, and move it to the lower left corner of the Form. Then create a Label Control by double-clicking on the "A" in the Toolbox. Punch it around, too, until you come up with something like this:

Figure 5-7: Still Just Playing Around

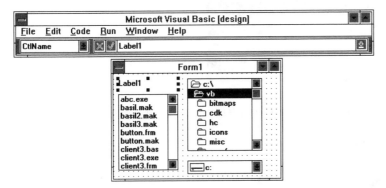

Did you notice how the File List Box is called "File1," and the Label Control is called "Label1"? Do you detect a pattern here?

We're almost done.

Double-click on the Directory List Box Control. Visual Basic guesses that you're going to write a subroutine to handle the Dir1_Change Event, that is, a subroutine that will be run whenever you change the directory in the "Dir1" Control.

Figure 5-8: The Dirs They Are a-Changing

Whenever the "Dir1" path changes, we want the "File1" path to pick up on the new directory—that way the "File1" Control will always show the files in the "Dir1" path. Piece of cake. On the line after "Sub Dir1_Change()," type:

```
File1.Path=Dir1.Path
```

And just to add a bit of icing to the cake, let's display the name of the file the user picks. Double-click on the File List Box Control. Visual Basic guesses that you want to work with the File1_Change() event. *Right again!*

File List Box Controls have a property called "FileName," which is the name of the selected (highlighted) file. Label Controls have a property called "Caption," which corresponds to the text displayed in the label. To set the "Label1" caption to the "File1" file name, whenever there's a change in "File1," all it takes is—you guessed it—one line:

Figure 5-9: The Final Link

That's all she wrote. Push F5 or click on "Run," then "Start."

Figure 5-10: Not Bad for a Toy Language

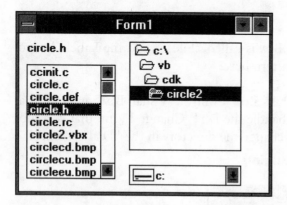

Try clicking on anything and everything; scroll through the files; minimize the window by clicking on the down-arrow; resize the window; maximize the window by clicking on the up-arrow; you can even stop the program by double-clicking on that little hyphen-thing in the upper left corner.

Remember Windows 3.0? Well, you've just written the foundation of a File Manager that's much, much better than the Windows 3.0 File Manager.

All of this *from a three-line program!*

When you're through gazing in wonderment at your work, get rid of this "toy" application by leaving Visual Basic (click on "File," then "End"). When asked if you want to save stuff, just click "No."

We'll build a better Drive-Directory-File Troika here in just a bit.

Events Happen

Okay. Time to stop playing. Time to start working.

*What, you couldn't tell the difference? Good. You've learned an important lesson—perhaps **the most** important lesson—about Visual Basic programming!*

Let's take a look at what you just did.

First, Visual Basic forced you to set up the user interface before you could start writing your program.

Second, your program was inseparable from the user interface; it "hung on" the user interface's Controls. All of the code you wrote—indeed, most of the code in Visual Basic—is tied directly to a Control.

Third, your program wasn't linear. No input-process-output. You graduated to the land of Event-Driven programming by writing little snippets of code (or subroutines or procedures, if you prefer) that take care of Events: if the disk drive changes in the Disk Drive Control, your subroutine changes the path in Directory Control; if the path changes in that Directory Control, another subroutine changes the path in the File Control; if the file name changes in the File Control, your subroutine pastes the file's name into the Label Control.

That's the heart of Event-Driven programming. Something happens—an Event—and one of your subroutines kicks in to handle it. Automatically.

You'll be forgiven for believing that Event-Driven programming really isn't all that tough! At least, it isn't that tough when you use the right tools. Try doing this in C. Nasty! Sure would be nice to have Visual C. . .

Projects

Let's back off for a second and get the "big picture," an idea of how all the pieces of a Visual Basic program come together.

Forms

We've talked about Forms. They're just the windows that hold all your Controls. A Form is the "canvas" onto which your program is drawn. While we were playing around a few minutes ago, the Form was the "thing" that held the Drive, Directory, File, and Label Controls.

Visual Basic stores each Form, and the Controls and code associated with each Form, in a single file. That's a rather revolutionary idea: the Form, the Controls on the Form, and the code "hung on" each Control, all get put in the same place, in the same file.

You can always pick out the Form files: unless you go way out of your way to change them, they're the ones that end with ".FRM."

It is possible to create a Form that will work with more than one Visual Basic program. If you try that—and in some cases it's a good idea—you'll have to keep track of the Form. There's no cataloging system for Forms, no version tracking or revision support worthy of the name. Any third-party vendors listening?

■ **T I P**

In general, it's a whole lot easier to keep track of your Visual Basic programs by sticking each one or each group of related programs in its own subdirectory. That isn't a requirement by any means, but it's worth considering.

Modules

What if you want to write some code that isn't associated with a Control or doesn't go with a Form?

Maybe you have a favorite function that turns a number like "1000" into words like "One Thousand," or perhaps you have a routine custom-designed for the boss, who likes to have all dollar figures rounded to the nearest tenth of a cent.

Those kinds of routines aren't really associated with a Control. For lack of a better term, they belong in a Subroutine Library, a library that floats around, detached from everything, but is available to all the Forms and all the Controls in your program.

In Visual Basic, a collection of subroutines—a Subroutine Library, if you will— is called a "Module." Like good Subroutine Libraries everywhere, they only exist for your convenience; you don't have to use them; you can forget about them completely, with impunity. They're just a handy way to get organized, if you like.

Each program can have as many Modules as you like. They're easily identified by the ".BAS" extension on the file name.

Modules are very convenient places to stick stuff that can be used by any number of Forms and Controls. Why they aren't called "Subroutine Libraries"—who knows?

Global Module

Every program has exactly one Global Module.

■ T I P

Now, here's the clincher: the Global Module isn't a "module," in the normal Visual Basic sense of the term, at all! It is emphatically *not* a collection of subroutines, *not* a Subroutine Library, like the garden-variety modules we've been talking about.

The Global Module contains global declarations: variables used throughout the program, say, maybe an occasional Windows API "Declare" statement. The Global Module does *not* contain any subroutines or functions. If you want a subroutine or function to be accessible by all the Forms and Controls in your program, it has to go in a regular module.

Make File

So now your program consists of a Global Module, a handful of Forms, and maybe a Module (neè Subroutine Library) or two. You have files all over the place. How do you keep track of them?

Well, if you stick with a few simple Visual Basic rules, you won't have to keep track of them at all. Visual Basic will do it for you.

The "Make File"—*bet you'd never guess that's a bit of C terminology*—keeps track of which files make up your program. It's nothing more or less than a packing list, a simple delineation of all the files that, together, constitute your program.

Make Files (again, unless you try really hard to change them) always end with ".MAK."

■ T I P

As long as you use Visual Basic to rename files, or move them around to different directories, the .MAK File will be updated for you. But the minute you rename or move a .FRM or .BAS file using a utility outside of Visual Basic-–in File Manager, say, or DOS—you're begging for trouble. The .MAK file may get all confused. And if the .MAK file gets confused, you will, too. Guaranteed.

Projects

Saving the greatest obfuscation for last.

For some reason, Visual Basic calls a program a "Project."

Microsoft thinks there are good reasons for saying "Project," instead of "Program"—and they say an "Application" is something different, still. Don't sweat the little stuff. A "Project" is just a Visual Basic program, much as a "Module" is just a Subroutine Library.

■ **T I P**

We'll lapse into Visual Basic-speak here, to keep from confusing you when you start building Visual Basic programs. But keep this in the back of your head:

- A "Project" is just a program.
- A "Module" is just a Subroutine Library.
- The "Global Module" isn't really a "Module"; it's a collection of global variable declarations and "Declare"s for outside subroutines.

Got that straight? OK. Now for the detailed anatomy.

A "Project" consists of exactly one Global Module, one or more Forms (well, you can have a Project without any Forms, but that's pretty weird), and as many Modules as suits your fancy.

Each Project has a .MAK file; each .MAK file is for one Project.

When you crank up Visual Basic it starts out with a brand-spanking new Project. You don't open a file in Visual Basic, you open a Project.

■ **T I P**

Surprisingly, you can't close a Project. The current Project is saved whenever you start a new Project or open another existing one. The only way to close a Project without opening another one is by exiting Visual Basic entirely.

Are We Having Fun Yet?

Has all of this Project, Module, Make File stuff got you confused? Well, you aren't alone. Unfortunately you need to know the terminology to get off the ground in Visual Basic, so let's go over it again, one more time, slowly, *with feeling*.

A Visual Basic program is called a Project.

Visual Basic assigns each Project a .MAK file—which is nothing more than a packing list of all the files that go into the individual Project. If you mess around with Visual Basic files using, say, File Manager to change file names or to move files to different directories, you'll confuse the .MAK file, and thus confuse Visual Basic.

Each Project has exactly one Global Module. It contains global variable declarations and "Declare"s for subroutines—including Windows API calls—that exist in the outside world.

Each Project (usually) has at least one Form. The Form is the canvas on which Controls are painted. Bits of code are "hung on" the Form and Controls, specifically attached to Events that happen to the Form and its Controls.

Each Project may have as many Modules as you like. Modules are just libraries of subroutines and functions, available to all Forms and Controls in the Project.

End of the lecture. Let's see how this all works. Roll up your sleeves.

WinLHA 1—The File Troika

One event happened to them all.

—*Ecclesiastes* ii, 14

That little Drive/Directory/File List Control threesome you put together while you were playing a while ago—that's probably the most common combination of controls you'll see in Visual Basic.

Let's assemble another File Troika (for lack of a better term); this time we'll add a couple of bells and whistles.

Crank up Visual Basic. (Yes, this part of WinLHA is on the Companion Disk, but you'll get the hang of things much more quickly if you build it first, all by yourself, then pull the finished product off the disk afterward. Constructing Forms is quite tactile, and you won't get the "feel" of it if you just copy off a disk.)

The Event-Driven stuff is simplicity itself: if the user changes the drive, we want to reset the list of directories so they match the new drive. If the directory changes, we need to reset the list of files so they match the new directory.

So we'll set up a File Troika that lets the user pick a file. Double-click on the drive icon in the Toolbox—that's the second picture from the bottom, on the right-hand side. You should get something like Figure 5-11 on the following page.

Now, without doing anything else, simply type "PickDrive" (without the quotation marks), and you should get something like Figure 5-12 on the following page.

Take a look at the Control Name—CtlName—up on top. Neat, huh?

In many, many cases you'll find Visual Basic is extraordinarily "smart." It makes an honest effort to interpret your actions in a way that makes sense—and in a way that saves you time.

In this case, Visual Basic was smart enough to realize that you were typing in a new value for CtlName. You could have highlighted "Drive1" with your mouse, or clicked at the beginning of "Drive1," erased it, and typed in "PickDrive;" either of those will work. But all you *really* need to do is type!

Figure 5-11: The Pick Drive Control

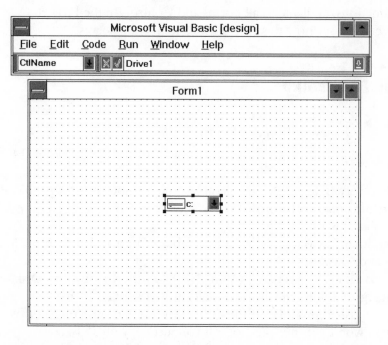

Figure 5-12: Pick Drive Renamed

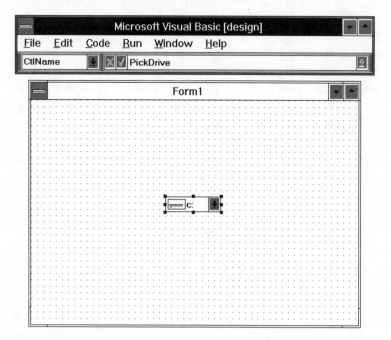

Now, stretch out the Form a bit, move the Drive List Control down, double-click on the Directory List Control (which looks like a file folder, at the lower left corner of the Toolbox), stretch it around, and arrange things so they look like this, more or less:

Figure 5-13: Two Parts of the File Troika

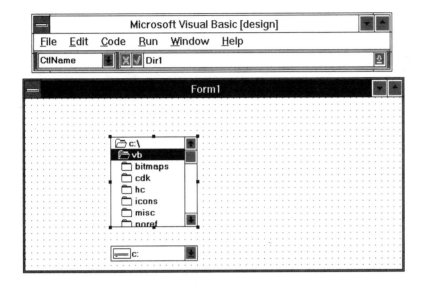

That Drive List Box Control deserves a name, so (again, without clicking the mouse) just type "PickDirectory."

Next, let's get the File List Box Control working. Double-click on the picture of a sheet of paper with dog eared corner. Stretch and move it a bit. Then type in "PickFile."

Your Form should look something like Figure 5-14 on the following page.

Now for the two lines of code that make the Troika work.

Double-click on the Drive List Box Control. Up pops a little box, like the one in Figure 5-15 on the following page, for code that will be run every time the Pick-Drive is changed. Type in the magic line that will change PickDirectory's path to the new drive in PickDrive.

Figure 5-14: The File Troika

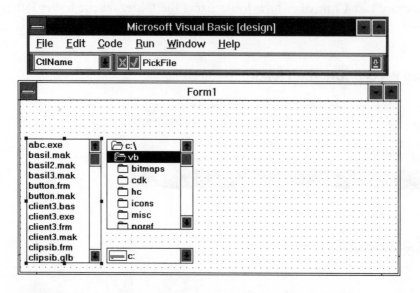

Figure 5-15: PickDrive_Change () Event Handler

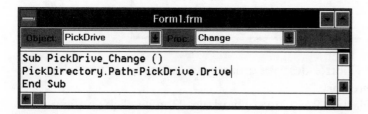

Next, double-click on the Directory List Box Control. Here comes another little box, for code that runs every time the PickDirectory changes. This is the line that will change PickFile's path to the new PickDirectory path:

Figure 5-16: PickDirectory_Change () Event Handler

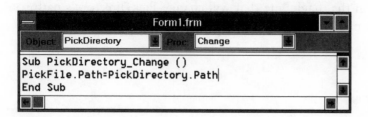

Finally, let's make the Form a little prettier.

Click anywhere on the Form, outside of those three Controls. The Visual Basic command bar should look like this (yours will probably be a little longer, with some weird numbers on the end; not to worry):

Figure 5-17: What a Caption!

Type in a good title for this Form. Maybe "WinLHA—Pick Files to be Compressed."

Figure 5-18: Form Caption

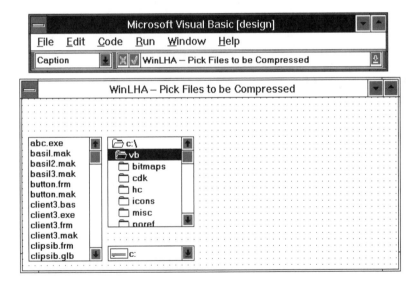

Let's put some labels in there, so your users will know what they're supposed to do.

Labels are easy. Double-click on the "A" in the Toolbox. Resize and move the label wherever you want it.

To change the caption—the text that appears in the label—click once on the LabelControl you'd like to change. Then click the down-arrow underneath "Code" on the menu. See it?

Whenever you click on that down-arrow, you'll get a list of all the Properties associated with this particular Control. (Well, that isn't quite true—what you get is a list of all the Properties you can change *during design time*, but you get the idea.)

The Property you want is called "Caption." Click on it once, and type whatever Caption seems best. Don't worry, you can change it any time you like by clicking once on the Control, clicking the down arrow, and clicking on Caption.

■ **T I P**

There's a fancy name for that first drop-down box under the "File ... Help" menu bar, the one you just flipped through to find the "Caption" Property: it's called a "Properties List Box" or "Properties Combo Box." Some people insist on the latter, which is a really lousy name because this isn't a Combo Box at all (it's a List Box), but such subtleties seem to have passed by the folks who name things.

We won't burden you with Official Names unless they become absolutely necessary. They're just more senseless things to clutter your head.

Four well-chosen labels can look like this:

Figure 5-19: The Final File Troika

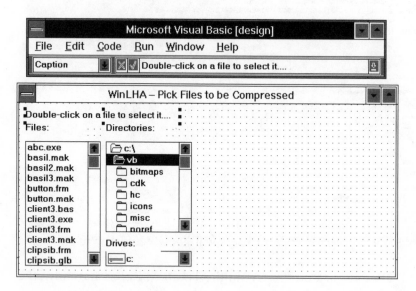

Now, double-check what you've done by pressing F5 or clicking on Run, then Start. Do all your controls behave properly? Great!

You can keep the Form you just made, or if you'd feel better about it, you can retrieve a prebuilt copy of this Form from your Companion Disk.

To save your own Form in a way that will minimize housekeeping headaches: first, make sure you have a new subdirectory created for your WinLHA. (Double-click on "Program Manager," then "File Manager," then scroll to wherever you want the new directory, and click on "File, Create Directory.") No, a brand new subdirectory isn't necessary. But you'll be glad you did.

Once you have that brand new subdirectory, go back into Visual Basic, and click on "File," then "Save Project." Visual Basic will ask you for a name for the Form. Make sure you're in the new subdirectory, then type in a good name for the form: PICKIT comes to mind. Then Visual Basic will ask you for a name for the Project (which is actually the name of the .MAK file). You could give it a name like MYWINLHA.

To toss away all your work and bring in the Companion Disk version of this Form: from inside Visual Basic click on "File," then "Open Project." Scroll to the subdirectory that holds the WinLHA programs (described in Appendix 3; it's probably something like "C:\VB\WINLHA"). Then double-click on "C5PGM1.MAK," which is just shorthand for "Chapter 5, Program 1." When Visual Basic asks if you want to save the changes you've made to Form1.Frm, click "No."

Finally, if you're using the Companion Disk, take a look at the window on the right-hand side, the one that says "C5PGM1.MAK." That's the packing list . . . er . . . the .MAK file listing of all the Forms and Subroutine Libra . . . er . . . Modules in this program . . . er . . . Project. Double-click on C5P1PICK.FRM, and you'll see the Pick Form, ready for the next round of hacking.

WinLHA 2 Making a List, Clicking It Twice . . .

The next step in WinLHA is pretty obvious: we have to keep track of which files have been "picked."

BUG

In doing so we're going to bump into one of the worst design decisions confronting all the Microsoft Basics—the "trailing backslash" bug feature.

Function Smash$()

Whenever you ask Visual Basic for a path name, you may or may not get a "\" backslash at the end of the name. It's infuriating because every single time your program constructs a fully qualified file name, you have to go through the gyrations to determine if there's a final backslash—and add one if there isn't—*every bloody time*.

If you knew there would *never* be a "\" on the end of the path name, your program could always construct a file name like this:

```
LongFileName$=PathName$ + "\" + ShortFileName$
```

Contrariwise, if there were *always* a "\" on the end of the path name, we could get away with something simple like:

```
LongFileName$=PathName$ + ShortFileName$
```

But, of course, we can't depend on either, so much Visual Basic code appears like this abomination:

```
Sep$=""
If Right$(PathName$,1)<>"\" Then Sep$="\"
LongFileName$=PathName$ + Sep$ + ShortFileName$
```

That's simply ludicrous. So we're going to write a function to handle the problem and cure the problem once and for all.

Function Smash$(Path$,File$) simply takes the Path$ and looks to see if there's a "\" backslash on the end of it. If not, it adds one. Smash$ then smashes the Path$ and File$ names together, to produce a fully qualified file name.

And while we're building Smash$(), we'll take a look at how to use Modules.

Your First Module

Get back to WinLHA program number 1. If you're working from the Companion Disk, crank up Visual Basic, click on "File," "Open Project," go into the WinLHA subdirectory, and double-click on C5PGM1.MAK.

We need a home for Smash$(). Because it's a function—and it will be called many times, in many different places—the only place to put it is in a Module, that is, in a Subroutine Library.

Nothing to it.

Click on "File," then "New Module." You'll see Figure 5-20 on the following page.

Now you can type in Smash$() much as you would WordBasic Function. Type in the first line of Smash$(), which looks like this:

```
Function Smash$ (ByVal Path$, ByVal File$)
```

Figure 5-20: Module 1 on the Make

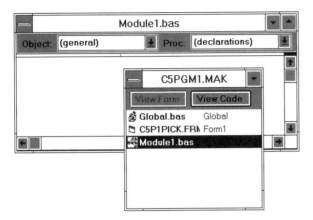

Hit Enter. If this doesn't impress you, nothing will!

Figure 5-21: Simply Smash$_ing!

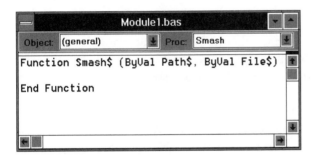

Here's what happened when you hit Enter. First, Visual Basic scanned the code you entered and checked for errors. There weren't any, because you typed carefully.

Second, Visual Basic interpreted the code far enough to understand that you were starting a new Function. Visual Basic was smart enough to toss the "End Function" together, give you a line to start typing on, and put the cursor where it belongs.

Third—as if the others weren't enough—Visual Basic created a neat little cubbyhole for Smash. See the "Smash" listed in the "Proc:" drop-down list box? Visual Basic keeps all the functions and subroutines sorted out, automatically. You don't have to do a thing. If you want to find Smash$ again sometime, just click on the drop-down box's arrow, and click on "Smash." What could be simpler?

Take a deep breath. Don't get your expectations up too high. Not all of Visual Basic is this smart, but much of it is.

Type in the Smash function, like this:

```
Function Smash$ (ByVal Path$, ByVal File$)
    While Right$(Path$, 1) = "\" Or Right$(Path$, 1) = " "
        Path$ = Left$(Path$, Len(Path$) - 1)
    Wend
    If Path$ = "" Then
        Smash$ = File$
    Else
        Smash$ = Path$ + "\" + File$
    End If
End Function
```

If you think this program looks a lot like WordBasic, well, don't be surprised. With one exception, the commands here are identical to those in WordBasic, and they behave in the same way: loop while there's a backslash or a space at the end of Path$, stripping off the final character; when you get down to the bone, slap on a backslash and the file name; return the result as "Smash$."

ByVal

The only new statement here is ByVal.

WordBasic, you may recall, is quite cavalier in how it treats variables passed to subroutines. It's a real jungle—subroutines and functions may change the values of parameters passed to them. WordBasic demands you respect jungle rules: if you want to make sure your variables aren't touched, you don't pass them!

Visual Basic, on the other hand, lets each subroutine or function decide for itself if it will change the value of variables. By putting "ByVal" in front of a variable, you tell Visual Basic, "Don't touch this variable; take the value being passed into the routine, and do with it what you will, but if you play around with this variable don't pass a new value for the variable back to the calling routine."

■ **TIP**

Unless you have a very definite reason for doing otherwise, it's always safest to declare all subroutine and function parameters as ByVal.

Now that we have the File Troika at our disposal and a function that compensates for Visual Basic's hokey backslash flim-flam, let's fill out the rest of the "Pick" form.

Picked List

We're going to create a List Box Control that contains a list of all the files the user has chosen to compress together. As usual, we'll start by drawing the Control, then adding code in the appropriate places.

Get the WinLHA Pick Form out in front, then double-click on the List Box icon over in the Toolbox—that's the fifth one down on the right, the one that looks a little bit like a list box.

Stretch and drag it out so it looks like this:

Figure 5-22: List Box for Picked Files

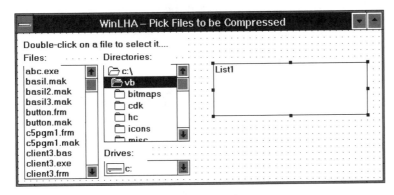

Change the CtlName on that List Box Control to something like "PickedList." (All you have to do is type it, remember?)

There should be a Label identifying the PickedList. Double-click on the picture in the Toolbox that looks like an "A," stretch it out, and click on that down-arrow under "Code," so you can assign the Caption to say, oh, "Double-click on a file to remove it . . . ."

Your Pick Form should like something like this:

Figure 5-23: Picked List in Place

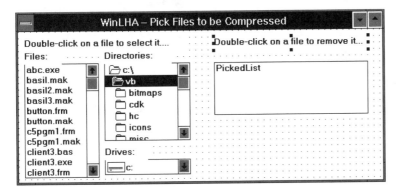

Lights, Camera, Action!

The final step in developing this part of the user interface—this Form—is figuring out how the user is going to tell WinLHA what needs to be done. *(And you thought we forgot about that little detail!)*

There are four things the user should be able to do:

- Tell WinLHA to create (or modify) a compressed file.
- Tell WinLHA to create (or modify) a compressed file, then go ahead and turn it into a self-extracting file. Self-extracting files are very nice because they don't require any special software to decompress. This is a two-step process in LHA land, but we don't have to tell the user that.
- Set WinLHA Defaults: starting directories, the location of the LHA archiving program, that sort of thing.
- Quit. This should *always* be an option.

We'll assign each action its own Command Button. Remember Command Buttons from Chapter 3?

Make sure the Pick Form is on top of the pile, and double-click on the Command Button icon in the Toolbox. The Command Button is third down on the right: it looks like a pregnant oval.

Stretch the Command Button and move it over to the right. Give it a reasonable CtlName like "MakeEXE," and set the Caption to, "Create Self-Extracting File." Something like this:

Figure 5-24: Create a Self-Extracting File

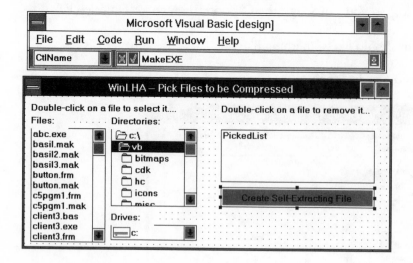

Add three more Command Buttons: CtlName MakeLZH (with a caption of "Create/Modify Archive File"), CtlName SetDefaults (caption "Set Defaults"), and CtlName Quit (caption "Quit"), and the hard part of this Form is done!

It should look like this:

Figure 5-25: The Pick Form in Fighting Form

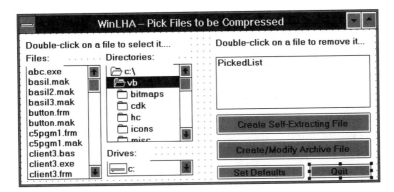

Not bad for a few clicks and drags.

What Hath This Ungodly Rot?

Sit back for a second and *grok* this little hummer. Could you imagine doing this in C? Can you imagine doing it without Windows?

If you're working from the Companion Disk, now is a good time to click on "File," then "Open Project," find the WinLHA subdirectory, and double-click on C5PGM2.MAK. Then you can follow along as we put together the program—the glue behind this pretty picture.

Methods and Madness

You're already accustomed to Controls' Properties. Properties can be rather obvious: size, location, color, that sort of thing. They can also be a tad more subtle: we've seen "Path" and "FileName" as Properties, for example, and there are many other odd Properties.

In addition to Properties, Controls can also have "Methods."

A Method, quite simply, *does something to* a Control. For example, the AddItem Method adds an item to a List Box Control. Pretty simple stuff.

Visual Basic has a strange way of indicating when a Method is supposed to be invoked. It looks like this:

```
ControlName.Method Arguments$
```

To add the item "C:\HELP.ME" to the PickedList List Box Control, for example, your program would contain a statement like this:

```
PickedList.AddItem "C:\HELP.ME"
```

No doubt you can think of a thousand more intuitive ways to tell Visual Basic that you want to add an item to a List, but we're stuck with this one.

Adding Items to PickedList

Now that you know how Visual Basic adds items to List Box Controls, you can almost guess how to hook in the code to move the name of a file from the PickFile Control over on the left to the PickedList Control over on the right.

Every time the user double-clicks on a file in the PickFile Control, we want to move the name of the file over to the PickedList Control. So we're going to hook into the Double-click Event in the PickFile Control. Easily done.

Get the Pick Form on top again, and double-click on the PickFile Control, there on the left. Here's what you get:

Figure 5-26: PickFile_Click()

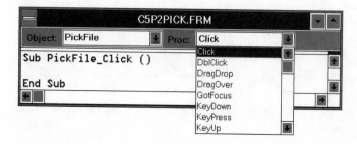

Visual Basic assumes that you want to write a program that kicks in whenever there's a Click Event on the PickFile Control. *Wrong!* We want to write code to handle the double-click event; we couldn't care less about a single click.

Again, Visual Basic makes it easy. Click the down-arrow on the "Proc:" list, and look for the "DblClick" Event. Click on it.

Figure 5-27: PickFile_DblClick ()

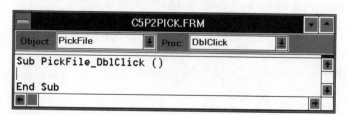

That's where we want the code to go.

Whenever the user double-clicks on a PickFile FileName, WinLHA should put the file's name over in the PickedFile List. Armed with Smash$(), it's easy. Just type this in the PickFile_DblClick () procedure:

```
PickedList.AddItem Smash$(PickFile.Path, PickFile.FileName)
```

One line. That's all it takes. Hit F5 and play with it a bit. See how the double-click on a file name there on the left triggers a DblClick event, which runs an AddItem on the right? Spiffy.

Click on "Run," then "Stop," and let's go fill in a few more gaps.

Deleting Items from PickedList

*Stifle that yawn! Wake up! This is **difficult stuff**, remember? You're writing Event-Driven programs! If you fall asleep, we'll get the Event Police to toss you in C school, and you can spend the next year there wondering what you ever did to deserve such a fate!*

Yes, deleting a file from the PickedList is another one-liner. But there's a neat little Property attached to List Boxes that we haven't worked with yet. It's called "ListIndex," and it's just the number of the item that's been selected in the List Box (starting at zero).

Removing an item from a List Box Control is as easy as this command:

```
ControlName.RemoveItem ItemNumber
```

We want the user to be able to remove items in the PickedList by simply double-clicking on them. Couldn't be easier. Double-click on the PickedList Control. Visual Basic guesses you want to write code to handle the Click Event. Actually what we're after again is the DblClick Event, so click the down-arrow on the "Proc:" box, and click on "DblClick."

Type in one line. Like this:

Figure 5-28: PickedList Taketh Away

That line simply tells Visual Basic to take the selected List Box item—Picked List.ListIndex—and remove it.

Quit!

One last little Event handler—that Command Button called "Quit"—and we'll be done with WinLHA Program 2.

Again, it's a one-liner. Double-click on the Quit Command Button. Visual Basic guesses that you want to write a handler for the Quit_Click Event.

The correct command to quit is . . . nope, not "Quit" . . . it's "End." Duh.

Figure 5-29: Quit, I Say!

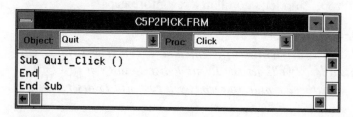

Play Time

Push F5 and give WinLHA program 2 a run.

This time, when you're done, instead of clicking on "Run," then "End," all you have to do is click the "Quit" Command Button. Careful! That's a real Event-Driven program you're playing with there. People who write Event-Driven programs have years of experience. Gray hair. Ulcers. Corner offices.

Finding Properties

By now you're probably wondering how you're supposed to know that a List Box has Methods called "AddItem" and "DeleteItem" and that a File List Box has Properties called "Path" and "FileName."

Sure, you can look it up in the manual, but that's *archaic*.

Visual Basic has a good (but not excellent) context-sensitive on-line help. In general, you can click on most anything, then hit F1, and a very detailed explanation of whatever confuses you will pop up.

■ T I P

There are two problems with the on-line help. First, it isn't context-sensitive enough. If you click on, say, a List Box Control, then hit F1, you'd expect to get an explanation of List Box Controls. Alas, it doesn't work that way. Visual Basic only goes as far as to explain Forms. From the Form explanation, you'll have to click on "Search," then type in the first few letters of the name of the Control that interests you.

■ T I P

Second, in far too many cases, the Visual Basic on-line help—indeed, the Visual Basic manuals and most Visual Basic books!—assume that you already understand the terminology and then mumble little cyclic excuses for definitions. Following the semantic machinations that differentiate between an "application," a "project," and a "program" in the Visual Basic on-line help, for example, would bring a big grin to all but the most jaded linguist. Don't worry about fundamental definitions; don't expect to learn concepts drom the on-line Help; don't sweat the little stuff. If you can't figure out a definition, try something—anything!—and see what happens. Sooner or later it'll become clear.

WinLHA 3—The Working Form

Now that we have the first Form in WinLHA pretty much figured out, let's try to take on the Form that does bring it all together—the one that picks up all the information and invokes LHA; the one that does the work; the WorkinForm.

Along the way we'll keep some notes about what we need in order to bridge the gap between the PickForm and the WorkinForm.

How to Use LHA

Let's take a few minutes here to scout out where we're headed.

Ultimately, WinLHA will construct a little batch file—an honest-to-Gates DOS .BAT file. After all, LHA *is* a DOS application. No DLLs, no API calls, none of that Windows stuff. Just a plain DOSapp. We could've written WinLHA to avoid the batch file, but it gives us some flexibility and makes a good excuse to introduce file handling commands.

If you wade through the LHArc documentation long enough (*good luck!*) you'll discover that a one-line batch file is all it takes to create or modify an LHA archive file. That line looks like this:

```
c:\...\lha.exe a c:\....\archive.lzh @c:\...\response.fil
```

Let's take that apart one piece at a time.

```
c:\...\lha.exe
```

is just the fully qualified name of the LHArc program. WinLHA needs to find LHA.EXE and insert the fully qualified name into the .BAT file. That's a good job for the "Set Default" button.

a

This "a" tells LHA how to handle the archive files. LHA has several options, several different ways of grabbing files and compressing them, including an "update," a "move," and several more esoteric options. ("Update" is just like "add," except it only replaces files with newer time stamps; "Move" is like "Update," except it deletes all the files after compressing them into the archive.)

WinLHA will concentrate on the most basic function: add. You might enjoy retrofitting WinLHA for other options once we're done. You'll be amazed how simple the retrofitting can be.

```
c:\...\archive.lzh
```

The third item on the batch line is simply the fully qualified name of the archive file.

Yes, it's possible to use extensions other than ".LZH" for LHArced files, but why confuse things? WinLHA will only deal with archived files with an extension of .LZH. By management edict.

If the user picks an existing .LZH file, they surely want to modify it. If the user types in a new name—a file that doesn't currently exist—we'll assume they want to create a new archive. Let's keep it simple and reasonably intuitive.

```
@c:\...\response.fil
```

This is the tricky one.

LHArc uses something called a "response file," to get around the DOS batch file limitation of 256 characters on a line.

Normally, people use LHArc by sitting down at the DOS "C:>" prompt, and typing in "LHA a some file" and a list of all the files they want to compress on the end of the DOS command line. That works fine if you have one or two files; it's a real pain if you have ten or twenty.

By using the "response file"—which is a simple text file, brought to LHArc's attention by placing an "@" at-sign at the beginning of the file name on the DOS command line—LHArc will start taking its input from the response file. That's a big help for people with lots of files to compress; it's nearly indispensable for WinLHA.

Because all the "to-archive" files are chosen on the PickForm—the first Form—it makes sense to have the PickForm create this response file *before* shifting the user over to the WorkinForm.

Finally, changing a .LZH file to a self-extracting .EXE file takes but one more LHA command:

```
c:\...\lha.exe s c:\...\archive.lzh
```

That takes the file ARCHIVE.LZH and produces a file called ARCHIVE.EXE, which is a self-extracting compressed file.

Now you know why it's so much easier to point and click!

Back to WinLHA.

A New Form

If you're using the Companion Disk, get the C5PGM2.MAK project cranked up. Follow along as we add the next Form.

We'll need a Form that allows users to select a name and location for their compressed file. Sounds tough, huh?

Click on "File," then "New Form."

Figure 5-30: WorkinForm, Ready to Go

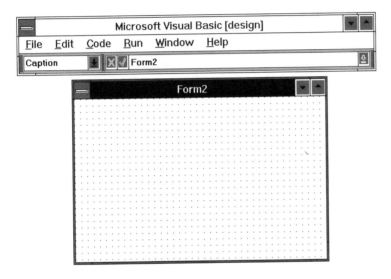

That wasn't hard, was it?

Let's give that new Form a decent Caption. Say, "Specify Archive File." All you have to do is type it.

Now get the Controls out for a File Troika, over on the left side. Double-click on the Drive Control in the Toolbox, and give it a CtlName of ArchiveDrive. Double-click on the Directory Control in the Toolbox and call it ArchiveDirectory. Double-click on the File Control in the Toolbox and call it ArchiveFile.

Add the three traditional File Troika labels and you should have something that looks like Figure 5-31 on the following page.

Figure 5-31: The WorkinForm Troika

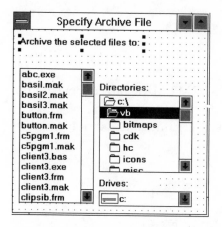

Now let's throw a monkey wrench into the works.

Typing in a File Name

In all our previous work with File Troikas, we've been interested in letting the user select from among existing files. For this Form, though, we have to let the user type in a new file name—to set up a brand new archive file.

That's what Text Box Controls do for a living: sit out there and wait for the user to type something. So we'll pick a Text Box.

Double-click on the Text Box icon over in the Toolbox. It's the second one down on the right, the one with an "ab" and what looks like a cursor inside a rectangle.

Drag that Text Box up into the upper left corner of the Form. Then try to squish it down so it's about the same size as a Label. No luck? That's one of the problems with Text Boxes; they don't quite set right with Label Controls.

The easiest solution is to make Text Boxes short and line them up with each other. (You can do all sorts of neat stuff with that Text Box Control if you want to, but we're going to keep this one simple. Walk before you run.)

This calls for a little surgery. Click on that down-arrow underneath "Code." Then click on "Height." We want to make that Text Box as short as possible. So use your mouse, delete the current "Height" setting, and type in a ridiculously small number—like "1." Hit Enter. Take a look at Figure 5-32 on the following page.

Figure 5-32: Not with My Twips, You Don't

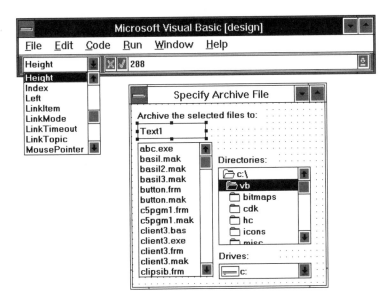

Visual Basic won't let you go all the way down to "1," but it will oblige a bit by making the Text Box just as small as it can. On this system, the smallest Text Box has a height of 288: you can see it in the "Height" box. Your system may be different.

Were you wondering what the measurement scale is? The numbers commonly used in Visual Basic measurements—unless you change them—are *twips.* There are 1,440 twips to the inch.

Let's give that Text Box a name. Click on the down-arrow again, click on "CtlName," and type "ArchiveFileText" (no quotes). We now have a place where the user can type in a file name.

Following that box for a file name, it would be nice if we could warn the user that they're going to be dealing with .LZH files—and .EXE files, too, if they chose to make a self-extracting file back on the PickForm.

■ **TIP**

Here's one way to do it. It relies on disguising a Text Box Control, making it look like a Label Control. There are many ways to accomplish essentially the same thing: if you can think of a better way, that's what hacking is all about.

Create another Text Box by double-clicking on the appropriate icon in the Toolbox. Use the "Height," "1" trick we just went through to make the Control as short as possible. Butt it up against the ArchiveFileText Control, and stretch it out a bit. Give it a CtlName of, oh, ArchiveFileExtension.

Here's what the Form should look like:

Figure 5-33: Text Box as Label

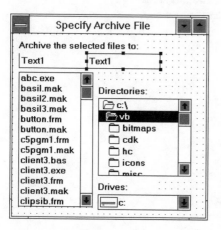

Now to make the transition from Text Box to ersatz-Label, click on the down-arrow under "Code" again to bring up the "Enabled" Property. Click the down-arrow on the right (at the end of the long box that says "True"), and set it to "False." With the Enabled Property set to False, Visual Basic will automatically gray-out the text in this Control and thus keep the user from changing it. It's a neat visual effect.

Command Buttons

Even though the Form looks bodacious, it's still lacking. How can the user tell WinLHA to go do its thing?

We need two Command Button Controls. Double-click on the Command Button icon over in the Toolbox—the one that looks like a pregnant oval—and give this first Command Button a CtlName of "Go," and a Caption of "Go!." Then pull out another Command Button, again by double-clicking on the icon in the Toolbox, and call this one "Quit," with a Caption Property set to, oh, "Quit."

It would be nice to rig things so that pressing Enter is the same as clicking on "Go." Easily done. Click on the Go Command Button. Hit the down-arrow under "Code," and look for a Property called "Default." Click on "Default." Go over to the right and click the other down-arrow, setting "Default" to "True." That's all it takes: any Command Button Control with its Default Property set to True will be "clicked" whenever the user hits Enter.

Here's the final WorkinForm:

Figure 5-34: WorkinForm

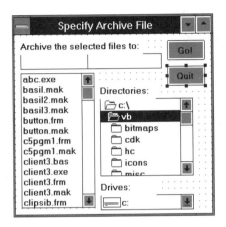

Code? What's That?

Before we jump on to the final Form—DefaultForm, the one that lets the user assign defaults—let's add a few bits of code to the WorkinForm.

Naturally, we want the Quit Command Button to quit, so double-click on the Command Button. Visual Basic guesses (correctly!) that you want to work with the Quit_Click Event. Simply type in the End command, like this:

Figure 5-35: Quit, I Say!

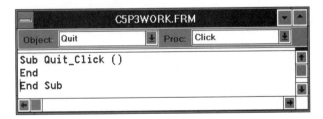

Then fill out the File Troika by first double-clicking on the ArchiveDrive Control, typing in the path changing mantra:

Figure 5-36: ArchiveDrive_Change Event Handler

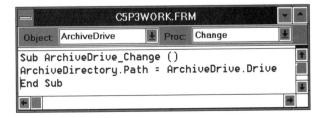

And then double-clicking on the ArchiveDirectory Control, typing in the file path change one-liner:

Figure 5-37: ArchiveDirectory_Change Event Handler

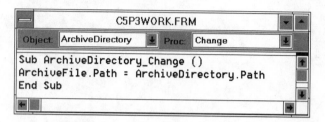

Finally, let's allow the user to click once on any file name and have that file name—stripped of its extension—show up in the ArchiveFileText text box.

Double-click on the ArchiveFile Control (that's the File List Box, the big one on the left), and type in these two lines:

Figure 5-38: The ArchiveFile_Click Event Handler

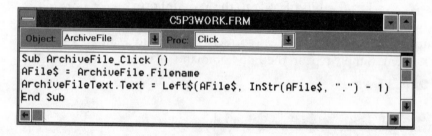

(You don't really need two lines—don't need the variable Afile$ at all, for that matter—but we split it out this way to make it a bit easier to read.)

Look familiar? Thought so. Except for the ControlName.PropertyName funnies, you've already seen all of these commands . . . in WordBasic. In a nutshell, these two lines take the ArchiveFile's Filename (i.e., the name of the file selected by the user), strips off everything in the filename from the "." period onward, and writes the resulting string in the ArchiveFileText Control, by setting its Text Property.

One more Form to go.

WinLHA 4—It Ain't *My* Default

The final Form allows the user to pick a few defaults, that is, establish settings that WinLHA will use whenever it's started. If you go back over the earlier parts of this chapter, you'll see that there are three things that make sense as WinLHA defaults:

- The PickForm's "Pick-From" directory.
- The WorkinForm's "Archive-To" directory.
- The location of LHA.EXE, the LHArc program.

Everything else in WinLHA changes every time it's run, so there's not much sense in saving any of the other stuff as defaults.

DefaultForm

If you're working from the Companion Disk, crank up Visual Basic and File/Open Project on the C5PGM3.MAK file.

If you've been typing from the book, don't do anything. We're going to build on Program 3.

Click on "File," then "New Form." Visual Basic correctly identifies this as Form3, our third form. We're going to call it the DefaultForm.

Where's LHA.EXE?

Give the Form a Caption—say, "Specify Defaults." Then, double-clicking on the Drive icon, the Directory icon, and the File icon over on the Toolbox, assemble a File Troika.

We're going to build the fully qualified name of the LHA file, to show the user precisely what's been selected. Make a Label (double-click on the "A" in the Toolbox), clear out its Caption, and give it a CtlName of LHAFileName.

Stick in one more label, with a Caption of "Location of LHA.EXE;" with some liberal rearranging, you'll have something that looks like Figure 5-39 on the following page.

Click on each of the three List Controls in turn, switch over to the CtlName Property, and give the Controls reasonable names, like "LHAFile," "LHADirectory," and "LHADrive."

Pick-From, Archive-To

For the Pick-From and Archive-To default directories, we don't need the "file" part of the File Troika. So bring out drives and directories (double-clicking on the appropriate Toolbox icon), and a few labels, rearranging them so they look like Figure 5-40 on the following page.

Figure 5-39: The Default Troika

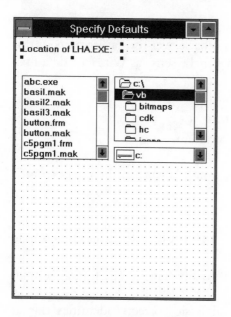

Figure 5-40: Three Troikas, Mostly

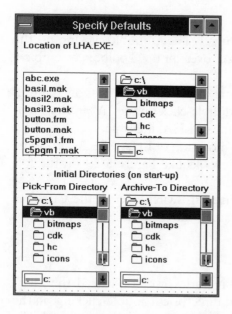

Click around again, assigning CtlNames: "PickDirectory," "PickDrive," "ArchiveDirectory," and "ArchiveDrive" should fit the bill nicely.

One final touch—once again we have to let users indicate when they're done.

Double-click on the Command Button icon in the Toolbox. Squish the button down so it fits on the Form. Give it a CtlName of OK, and a Caption to match. Then double-click again on the Command Button icon; make this one with a CtlName and Caption of Quit.

Here's the final DefaultForm:

Figure 5-41: The Final DefaultForm

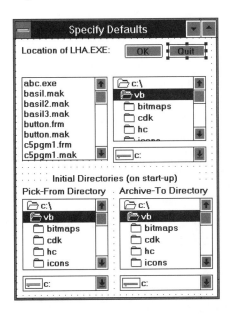

Tie together the Troikas with the usual code—adding one-liners to keep the LHAFileName Label Control updated—by double-clicking on the appropriate Control and typing the following code:

```
Sub LHADrive_Change ()
LHADirectory.Path = LHADrive.Drive
LHAFileName.Caption=LHADrive.Drive
End Sub

Sub LHADirectory_Change ()
LHAFile.Path = LHADirectory.Path
LHAFileName.Caption = LHADirectory.Path
End Sub

Sub LHAFile_Click ()
LHAFileName.Caption = Smash$(LHAFile.Path, LHAFile.List(ListIndex))
End Sub
```

```
Sub PickDrive_Change ()
PickDirectory.Path = PickDrive.Drive
End Sub

Sub ArchiveDrive_Change ()
ArchiveDirectory.Path = ArchiveDrive.Drive
End Sub
```

Then make sure "Quit" quits by double-clicking on the Quit Command Button and typing one line:

```
Sub Quit_Click ()
End
End Sub
```

And we've completed the skeleton of the DefaultForm.

What's Next, Boss?

Having fun playing with all the pretty pictures?

Yes, it's addictive. There's a constant temptation to tweak and stretch and slide. Not to mention add color—which is usually as simple as clicking on the "BackColor" Property, and selecting from a palette of colors or customizing your own!

Don't get the idea, though, that the rest will be easy. It won't. The code necessary to tie these three Forms together gets a touch complicated, and it's *very* Event-Driven.

Before we get back to the keyboard, let's pause for a second and take a look at what you've put together.

You've created three windows—three Forms—each with a complicated web of interrelated Controls. You've done all of it by clicking here, double-clicking there, using Visual Basic to keep track of all the pieces, all the Property settings.

Most important, Visual Basic *forced* you to think through the user interface. Yes, you can go back and change things later; nonetheless, Visual Basic has *forced* you to put the horse before the cart, to think of your users before you think of your code!

It's no exaggeration to say that moderately experienced C programmers would have taken five to ten **times** as long to get to this point—and they would have been bogged down in WM_MESSAGE codes.

A *novice* C programmer would still be struggling to slap together a window that says "Hello, World!"

Not you.

WinLHA 5—Time to Write the Program

Get ready to write a little code.

Most of all, though, get ready to switch your head around to the Event-Driven way.

If you're working with the Companion Disk, retrieve the C5PGM4.MAK project. (Click on "File," then "Open Project," scroll down to where you've stuck the Companion Disk programs, and double-click on C5PGM4.MAK.) We'll be building on C5PGM4, creating the next version, WinLHA compression routine, C5PGM5.

In the Beginning There Was Logos . . .

> One God, one law, one element,
> And one far-off divine event,
> To which the whole creation moves.
>
> —Alfred, 1st Lord Tennyson, *In Memoriam,* ca. 1890

The very, very first Event in any Visual Basic program's life is the Form_Load of the initial Form. In WinLHA's case, the initial Form is what we've called the Pick-Form.

Any initialization that needs to be done for the Form has to be done in the Form_Load procedure—or at least it has to be initiated by the Form_Load procedure. The PickForm's initialization isn't too bad, as such things go: only two things really need to be done.

First, we need to retrieve the default settings for the PickDirectory—the ones set on the DefaultForm. If there aren't any default settings (for example, if this is the first time WinLHA has been run), well, WinLHA better prod the user and get some!

Second, WinLHA needs to set the PickDirectory to match the default. That's it.

Pick's Form_Load

Let's translate that into some code. Double-click on the PickForm, someplace outside of the Controls. Visual Basic guesses that you want to write some code to be executed on a single click. Wrong. Click that right-hand "Proc:" down arrow, scroll to Load, and click once. You should see something like Figure 5-42 on the following page.

We're going to store all of the defaults in a Windows .INI file—appropriately named WINLHA.INI—but we'll worry about all of that when we work on the

DefaultForm. For now, all that's needed is a call to an (as yet unwritten!) subroutine. Let's call it "GetDefaults."

Figure 5-42: PickForm's Form_Load Event Handler

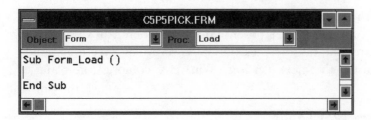

There are three defaults to get, three things stored away by the DefaultForm: the PickDirectory, ArchiveDirectory, and LHAFileSpec. A subroutine call that looks like this should work just fine:

```
GetDefaults(PickDir$,ArchiveDir$,LHAFileSpec$)
```

Now, how are we going to know if there *are* no defaults? One sure-fire sign would be if the LHAFileSpec$ didn't exist—without the location of LHA.EXE, WinLHA will just be pounding sand. Thus:

```
If LHAFileSpec$="" Then
```

If that IF statement evaluates to true, WinLHA has to force the user to set defaults—at a bare minimum, they must find LHA.EXE.
Ready for something spectacular?
Look at Figure 5-25. See the "Set Defaults" button, down near the bottom right? At some point we'll have to write the code behind that button—code that whisks the user off to the DefaultForm and lets them set the defaults.
What if there *are* no defaults? What if it's the first time WinLHA has been run? What if the user clobbered all the settings in WINLHA.INI, or deleted the file?
Your first reaction, probably, is: if there aren't any defaults, we need to write something that will whisk the user off to the DefaultForm and let them set the defaults.
Wait a second. Doesn't that sound familiar?
Your second reaction, probably, is: Hey! Why write the same code twice? Why not write a subroutine or something that we can call here—when no defaults have been set, and the user really *should* click that stupid "Set Defaults" button anyway?

If all the code is in a subroutine we can call the same subroutine here *and* when the user clicks the "Set Defaults" button . . . . Reusable code and all that.

Ahhhh but there's a better way. Visual Basic has this giant invisible hand, you see. That hand can do just about anything it pleases, anywhere it pleases. It lurks behind the scenes, gives you great power, lets you get into all sorts of trouble.

Why don't we just reach right over—the user will never know that the giant invisible hand is working here behind the scenes—why don't we just reach over to that "Set Defaults" button and *click* the sucker?

That's what you really want to do anyway, isn't it? If there aren't any defaults, you want to "Set Defaults". So why not reach out and just do it? Push the button *for* the user.

It's another one-liner.

```
SetDefaults.Value=-1
```

Setting the "Value" Property of a Command Button Control to -1 is precisely the same thing as clicking on the button. There's absolutely no difference. Clicking on the "SetDefaults" button triggers an Event. Setting SetDefaults.Value to -1 triggers *the same Event.*

Now you can start to see some of the immense power inherent in Event-Driven programming. One Event can trigger another Event, which can trigger twenty more, and on and on.

Compared to that little trick, the rest of PickForm's Form_Load is pretty mundane. Here's how the whole thing looks:

Figure 5-43: PickForm's Load Event Handler

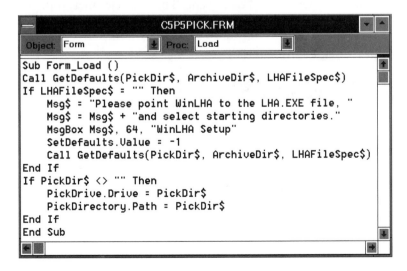

```
Sub Form_Load ()
Call GetDefaults(PickDir$, ArchiveDir$, LHAFileSpec$)
If LHAFileSpec$ = "" Then
    Msg$ = "Please point WinLHA to the LHA.EXE file, "
    Msg$ = Msg$ + "and select starting directories."
    MsgBox Msg$, 64, "WinLHA Setup"
    SetDefaults.Value = -1
    Call GetDefaults(PickDir$, ArchiveDir$, LHAFileSpec$)
End If
If PickDir$ <> "" Then
    PickDrive.Drive = PickDir$
    PickDirectory.Path = PickDir$
End If
End Sub
```

Note how WinLHA is nice and polite: "Please" it says. Also note the sincere effort to translate computerese into something real folk can understand. That sort of stuff is important and too readily overlooked in the rush to get a product out the door.

Before we get too worried about assigning and retrieving default values from WINLHA.INI, let's finish off the coding for this Form.

The Set Defaults Button

Double-click on the Set Defaults Command Button. We're ready to write the Event Handler for a SetDefaults_Click Event.

When the user clicks on the Set Defaults Command Button (or it's "clicked" *for* them when the PickForm is loaded), we want to crank up the DefaultForm and hold the users' feet to the fire until they make some decent choices for defaults or until they give up in frustration.

That's a one-liner:

```
Form3.Show 1
```

"Form3" is the name of the DefaultForm. "Show" is a Method that tosses the Form on the screen. And that "1" tells Visual Basic that Form3 should be treated as modal. (Don't go scrambling for the Glossary. "Modal," you may recall, just means the Form takes control of everything; the user won't be able to do anything else until that Form goes away.)

Once the user has clicked on the Set Defaults Command Button, then gone through all the effort to pick some reasonable defaults, it's only polite that WinLHA re-initialize the PickForm to reflect all those new defaults.

Sound tough? It isn't. Take a look. In order to re-initialize everything, all your program has to do is trigger another Form_Load event! That's a one-liner, too.

Here's the complete SetDefaults_Click Event Handler:

Figure 5-44: SetDefaults_Click Event Handler

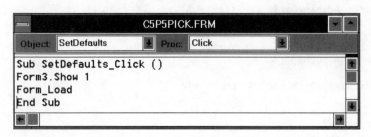

When it's running up to two lines per subroutine, things have to be getting complicated.

Create/Modify Archive File Button

This is the toughest Button of the bunch.

If you recall the earlier discussion, when the user clicks this Button, WinLHA has to take all the files listed in the PickedList and create an LHArc-style "@" response file. Once that file's out and available for LHArc to use, it's time to switch over to the WorkinForm.

What's that, you say? Sequential File I/O—pretty archaic.But LHArc demands it.

First problem: what if the user forgot to select any files? We better provide a Message Box, and warn them. Not surprisingly, Visual Basic Message Boxes are quite similar to WordBasic Message Boxes.

Second problem: where to stick the "@" response file? There are several reasonable choices. We'll put it in the subdirectory that contains LHA.EXE, just because it's easy to find.

Double-click on the Create/Modify Archive File Button—the one with a CtlName of "MakeLZH." Type in all this:

Figure 5-45: MakeLZH_Click Event Handler

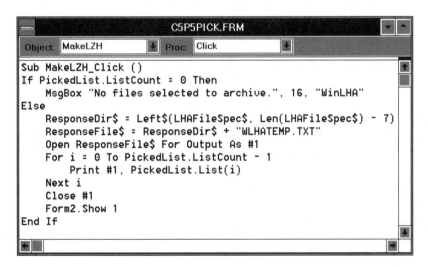

Let's step through that one slowly.

```
If PickList.ListCount = 0 Then
    MsgBox "No files selected to archive.", 16, "WinLHA"
```

That code says if there are no items in the PickList, put up a MsgBox with a warning. The "16" tosses a Stop Sign in the MsgBox.

But wait . . . isn't that backwards?

Well, as a matter of fact, it *is* backwards! When you use WordBasic, the MsgBox title comes before the number that specifies icons, buttons, and defaults. But when you switch over to Visual Basic, the number is in the middle and the title is on the end.

```
ResponseDir$ = Left$(LHAFileSpec$, Len(LHAFileSpec$) - 7)
ResponseFile$ = ResponseDir$ + "WLHATEMP.TXT"
Open ResponseFile$ For Output As #1
```

The first two lines here just strip "LHA.EXE" off the end of the LHAFileSpec$, substituting "WLHATEMP.TXT."

There's a new command here: Open. It's valid in both WordBasic and Visual Basic. Files may be Opened for Input, Output, or Append. (In Visual Basic you also get several additional modes that allow random access to everything in the file and support file-sharing.) The "As #1" helps Visual Basic identify which file is which, should you open more than one at a time.

```
For i = 0 To PickList.ListCount - 1
    Print #1, PickList.List(i)
Next i
Close #1
```

■ **TIP**

Here's another oddity that harkens back to Basic's schizophrenia over starting some things (like subscripts and counts) at zero and other things at one. While it's true that PickList.ListCount gives the total number of items in the PickList Control, if you want to *use* those items, your program must refer to them as PickList.List(i), with "i" running from zero to the ListCount minus 1!

The "Print #1, PickList.List(i)" tells Visual Basic to write out the "i"th item in the PickList, followed by a carriage return. Which just happens to be precisely what LHArc wants in a "@" response file.

Finally,

```
Form3.Show 1
```

cranks up the WorkinForm, as a "modal" window.

Variable Scope

There's a little problem with the MakeLZH_Click procedure we just finished. You may have noticed. It concerns something called "Variable Scope" and the variable LHAFileSpec$.

There's a simple way of looking at it: each Procedure—each Event Handler—has its own variables. If you want to pass the value of a certain variable among Procedures, that variable must be declared at the Form level. Similarly, if you want to pass the value of variables back and forth between Forms, the variables have to be declared at the Global level.

Bet you've been wondering when we'd get around to the so-called Global Module. We just hit it.

Modules work the same way: each subroutine or function in a module has its own variables. If you want to pass values among subroutines or functions, the variables must be declared at the Module level. If you want to pass the value of variables back and forth between Modules, the variables have to be declared at the Global level.

The MakeLZH_Click Event Handler uses a variable called LHAFileSpec$. Visual Basic assumes that LHAFileSpec$ is a variable that only exists inside MakeLZH_Click, unless we tell it otherwise.

We could make LHAFileSpec$ a Form variable, specific to the PickForm. But, looking around a bit, it's apparent that we're going to want LHAFileSpec$ in *all* the Forms: we'll want to know the location of LHA.EXE in PickForm, WorkinForm, and DefaultForm. May as well make LHAFileSpec$ a global variable.

Here's how you make a variable global—how you tell Visual Basic that this particular variable should be made available to all the Forms, all the Procedures, all the Modules, and all the Subroutines and Functions.

Take a look at your packing list, what's called the "project list." It looks something like this:

Figure 5-46: The .MAK file Project List

Double-click on "GLOBAL.BAS." That's the Global Module. Then type this to make PickDir$, ArchiveDir$, and LHAFileSpec$ all global:

Figure 5-47: Global Variables

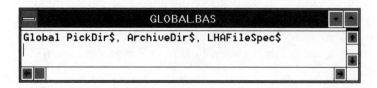

Note that there's no "Sub," no "End Sub," no parameter list or Object/Proc drop-down arrows. The Global Module is very basic.

That's all it takes to make those three variables global. We won't have to worry about passing them among Forms.

Create Self-Extracting File Button

Well, you'd probably think this will be the toughest Button of all. And you'd be dead wrong!

All this Command Button has to do is what the Create/Modify Archive File Button *already does*, except it needs to notify the WorkinForm that a self-extracting file should be constructed from the .LZH archive file.

How to set a flag of some sort that the WorkinForm can check? Why, it sounds like another Global variable!

Let's call the variable "MakeEXEFlag" and stick it in the Global Module:

Figure 5-48: Another Global

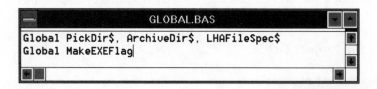

Now we're ready for the whole program. Double-click on the Create Self-Extracting File Command Button—its CtlName is MakeEXE, and the Event is MakeEXE_Click—then type in this two-liner shown in Figure 5-49 on the following page.

Figure 5-49: MakeEXE_Click Event Handler

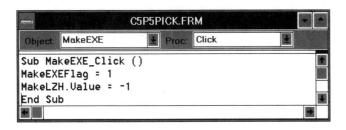

This procedure sets a flag, warning the WorkinForm that it needs to make an .EXE file, and then "clicks" the Create/Modify Archive File Command Button. *And that's all it takes!*

You've just finished all of the programming for the PickForm. WinLHA now consists of about three dozen lines of program code; maybe a little more if you include the File Troika stuff, which you probably consider pretty trivial by now.

DefaultForm Procedures

The DefaultForm is a piece of cake.

We're only concerned with two Events: the Form_Load, which is mighty similar to PickForm's Load, and the OK_Click, which has to store away new default settings.

For Form_Load, bring the DefaultForm to the top of the pack (double-click on it in the packing list if you have to). Double-click on the Form, outside of any Controls. Visual Basic guesses Form_Click; you have to hit the rightmost down-arrow and click on Load.

The DefaultForm Load Event Handler is shown in Figure 5-50 on the following page.

There are only three parts of this Form_Load procedure that differ from what we've seen before.

First, this Form_Load has to set up the File Troika for the LHA file spec. The LHADirectory.Path is a touch tricky: it relies on the fact that the last eight characters of the LHAFileSpec$ are "\lha.exe".

■ **T I P**

While you can feed almost anything to a .Drive Property (throughout WinLHA we just set it to a path or a fully qualified file name), you have to be very careful assigning values to the .Path Property. For rather debatable reasons, .Drive is smart enough to strip off any extra characters, but .Path is not so clever.

Figure 5-50: DefaultForm's Form_Load Handler

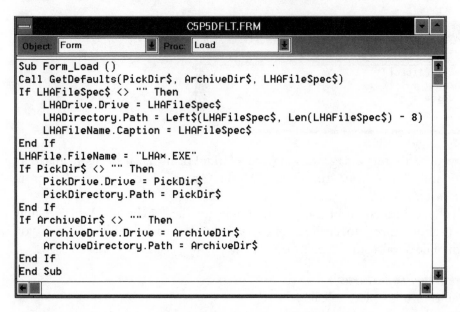

```
Sub Form_Load ()
Call GetDefaults(PickDir$, ArchiveDir$, LHAFileSpec$)
If LHAFileSpec$ <> "" Then
    LHADrive.Drive = LHAFileSpec$
    LHADirectory.Path = Left$(LHAFileSpec$, Len(LHAFileSpec$) - 8)
    LHAFileName.Caption = LHAFileSpec$
End If
LHAFile.FileName = "LHA*.EXE"
If PickDir$ <> "" Then
    PickDrive.Drive = PickDir$
    PickDirectory.Path = PickDir$
End If
If ArchiveDir$ <> "" Then
    ArchiveDrive.Drive = ArchiveDir$
    ArchiveDirectory.Path = ArchiveDir$
End If
End Sub
```

Second, by setting LHAFile.Filename to "LHA*.EXE," WinLHA is telling Visual Basic to only show files matching the "LHA*.EXE" in the LHAFile Control.

■ **T I P**

The .Filename Property is another picky one. If you set it to a pattern—something with a "?" or "*" wildcard—your program will never have a problem. But if you set it to a specific name, and that name doesn't exist in the File List Control's list, you'll generate a run-time error. Whenever possible, and unless you're absolutely sure there's a file around with the correct name, set Filename to a pattern rather than to a specific name.

Third, Visual Basic isn't smart enough to automatically scan Modules to see if subroutines are stored away there. That's why you need "Call" in front of some subroutine calls. Yes, you can declare them, but why bother? "Call" works just fine.

Once the user has chosen defaults, all that's needed is a function to store away the default values. We'll call it WriteDefaults( ).

Double-click on the OK Command Button. The OK_Click Handler is shown in Figure 5-51 on the following page.

Figure 5-51: OK_Click Event Handler

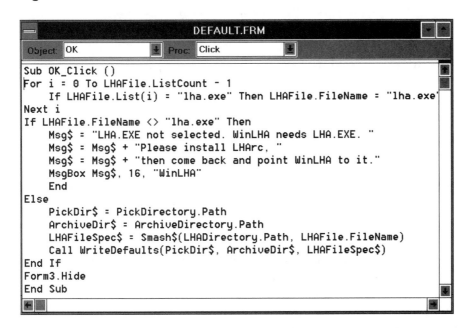

```
                        DEFAULT.FRM
Object: OK              ±  Proc: Click           ±
Sub OK_Click ()
For i = 0 To LHAFile.ListCount - 1
    If LHAFile.List(i) = "lha.exe" Then LHAFile.FileName = "lha.exe"
Next i
If LHAFile.FileName <> "lha.exe" Then
    Msg$ = "LHA.EXE not selected. WinLHA needs LHA.EXE. "
    Msg$ = Msg$ + "Please install LHArc, "
    Msg$ = Msg$ + "then come back and point WinLHA to it."
    MsgBox Msg$, 16, "WinLHA"
    End
Else
    PickDir$ = PickDirectory.Path
    ArchiveDir$ = ArchiveDirectory.Path
    LHAFileSpec$ = Smash$(LHADirectory.Path, LHAFile.FileName)
    Call WriteDefaults(PickDir$, ArchiveDir$, LHAFileSpec$)
End If
Form3.Hide
End Sub
```

The only trick here is in LHAFile.FileName. Because there can only be one "LHA.EXE" in any single directory, we're being a bit sloppy. Users needn't actually click on "LHA.EXE"—they only have to put WinLHA into the right directory. That should make life pretty easy.

Are you getting a little bit worried about bugs? It's easy to see why. We haven't tested anything yet!

Ah, you want proof. Now's as good a time as any to put together the GetDefaults() and WriteDefaults() subroutines. With those in hand, we can take the first part of WinLHA for a little test drive.

Get/WriteDefaults

Remember how WinExplorer reached into WIN.INI, using a Windows API call? We used GetProfileString. This bit from Chapter 4 might refresh your memory:

```
LengthOfString = GetProfileString("windows", "load", " ","\
 LoadString$, 200)
```

That translates into English something like: *Go out to WIN.INI, where the ProfileStrings are stored. Look for a section called [windows]. Then look for a line that says "load=." If there is no "load=" line, stick a " " in the variable called "LoadString$." If there is a "load=" line, pick up the stuff to the right of the equals sign, stick it* *in a variable called "LoadString$," up to a maximum of 200 characters. Finally, put the length of "LoadString$" in a variable called "LengthOfString."*

Windows has another API call that's very similar to GetProfileString. It's called Get**Private**ProfileString. The only difference? It sets up and maintains a separate .INI file; it doesn't play around with WIN.INI.

> ■ **TIP**
>
> Keep your hands off WIN.INI! The very best way to maintain "default" or "initial-ization" data in Windows is with your *own* .INI file. While it's possible to keep that information in WIN.INI, your users will curse you to your dying breath if some-how your program inadvertently messes up WIN.INI.
>
> Much better for all concerned is the Private .INI file. It is every bit as easy to use as WIN.INI. And if your program goes berserk and trashes an .INI file, you'll be forgiven if it's only a Private .INI file.

Because GetDefaults and WriteDefaults will be used by all the Forms in WinLHA, we have to put them in a Module. We can't put them in the Global Module (can't put any subroutines or functions in the Global Module for that matter), so we may as well use the Module that already contains Smash$.

Bring your Packing List (or Project List, if you insist) up to the front, and dou-ble-click on the Module. You're automatically propelled into the Module's General Declarations area, which is precisely where we want to be.

Figure 5-52: The Module's General Declarations.

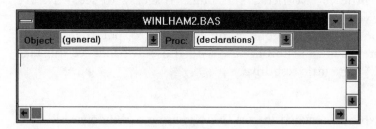

Are you curious about where Smash$ went? Just click on the "Proc:" down-arrow. There it is. Not to worry. Visual Basic will take care of you.

As you no doubt recall, Windows API calls can be terribly long winded. We're interested in two that are very similar to the GetProfileString we used so much in Chapter 4. They are shown in the code listing on the following page.

```
Declare Function WritePrivateProfileString Lib "Kernel" (ByVal\
  AppName$, ByVal KeyName$, ByVal KeyValue$, ByVal FileName$) As\
  Integer

Declare Function GetPrivateProfileString Lib "Kernel" (ByVal\
  AppName$, ByVal KeyName$, ByVal DefaultKeyValue$, ByVal\
  ReturnedKeyValue$, ByVal nSize As Integer, ByVal FileName$) As\
  Integer
```

In general, you can pull Visual Basic API declarations straight from the WINAPI.TXT file, located on the Companion Disk. They're heavily laden with junk—long pointers, "As String" declarations, that kind of thing—so they're a touch unwieldy. But they have one definite advantage: you can plop them in your program and they'll work!

We've taken some liberties with the WINAPI.TXT definitions of WritePrivateProfileString and its Get cousin: we changed some variable names around so they make more sense; we used "$" on the end of the variable names instead of "As String"; we got rid of the (generally) arcane "lp" Long Pointer terminology.

Once you're through typing or copying-in these "Declare"s, it's time to construct the WriteDefaults and GetDefaults subroutines. Ready for something really mondo-cool? Type this and hit enter:

```
Sub WriteDefaults(PDir$, ADir$,LHAfs$)
```

There goes Visual Basic again!

Figure 5-53: GetDefaults—Automatically!

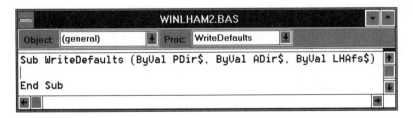

Man, it's like this program can read your mind. Here Visual Basic has determined that you want to start a new Subroutine; it's set up everything to keep track of the subroutine, tacked on an End Sub, and put your cursor right where it belongs.

Fantastic.

Here's the WriteDefaults code. Go ahead and type it:

```
n = WritePrivateProfileString("winlha", "lha", LHAfs$,\
"winlha.ini")
n = WritePrivateProfileString("winlha", "pickdir", PDir$,\
 "winlha.ini")
n = WritePrivateProfileString("winlha", "archivedir", ADir$,\
 "winlha.ini")
```

The WritePrivateProfileString Windows API call is quite simple. In this case, we're telling Windows to (1) go out to the Windows directory and find WINLHA.INI; if it isn't there, create it. (2) Look for the section marked [winlha]; if it isn't there, create it. (3) Look for "lha=," "pickdir,=" or "archivedir=," and stick in the new values.

Pretty easy, eh?

In fact it's so easy, it makes you wonder about people who insist upon using WIN.INI to store all their flotsam and jetsam.

GetDefaults is only a few lines longer. Start by typing, after WriteDefault's "End Sub," this one line, then hit Enter:

```
Sub GetDefaults (ByVal PDir$, ByVal ADir$, ByVal LHAfs$)
```

Visual Basic kicks in again, storing away WriteDefaults and setting you up with GetDefaults. Amazing, eh?

GetDefaults looks like this:

```
SpaceHolder$ = String$(255, 0)
ReturnLen = GetPrivateProfileString("winlha", "lha", ","\
 SpaceHolder$, 255, "winlha.ini")
LHAfs$ = Left$(SpaceHolder$, ReturnLen)
ReturnLen = GetPrivateProfileString("winlha", "pickdir", ","\
 SpaceHolder$, 255, "winlha.ini")
PDir$ = Left$(SpaceHolder$, ReturnLen)
ReturnLen = GetPrivateProfileString("winlha", "archivedir", ","\
 SpaceHolder$, 255, "winlha.ini")
ADir$ = Left$(SpaceHolder$, ReturnLen)
```

This is all very familiar—virtually identical to WordBasic's method for using the GetProfileString API—with one exception, that variable called SpaceHolder$. It's a . . . well, it's a space holder!

■ T I P

In a rare display of virtuosity, WordBasic has Visual Basic beat on this score. WordBasic takes care of these C string oddities behind the scenes; Visual Basic doesn't.

All Visual Basic DLL calls that expect returned strings should clear out an area where the called program sticks the string. The statement

```
SpaceHolder$ = String$(255, 0)
```

clears out 255 characters of memory, assigns it the name SpaceHolder$, and fills it with zeroes.

■ **T I P**

The Visual Basic Programmer's Guide hems and haws about it a bit, but ultimately recommends you use a 255-character string to reserve space for most DLL calls. Naturally, some custom DLL calls may need more space for returned strings, and you must always keep that possibility in mind. But for Windows DLL calls, you're usually covered with 255 characters.

B U G

Earlier versions of Windows exhibited a most distressing trait: if they were called with space-holder strings up around 300 characters, they would crash—or, worse, they would refuse to execute the DLL call *and not tell you what was happening!* Be **extremely** cautious using space-holder strings longer than 255 characters.

Play Time

Okay. You were the skeptical one. If you've been typing along, push F5 or click on "Run," then "Start." Play around with it a bit. If you'd rather pull it off the Companion Disk, do a File Open Project on C5PGM5.MAK, then push F5.

Do you get the "feel" of the Event-Driven shtick? Click on the Create Self-Extracting File Button. See how it works behind the scenes—how the first Form_Load Event "clicks" the Set Defaults Button, how the user never realizes that the MakeEXE_Click Event Handler "clicks" the Create/Modify Archive File Button?

Neat. And powerful.

Surely Event Driven. Almost Object-Oriented. But most of all, it's something mere mortals can handle!

You might want to play with some of the Visual Basic design-time capabilities. Edit Cut and Edit Paste, for example. They work just the way you think they would. Another good one, if you're curious: click on "File," then "Print." See how Visual Basic constructs program printouts? Pretty poor, eh? At the very least you'd think Visual Basic would print out the Properties for all the Controls and figure out how to print inside the page margins. *Version 1.0 software.*

No, you won't be able to do anything with the WorkinForm yet. We'll get there momentarily.

WinLHA 6—The Finishing Touches

You're probably tired of typing all this stuff. Let's cut to the chase. Click on "File," "Open Project," scroll to the WinLHA subdirectory, and double-click on WINLHA.MAK.

That's the final version of WINLHA.

Now that you know how to cheat, you can sit through the lecture, eh? If you have the Companion Disk, you can just follow along.

WorkinForm Code

We have one Form left, the WorkinForm, the one that's supposed to do all the hard work.

Go over to the Packing List and double-click on the WorkinForm. We'll start with the Form_Load Event Handler, so double-click on the Form outside any Controls and scroll down to Form_Load.

Here's the code:

```
Call GetDefaults(PickDir$, ArchiveDir$, LHAFileSpec$)
ArchiveFile.Filename = "*.lzh"
If ArchiveDir$ <> "" Then
    ArchiveDrive.Drive = ArchiveDir$
    ArchiveDirectory.Path = ArchiveDir$
    If ArchiveFile.ListCount > 0 Then
        ArchiveFileText.Text = Left$(ArchiveFile.List(0),\
        InStr(ArchiveFile.List(0), ".") - 1)
        ArchiveFileText.SelStart = 0
        ArchiveFileText.SelLength = 8
        ArchiveFileText.TabIndex = 0
    End If
End If
If MakeEXEFlag = 1 Then
    ArchiveFileExtension.Text = ".LZH and .EXE"
Else
    ArchiveFileExtension.Text = ".LZH"
End If
```

Let's step through that once over, lightly.

The second line ensures ArchiveFile File List Control will only display .LZH files. That's a good guess: all LHA files, far as we're concerned, end in .LZH. Even the .EXE self-extracting files must have an intermediate .LZH file made for them.

Then the File Troika is set up with the defaults—with one important exception.

Focus on the File

Do you ever get really ticked off at how Windows handles File Save As dialogs? Things start out great: the dialog box comes up with all the directories and files showing and the name of the current file in the box. But then if you change directories or drives, all of a sudden the focus goes off the file name. Remember that?

Why the File Save As dialog works like that is anybody's guess—normal folk would want the focus to stay on the file name box, so you can type in a new name.

Somebody at Microsoft decided that WinNuts wanted to have the focus shift so that you could pick a subdirectory by typing a letter. Sounds like the result of some usability test, conducted on people who've never seen a mouse.

Well, now that the inmates are in charge of *this* asylum, we can build our Form to do anything we please. And one of the things this WinLHA Form will do is keep the focus on the file name—where it belongs!

That's why we need these three lines in the Form_Load Event Handler:

```
ArchiveFileText.SelStart = 0
ArchiveFileText.SelLength = 8
ArchiveFileText.TabIndex = 0
```

By using one of the most intriguing Visual Basic Text Box Properties—the Selection—we can keep the focus, keep the faith, and keep things simple. Visual Basic gives you the ability to select text inside a Text Box. Simply set the .SelStart Property to the number of the character at the beginning of the selection (or zero for the beginning of the Box), set the .SelLength Property to the number of characters you'd like to have Selected, and voila! Instant selection.

The other new Property here is TabIndex. Visual Basic numbers all the Controls on your Form, so mouse-less people can Tab-Tab-Tab between Controls. The TabIndexes run from zero to the number of Controls on your Form. By forcing the .TabIndex of the ArchiveFileText Control to zero, you guarantee that when the Form is loaded, ArchiveFileText will receive the focus.

Yes, you can (and probably should) set ArchiveFileText.TabIndex to zero during design time—before the program is run. But it's a whole lot easier to explain here in Form_Load than it was earlier in this chapter, when you were struggling with stretching Text Boxes!

So much for Form_Load.

We've already put together the basic File Troika code for this Form. But since it's been decided (again, by management edict!) that the focus will always return to ArchiveFileText, a few changes are in order.

```
Sub ArchiveDirectory_Change ()
ArchiveFile.Path = ArchiveDirectory.Path
ArchiveFileText.Text = ""
On Error Resume Next
ArchiveFileText.SetFocus
On Error GoTo 0
End Sub

Sub ArchiveDrive_Change ()
ArchiveDirectory.Path = ArchiveDrive.Drive
ArchiveFileText.Text = ""
On Error Resume Next
ArchiveFileText.SetFocus
On Error GoTo 0
End Sub

Sub ArchiveFile_Click ()
AFile$ = ArchiveFile.Filename
ArchiveFileText.Text = Left$(AFile$, InStr(AFile$, ".") - 1)
ArchiveFileText.SelStart = 0
ArchiveFileText.SelLength = 8
ArchiveFileText.SetFocus
End Sub
```

No doubt you recognize the Error-check disabling we hit in WordBasic. (That's what "On Error Resume Next" does, remember?) Unfortunately, Visual Basic generates an Error Condition if your program tries to change Focus during a Form_Load procedure; because both the ArchiveDrive_Change and ArchiveDirectory_Change Events are triggered during a Form_Load (when they're set to the defaults), we have to step gingerly over those parts.

Short Cuts

Users rapidly grow accustomed to Windows shortcuts: double-clicking on a file name in a File Open, for example, is the exact same as clicking on the file, then clicking OK.

So why don't we build a shortcut, too?

If the user double-clicks on an Archive file, why don't we just take it away—as if they had clicked once on the file, and then clicked on the Go! Button.

Ah, another one-liner.

Look for the ArchiveFile_DoubleClick Event Handler.

You've probably already discovered that you can scroll down the "Objects" to search for Controls. If not, give it a try. Like Figure 5-54 on the following page.

Figure 5-54: Pick an Object, any Object

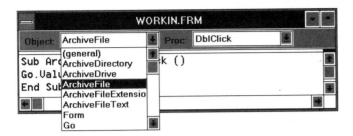

In the ArchiveFile_DblClick Procedure, just type:

```
Go.Value=-1
```

To translate: whenever an ArchiveFile_DblClick Event is generated, Visual Basic should "click" the Go! Button. What could be simpler?

The Final Coding Shoe Drops

All that's left now is the "meat" of the program: WinLHA creates a DOS batch file and runs it. No problem.

Find the Go_Click procedure—you can double-click on the "Go" Button on the WorkinForm, or you can just rifle through the Objects until you find "Go," then through the Procs until you find "Click."

```
If Len(ArchiveFileText.Text) < 1 Or Len(ArchiveFileText.Text) > 8 Then
    MsgBox "Invalid File Name. Please try again.", 16, "WinLHA"
Else
    ArchiveFileSpec$ = Smash$(ArchiveFile.Path,\
ArchiveFileText.Text + ".LZH")
    ResponseFile$ = Left$(LHAFileSpec$, Len(LHAFileSpec$) - 7) +\
"wlhatemp.txt"
    BatFile$ = Left$(LHAFileSpec$, Len(LHAFileSpec$) - 7) +\
"wlhatemp.bat"
    Open BatFile$ For Output As #1
    Print #1, LHAFileSpec$ + " a " + ArchiveFileSpec$ + " @" +\
ResponseFile$
    If MakeEXEFlag Then
        Print #1, Left$(ArchiveFileSpec$, 2)
        Print #1, "CD " + ArchiveFile.Path
        Print #1, LHAFileSpec$ + " s " + ArchiveFileSpec$
    End If
    Print #1, "@Pause"
    Close #1
    ReturnVal = Shell(BatFile$, 1)
    End
End If
```

There's one rudimentary file name check—to see if the name is between one and eight characters long—and all the rest is DOS!

The LHA "@" response file name is reconstructed. The file itself was saved in the PickForm, if you recall. Then WinLHA tosses together a name for the batch file that will be constructed to run LHA.EXE. That file is opened, and the LHA command line is "Print"ed to the file. The command line looks something like this:

```
c:\...\lha.exe a c:\...\archive.fil @c:\...\response.fil
```

That's what LHA is expecting.

Then, if the MakeEXEFlag has been turned on—and it could only have been turned on when the user pushed the Create Self-Extracting File Button on the PickForm—WinLHA adds a few lines to the batch file. Those lines change the directory to the directory of the archived .LZH file (so the .EXE file will end up in the same directory as the .LZH file—LHArc has no fancy method for moving .EXE files around), and then the LHArc "create self-extracting file" command is issued:

```
c:\...\lha.exe s c:\...\archive.fil
```

Finally, the constructed batch file ends with a DOS Pause command, so the screen will stop scrolling for a second!

The Go_Click procedure then closes this batch file and invokes the Visual Basic shell command. Shell simply starts a program—in this case, a .BAT file—in its own window. The "1" forces Windows to run this .BAT file in a normal window, with focus, so the user can watch LHArc's progress.

There are two little things we need to cover, but by and large, WinLHA is now complete.

Except for the error handling routines, you've just written a fully functional, commercial-quality front-end, in a few hours. It took about 100 lines of executable code.

Error Handling

We skimped a bit on the error handling. In particular, clicking on a drive that doesn't contain a disk will raise a Visual Basic error condition.

The very first Form, PickForm, has a Drive List Control. If you click on, say, "a:," when there's no disk in drive "a:," Visual Basic halts the program on an execution error, as shown in Figure 5-55 on the following page.

Figure 5-55: No Disk

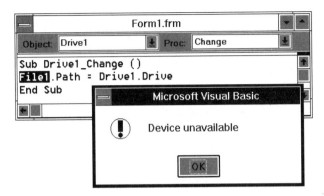

It's easily solved, though. In PickForm's PickDrive_Change procedure, try this:

```
Sub PickDrive_Change ()
On Error GoTo ErrHandler
PickDirectory.Path = PickDrive.Drive
GoTo Bye
ErrHandler:
MsgBox "Please insert a disk in the drive and close the door.",\
 48, "WinLHA"
PickDrive.Drive = PickDirectory.Path
Resume
Bye:
On Error GoTo 0
End Sub
```

The "On Error Goto x" and "On Error Goto 0" statements should be familiar from WordBasic. What's new here is the "Resume" statement. Visual Basic won't clear the Error Condition until it hits a Resume. If your program tries to leave a procedure without clearing the Error Condition, Visual Basic comes to a grinding halt, just as if you had no error handler in the first place.

Figure 5-56: No Resume

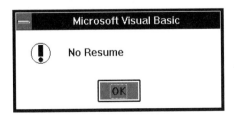

Similar error procedures are needed in the DefaultForm and WorkinForm. TheDefaultForm entries look like this:

```
Sub LHADrive_Change ()
On Error GoTo LHAErrHandler
LHADirectory.Path = LHADrive.Drive
LHAFileName.Caption = LHADrive.Drive
Exit Sub
LHAErrHandler:
MsgBox "Please insert a disk in the drive and close the door.",\
 48, "WinLHA"
LHADrive.Drive = LHADirectory.Path
Resume
End Sub

Sub PickDrive_Change ()
On Error GoTo PickErrHandler
PickDirectory.Path = PickDrive.Drive
Exit Sub
PickErrHandler:
MsgBox "Please insert a disk in the drive and close the door.",\
 48, "WinLHA"
PickDrive.Drive = PickDirectory.Path
Resume
End Sub

Sub ArchiveDrive_Change ()
On Error GoTo ArchiveErrHandler
ArchiveDirectory.Path = ArchiveDrive.Drive
Exit Sub
ArchiveErrHandler:
MsgBox "Please insert a disk in the drive and close the door.",\
 48, "WinLHA"
ArchiveDrive.Drive = ArchiveDirectory.Path
Resume
End Sub
```

And the WorkinForm error handler looks like this:

```
Sub ArchiveDrive_Change ()
On Error GoTo ArchiveErrHandler
ArchiveDirectory.Path = ArchiveDrive.Drive
ArchiveFileText.Text = ""
On Error Resume Next
ArchiveFileText.SetFocus
Exit Sub
ArchiveErrHandler:
MsgBox "Please insert a disk in the drive and close the door.",\
 48, "WinLHA"
ArchiveDrive.Drive = ArchiveDirectory.Path
Resume
End Sub
```

You can trace through the logic if you like. The trick is when to Resume Next. Not too bad.

Give WinLHA an Icon

Once again we saved the very best for last. Visual Basic lets you assign an icon to your program—an icon that can sit proudly on your desktop, ready for your beck and call. Here's how.

Crank up the PickForm, then click on the arrow under "Code." Scroll down to "Icon":

Figure 5-57: WinLHA Family Photo

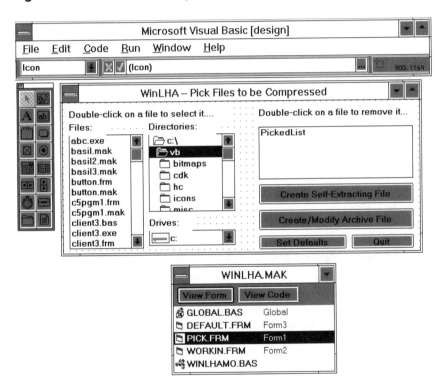

See the ellipses (. . .) way over on the right? Click on it. You'll get a dialog box that lets you pick an icon for the program. Scroll around. Take a look at Visual Basic's own icons (which are listed in the manual). Choose one you can live with. We're partial to the stick of dynamite, ready to explode; it's in the c:\vb\icons\misc subdirectory, file MISC39A.ICO.

Make It Executable

Final step. Make WinLHA an executable file.

Make sure you've saved any changes to WINLHA.MAK. Then click on File, and Make EXE. Type in a name you like—WINLHA will do just fine—and choose the icon from Form 1 (which is the PickForm).

It only takes a few seconds. And once you're done, anybody with a copy of VBRUN100.DLL—the Visual Basic run-time Dynamic Link Library—can run WinLHA. No matter how much you customize it, your copy of WINLHA.EXE will probably stay well under 20K. It's small, it's fast, and it's easy to customize!

The guy who was trying to write WinLHA in C? He just called us, up here on the mountain. He's all out of breath. The guy finally figured out how to get "Hello World" up on the screen. Now he's struggling with registering window classes. He thinks he'll have the WinLHA clone done in a few weeks. He's very excited about it—something about how it'll run 1.5 times faster than WinLHA, and take up 20% less disk room, because it's in "C"—but he wonders why such a complicated 1,000-line program would be included in a book for mere mortals.

WinLHAE—The Extractor

If you have the Companion Disk, bring up WINLHAE.MAK. (Click on "File," "Open Project," scroll to the subdirectory containing the WinLHA files, double-click on WINLHAE.MAK.)

We're going to run through the LHA Extractor, WinLHAE, rather quickly. It's quite similar to WinLHA.

Note how the DefaultForm and the Module in WinLHAE are identical to their counterparts in WinLHA. Using the Visual Basic File / Add File command lets us press the very same files into service!

Go ahead. Give it a try. Click on "File," then "Add File." See how you can add any Visual Basic file to your project? Good. If you accidentally added a Form and want to get rid of it, click on the file in the Packing List, then click "File," then "Remove File."

The ExtractorForm

While it's no work of art, the Extractor Form is certainly functional. Basically a File Troika-and-two-thirds, it looks like Figure 5-58 on the following page.

In the Extractor, double-clicking on the file name is not the same as clicking on the file, then clicking "GO." Why? Because in our exhaustive usability lab tests we discovered that far too many people would absent-mindedly double-click on the file before they set the correct Destination directory. One guess as to who's the worst offender.

Figure 5-58: The ExtractorForm

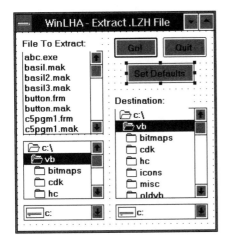

Extractor Code

The Form_Load procedure is just a touch different from, say, PickForm's. Taking an educated guess, the WinLHA Extractor starts the user in the "Archive To" directory stored away as a default. Naturally we want to limit the list of files to those with an .LZH extension.

```
Sub Form_Load ()
Call GetDefaults(PickDir$, ArchiveDir$, LHAFileSpec$)
If LHAFileSpec$ = "" Then
    Msg$ = "Please point WinLHA to the LHA.EXE file, "
    Msg$ = Msg$ + "and select starting directories."
    MsgBox Msg$, 64, "WinLHA Setup"
    SetDefaults.Value = -1
    Call GetDefaults(PickDir$, ArchiveDir$, LHAFileSpec$)
End If
If ArchiveDir$ <> "" Then
    ExtractDrive.Drive = ArchiveDir$
    ExtractDirectory.Path = ArchiveDir$
End If
ExtractFile.Filename = "*.lzh"
End Sub
```

The Global module is mighty simple:

```
Global LHAFileSpec$
```

The Drive and Directory Event Handlers are just as you would expect, including error trapping for missing diskettes:

```
Sub ExtractDrive_Change ()
On Error GoTo ExtractErrHandler
ExtractDirectory.Path = ExtractDrive.Drive
Exit Sub
ExtractErrHandler:
MsgBox "Please insert a disk in the drive and close the door.",\
 48, "WinLHA"
ExtractDrive.Drive = ExtractDirectory.Path
Resume
End Sub

Sub ExtractDirectory_Change ()
ExtractFile.Path = ExtractDirectory.Path
End Sub

Sub DestinationDrive_Change ()
On Error GoTo DestinationErrHandler
DestinationDirectory.Path = DestinationDrive.Drive
Exit Sub
DestinationErrHandler:
MsgBox "Please insert a disk in the drive and close the door.",\
 48, "WinLHA"
DestinationDrive.Drive = DestinationDirectory.Path
Resume
End Sub
```

No surprises with the Quit and Set Defaults Command Buttons:

```
Sub Quit_Click ()
End
End Sub

Sub SetDefaults_Click ()
Form3.Show 1
Form_Load
End Sub
```

The Go_Click Event Handler is a bit complicated, but only because it has to deal with DOS. It creates a DOS batch file that switches to the "Destination" directory, then runs LHArc with this:

```
c:\...\lha.exe e c:\...\archive.fil
```

The "e" tells LHArc to extract. WinLHAE also puts in a DOS Pause command to stop the screen and let the user see what happened.

```
Sub Go_Click ()
ArchiveFile$ = Smash$(ExtractDirectory.Path,\
 ExtractFile.List(ListIndex))
BatFile$ = Left$(LHAFileSpec$, Len(LHAFileSpec$) - 7) +\
 "wlhatemp.bat"
Open BatFile$ For Output As #1
Print #1, Left$(DestinationDirectory.Path, 2)
Print #1, "CD " + DestinationDirectory.Path
Print #1, LHAFileSpec$ + " e " + ArchiveFile$
Print #1, "@Pause"
Close #1
ReturnVal = Shell(BatFile$, 1)
End
End Sub
```

And that's all she wrote!

WinLHA Redux

> "...if he who desires to have before his eyes a true picture of the events
> which have happened, and of the like events which may be expected
> to happen hereafter in the order of human things, shall pronounce
> what I have written to be useful, then I shall be satisfied."
>
> —Thucydides, *Peloponnesian War,* ca. 440 BC

So there you have it. A full-featured Windows front-end to a DOS product. You built it yourself, with a little help from your friends.

Along the way, you've hit almost every major Visual Basic command, used a fair percentage of all the available Controls and many of their most common Properties. You've played with the files and their association through .MAK. You've created a rather sophisticated Module, replete with Windows API calls. You've used the Global Module, albeit sparingly.

You've also had a chance to see how a real-world Visual Basic application can be put together. We've taken some pains to step you through WinLHA much as a developer would approach the problem and its solution.

While it's true that the original version of WinLHA took more than a week to complete—and that development included its fair share of frustrations and blind alleys, mercifully not apparent in the final telling—it's still undeniably true that a similar effort in C would take most mere mortals many weeks, possibly many months.

Visual Basic's strong suit is quite apparent.

With a little luck, you've also seen how WordBasic and Visual Basic are so very similar—in syntax—but how the Event-Driven twist makes Visual Basic so much more powerful.

If you've been typing the code as we went along, you've also seen how the WordBasic coding editor (which is basically Word for Windows) works a whole lot better than its Visual Basic counterpart.

And you've seen how easy it is to use the Windows API. In WordBasic and Visual Basic, most DLL calls are only slightly more difficult than any other subroutine calls. You needn't be a guru to dig into Windows and dissect it with relish!

Most importantly, you should have a very good feel for the Event-Driven way of looking at the world. That's a Big Deal. It's something not easily taught or learned.

There's one problem, though. Now that you've seen the wonders that await, you may never go back to input-process-output!

CHAPTER 6

A Dynamic Data Exchange Primer

We're going to tackle Dynamic Data Exchange in the abstract, before using it in a real program.

The first part of this chapter takes you through several straightforward DDE conversations. The middle part concentrates on some of the variations and side issues. Finally, the last section of this chapter, the **DDE Cookbook—Caveat au Gratin,** is designed to be an ongoing reference.

Keep the cookbook by your side when you try to program (or even use!) DDE. Many DDE secrets, some of the traps, and at least a few bug warnings will be at your beck and call. Kind of a *WinMortals* "information at your bleeding fingertips."

Programming Pillars

Windows programming rests on four pillars: the Four Pillars of Windows Faith, as it were.

First is the Event-Driven way of looking at things. Second is the use of Dynamic Link Libraries to organize and handle routines. Third is Dynamic Data Exchange, which lets programs and applications talk to each other. Fourth is Object Linking and Embedding: DDE, the next generation.

We stomped on the First Pillar, Event-Driven programming, when we built WinLHA. Chapter 7 will take the Event-Driven paradigm further, with CoolCons, another real, commercial application that we'll build from scratch.

You've seen the Second Pillar in action. Many Dynamic Link Library calls (indeed, many Windows API calls) are quite straightforward. A DLL call is usually no more difficult than finding the correct library, looking up the right variable definitions, and adding "Declare" to the beginning of "Function" and "Sub" statements. Now that you know the "Declare" secret, you'll probably find it easier to use DLLs than to write your own routines. That's quite a revelation: most manuals relegate DLL information to the back of the book because DLLs are "too hard"!

OLE, the Fourth Pillar, hasn't yet reached the mainstream. Although more and more Windows applications claim they support OLE, getting at the OLE interface itself remains exceedingly and unnecessarily difficult. Visual Basic—with the extra-cost Professional Developer's Kit we'll discuss in Chapter 9—opens the door to OLE, if you're willing to use Visual Basic as a Client, and you're willing to put up with one of the other Windows applications as a Server.

Ultimately, the next version of OLE will provide the glue and the structure for Macro Manager, what we've called The Monster Basic from Hell. But until OLE Servers get better, OLE Clients more widespread, and until the whole functions in concert with a Basic Cereberus, OLE will remain much more art—black art—than science. *Lasciate ogni speranza voi ch'entrate! Abandon all hope ye who enter here!*

That leaves the Third Pillar, the subject of this chapter, the Windows Holy Grail: Dynamic Data Exchange.

DDE—The Living Link

> 'Twas not for every Gawain to gaze upon the Grail!
>
> — Robert Browning, *Fifine at the Fair,* 1872

Unfortunately, very little has been written about DDE, and almost all of the stuff that's out there is jargon-laden, stilted, inconsistent, and riddled with errors.

Like DLLs, like Windows programming in general, DDE is considered "too hard" for ordinary folks like us.

Ha!

DDE, Phone Home

Way back in Chapter 2 we went over the basics of a DDE conversation. It's really no more complicated than a telephone call. The sequence:

- *The Client looks up a phone number, picks a topic of conversation, and dials the phone.*

- *If the Server is home (i.e., it's running) it answers the phone.* The Server checks to see if it likes the topic of conversation. If the topic is not one the Server wants to talk about, it immediately hangs up the phone.

- *The Client asks the Server to do its bidding.* Usually this involves requesting a certain piece of information from the hapless Server or telling the Server to run a specific macro. Sometimes, though, the Client can just shove a bit of information at the Server and tell the Server where to put it.

- *The Server acknowledges that it has completed the task.*

- *The Client may ask the Server to do its bidding again, over and over, and may issue as many commands (pertaining to the current topic of conversation) as it likes.*

- *Finally, if they're polite, either the Client or the Server hangs up the phone.* If they're extraordinarily rude, one or the other may just walk away from the phone and leave the line open!

We'll have to translate all of that into code, of course. But at its heart, DDE is no more difficult than that imaginary telephone call.

DDE Bafflegab

So much of what has been written about DDE is astoundingly convoluted. Writers love to get tied up in Acks and Pokes and Unadvises and dynamically adjusted Timeouts. In the process, they tend to lose sight of the basic simplicity of DDE.

Worse, many folks get confused when they digest some of what the original DDE architects intended and then try to superimpose that grand design on real, working products.

Learning DDE by reading the original specs is like learning how to dial a phone by studying Switching Circuit Theory: you can do it, but why bother?

Some writers go so far as to say (or at least intimate) that DDE requires a team of specialists, hot-shot programmers who are willing to struggle with obscure bits and perplexing protocols. That's pure porkswill. DDE is well within the grasp of the shade-tree weekend hacker, the Mere Mortal.

We're going to concentrate on what works. If you're worried about establishing self-correcting Warm Links to remote redundant SQL servers, well, good luck! Just wading through all the errors in the documentation should keep you going in circles for a few weeks.

The Reality of It All

There are two big obstacles to getting DDE working.

First is the bloody, stupid variation in terminology. Visual Basic says "tomato," WordBasic says "tomahhhhto," Amí Pro insists on "termaytuh," and EXCEL says "= (red squishy thingy)."

The People Who Decide Such Things refuse to get together and keep their terms straight; we're the ones who suffer for it. Imagine the pandemonium if telephone numbers worked that way!

The second obstacle: different languages implement different parts of the DDE standard, and no two do it in the same way. Some things are ignored in, say, Visual Basic, but are required in WordBasic; others are implicit in both—in obscure ways.

That's why we're going to eavesdrop on a couple of DDE conversations. (Don't worry, we'll start out easy.) That should get you started. Then we'll boil down all the tips and bugs and hints and such, and put them in one place so you can come back and refer to them later. Finally, in Chapter 7, we'll build CoolCons, and see what can go wrong in the real world.

Visual Basic Calling WordBasic

Let's step through a conversation between Visual Basic and WordBasic. Visual Basic will be our Client, the one dialing the phone, and WordBasic will be our Server.

Visual Basic Dials the Phone

Whenever Visual Basic operates as a Client, the DDE conversation has to be "hooked" to a Control, just as Visual Basic code in general is usually "hooked" to a Control. The Control may be a Label, a Picture Box, or a Text Box—think of them as the Controls that can hold incoming data. And a DDE Control can be on any Form.

Say you have a Visual Basic Text Box—with a CtlName of, oh, "DDETextBox"—and you want to fill it with some text from Word for Windows. Let's say that text is in a file called "ANYDOC.DOC" and is marked with a Word for Windows bookmark called "SomeBookmark." (Word for Windows bookmarks are used to mark locations or sections of text in a document. They act like . . . well, they act like bookmarks!)

You'll be surprised how simple it is to lasso that data.

- *The Client looks up a phone number, picks a topic of conversation, and dials the phone.*

In Visual Basic, that sequence takes two lines of code:

```
DDETextBox.LinkTopic="WinWord|Anydoc.doc"
```

English Translation: Let's start a conversation with the application called "WinWord." (In effect, "WinWord" is the Client's phone number; we don't want to talk to anybody else.) We're looking for data in the document called "ANY-

DOC.DOC." In DDE-speak, that document name is a "Topic." (Throughout DDE uppercase is treated the same as lowercase, so "Anydoc.Doc," "aNY-doc.DOC," and "anydoc.doc" are all identical.) Finally, we want to hook this conversation up to the Control called "DDETextBox"; when the stuff comes back from this DDE conversation, the DDE gods should stick it in "DDETextBox."

No doubt you're wondering at this point how to find telephone numbers, how to make sure WinWord can locate "ANYDOC.DOC," and a thousand other things. Well, put a cork in it for a minute. You'll see. Let's learn how to dial this high-tech telephone first, before we delve into speed-dialing and call waiting.

```
DDETextBox.LinkMode=2
```

English Translation: Dial the phone. (The "2" signifies a "Cold" link. If you don't remember the difference between Hot and Cold, we'll go over them again—and the Case of the Mysterious Disappearing Warm Link—later in this chapter.)

WordBasic Answers the Phone

■ *If the Server is home (i.e., it's running) it answers the phone. The Server checks to see if it likes the topic of conversation. If the topic is not one the Server wants to talk about, it immediately hangs up the phone.*

This all happens automatically, behind the scenes. You don't have to code a thing.

If Word for Windows isn't running, the DDE gods simply raise an Error Condition in the Visual Basic program. If Word for Windows is running, it checks to see if there is an open document that matches the Topic file name. If no such file is open, WinWord refuses to "answer the phone"—if you will—and the DDE gods raise an Error Condition back in the Visual Basic program.

Ah, but if Word for Windows is running, and it has the Topic file open, we're in high clover. WinWord answers the phone; the DDE link is established; WinWord is officially a Server; and we're ready to get some work done.

Visual Basic Asks for Information

Now that the phone . . . er . . . DDE link is up and running, Visual Basic, as the Client, can go after whatever information it wants.

■ *The Client asks the Server to do its bidding. Usually this involves requesting a certain piece of information from the hapless Server or telling the Server to run a specific macro.*

We'll work with a simple request for info here. All it takes is two more lines of Visual Basic code:

```
DDETextBox.LinkItem="SomeBookmark"
```

English Translation: We're interested in the stuff contained in a Word for Windows bookmark called "SomeBookmark." In DDE-Speak that's an "Item."

Word for Windows and Amí Pro use bookmarks to identify Items that'll be involved in DDE. Visual Basic uses Controls. EXCEL uses cell names or ranges of cells. Superbase uses field names. To each its own.

```
DDETextBox.LinkRequest
```

English Translation: Go get it, tiger!

A DDE Request is nothing more than a "Read"—or a "Peek," in old-fashioned (that is, pre–1991) computerese.

WordBasic: The Server as Servant

Word for Windows, the lowly Server, takes a look at the Topic document and checks to see if it contains the Item bookmark.

If there's no such bookmark in the document (in this case, if "ANY-DOC.DOC" does *not* contains a bookmark called "SomeBookmark"), Word for Windows burps and the DDE gods raise yet another Error Condition back in the Visual Basic program. (You're starting to get the idea that much can go wrong in a DDE conversation, yes?)

- *The Server acknowledges that it has completed the task.*

When all goes right, Word for Windows takes everything in the bookmark (text, pictures, whatever), and hands it to the DDE gods, who in turn slap it into the Visual Basic Control.

Et cetera, Et cetera

- *The Client may ask the Server to do its bidding again, over and over, and may issue as many commands (pertaining to the current topic of conversation) as it likes.*

Since it's in the driver's seat, Visual Basic as the Client may switch over to a new Item—a new bookmark in the Word for Windows document—and request more information. All it takes is two more lines:

```
DDETextBox.LinkItem="SomeOtherBookmark"
DDETextBox.LinkRequest
```

As long as the Item bookmark exists in the Topic document, Visual Basic can keep this up for hours on end. Each time there's a new DDE Request, the old contents of the "DDETextBox" Text Box Control is obliterated, replaced by the newly requested data.

Visual Basic Hangs Up the Phone

- *Finally, if they're polite, either the Client or the Server hangs up the phone. If they're extraordinarily rude, one or the other may just walk away from the phone and leave the line open!*

Hanging up the phone—breaking the DDE link—is a one-liner:

```
DDETextBox.LinkMode=0
```

that puts us right back where we started.

Is That All There Is to It?

That's a basic DDE conversation. Five lines of Visual Basic code. *No* WordBasic code.

Visual Basic picks up the phone, dials WordBasic, asks for information in a WordBasic bookmark, receives that information in a plain-vanilla Control, and hangs up the phone.

Not exactly quantum mechanics.

WordBasic Calling Visual Basic

Let's put the shoe on the other foot. Say we want to write a WordBasic program that will grab something out of a Label Control in a running Visual Basic program.

Ah, no sweat. WordBasic as Client. Visual Basic as Server. The terminology is different—surprisingly so!—but the concepts remain the same.

WordBasic Dials the Phone

Let's say you have a running Visual Basic program called, oh, "WayCool." (Visual Basic program names are determined by the name of the ".MAK" file if you're running from a Make File in Visual Basic's design time, or by the name of the

".EXE" file if you've used Visual Basic's File / Make EXE option to create a stand-alone program.)

In the "WayCool" program you have a Form called, oh, "Form1," which has a Label Control, with a CtlName of, say, "DDEStuff."

Here's how you pull "DDEStuff" into WordBasic, with WordBasic acting as the Client.

- *The Client looks up a phone number, picks a topic of conversation, and dials the phone.*

That took two lines in Visual Basic. It only takes one in WordBasic:

```
ChannelNumber = DDEInitiate("WayCool", "Form1")
```

WordBasic doesn't care about hot, cold, or warm links: you can have any kind you want, as long as it's cold!

Also, unlike Visual Basic, WordBasic requires that your program explicitly work with something called a "Channel Number." Just think of it as a number, with no meaning in and of itself, that helps Windows keep track of which DDE conversations are under way. Channel Numbers are assigned dynamically by Windows, starting at one, and going up with each active conversation.

Visual Basic Answers the Phone

- *If the Server is home (i.e., it's running) it answers the phone. The Server checks to see if it likes the topic of conversation. If the topic is not one the Server wants to talk about, it immediately hangs up the phone.*

Once again, the DDE gods do all of this for you. You don't have to code a thing.

If there's no "WayCool," WordBasic traps the error and presents your user with an informative message that looks like this:

Figure 6-1: WordBasic Can't Find WayCool

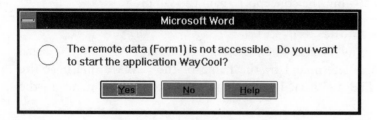

Perhaps *your* users can figure that one out. If so, they deserve a hearty pat on the back. But for all intents and purposes, the fact that "WayCool" isn't running, puts a big dent in your program's "user friendliness."

(For what it's worth, if your user clicks on "Yes" in response to that message box in Figure 6-1, WinWord will try to kick start the application. It takes the application name shown in the box—in this case "WayCool"—and uses the normal Windows method to try to start "WayCool," that is, it looks for WayCool.PIF, WayCool.EXE, WayCool.COM, or WayCool.BAT, and it only searches the current directory, plus the directories on your DOS Path. If WinWord doesn't find one of those files in one of those places, users get a "Can't establish link" error message. If they weren't confused before the Figure 6-1 message, they sure will be confused afterwards!)

If there *is* a "WayCool" but no "Form1," WordBasic pops up a message startlingly similar to the one in Figure 6-1. Your users will walk away perplexed.

If "WayCool" is running and it has a Form called "Form1," then it answers the phone—a DDE connection is established—and the Visual Basic "WayCool" form called "Form1" becomes a Server. In Visual Basic, Forms are Servers.

WordBasic Asks for Information
Armed with a DDE link—and a Channel Number—WordBasic is ready to request information.

- *The Client asks the Server to do its bidding. Usually this involves requesting a certain piece of information from the hapless Server or telling the Server to run a specific macro.*

WordBasic, the Client, has to tell Visual Basic, the Server, which Control contains the information that's of interest:

```
data$ = DDERequest$(ChannelNumber, "DDEStuff")
```

Visual Basic Goes to the Barn
Visual Basic rummages around in Form1 for a Control named "DDEStuff." If there's no such Control on WayCool's Form1, WordBasic is sure out of luck—it gets a big, fat Error Condition.

- *The Server acknowledges that it has completed the task.*

If all the ducks are in order, though, Visual Basic hands the contents of the "DDEStuff" Label Box Control to the DDE gods, and they pass it on to the WordBasic variable called "data$."

From that point, WordBasic may do with "data$" what it may.

WordBasic Slams Down the Phone and Stalks Off

*Just wanted to see if you were still awake. This stuff is supposed to be complicated. Remember—you're supposed to keep a **team** of programmers around to do DDE!*

The last step in a DDE conversation.

- *Finally, if they're polite, either the Client or the Server hangs up the phone. If they're extraordinarily rude, one or the other may just walk away from the phone and leave the line open!*

WordBasic hangs up the phone on this DDE conversation with a simple

```
DDETerminate ChannelNumber
```

So there's your complicated DDE conversation: three whole lines of WordBasic code. In contrast, this stuff is hideously complicated in C, even if you use a new, supposedly high-level DDE management library from Microsoft called DDEML. You're *a lot* better off doing DDE in BASIC rather than in C. A lot.

Quick Recap

You now know enough to start some real DDE conversations and get some real work done.

Let's look back for a second.

DDE Initiate   Every DDE Conversation starts with one Windows application—the Client—calling another—the Server.

In order to establish a connection, the Client must find the correct phone number (sometimes called an "Application Name" or a "DDE Name" or a "DDE Server Name") and a Topic (often a file name or a form name, but there's no real restriction) acceptable to the Server.

The Client starts the conversation by issuing a "DDE Initiate" command. In Visual Basic it looks like this:

```
ControlName.LinkTopic="ApplicationName|Topic"
ControlName.LinkMode=2
```

with a mode of 1 for a Hot link or 2 for a Cold link. In WordBasic (and Amí Pro 2.0), a DDE Initiate looks like this:

```
ChannelNumber = DDEInitiate(ApplicationName$,Topic$)
```

In EXCEL (introducing a new player here), it looks like this:

```
=INITIATE("ApplicationName", "Topic")
```

and in EXCEL the spreadsheet cell containing that command will receive the channel number.

What's most surprising about all of this is the variety, the lack of uniformity . . . and the fact that it works at all!

At first blush (and second and third blush), it would appear that every application developer has gone its own way.

Even the apps in the Microsoft stable vary: Visual Basic supports Hot and Cold links; WinWord and EXCEL are all Cold. (Yes, you can establish Hot links from WinWord and EXCEL, but not by using the macro language!)

WordBasic and EXCEL let you (*make* you!) keep track of the channel number; Visual Basic keeps track of things internally, based on the Control. In Visual Basic the ApplicationName/Topic combination is one field, with a "|" separator; in WordBasic and EXCEL it's two. And on and on.

The trustbusters think Microsoft talks to itself. Sure. You can bet the Feds have never seen a polyglot DDE Initiate. Is this any way to run a monopoly?

DDE Request Once the DDE channel is open, the Client may request data from the Server. The Client tells the Server which Item is required. An Item can be a cell or range of cells in a spreadsheet (EXCEL); it can be the contents of a bookmark (Word for Windows); it can be the contents of a Control (Visual Basic); it can be a field in a database record (Superbase); in fact, just like the Topic, it can be anything the Client and Server can agree on!

Don't get too wound up in the terminology: a DDE Request is just an old-fashioned "Read," dressed up with a fancy new name, except it's one application reading from another application—that part is new.

From Visual Basic, requesting/reading data is a two-step process:

```
ControlName.LinkItem= Item$
ControlName.LinkRequest
```

The requested data is placed in the "ControlName" Control.

In WordBasic it looks like this:

```
data$ = DDERequest$(ChannelNumber, Item$)
```

In Amí Pro 2.0:

```
data$ = DDEReceive$(ChannelNumber, Item$)
```

In EXCEL:

```
=REQUEST(ChannelNumber, "Item")
```

In WordBasic and Amí Pro, the variable "data$" gets the result of the Request; in EXCEL the result of the DDE Request is placed in the cell containing the command.

DDE Terminate When all the data has gone back and forth, either the Client or Server should hang up the phone. If the DDE link isn't terminated, a small amount of memory ("Free System Resources") gets eaten up and won't return until you restart Windows.

In Visual Basic:

```
ControlName.LinkMode=0
```

In WordBasic and Amí Pro:

```
DDETerminate ChannelNumber
```

In EXCEL:

```
=Terminate(ChannelNumber)
```

Many different ways of saying precisely the same thing.

DDE Poke

> Billy, in one of his nice new sashes,
> Fell in the fire and was burnt to ashes;
> Now, although the room grows chilly,
> I haven't the heart to poke poor Billy.
>
> —Harry Graham, *Tender-Heartedness*, 1899

If DDE Initiate, DDE Request, and DDE Terminate were the entire Dynamic Data Ballgame, DDE would be a remarkably powerful tool. But wait, there's more. If you order now. . .

Forget What You've Read

If you've struggled with DDE before—if you've read other books or articles on DDE and tried to make some sense out of them—chances are pretty good that Poke drove you nuts.

Somebody, somewhere in DDE's dim dank past, decided that there were "natural" things DDE "should" do. By inference, that meant there were "unnatural" things that DDE "shouldn't normally" do—as if DDE commands were regulated by Orwellian Thought Police.

Taking the DDE Thought Police point of view, Poke is an "unnatural" act. That absurd bias has propagated throughout the literature.

Petzold claims that a Poke involves "unsolicited data" and that the command is "rarely used." The official *Windows Programmer's Reference* (Microsoft Press) says a Poke "requests the server application to accept an unsolicited data item value."

First, DDE Pokes are quite common. Matter of fact, Poke may be the most commonly used DDE command.

Second, DDE Pokes don't involve "unsolicited" data; they have to be set up just like any other DDE data interchange, with the Client and Server working together to make things happen.

Third, DDE Poke, maligned as it is, may be the only reasonable way to get the job done!

Where a DDE Request is just an old-fashioned "Read," a DDE Poke is an old-fashioned "Write." That's all. It's pretty hard to imagine a computer setup confined to reads, with no writes.

So, please, if you've already looked into DDE Poke and come up with some crazy biases, forget what you've seen before you proceed with this chapter. Start with a clean slate. Poke is natural. Poke is good. Poke works fine. Poke is something you should use whenever you need it, regardless of what you may have read, no matter how many people perpetuate the "unnatural" myth.

The Poke Shtick

DDE Poke merely sends data over a DDE Link.

That's the whole shtick.

In old-fashioned computer lingo, Poke is just a "Write."

Let's take Visual Basic and WordBasic as examples again, with Visual Basic as Client and WordBasic as Server.

You've seen how wonderful Visual Basic's user interface can be. By comparison, WordBasic is woefully inadequate. Conversely, WordBasic works wonders with documents, while Visual Basic barely limps along.

More than a few people have recognized the enormous disparity and set out to even the playing field a bit. The result: applications that use Visual Basic to handle the user interface and Word for Windows to take care of the output. They work like a champ. And DDE Poke is the key.

Promissory Notes

Here's a real-world application: George Mair, esq., WordBasic fan and solicitor extraordinaire, has created a Visual Basic program that produces Promissory Notes. The user types a few things onto a Visual Basic screen, hits a button, and the program calculates payment periods and balances and such, DDE Pokes all the appropriate data into a fancy Word for Windows document, then prints it.

For this you'd pay a lawyer $100.

One tough part of George's Promissory Note program is transferring data from the Visual Basic form to specific spots in the Word for Windows document. The spots are marked with bookmarks.

Let's say there's a Text Box Control called, oh, "MakersName," on the Visual Basic Form, and a bookmark called, say, "Maker" in the Word for Windows document called, uh, "c:\winword\PromNote.DOC."

Here's all it takes to transfer the data from that Form to the document. The first two lines

```
MakersName.LinkTopic = "WinWord|c:\winword\PromNote.doc"
MakersName.LinkMode = 2
```

set up a Cold link with Word for Windows and the PromNote.DOC document; then

```
MakersName.LinkItem = "Maker"
```

establishes the bookmark that is to receive the data, and

```
MakersName.LinkPoke
```

sends it on down the line. Finally,

```
MakersName.LinkMode = 0
```

breaks the DDE connection.

After running that five-line Visual Basic program, the contents of the "MakersName" Control has been transferred to "PromNote.DOC," at the location of the "Maker" bookmark.

Tough, eh?

To set up a Poke in WordBasic or Amí Pro, you'd use the command

```
DDEPoke(ChannelNumber, Item$, StuffToBeSent$)
```

In EXCEL it's

```
=Poke(ChannelNumber, "Item," "StuffToBeSent")
```

That's all there is to Poke. It's a simple, old-fashioned "Write," with a new-age moniker.

DDE Time Out

Time Waits for No One

DDE won't wait forever.

In our imaginary phone call, if the Client or Server walks away from the phone (or, more aptly, dies of a General Protection Fault Heart Attack mid-conversation), the link won't work any more. Kaput.

If something goes haywire with a DDE link—usually, if one or the other participant in the link disappears—the DDE gods will capitulate, wringing their hands in despair. They raise an Error Condition, send it to whichever party is still on the line, and summarily hang up the phone.

We'll see momentarily how the Time Out can really bollix up a conversation. For now, keep in mind that there are all sorts of messages zipping back and forth during a DDE conversation that you, as a user or Basic programmer, won't normally see. In C, you get to see every last one. That's either a good thing or a bad thing, depending on your point of view and the day of the week.

When a Server picks up the phone, for example, there's a message behind the scenes ("Hello, it's me!") that establishes contact. When a Client sends a DDE Poke, there's another message that comes back saying "I got it." A DDE Request requires an answer, of course—that's why it's a Request. Even a DDE Terminate involves a confirming "OK, I'm hanging up the phone" from the other end of the line.

The DDE gods wait for all of those messages, for the specified amount of time. If the messages don't come in time, the gods get angry, raise an Error Condition, and break the link.

Who says patience is a virtue?

The Visual Basic Tesseract

Visual Basic lets you change the length of time DDE will just sit around, tapping its feet, waiting for a response:

```
ControlName.LinkTimeOut=200
```

That number is in tenths of a second; this particular command would set the DDE TimeOut to twenty seconds.

BUG

The manuals say that a LinkTimeOut value of minus one will make DDE in Visual Basic wait forever. Not true. With a "-1," DDE only waits 6,553.5 seconds—almost two hours—before giving up. *Somebody stays awake at night and tests these things.*

There's no simple way to change the DDE Time Out time setting in WordBasic, Amí Pro, or EXCEL.

You *can* do it, though, if you're feeling omnipotent. Check the DDETimeOut setting under [Microsoft Word 2.0] and other applications in your WIN.INI. The precise method is documented in a file called WININI.TXT, which you should be able to find in your Windows directory. And you can use WriteProfileString to change DDETimeOut from inside your program.

In general, most programs will wait between five and thirty seconds before timing out. Visual Basic defaults to a LinkTimeOut value of 50—five seconds. WordBasic tops out around thirty seconds.

DDE Execute

Here's the most powerful DDE command.

Your program can use DDE to tell another application to execute a macro, a command, even an entire on-the-fly program!

Visual Basic as Client

Let's start with something simple. WordBasic, Amí Pro, and EXCEL all have commands that insert the current date in a document, at the insertion point. In WordBasic the command is **InsertDateField**; in Amí Pro it's **InsertDate(2,1)**. In EXCEL it's **Formula("=Today()")**. (Yes, there are other ways of inserting dates in WinWord, Amí Pro and EXCEL, but let's work with these.)

Assuming Word for Windows is running and has a document called "c:\winword\TESTDATE.DOC" open, this Visual Basic code will insert the current date in TESTDATE.DOC:

```
ControlName.LinkTopic = "WinWord|c:\winword\TESTDATE.DOC"
ControlName.LinkMode = 2
ControlName.LinkExecute "[InsertDateField]"
```

Similarly, if Amí Pro is alive and well and it has opened a document called "d:\amipro\TESTDATE.SAM," here's the Visual Basic code that inserts the current date at the insertion point:

```
ControlName.LinkTopic = "AmiPro|d:\amipro\TESTDATE.SAM"
ControlName.LinkMode = 2
ControlName.LinkExecute "[InsertDate(2,1)]"
```

Finally, if EXCEL is active and has an open spreadsheet called "e:\excel\TESTDATE.XLS," this Visual Basic code will insert the current date in the active cell:

```
ControlName.LinkTopic = "excel|e:\excel\TESTDATE.XLS"
ControlName.LinkMode = 2
Label1.LinkExecute "[Formula(""=Today()"")]"
```

The general format, which you've no doubt discerned by now, involves the macro command being surrounded by [square brackets]. That's pretty silly—a throwback, no doubt, to EXCEL, which was the first application to really use DDE—but it's a fact of life in many Windows applications.

Just as an aside, if you're running these snippets of code, adding this line to the EXCEL code above will format the date so you can read it:

```
Label1.LinkExecute "[Format.Number(""mmm d, yyyy"")]"
```

Doubled Double-Quote Interlude

Time to get side-tracked for a bit.

DDE Execute statements tend to have lots of quotes in them.

Those doubled-up double-quotes in the LinkExecute command we just used, for example, are vital. EXCEL is looking for something that says [**Formula("=Today()")**]; without the quotes, it won't work.

Visual Basic is smart enough to recognize a pair of double-quotes (" ") within a literal string as being a single double-quote .

Was that confusing enough?

Here. Take a look at this Visual Basic message box:

Figure 6-2: Doubled Double-Quotes in Visual Basic

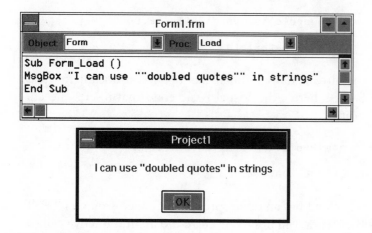

See how Visual Basic treats two double-quotes, back-to-back, as a genuine double-quote, not as the end of a string? That's one of those little programming things that can make your life much, much easier.

Amí Pro is smart enough to work with doubled-up double-quotes, too, just like Visual Basic.

Unfortunately, WordBasic hasn't gotten that far along yet. In WordBasic you have to mess around with Chr$(34) quotation marks, ANSI character number 34 being a double-quote. It gets real messy:

Figure 6-3: Chr$(34) Double-Quotes in WordBasic

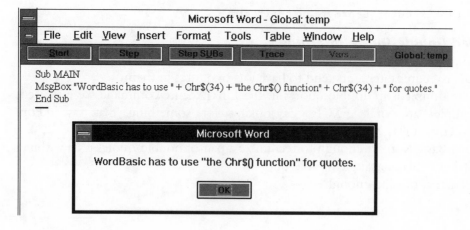

That's why you'll see a lot of Chr$(34)s in WordBasic DDE Statements. They really tend to clutter things up.

Back to DDE.

Visual Basic as Server

While Word for Windows, Amí Pro, EXCEL, Q+E, Crosstalk for Windows, and many other Windows applications require you to wrap those [square brackets] around DDE Execute commands, Visual Basic and DynaComm (among others) do not.

In fact, Visual Basic and DynaComm let you pass *any* argument through DDE Execute. There's just one trick: it's a two-edged sword. You have to write the program that intercepts those commands and runs them!

As you may recall, Visual Basic Server code is attached to a Form. When a DDE link is established with a particular Visual Basic Form, the Form_LinkExecute event is triggered. (Remember Events?)

You have to write the code to handle a Form_LinkExecute event. It really isn't as tough as it sounds. Here's an example, with WordBasic as Client and the Visual Basic program "DDETest," Form1, as the Server.

Figure 6-4: ShowMsgBoxAndQuitTurkey

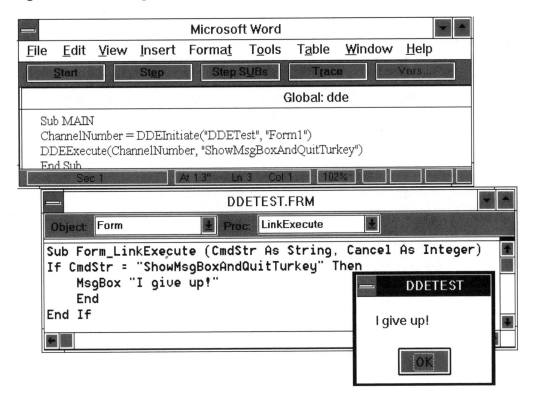

WordBasic starts up a DDE link with the DDE Initiate command. The link is with a program called DDETest, and in particular with DDETest's Form1. After the link is established, WordBasic, using a DDE Execute, tells DDETest's Form1 to execute a program called "ShowMsgBoxAndQuitTurkey."

Running that DDE Execute triggers a Form_LinkExecute event in DDETest's Form1. You've written a little Event Handler that checks to see if the command string being passed by DDE Execute has a certain value   "ShowMsgBoxAnd QuitTurkey." If the string checks out, DDETest slaps up a MsgBox with the caption "I give up!" and then quits with an "End."

We've skipped over a few of the finer points: we ignored the "Cancel" parameter in the Form_LinkExecute event—more about which later—and we didn't have either of them hang up the phone, but to a first order of magnitude a half-dozen lines of code can fully implement a DDE Execute from WordBasic to Visual Basic.

Using DDE, you can Execute any macro, any command, in any Windows program. Or at least any Windows program that supports DDE. That's one incredibly powerful capability. And once you get over the semantics, it's really not all that tough!

Quick Recap the Second

With DDE Execute, you've hit all the DDE commands (except for "Advise/Un-advise," which aren't implemented in very many application macro languages).

Everything from this point on is refinement, experimentation, consolation, and General Protection Faults.

We covered DDE Initiate, DDE Request, and DDE Terminate earlier. DDE Initiate, you may recall, starts a DDE conversation, providing the Server application is alive and it likes the Topic. DDE Request asks for specific data, specified by an Item generally the contents of a Control (in Visual Basic), a bookmark (in WordBasic and Amí Pro), a spreadsheet cell (in EXCEL), a field value (PackRat), whatever the application supports. DDE Terminate hangs up the phone.

DDE Poke The most maligned DDE command, Poke just sends data over the DDE line. You can Poke data into any Item that will accept it.

The Client specifies an Item. If that Item is acceptable to the Server, the Client can ask the Server to send along the contents of the Item, or the Client can send new data to the Server, to go into that Item.

That's the only difference between a DDE Request, which asks for data, and a DDE Poke, which sends data. In more pedestrian computer lingo, the difference between DDE Request and DDE Poke is the difference between "Read" and "Write." That's all.

Request=Read. Poke=Write. DDE folks sure do talk funny.

DDE Time Out DDE doesn't wait forever. Each interaction—and many interactions occur behind the scenes—must take place within an allotted time period, typically five to ten seconds. If the DDE gods don't get an answer in time, they raise an Error Condition and summarily shut down the DDE connection.

Of the major applications, only Visual Basic lets you change the Time Out interval without a direct Windows API call to change WIN.INI. The calls aren't difficult, but writing to WIN.INI must be undertaken with the utmost caution.

DDE Execute The most powerful DDE command, Execute lets you run any command, any macro, in any Windows program.

It's a mind-boggling capability.

Traditionally, DDE Execute commands are supposed to be placed in [square brackets]. So instead of telling WordBasic, oh, "FileOpen," you have to tell it "[FileOpen]."

WordBasic, EXCEL, and Amí Pro all insist on those corny [square brackets], and your programs are limited to executing existing commands or macros. But Visual Basic and the DynaComm macro/script language let you write *your own code* to handle Execute commands.

You may chain together DDE Execute commands by simply putting them one after the other, that is,

```
DDEExecute(ChannelNumber, "[Command1][Command2][Command3]")
```

in almost any application, with the notable exception of Toolbook. Those "Commands" don't have to be built-in commands; you can run custom macros with them, too.

Permutations and Combinations

From these simple building blocks—Initiate, Request, Poke, Execute, and Terminate—it's possible to build phantasmagorical castles of intertwined code. If you think you've seen spaghetti code before, well, Event-Driven DDE will set your head reeling.

Keep in mind that any application can be both a Client and a Server *at the same time.* More than that, applications can handle a nearly infinite number of DDE conversations concurrently.

IsAppLoaded, For Sure?

In order to make DDE conversations work, the Server should be kick-started before a Client tries to dial the phone.

While starting—the techie term is "loading"—an application isn't really a DDE problem, it's inextricably tied up in the whole DDE milieu. Let's take a break from DDE *per se* and give IsAppLoaded a quick whirl.

Novitiate No More

You may remember the training-wheel version of GetModuleHandle, the one recommended in the Word for Windows books:

```
Declare Function IsAppLoaded Lib "kernel"(AppName$) As Integer\
  Alias "GetModuleHandle"
```

The function GetModuleHandle returns the handle of the "AppName$" module, if "AppName$" is running. If "AppName$" isn't running, GetModuleHandle returns a zero.

By Declaring GetModuleHandle as a fun-and-games Alias in this fashion, an early WordBasic DDE pioneer discovered that programmers (the ones who think DLL calls are "too hard") could write statements like this:

```
If IsAppLoaded("EXCEL")=0 Then Shell("EXCEL")
```

That kind of statement is sweet and simple. Never mind the fact that a generation of WordBasic programmers has grown up wondering *why and how in the name of Gates it works!*

Since you're an old hand at Windows API calls by now, you know that, because of the Alias, "IsAppLoaded" is just "GetModuleHandle" in drag. And you know that GetModuleHandle returns a zero if it can't find the program. Mystery solved.

You might guess, though, that there are all sorts of nasty sharks swimming around just below the surface.

Let's take a look at some of those sharks and greet them by name.

Shark Names

> Oh the shark has pretty teeth, dear,
> And he shows them pearly white.
> Just a jack-knife has Macheath, dear,
> And he keeps it out of sight.
>
> —Bertolt Brecht, *Threepenny Opera*, 1928

When you start using macro languages to program Windows, you'll find yourself searching, over and over again, for ways to see if programs are running, start them if they aren't, and get the all-important "hWnd" handles to windows that are vital for you and your programs.

Windows, of course, has all sorts of ways to get in and around windows. We're going to take a look at some of the simpler ones. And while we're at it, we'll try to draw some distinction between all the different "names" that are floating around.

Window Titles

Ah, to have a nickel for every program that assumes Word for Windows windows— and only Word for Windows windows—have titles that start with "Microsoft Word".

You've already seen how easy it is to change a window title. It takes two shakes of a donkey's tail to make a Visual Basic window with a title like this:

Figure 6-5: Visual Basic in Disguise

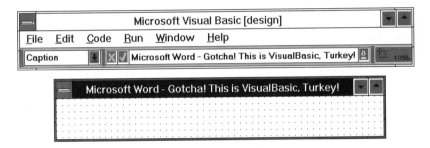

If you build a program that looks for WinWord windows by hopping through all the window titles and checking for "Microsoft Word," some day you may get burned.

Still, that approach is relatively easy to code. Something like this, perhaps, borrowed and slightly modified from the WinExplorer series:

```
hWnd = GetActiveWindow
hWnd = GetWindow(hWnd, GW_HWNDFIRST)
x = GetWindowText(hWnd, WindowText$, 200)
While hWnd <> 0 And Left$(WindowText$,14)<>"Microsoft Word"
     hWnd = GetWindow(hWnd, GW_HWNDNEXT)
     x = GetWindowText(hWnd, WindowText$, 200)
Wend
'Check here to be sure you have the right window
```

That's all it takes to find the hWnd of a Word for Windows window. By searching for a 15-character match with "Microsoft Excel," you can use the same code to stalk EXCEL windows.

But if you know the trick, there's a better way!

Class Names

If you had started Windows programming using C instead of the macro languages, you'd be struggling with window classes and class names right now.

Fortunately, we are "just" macro programmers; we can simply cut to the chase.

Every window has to be part of a class. That's how C programmers feed information to Windows—all windows in the "AlfredENeuman" class, say, have purple polka-dot backgrounds, need so much extra memory, do such-and-so when they're moved around, and minimize down to an icon with a wide, toothless grin. All sorts of garbage like that.

There is one thing about windows classes, though, that make them interesting for Mere Mortals. Windows classes have names. Not just any old names. Very specific names. Names we can use. In Windows, once you know something's name, you can control it.

In fact, if you know an application's class name, you can get at an hWnd with a one-line Windows API call! Here's how:

```
Declare Function FindWindow Lib "User"(ClassName$, n As Long) As\
  Integer

hWnd = FindWindow(ClassName$, 0)
```

FindWindow returns a zero if no windows of the indicated class are available. What could be simpler?

All you need is a list of Class Names. Here you go:

TABLE 6-1: CLASS NAMES

APPLICATION	CLASS NAME
Amí Pro	AmíProWndA
Cardfile	Cardfile
Clipboard	Clipboard
CorelDRAW! 2.0	CDraw2
EXCEL	XLMain
File Manager	WFS_FRAME
Notepad	Notepad
Paintbrush	pbParent
Program Manager	Progman
Print Manager	Printman
Visual Basic Design Time	ThunderForm
Visual Basic Run Time	ThunderForm
Windows Calculator	SciCalc

TABLE 6-1: CLASS NAMES (CONTINUED)

APPLICATION	CLASS NAME
Windows Help	MW_WINHELP
Windows Recorder	Recorder
Windows Write	MSWRITE_MENU
Word for Windows 1.x	OpusApp

Visual Basic apps can be run two different ways. We're listing them here as "Design Time"—that's when you click on "Run," then "Start," or push F5 while Visual Basic is alive—and "Run Time," after you've turned your Visual Basic app into a stand-alone package by clicking on "File," then "Make EXE File."

■ **TIP**

If you have more than one copy of a program running (or more than one Visual Basic program running), FindWindow may return an hWnd that doesn't correspond to the copy you thought you were getting. If that's a potential problem for you, make sure the copy you want can identify itself—with a Topic, perhaps, or an item that won't occur in other copies.

Admittedly, it isn't always easy finding class names. Some manufacturers seem to be a bit embarrassed by the creative names their programmers use. But if you try hard enough—and can find a tech support person who understands what a windows class *is*—you should be able to simplify your programming dramatically.

■ **TIP**

Alternatively, if you have a friend with the Windows SDK (you know, the guy who gave up a week in Cabo San Lucas to enrich Microsoft?), you can have your friend use the "Spy" application. It divulges Class Names in no time flat.

Module Names

If you're comfortable with the GetModuleHandle / IsAppLoaded Windows API call, you'll need module names.

The training-wheel approach:

```
If IsAppLoaded(ModuleName$)=0 Then ...
```

and the equivalent direct Windows API call:

```
If GetModuleHandle(ModuleName$)=0 Then ...
```

demand that you use a module name—not a window name or an application name or any other kind of name—even if you don't know a module name from a tuna fish sandwich.

Module names are established at a program's birth. The module name is set when a C programmer links a program. That's the last step in getting a C program to run. *Well, except for the debugging, of course.*

Part of the Link rigmarole is something called a module definition, and part of the module definition is a NAME for the module. If the programmer is nice to all of us, he, she, or it will forget to include the NAME parameter in the module definition. When there's no NAME specifically supplied, the module is assigned a very logical one: the eight characters that precede ".EXE" in the executable file.

Naturally, not all programmers are so kind.

Here are some of the most common module names, the ones you can use in GetModuleHandle or IsAppLoaded:

TABLE 6-2: MODULE NAMES

APPLICATION	MODULE NAME
Amí Pro	amipro
CorelDRAW! 2.0	waldo
DynaComm	dynacomm
EXCEL	excel
Visual Basic Design Time	vb
Visual Basic Run Time	name of the .EXE file
Word for Windows 1.x	OpusApp
Word for Windows 2.0	msword

Module names can be difficult to find, too. Usually the manufacturer can be coerced. If all else fails, find somebody with a copy of the Windows SDK and have him or her run Heapwalker. That lists Module Names of all active modules; with a bit of educated guesswork, you can usually find the right name.

Admittedly, "waldo" was a stretch!

B U G

If you rely on Module names to identify compiled Visual Basic programs, be careful. Because of the way Visual Basic registers its name internally, you should always include the ".EXE" in the Module name. For example, if you have a program called "JAWS", the correct way to look for that program is:

(Continued)

```
If GetModuleHandle("JAWS.EXE") Then ...
```

If you use the most logical Module name for JAWS you may or may not get the right answer! See how the executable file "excel.exe" is called "excel", "amipro.exe" is called "amipro", and so on? You might be tempted to use a call like this:

```
If GetModuleHandle("JAWS") Then ...
```

But if you do, the results are completely unpredictable. Some compiled Visual Basic programs will respond correctly; others won't. Even the usually infallible SDK Spy won't pick up the final ".EXE" in the Module name. It's infuriating if you don't realize what's happening... hell, it's infuriating if you do realize what's happening.

Application "Shell" Names
In the normal DDE way of doing things, once you've determined that a particular application is not running, you'll generally start it by shelling to it.

```
hWnd=FindWindow("OpusApp",0)
If hWnd = 0 Then
     Shell("winword.exe")
     hWnd=FindWindow("OpusApp",0)
End If
```

It probably won't surprise you that the name required in the Shell statement is not the same as the module name and it's not the same as the class name.

Nope. When you Shell, you're actually cranking up a program. A real program. Remember those? They're the ones with names that end in an ".EXE," or a ".COM," maybe a ".BAT"—even a ".PIF."

Shell file names obey all the old DOS rules: if the file isn't in your DOS Path, it better be in the current directory. If the file isn't on the Path or in the current directory, you better put the fully qualified file name in there. Like this:

```
If hWnd = 0 Then
    Shell("c:\winword\winword.exe")
```

One more name comes into play when attempting DDE.

DDE Server Names

Finally, before a Client can "dial the phone" in a DDE link, it has to know what name the Server will respond to. That name—the phone number of the Server, as it were—is called a DDE Server Name.

(Note that DDE *Clients* don't need names!)

Fortunately, some semblance of sanity reigns in the realm of Server Names. Most of the major Windows applications use the first characters of their Shell file name ".EXE" names as their Server names.

With one exception, of course. Toolbook. There's always one in a crowd:

TABLE 6-3: DDE SERVER NAMES

APPLICATION	DDE SERVER NAME
Amí Pro	amipro
Crosstalk	xtalk
Current	current
DynaComm	dynacomm
EXCEL	excel
Q + E	qe
PackRat	packrat
SuperBase 4	SB4W
Toolbook (TBOOK.EXE)	toolbook
Visual Basic Design Time	name of the .MAK file
Visual Basic Run Time	name of the .EXE file
Word for Windows 1.x and 2.0	winword

Finding DDE Server Names is remarkably difficult. In most cases, you're at the mercy of the manufacturer.

Una Rosa de Otra Nombre

> Rose is a rose is a rose is a rose.
>
> —Gertrude Stein, *Sacred Emily*, 1933

What do we have now, six *different* names?

Take Word for Windows, for example. *Please.*

There's the actual name of the application, the one we use every day (presumably "Word for Windows"). Then there's usually some variation of the application's name in window titles (like "Microsoft Word"). A class name

("OpusApp"). A module name ("msword"). A Shell file name ("winword.exe"). And now a DDE Server name ("winword").

Anybody got a scorecard?

Back to DDE.

The Real Story on Topics and Items

> Tout est pour le mieux dans le meilleur des mondes possibles.
>
> —Jean de Voltaire, *Candide*, 1759

In the best of all possible worlds, all Dynamic Data Exchange Servers would behave similarly.

Hey, we're talking Windows here. Not a chance.

Let's take a look at how the various major Windows applications behave as DDE Servers. But before we do, step back for a second and take in the big picture.

Why Sweat the Small Stuff?

You might think the nitty-gritty details of how each Windows application behaves under pressure—fending off the advances of DDE—makes little difference. After all, DDE is DDE is DDE, right?

Well, no. At least at this point, each Windows application has its own DDE personality. There's almost no uniformity in how the details are handled. In fact, the differences are so great that you may not be able to build your dream application because of the limitations! Before you take on a DDE project, it behooves you to test things a bit, look up the oddities here in Chapter 6, toss a DDE conversation out and see how that particular application behaves in that particular situation.

You'd be up the old creek without a paddle, for example, if you took on a project that required WordPerfect for Windows to act as a DDE Server. It doesn't. And nothing you can do (short of writing your own DDE interface!) will change that. You may get a great idea for feeding Ami Pro data from EXCEL function calls—and then discover that you need a really powerful 386 and a gazillion megabytes of memory to get both Ami Pro and EXCEL loaded, to initiate a DDE call.

Over the next few years, you'll probably discover that more and more of your programming time is taken up in making custom routines that work inside the major Windows applications, and custom routines that make those Windows apps talk to each other.

In a very real way, the Windows apps are just as much "Windows" as Windows itself! So if you're going to learn how to program Windows, you'll have to learn how to program the major Windows apps, too. And that means learning all the little, niggling details—and avoiding all the things that go bump in the night.

Awwwww, don't worry. It's really a lot of fun!

The System Topic

Whenever a Client tries to start a DDE conversation, it has to know two things: the DDE Server Name (or "phone number") and a Topic the Server will find acceptable.

In Visual Basic, WordBasic, and EXCEL, for example, the code for initiating a DDE conversation looks like this:

```
ControlName.LinkTopic = "DDEServerName|Topic"
ChannelNumber = DDEInitiate(DDEServerName$, Topic$)
=INITIATE("DDEServerName," "Topic")
```

Note how the DDE Server Name and Topic are absolute requirements. If either is missing, the link simply won't go through.

If Visual Basic wants to start a conversation with Word for Windows, say, using an (already open) file called "c:\winword\myfile.doc," the Visual Basic DDE Initiate command looks like this:

```
ControlName.LinkTopic = "winword|c:\winword\myfile.doc"
```

Which is all well and good, if your program *knows* that WinWord is running and it *knows* WinWord has an open document called "c:\winword\myfile\doc."

In the previous section of this chapter, we looked at myriad ways to determine if WinWord is loaded. We also saw how to get WinWord going if it isn't there.

But once our program knows WinWord is running, does it figure out which files are open? If WinWord only responds when fed a Topic that's an already-open file, how can our humble Visual Basic program discern which Topic will work?

It's a tough chicken-and-egg problem.

The designers of DDE provided a way to break the "I need a Topic to talk to you, but I have to talk to you in order to get a Topic" impasse. It's called the System Topic—and it is, quite literally, a Topic equal to "System."

Using the System Topic couldn't be simpler:

```
ControlName.LinkTopic = "DDEServerName|System"
ChannelNumber = DDEInitiate(DDEServerName$, "System")
=INITIATE("DDEServerName," "System")
```

Any DDE Client can try to get a link established with the System Topic.

Unfortunately, not every Windows application—not every Server—will respond to the System Topic. And among those that do, the response varies all over the place! The Lord must love standards, since He made so many of them.

Visual Basic's Response to the System Topic

Visual Basic doesn't support the System Topic, no way, no how. It won't respond to "System" during design time. It won't respond to "System" during run time. It won't respond to "System" at all, unless you write a custom program.

So much for Visual Basic.

WordBasic's Response to the System Topic

If you start a DDE conversation with Word for Windows using the System Topic, you can get at three different Items: "SysItems," "Topics," and "Formats."

That sounds complicated, but it isn't. Here's a Visual Basic program that starts a conversation with WordBasic using the System Topic, then asks for data from the Item called "Formats."

Figure 6-6: WordBasic System Topic, Formats

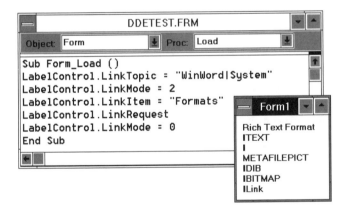

A couple of minor mysteries: those black blotches you can see in Form1 are Visual Basic's way of representing Chr$(9) tabs. WordBasic returns System Topic items in tab-delimited format, i.e., with tabs separating each entry. Oh, and you probably wondered what "Formats" these are! They're just the data formats Word for Windows supports when it passes data via DDE and in the Windows Clipboard.

Do you see now how the System Topic works? It gives your program a "hook" into WinWord, a way to establish communication when you don't really know which Topics are valid.

Here's what you get with the Item set to "Topics":

Figure 6-7: WordBasic System Topic, Topics

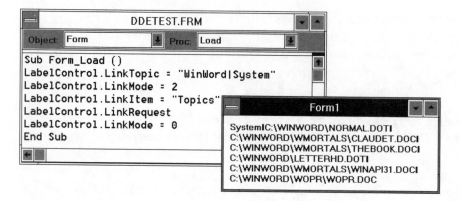

Aha! It's a complete list of all valid Topics for DDE conversations initiated, right *now*. WinWord really bends over backward on this one: it gives you fully qualified file names for all open documents, which is precisely what your program needs to set up a Topic in a DDE Initiate. And the list is truly complete: even the obscure behind-the-scenes WinWord templates (which don't show up normally on WinWord lists—but are still valid for DDE) and the System Topic (which is also perfectly valid as a DDE Topic) appear on the list.

For the third valid Item in the System Topic, with Item set to "SysItems":

Figure 6-8: WordBasic System Topic, SysItems

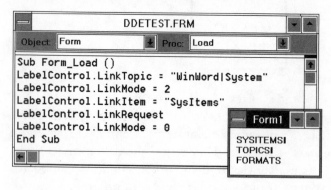

It's a list of all the "Items" that are valid while a conversation is under way with the System Topic.

Recapping for a second. When you start a DDE conversation with WordBasic using the System Topic, you can use DDE Request to get at three different tab-delimited lists, depending on the Item in that DDE Request:

- Item = "SysItems"—lists all of the valid Items, i.e., the three Items you see right here, "SysItems," "Formats," and "Topics."
- Item="Formats"—lists all of the formats Word for Windows currently supports for transferring data to and from the Clipboard. (If you ever need this list, be careful! The names are mixed upper/lowercase, and the abbreviations can be a tad nonstandard.)
- Item="Topics"—a very complete list of all valid Topics for initiating a DDE conversation. Includes "System" and all the hidden templates that WinWord usually keeps behind the scenes.

If you've been wondering all this time how to get at a list of valid Topics for initiating DDE with Word for Windows, well, now you know.

EXCEL's Response to the System Topic

EXCEL has all sorts of items set up and ready for a DDE System Topic inquiry.

Figure 6-9: EXCEL System Topic, SysItems

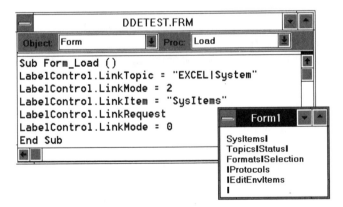

Note how this SysItems list is just a little bit different from the WordBasic list. Although EXCEL has a tab-delimited list just like WinWord, there's an extra tab at the end. That's not important—until you try to write a program that massages the SysItems list.

Let's take each of the EXCEL SysItems in turn. They're a touch different from WinWord's.

EXCEL SysItem "Topics" The "Topics" are . . . uh . . . valid Topics:

Figure 6-10: EXCEL System Topic, Topics

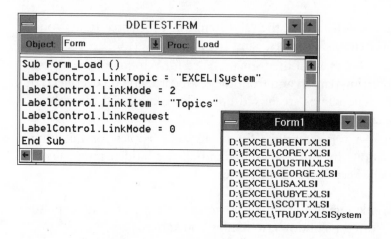

EXCEL gives a list of all valid Topics, just like WinWord. They're all fully qualified file names, and they'll all work immediately as DDE Initiate Topics. The "System" Topic appears at the end of the list. And, unlike SysItems, there's no dangling tab at the very end.

Pretty normal.

EXCEL SysItem "Status" The "Status" SysItem returns either "Ready" or "Busy"—character strings, without the quotes. Generally, there's no need to worry about whether EXCEL is ready: DDE commands just back up in the queue and get released when EXCEL is ready for them.

There are a few exceptions to that generalization, though:

- If the DDE command being shot at EXCEL requires some sort of acknowledgment—even a behind-the-scenes one—the Client may Time Out waiting for EXCEL to come to its senses. There's a trick you can use, though, and we'll talk about it here shortly.

- If there are lots of DDE commands backing up, the queue limit kicks in. In EXCEL, at most eight DDE commands can stand in line (unless you dig into the deep recesses of Windows and change it!). The ninth DDE command gets relegated to the unforgiving bit bucket, and EXCEL will never see it.

- If your program has some sort of weird time-dependent DDE command, *"Yo! EXCEL! Do this right now or you'll lose this data!,"* the Client would be well-advised to make sure EXCEL is Ready before sending the command.

EXCEL SysItem "Formats" Much like WordBasic, the EXCEL Formats are acceptable Clipboard and DDE data formats:

Figure 6-11: EXCEL System Topic, Formats

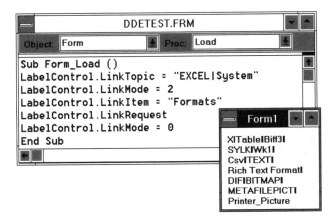

Note the hodgepodge of upper and lower case. The first Format listed, for example, is "XLTable," but the "L" is lowercase. If you're trying to program with this stuff, matching strings inside your program, be careful!

Surprisingly, WinWord 2.0 lists two DDE/Clipboard formats that are not listed in EXCEL 3.0—Device Independent Bitmaps, or DIBs, and the "Link" format.

EXCEL SysItem "Selection" This SysItem returns the current selection:

Figure 6-12: EXCEL System Topic, Selection

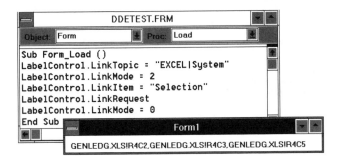

Note how a discontinuous selection is returned, with each fully qualified cell name separated by commas.

EXCEL SysItem "Protocols" Finally, EXCEL can tell you what sort of editing protocols are permitted. There are only two; StdFileEditing and Embedding, as shown in Figure 6-13.

Figure 6-13: EXCEL System Topic, Protocols

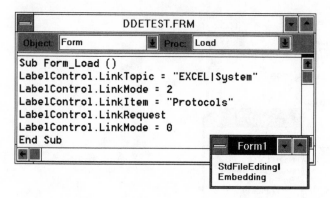

"Embedding" is a reference to Object Linking and Embedding.

The listing for "EditEnvItems" is equally enlightening. It returns "StdHost-Names" and "StdTargetDevice."

Amí Pro's Response to the System Topic

Amí Pro has a few tricks up its sleeve:

Figure 6-14: Amí Pro System Topic, SysItems

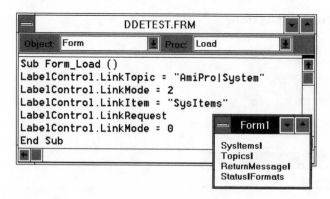

One of Amí Pro's Topics is "Remote Control"—and that's a dynamite idea. You'll see why in a second. The other SysItems are similar to what we've encountered before.

Using the System Topic for DDE Execute

Sometimes you don't care which WinWord files are loaded, whose EXCEL spreadsheets have been opened, which Superbase databases are available, when specific Visual Basic Forms or DynaComm scripts come up—in other words, you couldn't care less what Topic is appropriate.

That's particularly common when you want to take matters into your own program's hands, when you want to use DDE Execute to take control of the Server and do with it what you will. The "System" Topic is ideally suited for those occasions; we'll be using the System Topic exclusively inside CoolCons.

Here's a real-world example. Let's use Visual Basic as the Client and EXCEL as the Server (we'll assume for the moment that EXCEL is running). Say you want to use Visual Basic to open a specific spreadsheet, "d:\excel\genledg.xls," in EXCEL. You then want to retrieve the value in row 4, column 2 and place that value in your Visual Basic program's LabelControl.

Piece of cake.

Figure 6-15: Using System Topic to Load a Spreadsheet

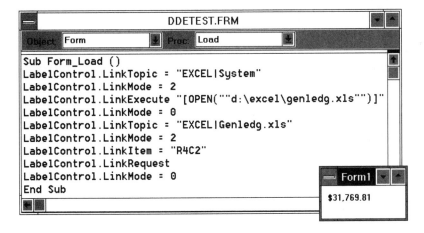

Let's step through that slowly.

First, Visual Basic establishes a Cold link with EXCEL, using the "System" Topic. Because we are assuming that EXCEL is already running, and we know that EXCEL always responds to the System Topic, all it takes is:

```
LabelControl.LinkTopic = "EXCEL|System"
LabelControl.LinkMode = 2
```

Next, we want EXCEL to run the command that will open the file we're look-ing for, OPEN("d:\excel\genledg.xls"). Using DDE Execute that's easy:

```
LabelControl.LinkExecute "[OPEN(""d:\excel\genledg.xls"")]"
```

Note how the doubled-up double-quotes make that command nice and short.

Now that we've opened up the file we need, the System Topic link loses its usefulness. Being good DDE citizens, we hang up the phone:

```
LabelControl.LinkMode = 0
```

All that's left is retrieving the contents of Genledg.xls, Row 4, Column 2, plac-ing it in the LabelControl, and hanging up once again:

```
LabelControl.LinkTopic = "EXCEL|Genledg.xls"
LabelControl.LinkMode = 2
LabelControl.LinkItem = "R4C2"
LabelControl.LinkRequest
LabelControl.LinkMode = 0
```

By any way of thinking, that's a nontrivial DDE application. And it took a whopping nine lines of Visual Basic code.

Remote Control in Amí Pro
In Amí Pro, the System Topic needn't do double duty. There's an almost-undocu-mented setting called "RemoteControl" that does everything the System Topic does, except return SysItems.

When using DDE Execute in Amí Pro, instead of relying on the System Topic, set the Topic to "RemoteControl" (all one word). It'll make the Samna/Lotus folks sleep better at night.

Hot, Cold, and the Missing Warm Link

Everything we've done so far has been based on Cold links.

That's good. Cold links are the ones least likely to go bump in the night.

Hot Diggety
A Hot link keeps data updated continuously. Whenever data in the Server changes, the Client is updated almost immediately.

Here's a simple demo of a Hot link, using Visual Basic as Client and EXCEL as Server. We'll set up a Hot link between the Control called LabelControl and the very first spreadsheet cell in "Sheet1.xls."

Once the Hot link is established, every time the user types something into that first spreadsheet cell, the Visual Basic control is updated, automatically and almost instantaneously. Like this:

Figure 6-16: Hot Link

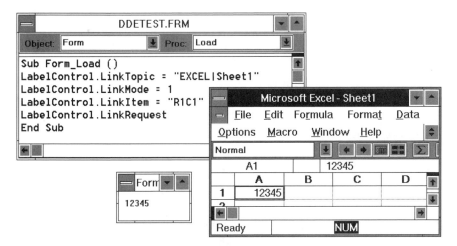

Four lines of Visual Basic code, and you have a working Hot link in place with EXCEL. Change cell A1 in EXCEL, and the Visual Basic LabelControl is immediately updated with that new value. This is incredible!

Where's the Warm Link?

You've seen Cold links in action. They just kind of sit there, waiting for the Client to do something.

You've just seen at least one Hot link in action. Hot links keep the Client posted on any changes in "DDE Request" requested data.

There's a hybrid link that you haven't seen, though. *A Missing Link.* The Warm link.

Why haven't you seen a Warm link? Because Warm links aren't implemented very well—if at all. Amí Pro has a Warm link capability (sort of, via the DDEAdvise command). Other Windows applications nibble at the edges of Warm links, with varying degrees of success. But by and large the Warm link isn't used very often. Visual Basic and WordBasic don't have *any support at all* for Warm links.

B U G

Some books and articles say the Visual Basic LinkMode setting of "1" is for a Warm link. No way. The Visual Basic LinkMode 1 is a Hot link, pure and simple.

In theory, the Warm link works something like this:

- The Client calls the Server, picks a Topic and Item, and specifies a Warm link. (In C-speak that's an fDeferUpd setting in the WM_DDE_ADVISE message. If it weren't for the C definition, you might thing that the Warm link was a figment of some manual writer's grotesque imagination!)
- Whenever the Item data changes in the Server application, the Server notifies the Client that there's new data available. (In C-speak, the Server sends a WM_DDE_DATA message to the Client with a null hData. *Aren't you glad you aren't using C to do DDE?*)
- If the Client decides it wants the new data, it sends a regular old DDE Request to the Server (in C that's a WM_DDE_REQUEST), asking for an update.

Check that sequence against your favorite DDE application. Chances are very good there is no way to make note of an incoming "Data Has Changed" message, much less automatically trigger or avoid a DDE Request.

Some Like It Cold

T I P

Unless you have a very, very specific reason for maintaining a Hot link, keep 'em Cold. Cold links are much simpler, much less prone to the accidents that seem to happen from time to time.

The DDE Execute Trick

Ah, the moment you've been waiting for!

There is one trick that can make a huge difference in your use of DDE, particularly if you use DDE Execute statements.

The trick just happens to be a key component of CoolCons. It's presented here for the first time.

The Time Out Problem

> You must remember this:
> A kiss is just a kiss,
> A sigh is just a sigh—
> The fundamental things apply
> As time goes by.
>
> —Herman Hupfeld, "As Time Goes By," *Casablanca*, 1942

There's a clock ticking behind every DDE interaction. The Time Out clock. The DDE gods start that clock ticking every time there's a DDE command tossed into the Windows ooze. If no response is forthcoming within the allotted time, the DDE gods shut everything down and hang up the phone.

Of the major Windows applications, only Visual Basic lets you set the amount of time on that infernal stopwatch. All the others just roll over and die after five to ten seconds. And there's nothing you can do.

Well, almost nothing. Which is to say, there is something you *can* do about it. A kludge. A trick. A lifesaver, should you be confronted with the Time Out blues.

Here's an example. Let's put Visual Basic in the Client's chair again, and WordBasic will serve as Server. Suppose you want to open a new document inside Word for Windows, insert some text, and then save the file, all under the control of Visual Basic.

After scouring through the WordBasic manual for a few minutes, you might be tempted to write a very simple program like this:

Figure 6-17: DDE Hello, Word!

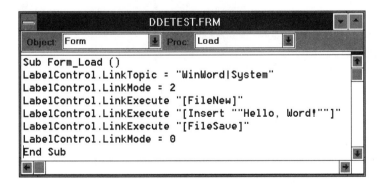

That sure looks like a good program. Short and sweet. Well, try running it. This is what happens:

First, the Word for Windows window (or icon) starts blinking like crazy. WinWord wants you. But no matter how hard you try clicking on the WinWord window (or icon), it won't respond. It keeps on blinking. The Visual Basic window in Figure 6-17 has the Focus and won't let go.

The flashing lights continue for about five seconds (sounds suspicious, eh?). Then this message box pops up:

Figure 6-18: Visual Basic Times Out

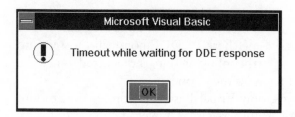

Something's wrong. You click OK to get rid of the Time Out message, and this pops up over your Word for Windows window:

Figure 6-19: Save As—The Culprit

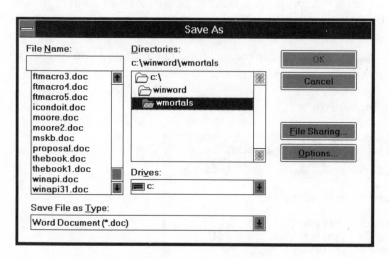

You click on Cancel and trigger yet another error, as is shown in Figure 6-20 on the following page.

Figure 6-20: You're Telling Me!

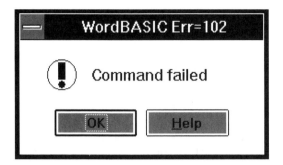

Once all the errors have cleared out and you can get back to your document, you discover that it hasn't been saved:

Figure 6-21: Document5 Isn't Saved

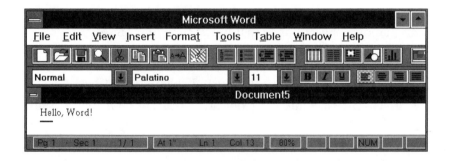

You know it hasn't been saved because "Document5" isn't a valid (eight-character-maximum) file name.

So, what went wrong?

Let's step through the Visual Basic code and see. The first two lines establish a Cold DDE link with WinWord's System Topic:

```
LabelControl.LinkTopic = "WinWord|System"
LabelControl.LinkMode = 2
```

Apparently that part went fine. You know the link was established because the next Visual Basic command was executed, and a new file ("Document5") was created:

```
LabelControl.LinkExecute "[FileNew]"
```

And you know *that* line worked fine, because the next line worked; "Hello, Word!" was inserted into Document5:

```
LabelControl.LinkExecute "[Insert ""Hello, Word!""]"
```

Looks like we've narrowed it down to one possibility.

The Problem with User Input

> When you have eliminated the impossible, whatever
> remains, however improbable, must be the truth.
>
> —Sir Arthur Conan Doyle, *The Sign of Four*, 1890

That FileSave must be the culprit.

```
LabelControl.LinkExecute "[FileSave]"
```

The problem with WordBasic's FileSave indeed, the problem with many DDE Execute commands in most applications, is that it demands a user response.

Here's what's happening behind the scenes:

- Visual Basic sends the DDE Execute command [FileSave] to WordBasic.

- The DDE gods start that infernal stopwatch: the Time Out clock starts ticking. *Tick. Tick. Tick.*

- WordBasic gets that [FileSave]. It needs a file name—this is a new file, it hasn't ever been saved before, so it needs a name. WordBasic slaps the File Save dialog box up on the screen, asking the user to pick a name. Tick. *Tick. Tick.*

- Visual Basic keeps the focus. Unless your program specifically changes focus over to Word for Windows, your Visual Basic program holds onto it. Meanwhile, the Visual Basic program is still "stuck" on the LinkExecute [FileSave] statement. WordBasic hasn't responded. The Word for Windows window starts flashing: it needs input. Could something be wrong? *Tick. Tick. Tick.*

- *Tick. Tick. Tick. BZZT.* Five seconds pass and the Time Out stopwatch goes off. The DDE gods intervene. WordBasic isn't responding. Something must be wrong. The DDE gods raise an Error Condition in Visual Basic and cut off the DDE link.

- Visual Basic gets the Error Condition and puts up its standard "Time Out" dialog box. It's a modal dialog box, so the user can't do anything until it's been satisfied. Word for Windows keeps flashing until the user finally has a chance to click on it, giving it focus. Ultimately the user gets back to Word for Windows, sees the File Save dialog box, and puts WinWord out of its misery.

Not a pretty sight.

The real clincher: this same sequence happens with *any* DDE Execute statement that requires user input. Which is to say it happens with a very large percentage of DDE Executable commands in any Windows application: Visual Basic, Word for Windows, EXCEL, Amí Pro, you name it. It's a congenital defect.

Unfortunately, DDE is set up so the Server has to send a message back to the Client saying, in effect, "Yes, Master. The DDE Execute you ordered has now finished."

It would all work fine if DDE were designed so that the Server could send a message back to the Client saying, "Yo! I got the DDE Execute, dude. Now *get off my back and let me run it.*" But it doesn't work that way.

That's the problem.

Some Possible Solutions

Several possibilities present themselves.

Yes, your program can send focus to the Server, using an hWnd and the Windows SetFocus(hWnd) API call. Your program can jack up the Time Out interval to thirty seconds, or two minutes, or an hour. You can do something like this:

```
Declare Function FindWindow Lib "user" (ByVal ClassName$, ByVal n\
  As Long) As Integer
Declare Function SetFocusAPI Lib "User" Alias "SetFocus" (ByVal\
  hWnd As Integer) As Integer

hWndWinWord = FindWindow("OpusApp", 0)
n = SetFocusAPI(hWndWinWord)
LabelControl.LinkTopic = "WinWord|System"
LabelControl.LinkTimeout = 100
LabelControl.LinkMode = 2
LabelControl.LinkExecute "[FileNew]"
LabelControl.LinkExecute "[Insert ""Hello, Word!""]"
LabelControl.LinkExecute "[FileSave]"
```

There are three problems (at least!) with that approach:

- Visual Basic can set the Time Out if it is the Client, but that method won't help one whit if WordBasic or EXCEL or Amí Pro is the Client.

- You don't *really* want to change the Time Out anyway. It's a safety net, a way to iron things out if the Server suddenly disappears in the middle of a DDE conversation. Take away that safety net, and your user could be confronted with The DDE That Wouldn't Die. And unless the user knows how to cancel an in-progress DDE conversation, it'll be Vulcan nerve-pinch time (Control+Alt+Delete).

- The SetFocusAPI call doesn't always behave the way you think it should. Triggering a dialog box in a DDE Execute, with focus shuffled to the Server application, can send Windows into an odd never-never land: you may think the dialog box has focus; it may look like the dialog box has focus; but your users may not be able to click on any of the buttons and have the click "take." It's bizarre behavior that occurs intermittently, but when it *does* happen, the only solution is to wait for a Time Out.

So much for things that don't work.

The OnTime Shoe Drops

WordBasic, EXCEL, and Amí Pro all have the ability to defer execution of a specified command or macro.

In WordBasic, for example, this little bit of code will run the "FileSave" command at 6:00 p.m.:

```
OnTime "18:00", "FileSave"
```

When WordBasic hits an OnTime like that, it stores the command away and schedules an Event *(remember Events? good!)* to take place at 6:00 in the evening. When the Event is triggered, the indicated macro is executed (assuming WinWord itself is still running of course): at 6:00, FileSave will be run.

There are some nuances: in WordBasic, only one OnTime can be active at a time—poor WinWord has but one clock it can shanghai. The command will actually be run any time *after* 6:00 p.m. There are some other switches and stuff you can tack onto the OnTime command.

In EXCEL there's a very similar command:

```
ON.TIME("6:00:00 PM", "Save()")
```

which behaves in precisely the same way. If EXCEL encounters that command at 6:30 p.m., it'll run the Save() immediately.

In Amí Pro, OnTime is only slightly different:

```
RunLater("Save()", "00:00.30")
```

RunLater specifies how long Ami Pro is to wait before running the indicated command. In this example, Ami Pro should wait 30 seconds before running Save( ).

By using OnTime, the DDE gods can be tricked!

DDE Götterdämmerung . . .

Instead of running the program in Figure 6-17 and worrying about whether the user will respond quickly enough, we need only change one line of code—and have the FileSave run as an OnTime!

It looks like this:

Figure 6-22: OnTime to the Rescue

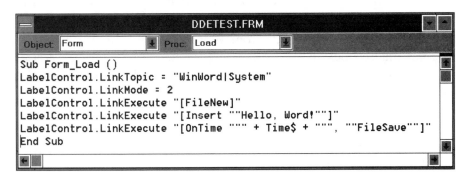

```
Sub Form_Load ()
LabelControl.LinkTopic = "WinWord|System"
LabelControl.LinkMode = 2
LabelControl.LinkExecute "[FileNew]"
LabelControl.LinkExecute "[Insert ""Hello, Word!""]"
LabelControl.LinkExecute "[OnTime """ + Time$ + """, ""FileSave""]"
End Sub
```

Here's the original line of code, the one that threw DDE into spasms:

```
LabelControl.LinkExecute "[FileSave]"
```

Here's the new line, the one that works:

```
LabelControl.LinkExecute "[OnTime """ + Time$ + """, ""FileSave""]"
```

Taking advantage of the Visual Basic Time$ function, which simply returns the current time, and collapsing all those wonderful double-quotes into something we humans can read, this new line sends a DDE Execute command to WordBasic that says:

```
[OnTime "12:34:56", "FileSave"]
```

where "12:34:56" is just the current time.

Visual Basic is saying to WordBasic, "Run this command—FileSave—at a specific time . . . and *that time is right now!*"

Here's what happens behind the scenes:

- Visual Basic sends the DDE Execute command [OnTime ...] to WordBasic.

- The DDE gods start that lousy stopwatch again. The Time Out clock starts ticking. *Tick. Tick. Tick.*

- WordBasic gets that [OnTime ...]. Oh goody. A real Event that needs scheduling. *(WordBasic doesn't see enough real Events, by half. You can tell by the light in its eyes.)* WordBasic posts the FileSave, to be run at the specified time. *Tick. Tick. Tick.*

- WordBasic has taken care of the DDE Execute [On Time ...] command. It sends a message back to the DDE gods that all is hunky-dory. *Tick. Tick. Tick.*

- The DDE gods see the message from WordBasic. Wow, that was quick. Just a few milliseconds and WordBasic is all done. *(And you were worried, huh?)* The DDE gods click off the stopwatch and send to Visual Basic the all-clear.

- In less than the blink of an eye, Word for Windows gets hit with an On Time event—after all, the time set for that Event is right *now*. WordBasic handles the Event by running the indicated command, File Save. The user gets a File Save dialog box and can take as long as he or she likes to play with it: there's no stopwatch clicking away.

- About the same time, Visual Basic gets an OK from the DDE gods and continues doing its thing. All is right in this, the best of all possible worlds.

That one little trick—OnTime in a DDE Execute—suddenly makes it possible to run any command with a DDE Execute, without fear of a Time Out. It's a pretty big deal, if you ever hit the problem.

DDE Daisy Chains

The basic, simple telephone-call underpinnings of DDE are so powerful, they will let you create totally awesome entwined masses of programs. It's a real hacker's delight, and you don't have to be a C programmer or Pascal guru to partake in the festivities.

Let's take a look at just one possibility: Visual Basic calls WordBasic and tells WordBasic to drop off some important information by calling back on a different line.

Sounds complicated? It isn't.

Here's the fun part: all it takes is *one* program—a Visual Basic program. With the necessary WordBasic program embedded inside.

Ever see "Alien"? Remember the first time one of those cool little aliens popped out of its human incubator? Minus a little gore and special effects, that's exactly what we're going to do right here.

Feed Me Bookmarks

Once again we'll draw on a problem posed—and solved, albeit somewhat differently—by George Mair.

The question is reasonable enough: working with Visual Basic as Client and WordBasic as Server, how can we find out which Items are available for a DDE Poke?

If you recall, WordBasic will accept a DDE Poke with an Item name that is a bookmark in the current document.

Our problem boils down to this: with Visual Basic as Client and WordBasic as Server, how can we coerce WordBasic to send Visual Basic a list of all the bookmarks in the current document?

You'd think such an obvious request would be mighty easy to fulfill. After all, if your program wants a list of all valid Topics, all it has to do is initiate a DDE conversation with the Topic set to "System," then set the Item to "Topics" and run a DDE Request. We did just that a few pages back. Nothing to it.

Retrieving a list of all valid Items isn't nearly so simple. Unless you know the trick, of course!

What Would WordBasic Do?

If all we had to worry about was WordBasic, shipping a list of bookmarks to Visual Basic would be easy.

After rummaging through the manuals and tinkering for a bit, you'd discover that this code creates a list of available bookmarks and puts them in a variable called Bmarks$, each one separated with a tab (Chr$(9)):

```
For i=1 to CountBookmarks()
Bmarks$ = Bmarks$ + Chr$(9) + BookmarkName$(i)
Next i
```

Once the list of bookmarks is complete, sending it to Visual Basic is easy. Let's assume we have a Visual Basic program called "DDETest"; it has one form, called "Form1"; and on that form there is a label control called . . . uh . . . LabelControl.

Slapping all the bookmarks into LabelControl is another three-liner (where "cn" is the Channel Number):

```
cn=DDEInitiate("DDETest","Form1")
DDEPoke cn, "LabelControl",Bmarks$
DDETerminate cn
```

Hate to tell you this, but you've already solved the whole problem!

Insert Tab "A" in Slot "B"

Once you've figured out the WordBasic code necessary to solve the problem, all that remains is shoe-horning the program into Visual Basic and setting up Visual Basic to DDE Execute the program over to WordBasic!

It's a whole lot simpler than it sounds.

Figure 6-23: A DDE Daisy Chain

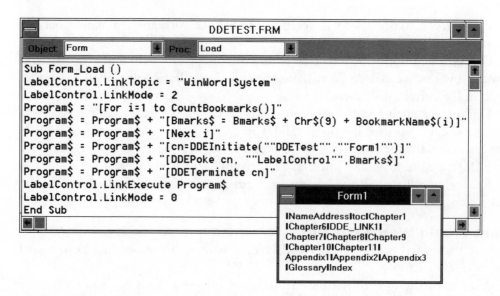

Let's step through that one slowly.

Recall that DDE Execute commands may be chained together. For example,

```
DDEExecute(ChannelNumber, "[Command1][Command2][Command3]")
```

is the same as running a program that looks like this:

```
Command1
Command2
Command3
```

First, the Visual Basic program in Figure 6-23 establishes a Cold link with Word for Windows. Using the "System" Topic guarantees that we'll be looking at the current active document.

```
LabelControl.LinkTopic = "WinWord|System"
LabelControl.LinkMode = 2
```

That's easy. Next we build up a long, long string called "Program$." Program$ is the six-line WordBasic program we worked out a few seconds ago to DDE Poke all the bookmark names into the LabelControl. (Actually, we could've put all this on one line, but it would've been harder to see here in the book.)

```
Program$ = "[For i=1 to CountBookmarks()]"
Program$ = Program$ + "[Bmarks$=Bmarks$ + Chr$(9) + BookmarkName$(i)]"
Program$ = Program$ + "[Next i]"
Program$ = Program$ + "[cn=DDEInitiate(""DDETest"",""Form1"")]"
Program$ = Program$ + "[DDEPoke cn, ""LabelControl"",Bmarks$]"
Program$ = Program$ + "[DDETerminate cn]"
```

Finally, with the Cold link already established, we DDE Execute that Program$ over in WordBasic and then hang up the phone.

```
LabelControl.LinkExecute Program$
LabelControl.LinkMode = 0
```

You can see the result in Figure 6-23. All of the current bookmark names—all of the valid DDE Poke Items—have been placed in LabelControl, in Form1.

Wow

The solution to the "What can I Poke?" problem is so simple and elegant that it's really quite amazing. And it only begins to hint at the power available to you through DDE.

Worth noting: it may not be immediately obvious, but the program in Figure 6-23 uses and re-uses Controls in various ways, and Visual Basic manages to keep it all sorted out. The Label Control called "LabelControl," in particular, is used both as a DDE Client and as a DDE Server, *at the same time*. While LabelControl is running the Visual Basic LinkExecute command—feeding commands to WordBasic—it's doing double-duty as the recipient of all the incoming data.

A DDE Cookbook—Caveat au Gratin

Here's the most-requested part of *WinMortals*. A truly quick and dirty guide to Dynamic Data Exchange.

For best results, read all of Chapter 6 before trying to use these snippets of code.

The concepts behind DDE are quite simple. Unfortunately, the actual *implementation* of those concepts can get pretty hairy. So make sure you understand how to dial the DDE telephone before you try to call-forward instructions to yourself about how to call-forward instructions to yourself about how to call-forward instructions to yourself.

Visual Basic as Client

In Visual Basic, Clients are Label, Picture Box, or Text Box Controls.

A typical Cold link DDE Execute goes like this:

```
AppName$ = "WinWord"
Topic$ = "System"
On Error GoTo BadApp
ControlName.LinkTopic = AppName$ + "|" + Topic$
ControlName.LinkMode = 2
On Error GoTo 0
ControlName.LinkExecute Program$
ControlName.LinkMode = 0
ExitSub
BadApp:
TaskID = Shell(AppName$)
DoEvents()
Resume
```

The .LinkMode Property actually establishes the DDE link: "Cold" is 2, "Hot" is 1. (Some books say there's a Warm link. They're wrong.) To break the link, set the .LinkMode to 0.

Note how the IsAppLoaded/GetModuleHandle approach isn't necessary.

The DoEvents() command forces Visual Basic to twiddle its thumbs for a few milliseconds while Windows catches up with pending activities. In this case, it gives Windows enough time to load the application before Visual Basic continues with the program.

A typical Cold link DDE Request goes like this:

```
AppName$ = "WinWord"
Topic$ = "c:\winword\AnyOpen.DOC"
On Error GoTo BadApp
ControlName.LinkTopic = AppName$ + "|" + Topic$
ControlName.LinkMode = 2
On Error GoTo 0
ControlName.LinkItem = "SomeBookmark"
ControlName.LinkRequest
ControlName.LinkMode = 0
ExitSub
BadApp:
TaskID = Shell(AppName$ + " " + Topic$)
DoEvents()
Resume
```

By Shelling to the Application Name and Topic, you'll *usually* get the Topic document loaded.

A typical Cold link DDE Poke:

```
AppName$ = "WinWord"
Topic$ = "c:\winword\AnyOpen.DOC"
On Error GoTo BadApp
ControlName.LinkTopic = AppName$ + "|" + Topic$
ControlName.LinkMode = 2
On Error GoTo 0
ControlName.LinkItem = "SomeBookmark"
ControlName.Caption = "The stuff that will be poked"
ControlName.LinkPoke
ControlName.LinkMode = 0
ExitSub
BadApp:
TaskID = Shell(AppName$ + " " + Topic$)
DoEvents()
Resume
```

When the Client Control is a Label, set the Caption Property. When it's a Text Box, set the Text Property. When it's a Picture Box, set the Picture Property.

You may change the DDE Time Out interval with:

```
ControlName.LinkTimeOut = 100
```

The Time Out period is in tenths of a second; this 100 would call for a 10-second Time Out interval.

BUG

Sometimes, when you're attempting a Windows API call, Visual Basic gives bogus "Argument Count Mismatch" errors—several lines above or below the offender. If you get that error message, make sure to check around the highlighted line to see if Visual Basic is off by a line or two.

■ TIP

Sometimes you want to Shell out to another application (to get it kick-started for DDE, for example), and then immediately bring the Focus back to Visual Basic. Try this:

```
Declare Function GetActiveWindow Lib "User" () As Integer
Declare Function GetWindowText Lib "User" (ByVal hWnd As Integer,\
 ByVal WindowTitle$, ByVal max As Integer) As Integer
SpaceHolder$=String$(255,0)
CurrhWnd=GetActiveWindow()
Len=GetWindowText(CurrhWnd, SpaceHolder$, 255)
```

```
WindowTitle$=Left$(SpaceHolder$,Len)
' Do your shelling here
AppActivate WindowTitle$
```

Using the Visual Basic AppActivate command seems to be more reliable than the Windows SetFocusAPI command.

B U G

Controls used as Clients in Visual Basic must be "attached" to the Form itself. A Client Control cannot be placed on another Control. Among other things, this means you cannot draw a frame around a Client Control (i.e., you cannot place a Frame on the Form, then place a Control on the Frame, and expect to use that Control as a Client). This is clearly a bug in Visual Basic. Microsoft has a workaround—use an invisible Control (one with the Visible Property set to zero), and rig the InvisibleControl_Change event so it copies the data received via DDE to whatever Control you like.

B U G

Always hang up the phone—set .LinkMode to zero—before closing a Form. Otherwise, the LinkClose Event can crash.

■ T I P

This should be obvious, but you never know. Before resetting the .LinkTopic on a Client Control, make sure there's no active DDE conversation going with that Control. Set .LinkMode to zero if need be.

Visual Basic as Server

In Visual Basic, Forms are Servers.

The Application name is either the name of the ".MAK" file (if Visual Basic is in design time), or the name of the ".EXE" file (if you're running a Visual Basic program that's been converted to an .EXE file).

Visual Basic will not respond to the "System" Topic.

Visual Basic responds to DDE Requests and DDE Pokes, providing the correct Form name is used as the Topic and an appropriate Control name is used as the Item.

If you want to change the Form name—that is, change the Topic that will respond to a DDE Initiate—set the .LinkTopic property on the Server form.

You may ensure that a Visual Basic Form does not respond to *any* DDE activity by setting the .LinkMode property to zero.

Visual Basic does not automatically handle DDE Executes. You must specifically write a routine that handles each individual Execute command string and attach it to the Form_LinkExecute Event. Here's an example from Chapter 6:

```
Sub Form_LinkExecute (CmdStr As String, Cancel As Integer)
Cancel=0
If CmdStr = "ShowMsgBoxAndQuitTurkey" Then
    MsgBox "I give up!"
    End
End If
End Sub
```

The Cancel variable in the LinkExecute Event gives you great control over the inner workings of DDE. If you set "Cancel" to any value except zero, DDE will report back to the Client that the Server (Visual Basic) refused to take on the DDE Execute. Of course, in the meantime your LinkExecute Event Handler could've done most anything.

BUG

The manual says that Cancel is automatically set to zero, or False. Wrong. Cancel starts out True. For best results, set it yourself.

Because you write the LinkExecute Event Handlers, you can have Visual Basic respond to any DDE Execute command. DDE Executes don't have to have the [hokey square brackets] that are *de riguer* with other applications.

BUG

Beware the LinkClose Event! (Now you know why we didn't talk about it.) Windows will crash if you use the LinkClose Event to change the Caption property of a Label Control, the Text Property of a Text Box Control, or the Picture Property of a Picture Control in any Form involved as a DDE Server. In other words, don't use LinkClose to change any property that *could* be changed by a DDE command. Windows dies, sure as the morning sun. It's a bug. Microsoft has a workaround: instead of changing the property in LinkClose, have LinkClose start up a timer and change the properties a split-second later in the Timern_Timer Event.

■ T I P

This one could really jump up and bite you some day. When an application sets up a Hot link with Visual Basic as Server, there are problems updating Picture Box controls. Visual Basic does just fine as a Hot link Server with Text data: the Client is notified immediately of any changes. But Visual Basic does not, will not, can not, notify the Client when a Picture Box Control changes. You have to do that manually with a .LinkSend method.

It looks like this:

```
PictureControl.LinkSend
```

There's one exception: the Client is notified on a LoadPicture event. Confusing? Yeah.

B U G

Always hang up the phone—set .LinkMode to zero—before closing a Form. Otherwise, the LinkClose Event can crash.

WordBasic as Client

All WordBasic links are Cold. (You can establish Hot links, but they must be done with Word for Windows fields.)

Here's a typical DDE Execute from WordBasic. Try this as an alternative to the IsAppLoaded/GetModuleHandle routine you'll find in the manuals. (Table 6-1 gives an extensive list of Class Names.)

The FindWindow approach will give you the "hWnd" window handle of the Server application, in case you need it:

```
Declare Function FindWindow Lib "user" (ClassName$, n As Long) As\
  Integer
AppName$="EXCEL"
ClassName$="XLMain"
Topic$="System"
hWndEXCEL=FindWindow(ClassName$,0)
If hWndEXCEL=0 Then
     Shell(AppName$)
     hWndEXCEL=FindWindow(ClassName$,0)
End If
ChannelNumber=DDEInitiate(AppName$,Topic$)
DDEExecute "[AppRestore()]"
DDETerminate ChannelNumber
```

Here's a typical DDE Request, going after, say, EXCEL cell A1 (R1C1) in the file c:\excel\anyopen.xls:

```
Declare Function FindWindow Lib "user" (ClassName$, n As Long) As\
  Integer
AppName$="EXCEL"
ClassName$="XLMain"
Item$="R1C1"
Topic$="c:\excel\anyopen.xls"
hWndEXCEL=FindWindow(ClassName$,0)
If hWndEXCEL=0 Then
     Shell(AppName$ + " " + Topic$)
     hWndEXCEL=FindWindow(ClassName$,0)
End If
ChannelNumber=DDEInitiate(AppName$,Topic$)
CellA1Stuff$=DDERequest(ChannelNumber,Item$)
DDETerminate ChannelNumber
```

And here's a DDE Poke, to the same cell:

```
Declare Function FindWindow Lib "user" (ClassName$, n As Long) As\
  Integer
AppName$="EXCEL"
ClassName$="XLMain"
Item$="R1C1"
Topic$="c:\excel\anyopen.xls"
hWndEXCEL=FindWindow(ClassName$,0)
If hWndEXCEL=0 Then
     Shell(AppName$ + " " + Topic$)
     hWndEXCEL=FindWindow(ClassName$,0)
End If
ChannelNumber=DDEInitiate(AppName$,Topic$)
CellA1Stuff$="Anything you want"
DDEPoke(ChannelNumber,Item$,CellA1Stuff$)
DDETerminate ChannelNumber
```

The Channel Number is assigned sequentially, starting at one. A Channel Number of zero signifies that no link could be established.

The WordBasic command

```
DDETerminateAll
```

terminates all Channels where Word for Windows is a Client. It has no effect on Channels where WinWord is a Server. Yes, much of the documentation is wrong again.

Hidden text ("Hidden" being a Word for Windows character format that makes the text invisible) will not be transferred during a DDE Poke.

■ **T I P**

Just as in Visual Basic, sometimes you want to Shell out to another application and then immediately bring the Focus back to WinWord. Try this:

```
WindowTitle$=WindowName$()
' Do your shelling here
Activate WindowTitle$
```

Using the WordBasic Activate command seems to be more reliable than the Windows SetFocus API command. It's easier, too.

Any time WordBasic brings in a table—even a one-cell table—as the result of a DDE Request, paragraph mark is automatically embedded in the document immediately before the table.

WordBasic as Server

Whenever possible, the Topic should give full directory and subdirectory information; without them, WinWord will only respond if the requested file is from the current directory.

If no extension is supplied in the Topic, ".DOC" is assumed. Topic$="THE-BOOK" is the same as Topic$="THEBOOK.DOC." Note that this is different from EXCEL.

All WordBasic Items are bookmarks. A Word for Windows bookmark may be inserted anywhere (except in headers and footers) by selecting the text to be book-marked and running the command "InsertBookmark," or clicking on "Insert," then "Bookmark."

■ **T I P**

Unfortunately, the standard Word for Windows bookmarks—including "\Sel" for the current selection, "\Para" for the current paragraph, "\Line" for the current line, and a dozen others—are not considered "bookmarks" for DDE. They cannot be used as Items in a DDE Request.

B U G

DDE Execute [Window n] (where "n" is an integer between 1 and 9) will activate Window "n" as it should, as the WordBasic "Windown" command always does. But for some reason the old window, the one active when that command is executed, will remain on top. Window "n" gets focus. The old window is visible. This may be intentional, but it sure seems like a bug.

Hidden text ("Hidden" being a character format that makes the text invisible) will not be transferred during a DDE Request.

■ T I P

Often Clients will provide unwanted paragraph marks at the end of the data they send to WordBasic in a DDE conversation. EXCEL and Visual Basic are particularly notorious. That extra paragraph mark can really screw up the fine formatting you've achieved in your WinWord document; its been a source of consternation for WordBasic DDE programmers since the dawning of time.

Well, there's a trick.

If you don't want the extra paragraph mark, you can take the situation into your own hands. Instead of doing a DDEPoke from Visual Basic, for example, turn the problem around: make WordBasic the Client and Visual Basic the Server, and have WordBasic DDERequest the data. That brings the data into a variable, where you can strip off the final paragraph mark before Inserting it into your document.

If you want to make it really fancy, you can use the same technique we developed in the DDE Daisy Chains section to have Visual Basic put together a WordBasic macro. That macro would initiate a DDE conversation, with WordBasic as Client and Visual Basic as Server, run a DDERequest to bring back the data, and shut down the channel. The technique and most of the code is identical to what you saw in Figure 6-23.

Far as we know, this is the toughest text handling problem with WinWord as a DDE Server. The question comes up over and over again—and the solution is to simply turn WinWord into the Client!

EXCEL as Client

As of this writing, rumors are flying that the EXCEL macro language will be changed (or perhaps a second macro language will be added) to make EXCEL macros . . . uh . . . more Basic.

In the meantime, though, here's a quick rundown on the EXCEL DDE commands. A DDE Initiate looks like this:

```
=INITIATE("Application,""Topic")
```

where the cell containing the INITIATE receives the Channel Number of the link, or an "#N/A" if the link can't be established.

A DDE Request looks like this:

```
=REQUEST(ChannelNumber,"Item")
```

The Request returns tabular data as an EXCEL array. If the Server does not recognize Item, you'll get a "#REF!" in response to the Request. If the link times out, you'll see a "#DIV/0!"—surely one of the most bizarre flags in DDE-land.

A DDE Poke looks like this:

```
=POKE(ChannelNumber, "Item," "Data")
```

Again, if the Server doesn't recognize Item, you'll get a "#REF!" (which stands for "#Refused!"), and if the link times out you'll get a "#DIV/0!." *When all else fails, divide by zero and punt, eh?*

A DDE Execute looks like this:

```
=EXECUTE(ChannelNumber, "Command")
```

The "#REF!" and "#DIV/0!" responses apply here, too. In addition, a "#N/A" signifies that the Server is busy. Don't confuse this command with the EXCEL EXEC command, which starts a program—"EXEC" is EXCEL-speak for "Shell."

The EXCEL documentation relies heavily on simulating keyboard input—Type, Type Type— when demonstrating DDE Execute capabilities. That's just a bias of the manual writers (and speaks volumes about the sequential, non-Event-Driven nature of EXCEL macros). EXCEL can DDE Execute any command that any DDE Server can handle.

Finally, to end the DDE conversation,

```
=TERMINATE(ChannelNumber)
```

If EXCEL can't terminate the link—most likely because you have the wrong ChannelNumber—you'll get a "#VALUE!" returned. (In fact, you'll get a "#VALUE!" in any DDE command with an incorrect ChannelNumber.)

B U G

Some documentation says that EXCEL Channel Numbers are assigned sequentially, starting at zero. That isn't true. They start at one.

EXCEL as Server

When EXCEL performs as a Server, the Topic must be a fully qualified file name, including the ".XLS" extension, if appropriate. (This is different from how WinWord handles things.) Whenever possible, give full directory and subdirectory information; without them, EXCEL will only respond if the requested file is from the current directory.

The default Topic, when EXCEL starts, is "Sheet1," with no extension.

EXCEL often starts a new copy of itself in response to a DDE Initiate. To avoid having multiple copies of EXCEL hanging around, always Initiate with the "System" Topic—which connects to EXCEL's main window, and use EXCEL macro commands to load the spreadsheet you need.

Items to EXCEL are cells in "R1C1" format, ranges in "R1C1:R5C10" format, or named ranges.

■ **T I P**

EXCEL data is provided in tab-delimited format. You may want to reformat the data as soon as it's inserted into a document—WinWord's "Convert Text To Table" command, for example, can be very useful.

■ **T I P**

Sometimes EXCEL returns DDE Requested data with an extra paragraph mark—Chr$(13) + Chr$(10)—tagged on the end. If that's going to be a problem in your Client application, check for it and strip it off.

It's not overly difficult to have EXCEL, working as a Server, accept DDE Poked data and (using DDE Execute commands) create a chart, then finally Poke it back into the Client. Hint: write the EXCEL code first, then translate it into DDE Execute commands in the Client's language, just as we did in the Figure 6-23 DDE Daisy Chain.

B U G

If EXCEL absolutely, adamantly refuses to respond to any DDE Initiate, your user may have inadvertently *turned off DDE!* (Yes, it's possible in EXCEL.) Click on "Options," then "Workspace," and make sure there's no check-mark in the "Ignore Remote Requests" box. This "design feature" means that any of your users, anywhere, at any time, may suddenly shaft all DDE by inadvertently clicking on a very obscure check box. And once "Remote Requests" are turned off, there's no way you can use DDE to turn them back on again.

DynaComm as Client

DynaComm commands are a bit different, although their general form is vaguely familiar. A DDE Initiate, for example, looks like this:

```
Access "ApplicationName" "Topic" %Channel
```

The variable %Channel comes back as the Channel Number if all went well; a "0" if there is no response; "-1" if there's an error in getting the link going; and "-n" *if "n" different Servers responded!*

A DDE Request looks like this:

```
Request $variable From %Channel "Item"
```

where the Channel Number and Item are as you expect. The DDE Requested data is placed in $variable.

DDE Poke goes like so:

```
Poke $variable To %Channel "Item"
```

for a single data element. DynaComm also supports a fast method for DDE Poking entire tables of data in DIF, SYLK, or TEXT format, i.e.,

```
Table Send table To %Channel "Item" As Format
```

where "table" is a number between 0 and 15 specifying the DynaComm table to be sent and "Format" is DIF, SYLK, or TEXT.

DDE Execute looks a bit different, too:

```
Instruct %Channel Command1, Command2, Command3,...
```

Here's a real time-saver: those Commands can be surrounded by single quotes. For example:

```
Instruct n '[FileNew]', '[Insert "Hello, Word!"]'
```

is a marvelously uncomplicated rendition of a two-command DDE Execute for WordBasic. The freedom to use single and double quotes as delimiters is . . . unexcelled . . . in the DDE world.

Finally, a DDE Terminate looks like this:

```
Access Cancel %Channel
```

If there's no %Channel specified, the Access Cancel command ends all ongoing DDE conversations, much as WordBasic's DDETerminateAll.

DynaComm as Server

DynaComm is regarded by many as the most sophisticated Windows communication package available. Part of the reason for that lofty reputation is DynaComm's ability to work with DDE, and we're going to poke around with that ability right here. (DynaComm is from FutureSoft Engineering; they're the same folks who make the Windows Terminal application.)

DynaComm will respond to a Topic of "Server," but it doesn't provide you with any "SysItems"-style information.

As mentioned earlier, DynaComm doesn't respond automatically to any DDE Request, DDE Poke, or DDE Execute.

The method for handling those commands is not unlike Visual Basic's approach to DDE Execute: you must write code to handle each individual possibility. DynaComm doesn't have the clean simplicity of Visual Basic's Form_LinkExecute Event handling ability, but the DynaComm method isn't difficult once you get the hang of it.

Your best source of information for DynaComm as a Server is the DynaComm script manual, but to give you a taste of what's in store, here's what you might write to handle a DDE Execute command of "ClearScreen":

```
When Initiate %Channel Display 'DDE Link Started', Return
When Execute %Channel $Command Perform DoDDE
When Terminate Display 'DDE Link Ended', Return
While True
     Wait Signal
Cancel
*DoDDE
If $Command="ClearScreen"
     Clear Screen
Return
```

DynaComm has a rich and powerful macro ("script") language, although its syntax is rather different from the Windows Basics.

PackRat as Server

PackRat is a powerful "Information Manager". You know the type . . . phone book, calendar, to-do lists, contact organizer, alarm clock, and on and on. It's one of the best available; the latest version even supports networking. One of the reasons for PackRat's success is its ability to do DDE. Or at least some DDE.

■ **T I P**

Caveat programmer! PackRat only works as a DDE Server, and only with the Topic set to "System." If you try to DDE Initiate a conversation with PackRat, using the "System" Topic, and PackRat has no files open, the Initiate will fail.

B U G

At one point, trying a DDE Initiate with PackRat as Server and no files open could even trigger a Windows crash. That may have been corrected by the time you read this, but don't bet on it!

Since PackRat has no embedded macro language, PackRat commands—actions you would normally expect to start with a DDE Execute—can be accessed with a DDE Poke to specific Items. It's an unusual approach, but not without some merit. For example, instead of a DDE Execute command specifying "[Search(PhoneBook)]" or some such, PackRat has you Poke, like this:

```
DDEPoke(ChannelNumber, "STARTSEARCH","P")
```

where the "P" stands for "Phone book."

Before you try to re-invent the wheel, look at PRIME, an impressive (and pioneering) suite of Word for Windows-PackRat-DDE macros written by T.J. Lee and Lee Hudspeth. For more information, write: Lee Hudspeth and Associates, 2629 Manhattan Avenue, Suite 273, Hermosa Beach, California USA 90254.

Toolbook/Daybook as Server

■ **T I P**

Julianne Sharer reports that Daybook won't take the standard DDE Execute format for stringing together commands. Instead of the common "[Command1][Command2][Command3]" style we used earlier, Daybook insists upon "[Command1];[Command2];[Command3]".

Tricks of the Trade

Send Keys
Yes, all of the DDE applications support Send Keys.

Send Keys (the exact name of the command varies just a bit) simulates a user pressing keys and feeds the keystrokes to other applications.

Using Send Keys in DDE is like using your fingers at *Tour d'Argent*. Go ahead and do it if you must—the manuals will show you how—but be aware that Send Keys is the ultimate sequential kludge in an Event-Driven world.

If you think through the problem, you'll almost never need Send Keys. That's why we didn't talk about it.

But . . . who has time to think? SendKeys can be useful.

DDE Watch

Sooner or later, if you get into the DDE swing of things, you're going to wonder exactly what is going on behind the scenes. Maybe a DDE Execute doesn't work right, and you wonder if the DDE gods lopped off part of the command. Maybe you're buried ten deep in nested double-quotes and just *have* to know what's really going out over the DDE wires.

When you reach that point—especially if you're bucking bugs in applications or DDE itself—you need some help.

If you own the Windows SDK, there's a great little utility called "DDE Spy" that actually monitors and reports on all DDE conversations as they happen.

If you'd rather not spend all that much money, there's a good alternative: a product called *DDEWatch* from TechSmith Corporation.

Let's say you're trying to use DDE to bring the cell R1C1 from EXCEL's "Sheet1" into Word for Windows. For some reason, the contents of R1C1 always get imported with a paragraph mark a Chr$(13)+Chr$(10) on the end of the data, and you can't figure out what's wrong.

If you'd read the section up above on EXCEL as a Server, you'd already know that EXCEL just does that; the paragraph mark is bogus. But let's suppose for a second you didn't have the DDE Cookbook handy, and you'd been beating your brains out trying to figure out why there's an extra paragraph being tossed into your WinWord document.

Well, crank up DDEWatch. Let it run while WordBasic establishes the DDE link, then DDE Requests the data in EXCEL's cell R1C1. Figure 6-24 on the following page shows what DDEWatch reports.

Fascinating, no?

First, look at how the DDE gods establish a DDE link. It's the brute force approach: the DDE Initiate string, in this case "excel|sheet1" is broadcast to every Tom, Dick and Harry application, in the hope that somebody sticks up their hand and says "I'll take it."

After sending out all those messages, one application responds—sends an "Ack"nowledgment. It's application 2f54. (All the numbers are in hexadecimal; don't worry about it.) A DDE link is established between application 2f54, EXCEL, and application 2bc8, WinWord.

Figure 6-24: DDEWatch

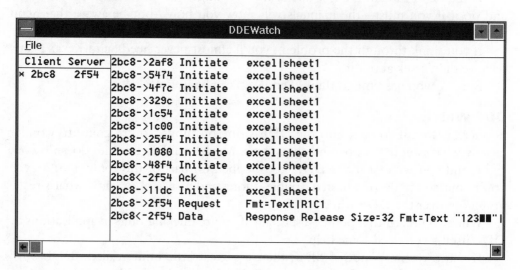

WinWord immediately sends out its DDE Request. It's asking for Item R1C1 in Text format. EXCEL can handle Text format, and it understands R1C1. *(It can get very interesting watching the Client and Server duke it out over data formats. It's like watching two drivers jockeying for the same parking spot.)*

EXCEL sends back the contents of R1C1, in this case "123" in Text format. But wait! What's that? Those two black blotches? That must be the bogus Chr$(13) and Chr$(10) we've been getting. Hey, how about that. EXCEL is screwing up.

End of mystery.

The product is DDEWatch, and if you do DDE, you need it. It's $85 from TechSmith Corporation, 1745 Hamilton Road, Suite 300, Okemos, Michigan USA 48864. And, no, the older Shareware version doesn't work as well.

TechSmith is considering building a similar product to let you take a peek into DLL calls—including Windows API calls. Code name is DLLWatch. If you order DDEWatch and would like to see a DLLWatch, tell TechSmith about it! And tell them Woody sent you.

Developers' Tools Conference Proceedings

One wide-ranging source of information, assembled by Steve Wexler (of WexTech Systems, "Using WordBasic" and DOC-to-Help fame) for the 1991 Developers' Tools Conference, is available directly from Microsoft. Call 1-800-227-4679, extension 11771 (206-54-2030 outside North America) and ask for *The Proceedings of the Word Developers' Conference, 1991*, part number 034-000-060.

It's $15 and considered by many to be the seminal work on DDE for Mere Mortals.

Make an Icon to Crank Up This Document

We've only scraped the surface of DDE. In fact, to really dig into all of DDE, you'd have to learn *all* of the macro languages behind *all* of the applications—a daunting task if ever there were.

But just to give you a taste of what else you can do, consider a little macro . . . "just" a macro.

This WordBasic macro talks to the Program Manager. Run this macro while inside Word for Windows, with an important document showing. The macro will create a new icon in the Program Manager's "WinWord" group. Double-clicking on that icon will *automatically start WinWord with that important document loaded and ready to go!*

```
ChannelNumber = DDEInitiate("progman", "progman")
DDEExecute(ChannelNumber, "[ShowGroup(WinWord)]")
DDEExecute(ChannelNumber, "[AddItem(C:\winword\winword.exe " + \
 Files$(.) + FileName$(), Some Description, c:\iconpath\icon.ico)]"
DDETerminateAll
```

"Some Description" will appear beneath the "c:\iconpath\icon.ico" icon in the "WinWord" group. Double-clicking on that icon will crank up "c:\winword\winword.exe" with an initial file in this case, the fully-qualified name of the current document. You can change any or all of those settings, of course.

A powerful, custom icon is five lines of code away . . . *from inside a word processor!*

CHAPTER ■ 7

CoolCons—DDE in Action

Even though there's a lot less to Visual Basic than meets the eye—
it's really just an interface builder (and a great one), not a
complete automated-programming tool—there's this wave
of hype coming up again, encouraging ordinary PC
users to learn to program. It's a waste of their time.

—Jim Seymour, *PC Computing*, January 1992

Excuse me, Jim. Is *any* programming language anything more than "just an interface builder"?

Okay, class. Let's get back to wasting our time.

Ready to build another commercial application?

This time our target is CoolCons—a fully customizable icon box which will work with any application that supports Dynamic Data Exchange. We're going to build a version to work with Word for Windows. With a little nip here and a little tuck there, though, you can change it to work with just about any decent Windows program.

While we're building CoolCons, we'll hit a fair percentage of the remaining Visual Basic and WordBasic commands. At the same time, you'll get another chance to see how to approach building a real, fully functional, Event-Driven Visual Basic program.

If you're just looking for the lowdown on customizing CoolCons, skip on down to the "Quick Customizing Instructions" section of this chapter. But while you're leafing through, pause every now and then and take a look at the parts of Visual Basic that make this all possible. If you skip the meat of this chapter, you're missing the fun part!

WHY MoreCons?

Have you noticed how all the hot-shot expensive Windows programs now sport icon boxes? Whether it's called a Toolbar (Microsoft) or SmartIcons (Lotus) or a Button Bar (WordPerfect) or SmartButtons (Polaris) or whatever, all the icon boxes have two traits in common:

- They really sell the program; and
- They're all different!

That should tell you something.

Icon Box as Marketing Feature

People just love those little icon boxes. They look sexy, especially in ad copy. Moreover, they *really work*.

If you've spent more than just a few hours with an icon box you'll see why: it's much, much easier to click on a button than to wade through a menu. This is one of the few places where reality almost approaches marketing hype: the icon box can really speed things up—if you can see the icons and tell what they're supposed to do.

Icon boxes seem to be most popular in word processors and spreadsheets at the moment, but you can bet they'll infect other types of Windows programs before long.

SmartIcons The Lotus/Amí Pro SmartIcons are very, very small—a challenge to your mousing dexterity. Not so good. On the other hand, you can always tell what a SmartIcon will do by clicking the right mouse button while your cursor is properly positioned: the icon's "description" appears as Amí Pro's window title.

You can position the icons anywhere you like: at the top, bottom, left, or right of the screen. Unfortunately, this works against the description capability: put the icon bar on the bottom of the screen, for example, and you'll get whiplash banging your eyes up and down, trying to see both icon and description simultaneously.

Remarkably, you can also turn the single-line icon bar into a box, position it anywhere on the screen, and make it stick.

Finally, SmartIcons are configurable: you choose new icons by dragging and dropping from a big pool, although the description that goes along with custom macros is limited to the macro name—all of eight characters.

That's pretty good. In fact, Lotus holds the blue ribbon for icon boxes—at least as of this writing.

Toolbar Microsoft Toolbar icons are a bit larger than Lotus SmartIcons and thus less likely to cause early myopia. But they're still mighty small, especially if you're working on a Super VGA monitor at 800 x 600 resolution or higher.

The Toolbar icons are stuck in one place: you can have the Toolbar anywhere you like, as long as it's the third line on the screen.

There are no hints about the meaning of the pictures: nothing short of a Vulcan Mind Meld will divulge the purpose of the less scrutable pictures.

You're limited to a very small collection of prebuilt icons (unless you use the Word for Windows Office Power Pack Toolbar Editor to build your own), and few of the existing ones use any color.

Changing icons can become a full-time job: try adding a "File Close" icon between "File Open" and "File Save," bumping all the other icons down one slot, and you'll see what we mean. You may assign a Toolbar icon to any built-in command, or even a macro you've written.

If you're looking for the ultimate icon box, you can keep looking, although (at this writing) EXCEL 4 should advance the state of the Microsoft art a bit—soon as the marketing folks figure out that icons sell programs, the development folks get religion, real fast.

Button Bar The WordPerfect Button Bar adds a few interesting capabilities.

You can choose between tiny buttons with text but no pictures (not exactly icons, not exactly menus); little buttons with pictures but no text; and bigger buttons with pictures and text. A big button might say "File Close," while a little button would only have a picture of a file folder. That's an innovative way to solve the "big vs. small" and "description vs. intuition" problems.

The Button Bar can appear at the top, bottom, left, or right of the screen, but it won't float.

If there are more icons than will appear in the allotted space, WordPerfect adds arrows, to let you scroll through the icons—at some point, though, the scrolling is more work than using a menu.

There's some customizing capability, but not much.

Button Bar is still in its infancy.

A Better Way

People can—and do!—debate the pros and cons of various manufacturers' icon boxes. Some think one is too big, others too small. Some want descriptions; others think the picture should be sufficient. Some are willing to give up the screen real estate necessary for bigger buttons; others want the bare essentials, so they can have more buttons. Some want to move them; others think they should stay put. Some want to draw their own pictures; others think all the pictures should be provided.

And so it goes.

There's no standard icon box; manufacturers' designs vary all over the place, and each new implementation has its own twists and turns. That's a reflection of one simple fact: nobody knows if there's one "best" kind of icon box. At this point anyway, the "best" is still a very personal choice.

The hacker's search for the ultimate icon box, like the Theravadan assault on nirvana, must allow for individual differences, preferences, idiosyncrasies. No single goal will satisfy all.

The ultimate icon box would let the user *choose*. Choose the size of the buttons. Choose the location and size of the box. Choose the number of buttons to be displayed. Choose the action associated with each button. Choose whether and how a description would be displayed.

Too Cool

CoolCons should behave like a typical icon box: click on an icon, and a Word for Windows command is executed. If we do things right, CoolCons will feel like a part of WinWord itself; nobody will know (or at least care) that it's a Visual Basic program talking to WinWord with DDE.

We want CoolCons to come as close to the "ideal" icon box as is possible with the tools we have at hand. While CoolCons is far from the ultimate icon box—among other things, customizing it requires some knowledge of Visual Basic—CoolCons gives users an enormous amount of flexibility.

CoolCons will let you make your own icons, any size, any shape, in any of the common Windows picture formats. You can make some icons big, others tiny, if you like, and you can put just as many icons in the box as you like.

The CoolCons icon box itself is configurable: twist it, resize it, move it anywhere you like and it "sticks", even between Windows sessions. When your mouse passes over an icon, a description of that icon's action appears in the title bar. When you aren't using CoolCons, it retreats to a single-line status bar that shows you the time, the date, free system resources and available memory.

You can set things up so clicking an icon runs a series of WordBasic commands, any WordBasic commands, or any WinWord macros you may have written.

Although we're building CoolCons to work with Word for Windows, the same ideas—even the same code—can be used to make it work with any Windows application that supports DDE.

Design Goal

If there's one lesson that Windows has taught designers over and over again, it's this: people are different; everybody likes to do things their own way. If hackers take the time to build programs that people can adapt to their own way of working, users will appreciate the effort, day in and day out.

Ergo, our number-one design goal for CoolCons: make it flexible.

Constraints

After playing with several prototypes of CoolCons we hit a few difficulties that will dictate how the program is built. Here are the major obstacles we'll have to face:

- Allowing the user to change icons during Visual Basic's run time is quite complicated. While drag-and-drop icon changes would be ultra-cool, CoolCons only permits icon changes during design time and only using Visual Basic itself.

- There are fancy ways to manipulate pictures, using esoteric Windows commands like BitBlts and the like. Unfortunately the programming gets pretty hairy, and if we went that way, we'd miss the discussion of Control Arrays—an important Visual Basic concept, quite possibly the most important part of this chapter. So we'll stick with good ol' Picture Box Controls, eschewing the faster and more efficient alternatives.

- CoolCons is an exercise in Dynamic Data Exchange: it'll only work with applications that support DDE Execute statements. That counts out Word-Perfect for Windows (at least at this point). But almost any other major Windows program will work; in fact, CoolCons can work *with more than one Windows application at a time!*

We'll build CoolCons to work with Word for Windows 2.0—you have a working model of WinWord 2.0 on your WinMortals Companion Disk, so it's a good candidate. Don't let that hold you back, though: changing CoolCons to work with other DDE-conversant applications is not difficult.

A Cool User Interface

The *less* time you spend *designing* forms, the
more time you will spend *programming* forms.

—J.D. Evans Jr., *The Art of Visual Basic Programming*, 1991
(Original emphasis)

As you might imagine, grafting a new user interface onto existing Windows programs aren't easy. The big companies spend millions of dollars on usability tests, graphic artists, and machine interaction specialists.

Mere mortals like us have to rely on intuition—and the fact that we use the programs to get real work done! That's where we have the edge. Designers rarely have the time or inclination to become proficient in using their products, to become real power users. They may know the program; we know how to use it. There's a difference.

So what can we working folk do better than the big guys?

Quite a bit, it turns out. And it all hinges on the user interface.

Keep It Simple

If our number-one design goal is to make CoolCons flexible, number two is to keep CoolCons simple. It may be necessary to step the user through the operating procedure once, but it shouldn't take more than twice for anybody to "get the hang" of a utility program.

The big guys have to please everybody. That leads to gargantuan programs with rarely used nooks and crannies and enormous overhead in the design, implementation, and support of the behemoths. The programs become so bloated that they *have* to be programmed in C or assembler or something similar, so the poor user won't spend eons staring at an "hourglass" cursor.

Ah, but we Mortals can be more selective. We can make programs that solve very specific problems—and solve them well.

While the Windows market may only support a few spreadsheet programs or word processors or databases, there are enough niches in the Windows biz for thousands and thousands of successful, well-designed, well-executed small programs that work with, and complement, these larger programs.

Put a dynamite Windows program out on the market, and you'll hear the same thing over and over again: "Why didn't Microsoft think of that?" or "How can a little company in Timbuktu make something so much better than Lotus?" or "These people really know what they're doing; look at how this works so much better than WordPerfect."

Design the perfect app for your office and you'll hear the same refrain: "Why can't those mainframe guys do this?" or "You ought to reprogram that in a real language like dBase; I'd take it on, but it would take six months!" or "What do you mean you did this in Visual Basic and a macro language? You can't do that in a macro language."

It's one of the wonderful consequences of solving problems—real problems that real people face every day.

And *you* can do it. By keeping it simple.

Design Considerations

With the two big considerations, flexibility and simplicity, taken as given, let's look at other aspects of CoolCons' design. There are some general issues involved here—some things you might consider no matter what kind of Event-Driven program you have in mind—so follow along while we dissect the beast.

Screen Real Estate An early version of CoolCons drew attention, but it simply took up too much space. People are willing to put up with quite a bit to get lots of fancy, usable icons, but they don't want to sacrifice 20 or 30% of the surface of the screen, especially if they're using a word processor or spreadsheet, applications where real estate is at a premium.

That's a big challenge: how do you give people lots of choices, without taking up lots of room?

Form Placement Icon box positioning can be a real bugaboo. WordPerfect lets you position the Button Bar on any edge, top, bottom, left, or right. Those work well enough, but there's no obvious place to put icon descriptions, except on the icons themselves.

Lotus SmartIcons can go on any edge, too, or they can float in a resizable box. That box looks nice in Amí Pro—until you actually try to *use* it! If you're typing along in a document and your typing goes under the box, the box doesn't move out of the way.

That's a tough one. It's most disconcerting to suddenly lose sight of your work. But the alternative—automatically sliding the box around to get out of the way—is also fraught with problems: where should the box go? Move it a little bit and any speed typist will make the box hop around like a tree frog. Move it a lot and the program may obscure something else that's equally important to the user.

You could consider using the right mouse button, but that, too, has its problems. It slows the user down: for most Windows mouse users, it still takes a moment of hesitation and thought to get that middle finger working. Worse, nobody knows at the moment if the right mouse button will become some sort of standard input option. If you build an application to use the right mouse button and six months later Microsoft suddenly attaches some significance to that button, you could be leading your users down a primrose path.

Quid Pro Quo Finally, an almost philosophical consideration: if we take something away (like, say, a bit of screen space), we should give the user something back. Something they can use all the time. Something that will inform or entertain, or at least make the day go better.

It's only fair.

The CoolCons Hot Bar

After weeks of wrangling and a handful of working prototypes bouncing around with several testers, we finally hit on a basic design for CoolCons. As you will see, it falls short of the ideal icon box. On the other hand, though, it packs a lot of power into a small space.

This particular implementation also demonstrates many features of Visual Basic, DDE, WordBasic, the Windows API, and Event-Driven programming in general, so in addition to being a neat little application, it's an ideal candidate for this chapter!

At the heart of CoolCons is the Hot Bar—a space on the screen that pops immediately to life whenever the mouse passes over it. That small space, which ideally consumes about as much room as one line of written text, is the only real estate hit the user suffers.

In the spirit of giving back more than has been taken away, we'll make the CoolCons Hot Bar show users things they might be curious about. Like this:

Figure 7-1: The CoolCons Hot Bar

CoolCons	12:48 PM	Tue 07 Apr 92	Free Sys Resources: 32%	Avail Memory: 20.6 MB

Microsoft Word - C:\WINWORD\WMORTALS\THEBOOK.DOC

File Edit View Insert Format Tools Table Window Help

That's a nice compromise. Take away a line on the screen, give back a little information.

All of this Hot Bar information is readily available inside Visual Basic, so why not use it? Everybody likes to have a clock. Most users will understand the "Avail Memory" figure; it includes the size of the Windows swap file and gives the user some feeling of control, illusory as it may be. Only a few users will understand the "Free Sys Resources" figure—and the ones who do will realize immediately that it's the most important number on the Hot Bar.

A little something for everyone.

We could've put the Hot Bar down at the bottom of the screen. In fact, one of the CoolCons prototypes did exactly that. After working with it for a while, though, it just *felt* awkward. Why? If the user can't find the icon they're looking for immediately, they'll go hunting in the menus. With the Hot Bar at the bottom of the screen, users were all over the place trying to get the mouse positioned.

Of course, you can put the Hot Bar at the bottom of the screen if you like. Or on the left or right, or smack in the middle of the screen for that matter. It's only a couple of lines of Visual Basic code. You'll see how to change it in just a bit.

The CoolCons Icon Box

Once the Hot Bar is designed and in place, the icon box itself is straightforward.

We're going to build a completely reconfigurable, resizable, positionable icon box. One with icons of any shape or size, including icons bearing any picture Visual Basic can handle. One that "sticks" where it's put. One that moves out of the way as soon as the user starts typing. One that shows descriptions of the action associated with each icon—with no user effort. In short, one that looks like this:

Figure 7-2: The CoolCons Icon Box

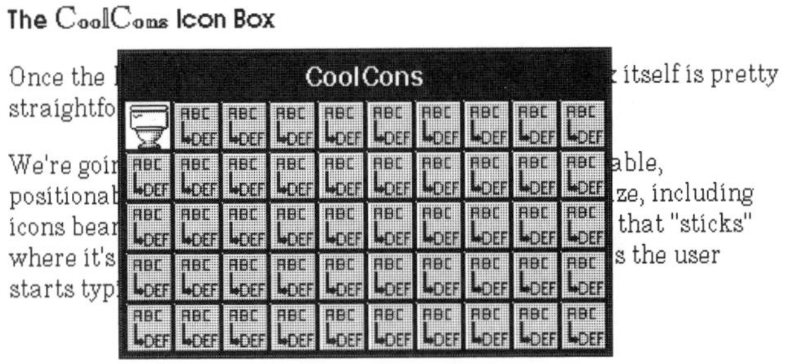

Since we're so emphatically committed to making the icon box malleable, there are very few specific design decisions that need concern us. Here are the two most important:

- We're going to program CoolCons to handle fifty icons. Since each icon is a Picture Box Control—a window in its own right—and since each Windows window takes its toll in Free System Resources, running much more than fifty icons can consume an inordinate amount of FSR. (Some fairly typical numbers: Word for Windows 2.0 takes 8 to 10% of FSR. CoolCons takes about 0.5% of FSR for each icon: fifty icons equates to 25% FSR, which is quite a hit!) If you can live with fewer than fifty icons, by all means, take some out. The "Quick Customization" section of this chapter shows you how.

- We're going to put descriptions in the icon box's title bar. We toyed with having the descriptions float above the icon as the mouse passed overhead, but it got very distracting very quickly. With the description in the title bar, there's a visual reference point that keeps the user's eyes from bumping against the top of their head. On the downside, though, the icon box title bar is quite small when CoolCons is configured as a tall, thin box. Can't win them all.

With those two exceptions, we'll try to make the icon box as flexible as humanly possible.

Visual Basic as Prototype Tool

Now, stand back for a second. Take a look at what we've been discussing.

On the first level, we've dug into the nitty-gritty of designing CoolCons to see where the programming will go. Fair enough.

But on a second level, we've examined the kinds of user interface questions that can pop up in the Windows world and the solutions that might be possible. The Event-Driven way is so very, very different from input-process-output that entire *categories* of design may go right over your head, until you play with Visual Basic a bit. The Hot Bar is a great example: can you imagine what it would take to make a robust Hot Bar in a DOS program? In Visual Basic, it's just one form and a handful of code.

On a third level, reading between the lines—and working behind your back—we did something else that's very important: we built and tested *dozens* of fully functional prototypes!

Some of the prototypes only lasted a few minutes. "Oops. No, that doesn't feel right. Let's try something else." Some of them lasted weeks. We smashed and battered and bent and tore at the prototypes until they worked the way we wanted.

Constructing a new prototype typically took minutes; even the first working CoolCons prototype only took a few hours. By comparison, prototyping and refining the Word for Windows Toolbar—or the Amí Pro SmartIcons or the Word-Perfect Button Bar—*took thousands of hours and hundreds of thousands of dollars, or more!*

You be the judge: as you work through this chapter, keep asking yourself, "Is the Toolbar/SmartIcons/Button Bar I know that much better than CoolCons? Is it *any* better than CoolCons? For that matter, why isn't it *as good as* CoolCons?"

The difference is in the tools. You picked the right one.

The Hot Bar Form

Time to get to the keyboard. Make sure you have the WinMortals Companion Disk data moved over, per the instructions in Appendix 3. You should have a sub-directory called something like "C:\VB\COOLCONS" that holds all the programs you'll need to follow along.

Since you were good in Chapter 5 and actually played with the Visual Basic Toolbox, got your hands dirty with clicking and dragging and sizing and all that, we'll save you a bit of headache and explain how to bring up the Companion Disk material before it's used.

The Headless Forms-man

The Hot Bar in Figure 7-1 is a Form without a Head.

There's no up-and-down maximize-and-minimize arrows. No hyphen-thing in the upper left corner. No title—no title *bar* for that matter. A most unusual Form. But one that's easily constructed.

If you're working from the Companion Disk, crank up Visual Basic, and click on File/Open Project, go into the CoolCons subdirectory, and open up C7PGM1.MAK.

Here's what you'll find:

Figure 7-3: Nascent Hot Bar

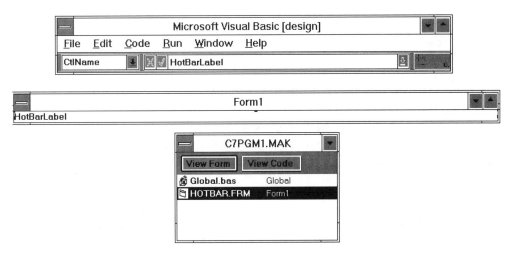

If you're working manually, you need to add one Label Control to Form1.

The Hot Bar Form should be just as wide as you can make it—way over to the left and right edges of the screen.

Inside the Hot Bar Form there's a Label Box Control we've called HotBarLabel. This Label Box Control should be just barely tall enough to show one line of text, and it should be as wide as the Form itself.

Finally, the Form needs to be closed in from the bottom, made as short as possible without bumping into the HotBarLabel.

There. We now have a single Label Control that takes over the entire Form. It's as wide as the screen. And it's as short as possible, while still clearly showing a line of text. Perfect.

Now we have to get rid of that big, fat head. That's done by setting the Form's BorderStyle Property to zero. Like this:

Figure 7-4: Off with His Head!

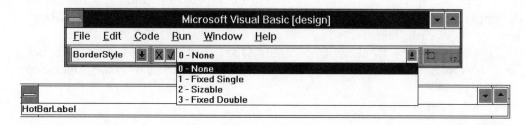

The transformation to a Headless Form isn't apparent during design time: no matter how hard you try, the title and arrows and all that stuff stick around until you push F5 or click on "Run," then "Start."

Hot Clock

We'll have to set up a Timer Control to periodically update the Hot Bar clock and all the other information.

If you're working from the Companion Disk, the Timer Control is already there. If you're working from scratch, bring one over by double-clicking on the clock in the Toolbox.

Figure 7-5: The Hot Clock

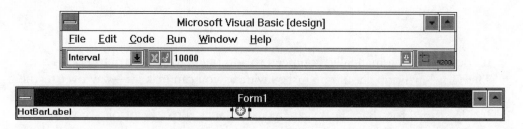

If you squint, you can just barely see the Timer control. We'll give it a Control Name (CtlName) of HotClock, and an interval of 10,000 milliseconds—in other words, the clock will "tick" every ten seconds.

Timer controls never show up on the Form when you run a Visual Basic program, so there's no need to adjust any other Property.

Now we're ready to set up the HotTimer_Timer Event handler. Double-click on the clock to bring up HotTimer_Timer:

Figure 7-6: HotTimer Ticks

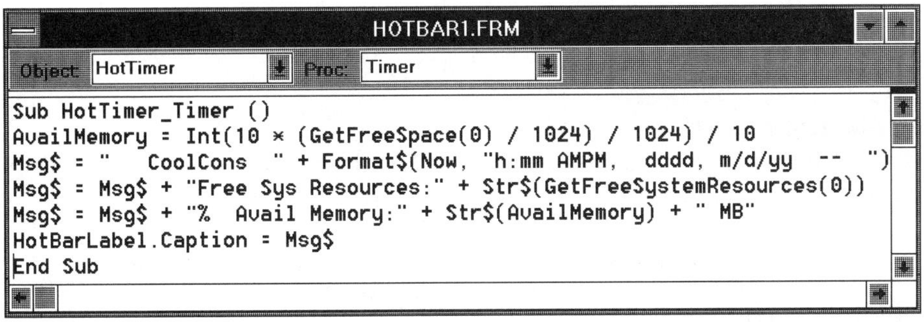

```
┌─────────────────────────────────────────────────────────────┐
│ ▬                     HOTBAR1.FRM                       ▼ ▲ │
├─────────────────────────────────────────────────────────────┤
│ Object: │HotTimer        │ ▼│ Proc: │Timer          │ ▼│    │
├─────────────────────────────────────────────────────────────┤
│ Sub HotTimer_Timer ()                                     ▲ │
│ AvailMemory = Int(10 × (GetFreeSpace(0) / 1024) / 1024) / 10│
│ Msg$ = "  CoolCons  " + Format$(Now, "h:mm AMPM,  dddd, m/d/yy  -- ")│
│ Msg$ = Msg$ + "Free Sys Resources:" + Str$(GetFreeSystemResources(0))│
│ Msg$ = Msg$ + "% Avail Memory:" + Str$(AvailMemory) + " MB"│
│ HotBarLabel.Caption = Msg$                                   │
│ End Sub                                                    ▼ │
│ ←▮                                                      → │
└─────────────────────────────────────────────────────────────┘
```

Let's step through that code lightly.

The first line

```
AvailMemory = Int(10 * (GetFreeSpace(0) / 1024) / 1024) / 10
```

calculates available memory in megabytes and rounds the amount to one decimal place.

GetFreeSpace(0) we've seen before, in WinExplorer. It returns the currently available memory including swap file memory, if any.

Visual Basic suffers from the same integer arithmetic overflow problems we hit in WinExplorer, so all the division and multiplication must be carefully crafted to avoid exceeding the "Int" function's 32,768 maximum. And the shenanigans with "Int" and 10 simply perform the single-decimal-place round-off in one step. You can work through the arithmetic if you like or just take our word for it.

Visual Basic Format$()

The next line

```
Msg$ = "  CoolCons  " + Format$(Now,"h:mm AMPM,  dddd, m/d/yy -- ")
```

takes advantage of one of Visual Basic's most powerful functions, Format$(). Format$() takes a number and applies a formatting rule to it, returning a formatted string. It's a remarkably flexible function, with the ability to suppress zeros, insert commas, insert literals (like the "-" in a telephone number), mix and match formatting for positive and negative numbers, and much more. Smart little sucker.

We're interested in the time and date formatting.

"Now" is a Visual Basic function that returns an inscrutable number with the very beneficial trait of being an ideal number to feed into Format$(). The "Now" number is transmogrified by the formatting pattern you see above, set off in quotes. In English, the formatting pattern can be interpreted as "hours:minutes AM/PM, day of the week, month/day/year -- ." See how the literal commas, dashes, and spaces all come through the formatting?

Hot Bar Message Final

The remaining lines simply construct the rest of Hot Bar's message, then slap it up on the screen as the Label Control's Caption property. Like so:

```
Msg$ = Msg$ + "Free Sys Resources:" + Str$(GetFreeSystemResources(0))
Msg$ = Msg$ + "%  Avail Memory:" + Str$(AvailMemory) + " MB"
HotBarLabel.Caption = Msg$
```

GetFreeSystemResources(0) is the same Windows API call we used in WinExplorer.

Just in case you were wondering. The entire Msg$ could've been put on one line. We've stretched it out here so it's easier to see.

Those two Windows API calls have to be "Declare"d somewhere. Since they're only needed on this Form, we'll stick them in the (general) (declarations) section of the HotBar Form:

Figure 7-7: Windows API Calls in General Declarations

The declarations are very similar to WordBasic's:

```
Declare Function GetFreeSpace Lib "kernel" (ByVal wFlags As\
  Integer) As Long
Declare Function GetFreeSystemResources Lib "user" (ByVal wFlags\
  As Integer) As Integer
```

Note how these functions—like all Windows API calls in Visual Basic—are set up to send variables By Value.

Where's the Rodent?

Here's the trick that makes the Hot Bar hot.

One of the fanciest Events tracked by Visual Basic is MouseMove. A MouseMove Event gets triggered whenever the mouse moves over a Form or Control. That makes it hot.

In theory, CoolCons should pop up its icon box whenever the user moves the mouse over the HotBar Form. In practice, though, it's not quite that simple.

You see, there are MouseMoves, and then there are MouseMoves. Does that make sense? Good. Just wanted to make sure you were awake.

■ **T I P**

If you have a Control on a Form and a mouse moving madly over the Control and the Form, you'll get two different kinds of MouseMove Events. Naturally, if the mouse moves over the Form, but not over the Control, the Form's MouseMove Event is triggered. That's as it should be. But here's the fun part: when the mouse moves over a Control, the MouseMove Event *for that Control* gets triggered—but there is no MouseMove Event generated for the Form! You have to read between the lines in the manuals to figure that out.

The upshot: CoolCons should monitor MouseMove events over the HotBarLabel. Since that Label covers all of the Form, waiting for a MouseMove Event on the HotBar Form would amount to an exercise in futility!

We'll build in the fancy features in the next section, but for now let's just set up something so you can see how the HotBar kicks in. Try using this for the HotBarLabel_MouseMove Event Handler:

Figure 7-8: HotBar Mouse Trap

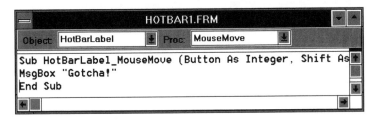

■ T I P

The MouseMove Event has a few other idiosyncrasies that'll keep you on your toes:

- If you move the mouse fast enough, no MouseMove Event is triggered. If it's important that you trap a MouseMove Event—even with Mario Andretti mice—stick your Form or Control all the way to the top, bottom, or side of the screen. The mouse "bumps up" against the side of the screen, and a MouseMove Event will almost always result.

- While MouseMove Events are triggered for Forms, Picture Box Controls, Label Controls, List Boxes, Combo Boxes, File List Boxes, Drive List Boxes, and Directory List Boxes, they are *not* triggered for Text Boxes.

- While MouseMove Events are triggered when the mouse moves over unoccupied territory on a Form (that is, areas where there are no Controls), they are *not* triggered when the mouse moves over a Form's title bar.

Check It Out

We'll be embellishing the HotBar Form shortly. Among other things, it has to initiate a DDE Conversation with Word for Windows, and it has to kick in the icon box at the appropriate time.

But for now, try playing with it. The HotBar MouseMove Event seems magical the first few times you see it.

To slap the HotBar Form up at the top of your screen, add these two lines to the Form_Load Event:

Figure 7-9: HotBar to the Top

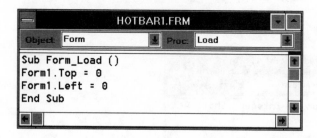

Now you're ready to play with the Hot Bar. Push F5 or click on "Run," then "Start." Slide your mouse up to the top of the screen. What happens?

Figure 7-10: HotBar Gotcha!

CoolCons 7:22 AM, Wednesday, 4/8/92 — Free Sys Resources: 57% Avail Memory:

Try moving your mouse up close to the HotBar, and see how close you can get without triggering the MouseMove Event. Then try moving your mouse quickly, all the way up to the top of the screen, and see how MouseMove captures it again.

Neat, huh?

The Icon Box Form

> . . . by the 7th century icon worship was an officially
> encouraged cult in the Byzantine Christian Church.
>
> —*New American Desk Encyclopedia*

We're going to build ourselves a righteous icon box, something that will give those multigazillion-dollar designed-by-committee icon boxes a real run for the money.

Using Control Arrays

A handful of Visual Basic concepts rate as "key" parts of the language. Control Arrays are among them.

You've seen arrays before—they're just subscripted variables, like, say:

```
Address$(i)="1600 Pennsylvania Ave"
FontSize(k)=18
SortedList(n)=SortedList(n-1)
```

No surprises there. Practically every language uses arrays. They're very convenient when you have a bunch of things that are quite similar and you want to handle them as a group.

Visual Basic takes the concept of "array" one step further on the evolutionary scale: it lets you create arrays *of Controls!*

You're wondering why somebody in their right mind would actually want to *use* an array of Controls. It seems like a mighty esoteric thing—like eating an array of corn flakes, or driving an array of Land Cruisers down an array of muddy roads.

Give the concept a while to soak in and you'll see. It just so happens that CoolCons needs arrays of Picture Box Controls to keep the programming from exploding into an unmanageable mess.

Any Control you can name may be turned into a Control Array—Check Boxes, Combo Boxes, Command Buttons, Frames, Scroll Bars, Labels, any kind of List Box, Option Buttons, Picture Boxes, Text Boxes, even Timer Controls. The whole nine yards.

Using Control Arrays couldn't be simpler.

An example: say you have five Picture Box Controls on a Form, with CtlNames of "PictureBox1," "PictureBox2," . . ., "PictureBox5." Changing the width of every Picture Box Control takes five lines of Visual Basic code:

```
PictureBox1.Width=NewWidth
PictureBox2.Width=NewWidth
PictureBox3.Width=NewWidth
PictureBox4.Width=NewWidth
PictureBox5.Width=NewWidth
```

But if your Form had an *array* of five Picture Box Controls called "PictureBox" and you wanted to change the width property on all of them, it's this easy:

```
For i=0 to 4
PictureBox(i).Width=NewWidth
Next i
```

(Note how Control Array indices start at zero and go up to the number of Controls minus one.)

Now imagine if your Form had fifty Picture Box Controls. See how things suddenly get much simpler? Well, the CoolCons icon box has fifty Picture Box Controls.

All of the benefits you've come to expect from arrays are available with Visual Basic Controls. It's a mighty powerful capability.

Creating Control Arrays

There are many ways to create Control Arrays. We'll use the simplest.

If you have the Companion Disk, resist the temptation to break out C7PGM2.MAK for a moment. This is another one of those things that you really have to "feel."

Let's create a Control Array of five Picture Box Controls.

Double-click on the Picture Box in the Toolbox—it's the one in the upper right corner, the one that looks like Sunset over Almogordo.

You get one Picture Box Control on your Form. Like this:

Figure 7-11: A Simple Picture Box Control

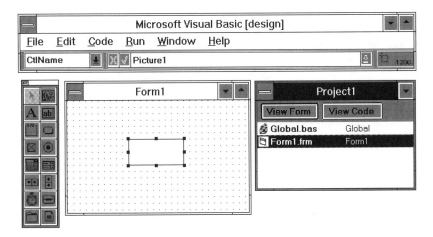

Next, click on "Edit," then "Copy." Yes, you're copying an entire Control—the Picture1 Picture Box Control.

Now click on "Edit," "Paste." You'll get a dialog box with a particularly strange message:

Figure 7-12: A Control Array Is Born

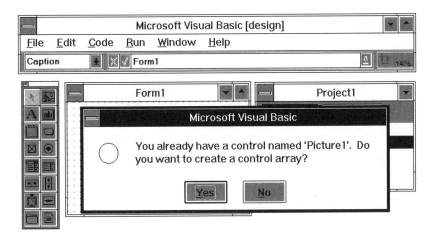

Why, yes, as a matter of fact, that's exactly what we're looking for. Click on "Yes," and you'll see Figure 7-13 on the following page.

Figure 7-13: A Second Picture1

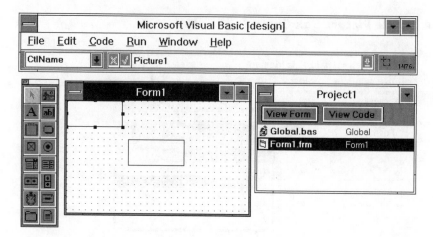

Congratulations! You now have a Control Array, called "Picture1," that consists of two Picture Box Controls.

Picture Box Edit Paste Oddity

Quick, before you do anything else. We're going to break something here, just to show you what can go wrong—and to warn you about the most common problem with creating Picture Box Control Arrays.

You haven't touched anything, right? The second "Picture1," the one in the upper left corner, is still selected, true?

Okay. Click on "Edit," then "Paste" once again. See how the next "Picture1" is propped on top of the first one? It doesn't look right. Try moving it.

Figure 7-14: Picture1 Peek-a-Boo

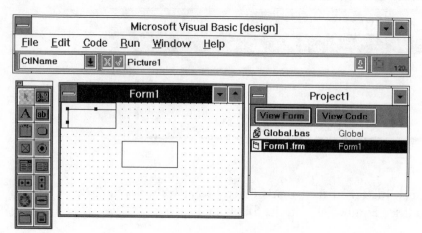

It's almost as if this new Picture1 got buried inside the old Picture1 and it can't get out! What happened?

Well, matter of fact, that's *exactly* what happened. The old Picture1 was selected when you clicked on Edit/Paste. Visual Basic thinks that you want to paste a new Picture Box Control *inside* the old Picture Box Control—even though you're pasting down another Control in the same Control Array, and it doesn't make one helluvalot of sense to put Arrayed Controls inside one another.

■ T I P

More than a few people think that paste-in-a-box behavior amounts to a bug. You can decide for yourself. It's certainly confusing. But remember: as you use Edit Paste to create a Picture Box Control array, make sure none of the old Controls are selected when pasting in a new one.

The Index Property

Now that you've seen how *not* to create a Picture Box Control Array, let's do it the right way.

Start with a new project—click on "File," then "New Project," and "No," you don't want to save changes to Form1.

Double-click on the Picture Box in the Toolbox, the one in the upper right corner. You get a simple old everyday Picture Box Control. Let's squish it down a bit and move it to the lower left corner of the Form to keep track of it. Like this:

Figure 7-15: Picture1 Reborn

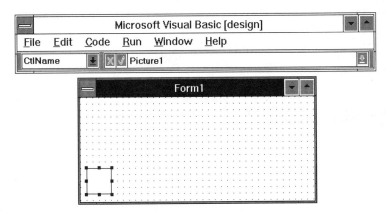

Once again, click on "Edit," then "Copy." All the properties of the Picture1 Control are copied—including its squished-down size. Now click on "Edit," then

"Paste," and say "Yes" when asked if you want to create a Control Array. Here's what happens:

Figure 7-16: The Second Picture1 Hides in the Corner

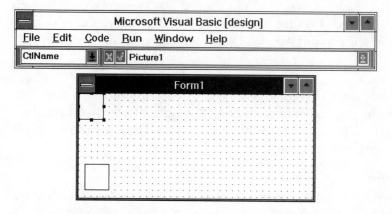

Move this new Picture1 down next to the original.

Double-check that you really have a Control Array by looking at the Index property. The Index property is precisely what you would expect—the subscript of this particular Control. Since the first Picture1 Control is Picture1(0), and the second one is Picture1(1), it shouldn't surprise you too much that the Index of the first Picture1 control is zero and the second is one.

Just confirming:

Figure 7-17: Picture1(1)

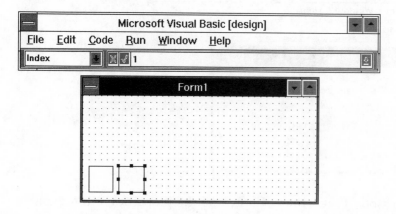

Let's put in the third Picture1 Control.

Listen up! This part is important!

Sorry. Didn't mean to wake you.

Click somewhere—anywhere—on the Form, so no other Control is selected. (Unfortunately, clicking on the Form's title bar doesn't work; you have to find a blank spot on the Form itself.) Once you're absolutely sure no Controls are selected, click on "Edit," then "Paste."

The third Picture1 Control appears:

Figure 7-18: Picture1 the Third

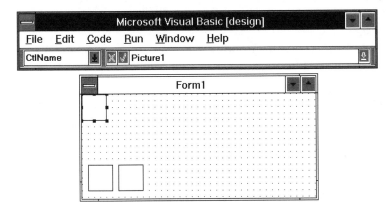

Move that Control down next to the other two. Click on the Form, click "Edit," then "Paste," and you have the fourth Picture1 Control. Move that one down, click on the Form, click "Edit," then "Paste," and you've completed the Picture1 Control Array:

Figure 7-19: The Picture1 Rogue's Gallery

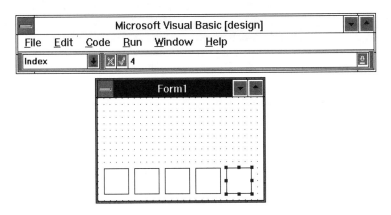

Note how the last Picture1 Control has an Index of 4. You would refer to it as Picture1(4).

We Need Fifty of Them

The CoolCons icon box has fifty icons—fifty Picture Box Controls.

If you're typing this all in from scratch, bring back the HotBar stuff and start a new Form. If you're using the Companion Disk, break out C7PGM2.MAK and follow along while we do some serious pasting.

Start by creating one Picture Box Control. Let's call it "CoolCon." The CoolCon Control can be any size you like, but if you want most (or all) of your icons to be a particular size, you'll save yourself a lot of time by making the first CoolCon Control that size.

We'll make this first CoolCon Control a little bit larger than a "normal" icon on this particular machine. With this Super VGA (800 by 600 pixel) monitor, a size of 380 by 380 twips works out just about right.

Picture Box Controls have a neat property that we need. It's called Autosize, and it simply tells the Control, "Readjust your size to fit the picture stuck on you." CoolCons lets you stick any picture you like on a Picture Box Control—in other words, you can have any size of icon you like; from 1 pixel by 1 pixel to the size of the entire screen, and then some! Thus, we need to set the Autosize property to True. Do that by clicking on the down arrow underneath "Code", finding Autosize, and changing it to True. Like this:

Figure 7-20: A Single CoolCon

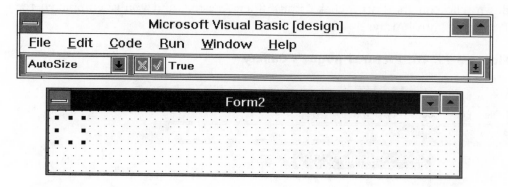

Remember that you set the Control's size by using the Height and Width properties.

Just as a matter of personal preference, we'll also turn the BorderStyle property to zero. You may like your icons drawn with boxes around them; if so, leave the BorderStyle on one ("Fixed Single").

Did you ever wonder what those numbers over on the right of the Visual Basic design window mean? They measure the current Control: the first pair of numbers tells you where the Control is located within the Form (in this case at 120 twips in the "x" direction and 120 in the "y"); the second pair tells you the size of the Control (380 by 380 twips).

From this point on, it's simply a matter of Edit Copy, clicking on the Form so we don't get any embedded Controls, then Edit Paste—and repeating it forty-nine times for a total of fifty Controls in the CoolCon array.

■ **T I P**

Actually, you can copy and paste several Controls at once. To see how, make the first ten Controls one at a time, as was just described. Click on the first one. Holding down the Ctrl key, click on the next one. And the next, and so on, until all ten Controls have been selected. Click on "Edit," then "Copy." And click "Edit," "Paste." Voila! You have twenty Controls. Next click on the Form, so you don't get any embedded Controls, and click "Edit," "Paste" again. That's thirty. And so on.

If you don't go blind or crazy first, you should have fifty CoolCons lined up, something like this:

Figure 7-21: Fifty Little CoolCons, All in a Row

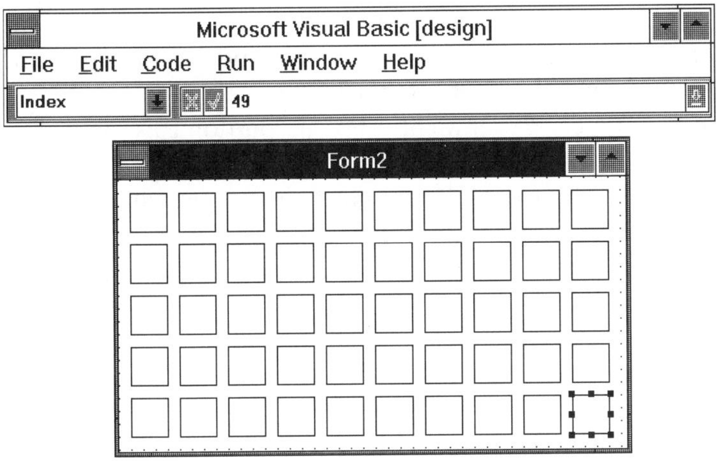

Finally, we're going to force the user to rearrange the icon box under our terms, so we want to get rid of the up-arrow, the down-arrow, and the hyphen-thing in the upper-left corner of this, the IconBox Form.

Scroll down the properties list and one by one choose "MinButton," "Max-Button," and "ControlBox" (that's the hyphen-thing). Set each one to False.

Like this:

Figure 7-22: No Control

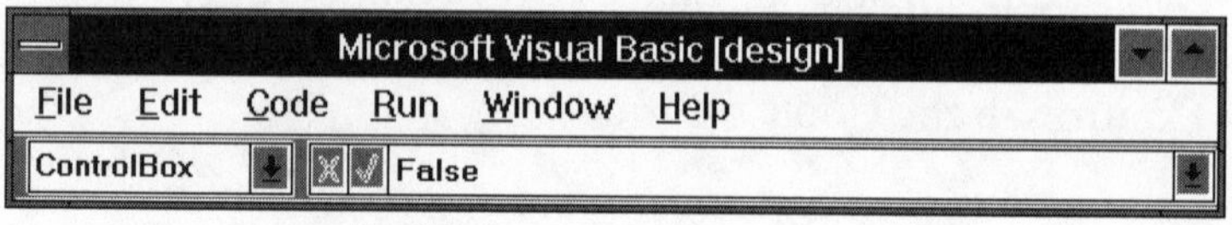

And with that the basic outline of the IconBox Form is complete.

Pulling in Pictures

All those little boxes, just waiting for icons. No doubt you're champing at the bit, ready to put your pictures up in lights.

Well, it's getting a bit ahead of things, but you've been mighty patient this far.

Each of those CoolCon Controls can be customized, changed to a different shape, emblazoned with its own picture. There are detailed instructions in the "Quick Customizing Instructions" section, but you can probably figure it out from this sketch.

To make any CoolCon larger or smaller, just grab it and stretch it. That's all it takes. You can move them around on the Form if you like, but when CoolCons takes over the icons will be rearranged in the "Index" order, running left to right, then top to bottom inside the Form. There's nothing to keep you from making each CoolCon Control a different size, but you'll probably find it more appealing visually if you keep groups of identical height together.

Don't worry about it too much. Experiment a bit. If you don't like what you see, come on back here (or look at the end of this chapter for step-by-step customizing instructions) and stretch the Controls around until you get what you like. It's that easy.

Far as pictures go, well, the sky is pretty much the limit. Any picture you can get onto a Visual Basic Picture Box Control will go on one of those CoolCon Controls. At a minimum, that includes any bitmap (.BMP), icon (.ICO), or Windows Metafile (.WMF) picture, plus anything you can coax onto the Windows clipboard.

Of course, icons are everywhere. There's a whole bunch that come with Visual Basic. (Check the subdirectory "VB\ICONS." Visual Basic also comes with one of the best icon editors in the business, so you can make your own or modify others'; look in "VB\SAMPLES\ICONWRKS.")

We've commissioned the wizard artists at Barry Keller Microsystems to put together a collection of CoolCons icons that you can use. Some of them are . . . uh . . . visually punny. "Save" is a baseball ump declaring a runner safe. "Save As" is a stop sign saving a donkey. "Save All" is lifebuoys from a ship. "Word Count" is *The* Count. "Insert Break" is a weak limb. "Insert Bullets" are 22 calibers. "Insert Table" has four legs. Finally, "Arrange Windows" is a juggler. Take a look. You'll get the idea.

Who says icons can't be fun?

If you're looking for more icons in this series—and of this quality, designed to work with CoolCons—contact Barry Keller Microsystems at 830 Arroyo Way, Taft, California 93268-3744.

To place an ".ICO" icon picture on a CoolCon, simply click on the CoolCon you want to adorn. Then click on the "Picture" property. See the ellipses ("...") over on the right? Click there. Then just find your picture.

As a general rule, we're going to make the very first CoolCon the "Exit" or "Stop" icon. It just so happens Visual Basic has a stop sign that would make a great "Stop" icon.

To put that picture on CoolCon(0), you need only click on the upper-left-corner CoolCon Control—that is, select CoolCon(0)—click on the Picture property, click on the ellipses, then scroll to where that "Stop" icon is stored—it's file "TRFFC14.ICO" in the Visual Basic subdirectory "VB\ICON\TRFFC."

Like so:

Figure 7-23: Trffc14.ICO Goes on the First CoolCon

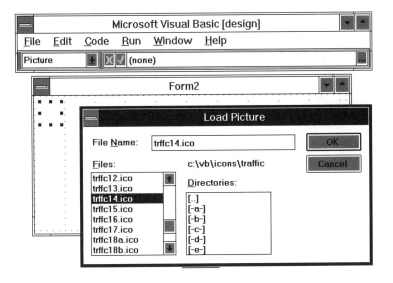

Click "OK" and your first icon is in place.

We're partial to using an "OOPS!" icon as the last of the bunch. Surprisingly, that same group of Visual Basic Traffic icons includes a "Do Not Enter" sign that fits the bill nicely. It's file "TRFFC13.ICO."

Using the same method to load the "Do Not Enter" picture gives you the alpha and omega of the icon box:

Figure 7-24: CoolCon(0) and CoolCon(49)

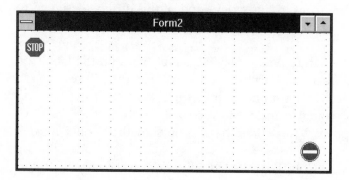

You can put any .BMP, .ICO, or .WMF picture on a CoolCon by clicking on the CoolCon Control, scrolling to the Picture property, clicking on the ellipses, and then finding the file containing the picture you want.

To import a picture from the Clipboard, simply click on the appropriate CoolCon Control, scroll to the Picture property, and click on "Edit," then "Paste."

So much for the hard part. All that's left is the code!

Making Contact

Time to polish off the Hot Bar.

We're going to draw on much of what came before. If you don't follow the Dynamic Data Exchange discussion here, flip back to Chapter 6 for a more detailed explication. *Extrication?*

If you have the Companion Disk in your hip pocket, crank up C7PGM3, and follow the bouncing ball.

Belly Up to the Hot Bar, Folks

"Six pints of bitter," said Ford Prefect to the barman of the
Horse and Groom. "And quickly, please, the world's about to end."

—Douglas Adams, *The Hitchhiker's Guide to the Galaxy*, 1979
(Quoted in *The Hacker's Guide to Undocumented Reality*, forthcoming)

Our primary concern is loading the Hot Bar. The Form_Load Event Handler must establish contact with Word for Windows, arrange things so the HotBar Form can be seen, and then transfer focus over to Word for Windows, so the user can start typing away.

As you might imagine, there are a few tricks.

Form_Load Here's the Form_Load procedure, minus the error routines:

Figure 7-25: HotBar Form_Load

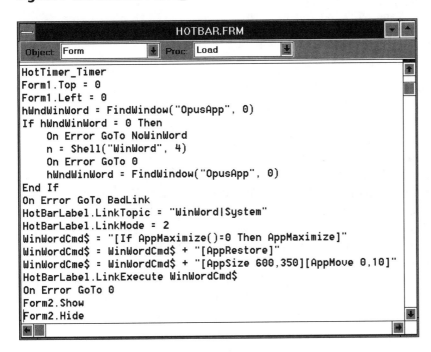

```
HotTimer_Timer
Form1.Top = 0
Form1.Left = 0
hWndWinWord = FindWindow("OpusApp", 0)
If hWndWinWord = 0 Then
    On Error GoTo NoWinWord
    n = Shell("WinWord", 4)
    On Error GoTo 0
    hWndWinWord = FindWindow("OpusApp", 0)
End If
On Error GoTo BadLink
HotBarLabel.LinkTopic = "WinWord|System"
HotBarLabel.LinkMode = 2
WinWordCmd$ = "[If AppMaximize()=0 Then AppMaximize]"
WinWordCmd$ = WinWordCmd$ + "[AppRestore]"
WinWordCme$ = WinWordCmd$ + "[AppSize 600,350][AppMove 0,10]"
HotBarLabel.LinkExecute WinWordCmd$
On Error GoTo 0
Form2.Show
Form2.Hide
```

That really isn't too bad if you take it in small doses.
The first three lines just set up the HotBar:

```
HotTimer_Timer
Form1.Top = 0
Form1.Left = 0
```

One point worth mentioning. It's an old trick, but one too often over-looked. If you want the user to think your program is really working hard, give the user something to look at—preferably something that moves. Put your dither windows up on the screen just as soon as you can, and leave them up there as long as you can.

That's why the very first action performed during a HotBar Form_Load is to update the HotBar (by setting off a HotTimer_Timer Event, making the Hot-Timer clock "tick") and then toss the HotBar Form up at the top of the screen. Although the Timer Event may not be processed quickly enough to beat Word for Windows onto the screen, at the very least all sorts of things will be flying around in short order!

The next seven lines get WinWord cranked up:

```
hWndWinWord = FindWindow("OpusApp", 0)
If hWndWinWord = 0 Then
    On Error GoTo NoWinWord
    n = Shell("WinWord", 4)
    On Error GoTo 0
    hWndWinWord = FindWindow("OpusApp", 0)
End If
```

We're using the "FindWindow" Windows API call (discussed in Chapter 6) because we're going to need that handle to the Word for Windows window, what we've called hWndWinWord.

As you'll certainly recall, "OpusApp" is the Class Name for Word for Windows windows. If Word for Windows isn't running, the FindWindow API call will return a zero, and it's time for CoolCons to punt.

The Form_Load procedure Shells to WinWord. (The "4" in the Shell command tells Windows to start WinWord in a normal window without focus.) If WinWord can't be found, i.e., if it isn't in the current directory, and it isn't in the DOS Path statement, Visual Basic branches to the "NoWinWord:" label, where we'll tell the users they have to have WinWord on the Path.

(Yes, we could've trapped a bad Shell, directed the user to point our program to WinWord, and stored away the path to WinWord in an .INI file—much as we did in WinLHA. But that seems like a lot of work, considering most people with WinWord will have it on their Path. It would be a worthwhile improvement, though, and is thus left to you the reader as "an exercise"!)

By the time we're done with this block of code, Word for Windows should be running, we should have a valid hWndWinWord that points to the Word for Windows window, and, most importantly, the On Error Goto flag should have been reset so errors are trapped.

CoolCons Calling WinWord Next, HotBar sets up the Dynamic Data Exchange link with Word for Windows:

```
On Error GoTo BadLink
HotBarLabel.LinkTopic = "WinWord|System"
HotBarLabel.LinkMode = 2
```

We're making the HotBarLabel Control do double duty, first as a real label (it's the one that displays the date and time and such), second as a DDE Client. Because we won't be bringing any information back from Word for Windows, there's no harm done. The Label won't be touched.

With an application of "WinWord," a Topic of "System," no Item, and a Mode of "2," Visual Basic CoolCons sets up a cold link with Word for Windows. Due to the "System" Topic, this link will go through no matter which documents WinWord has open. And without an Item, everything should be just fine for DDE Execute.

That's precisely what we want.

```
WinWordCmd$ = "[If AppMaximize()=0 Then AppMaximize]"
WinWordCmd$ = WinWordCmd$ + "[AppRestore]"
WinWordCmd$ = WinWordCmd$ + "[AppSize 600,350][AppMove 0,10]"
HotBarLabel.LinkExecute WinWordCmd$
On Error GoTo 0
```

The very first commands to be DDE Executed by Word for Windows are a string of cryptic WordBasic statements that translate, roughly, as follows:

- If the Word for Windows window is not maximized, maximize it. (We want to maximize the window so the next command will work properly.)
- Restore the window to a nonmaximized (and nonminimized) state. (The "Restore" command only works predictably if you already *know* that the window is either minimized or maximized. It's one of the most confusing commands in WordBasic.)
- Size the window so it's 600 points wide and 350 points high.
- Position the window so the upper left corner is ten points below the top of the screen. (Sizing and positioning only work if the window is not maximized and not minimized. That's why we had to jump through the hoops with AppMaximize and AppRestore.)

Those four commands may be the toughest, most convoluted ones in CoolCons—and they're in "easy" WordBasic, not "tough" Visual Basic!

Open the Kimono Finally, we want to flash the icon box up on the screen and then hide it.

```
Form2.Show
Form2.Hide
```

By taking care of this bit of housekeeping now, instead of waiting for the first time the user actually calls up the icon box, we can front-load all the time delays. User may tolerate a few seconds' delay during the start-up. But if that delay comes later, when they're waiting for the icon box to appear for the first time, it'll seem deathly slow.

When the icon box is shown, it'll be resized and repositioned to wherever the user last left it. Then when it's hidden, it'll be ready to show again in a split second.

It's almost always preferable to leave Forms alone until they're actually needed, and once they're used they should be thrown away—"unloaded"—as quickly as possible. Forms take up System Resources, memory, and all sorts of overhead. Unfortunately, we need the icon box to be available at a moment's notice. So we'll have to settle for showing it and hiding it: keeping it in the wings, consuming all those resources, simply so the Hot Bar is really hot.

If you're without a Companion Disk, the Form_Load event ends with a couple of simple error messages, thusly:

```
Exit Sub
NoWinWord:
    Msg$ = "Word for Windows must be in your "
    Msg$ = Msg$ + "DOS Path for CoolCons to work."
    MsgBox Msg$, 16, "CoolCons"
    End
BadLink:
    Msg$ = "Word for Windows is not responding "
    Msg$ = Msg$ + "to DDE. Terminating CoolCons."
    MsgBox Msg$, 16, "CoolCons"
    End
End Sub
```

Exit Sub is a nifty little command that just . . . exits the sub!

Eeek! I Saw a Mouse!

Earlier in this chapter we had you set up a simple MsgBox to demonstrate when a MouseMove Event occurred over the HotBarLabel Control.

It just so happens that the real code for the HotBarLabel_MouseMove Event handler is almost as simple. Take a look at Figure 7-26 on the following page.

Figure 7-26: Mouse_Move Event

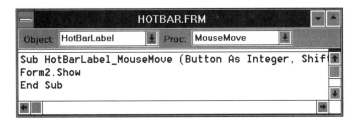

Whenever the user swings the mouse over the HotBarLabel, we want to show Form2, the icon box.

Would they were all so easy!

Switching Focus on Form_Load

The very last thing we want to do when the HotBar Form is loaded?

We have to switch focus over to Word for Windows. That way the user will be able to start typing normally and have what is typed zip straight through to WinWord.

You might think that switching focus would be pretty easy, what with all the Windows API calls at our disposal. It isn't necessarily so.

The fundamental problem: a Form_Load procedure grabs the focus and holds onto it. Even if you shift focus during the Load subroutine, Visual Basic grabs it back and leaves the loaded form with focus. Which leaves us up the old creek. Who wants focus on the HotBar?

Ah, but a solution exists! Actually, several solutions exist, but this one is mighty easy to implement.

What we need is another Timer Control. One that will wait a fraction of a second, until the HotBar Form is well and truly Loaded and then jump up and switch focus over to WinWord. We've got the hWnd for WinWord. How about that. Switching should be a piece of cake.

Bring up the HotBar Form, and double-click on the Timer Control over in the Toolbox. Set this second timer up as, say, "SetFocusTimer," and give it a very short interval—say 50 milliseconds. Like so:

Figure 7-27: The SetFocusTimer

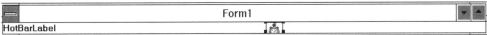

Since we know the SetFocusTimer "tick" event will occur just ever-so-slightly after the Form is loaded, we can use the hWndWinWord to set focus and have it stick.

Figure 7-28: SetFocusTimer Sets Focus

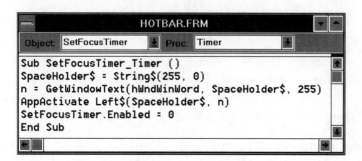

There are at least as many ways to set focus as there are hucksters at Comdex. We're using a particularly easy and reliable method, recommended in Chapter 6, that relies on the Visual Basic command AppActivate.

AppActivate doesn't really start (or activate) an application: it sends focus to a specific window, identified by that window's title.

The SetFocusTimer_Timer Event Handler uses the now-familiar SpaceHolder$ method to reserve enough room for the GetWindowText Windows API call. Feed GetWindowText the hWnd for WinWord and back comes the window title. Give that title to the Visual Basic AppActivate command, and WinWord gets focus.

Finally SetFocusTimer, having done its brief but crucial job, turns itself off by setting the Enabled property to zero.

Talking Turkey

In the earlier incarnation of the HotBox, we had to Declare two Windows API functions, GetFreeSpace and GetFreeSystemResources. Those provided numbers that end up being displayed inside the HotBoxLabel.

We need to add two more Windows API calls, FindWindow and GetWindow-Text, so SetFocusTimer can get its job done. And since hWndWinWord is established in the Form_Load procedure, then used in SetFocusTimer, we have to set up hWndWinWord as a variable shared throughout the HotBox Form.

Simply flip through the HotBox code, looking for (general) and (declarations), then make sure all of this appears:

```
Dim hWndWinWord
Declare Function GetFreeSpace Lib "kernel" (ByVal wFlags As\
  Integer) As Long
```

```
Declare Function GetFreeSystemResources Lib "user" (ByVal wFlags\
 As Integer) As Integer
Declare Function FindWindow Lib "user" (ByVal Class$, ByVal\
 Caption As Long) As Integer
Declare Function GetWindowText Lib "user" (ByVal hWnd As Integer,\
 ByVal WindowText$, ByVal nMax As Integer) As Integer
```

That should make the Form copacetic.

One Cool 'Con

Just one last step and HotBar is done. We need to give the Form an icon—something for the user to click on, to get CoolCons working, something cool.

Visual Basic obliges once again. The icon called MISC43 in their "Misc" collection depicts a skier (what could be more cool?), cavorting at 9,000 feet in the Colorado Rockies. The perfect Cool icon.

Click somewhere on the HotBar Form (you may have to stretch it a bit to find some unoccupied real estate; just make sure you shrink it back when you're done). Scroll down to the Icon property, and click the ellipses:

Figure 7-29: SchussCon

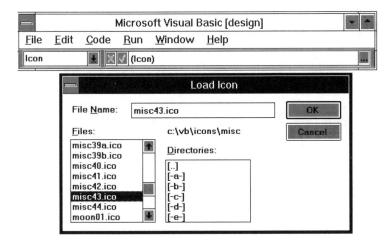

Of course, it looks as if the iconic skier is wearing a football helmet, but sometimes coolitude hath its cost.

HotBar In Action

If you have WinWord in your DOS Path, simply push F5 or click on "Run," then "Start." Slide your cursor up to the top of the screen.

There it is. Form2 lurks just beneath the surface:

Figure 7-30: Birth of the Cool

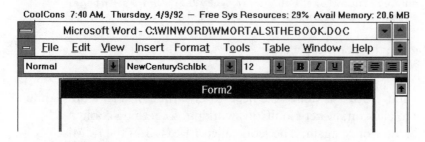

No, it doesn't really do anything yet. But it will. It will.

You can take a break now. Kick back and grab a cup of Java. This next section gets a bit hairy.

Icon See It

We're going to finish off the CoolCons Icon Box in this section. It's a long section, but once you see all the neat stuff Visual Basic can do, you'll probably feel it's worth the wading.

Keep in the back of your head the fact that although we're building this application for Word for Windows, the same principles—indeed, much of the same code—will work with *any* program that supports Dynamic Data Exchange.

If you have the Companion Disk, go ahead and bring in the whole enchilada, COOLCONS.MAK.

Icon Box Load

May as well begin at the beginning, the IconBox Form's Form_Load.

It's not complex. Take a look at Figure 7-31 on the following page.

The first line:

```
Para$ = Chr$(13) + Chr$(10)
```

should be an embarrassment to Visual Basic's designers. We want to set up a paragraph mark—you can call it a Carriage Return/Line Feed if you like; it's often abbreviated CrLf$ or CRLF$—so we don't have to keep typing "Chr$(13) + Chr$(10)" every time we turn around.

Figure 7-31: IconBox Form_Load

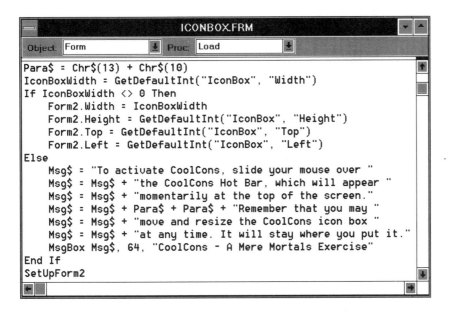

If there were ever a reason to have Global constants, this is it: a simple combination of characters, used over and over, that we'd like to set once and forget. It should be a one-liner in a Visual Basic Global Module,

```
Global Const Para$ = Chr$(13) + Chr$(10)
```

where the "Global Const" means "Global Constant."

Guess what? You can't do it!

B U G

Global constants cannot be set to values containing function calls. And while it stretches the terminology a bit, "Chr$()" is, quite literally, a function call.

B U G

Even if you could use "Chr$()," Global constants cannot be assigned values containing concatenated strings, either.

So in a very large percentage of Visual Basic programs, you'll find "Para$" or "CrLf$" defined as a Global variable, in the Global module, with its value assigned in the first convenient Form_Load Event handler.

Fortunately, Visual Basic doesn't have a lot of ridiculous arbitrary restrictions like this. But it makes the ones that remain all the more infuriating.

The next six lines

```
IconBoxWidth = GetDefaultInt("IconBox", "Width")
If IconBoxWidth <> 0 Then
    Form2.Width = IconBoxWidth
    Form2.Height = GetDefaultInt("IconBox", "Height")
    Form2.Top = GetDefaultInt("IconBox", "Top")
    Form2.Left = GetDefaultInt("IconBox", "Left")
```

check to see if we've stored away the size and location of the IconBox Form, much as we checked for default file names in WinLHA. We'll have to write a function for the CoolCons module-slash-subroutine library that stores and retrieves numbers in a Private .INI file. Call it, say, "COOLCONS.INI."

In WinLHA, a null ("") file name tipped us off that there was nothing in the WINLHA.INI file; here we're going to watch for a zero Icon Box Width. If the Width isn't zero, the rest of the numbers should be good, and this code resizes and repositions the IconBox Form to the specs in COOLCONS.INI.

That GetDefaultInt function is something to worry about later. At this point all that's important is realizing that the numbers will all be integers, so we can use a special Windows API call known as GetPrivateProfileInt, which only deals in integers.

If the user has never repositioned or resized the IconBox Form, the next few lines give a nudge. Most likely there's a new user at the controls, and we should be nice!

```
Else
    Msg$ = "To activate CoolCons, slide your mouse over "
    Msg$ = Msg$ + "the CoolCons Hot Bar, which will appear "
    Msg$ = Msg$ + "momentarily at the top of the screen."
    Msg$ = Msg$ + Para$ + Para$ + "Remember that you may "
    Msg$ = Msg$ + "move and resize the CoolCons icon box "
    Msg$ = Msg$ + "at any time. It will stay where you put it."
    MsgBox Msg$, 64, "CoolCons - A Mere Mortals Exercise"
End If
```

Finally, each individual CoolCon needs a description and a DDE Command assigned to it. The Description will flash up on the IconBox title bar, telling the user what will happen if they push that particular icon. The DDE Command is the precise WordBasic command that will be run if the icon is pushed.

For example, the "FileOpen" CoolCon should have a description that says something witty and informative, like, uh, "Open a File." The corresponding DDE Execute statement is just "FileOpen."

The code looks something like this, if CoolCon number 2 is the FileOpen icon:

```
Description$(2)="Open a File"
DDECommand$(2)="FileOpen"
```

Two variables. Times fifty CoolCons. At least 100 lines of code. Let's put it in a module / subroutine and call it:

```
SetUpForm2
```

Whew. Save the hard work for later.

Take a Load Off

So we need to save away the size and location of the Form, right? We could save that information every time the Form is moved or sized, but there's a simpler way.

There are four stages in a Form's life:

- A Form may be loaded with the "Load Form" statement. This puts the Form in memory, so your program can get at it quickly. It also triggers a Form_Load Event.

- A Form may be shown with the "Form.Show" command. (Show is called a "Method" in Visual Basic lingo.) If your program hasn't explicitly executed a "Load Form" statement for this Form, Visual Basic is smart enough to Load the Form and set off a Form_Load Event before the Form is actually shown. The last step of the Form.Show sequence is to set focus on the Form: that's precisely what made it so tough to send the focus to Word for Windows earlier in the HotBar's Form_Load Event Handler.

- A Form may be hidden with the "Form.Hide" command. (Yeah, "Hide" is a Visual Basic "Method," too.) "Hide" simply makes the Form invisible. Your program can get at the Form, but the user can't.

- Finally, a Form may be unloaded with the "Unload Form" statement. That takes the whole Form out of memory and reclaims any system resources devoted to it. A Form_Unload Event is also triggered.

Theoretically, any time your program ends, Visual Basic is supposed to unload all the Forms. In practice, it looks like that may not always be true (although some would argue otherwise). Regardless, it's simply a safe programming practice to explicitly unload big Forms before your program quits.

By any measure, the IconBox Form is a big Form. We'll be unloading it explicitly.

The easiest time to tuck away Form size and location information is at the very end of the Form's life, when the IconBox Form is unloaded. And that is when the Form_Unload Event is triggered.

Storing away the settings will take another subroutine in the module/subroutine library, called WriteDefaultInt:

```
Sub Form_Unload (Cancel As Integer)
Call WriteDefaultInt("IconBox", "Width", Form2.Width)
Call WriteDefaultInt("IconBox", "Height", Form2.Height)
Call WriteDefaultInt("IconBox", "Top", Form2.Top)
Call WriteDefaultInt("IconBox", "Left", Form2.Left)
End Sub
```

Pretty easy so far, huh?

Keep Them Descriptions Comin'

Every time the mouse passes over an icon, we'd like to flash a description up on the window title bar, explaining what that particular icon will do if it's pushed.

If we do this right, it'll be better than any other icon box around, simply because the hint will appear magically. Users don't have to click the right mouse button or try to remember what an eight-character macro name means in English. It'll be right there in front of them, in black and white.

There's a drawback, though. If the user resizes the icon box so it's narrow, many descriptions won't fit. While that isn't a technical problem, it makes the user interface less than perfect. Another place for improvement. Another exercise for you, dear reader!

As you've probably guessed, the code involved is almost trivial:

Figure 7-32: Icon Tells All

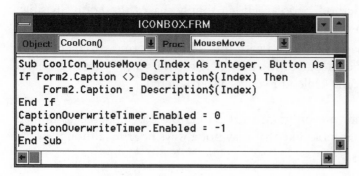

Everything here except the "Form2.Caption=" line is subtlety.

The CoolCon_MouseMove Event Handler first checks to see if the Form's Caption (that's the window title) has already been set to the description for this icon. Why? Because if you continuously reset the Caption, it flickers like a torch in a hailstorm. By checking to see if it needs resetting before actually writing over it, the flicker disappears.

CaptionOverwriteTimer

The next two lines in Figure 7-32 "reset the clock" on a new Control, called the CaptionOverwriteTimer. Turning a Timer Control off—by setting its Enabled Property to zero—then turning it back on—by setting Enabled to true, or minus one—has the effect of starting the Control's clock all over again.

But why a CaptionOverwriteTimer? To overwrite the Caption, natch!

Here's the problem: if the user swings the mouse over, say, the "File Open" icon, the Caption will almost immediately turn from "CoolCons" to "Open a File." That's good.

But if the user then moves their mouse off the "File Open" icon, and *off the Form entirely*, there's no Event triggered that will set the Caption back to "CoolCons." The user could walk away from *CoolCons* and come back ten years later, and the caption would still read "File Open."

That's not good.

During the original design and programming, futzing with this one little glitch took more time than all of the rest of CoolCons combined. We spent days trying to get Events triggered this way and that way, all to no avail. Visual Basic tracks many Events. "Mouse Just Left the Form" is not one of them.

So we settled on a decent—but not perfect—compromise.

Every three seconds the CaptionOverwriteTimer kicks in and writes the name "CoolCons" as the IconBox Form's title. Three seconds is a guess: any faster and the user may not be able to read the icon's description; any slower and the old, potentially bogus window title seems to hang around too long.

If you're using the Companion Disk, the CaptionOverwriteTimer is already there. If you aren't, bring up the IconBox Form and double-click on the Timer in the Toolbox. Set it up with a CtlName of CaptionOverwriteTimer and an Interval of 3000, or three seconds; like Figure 7-33 on the following page.

Timer Controls don't show up when the program is running, so you needn't worry about location or size of that little clock.

Figure 7-33: CaptionOverwriteTimer

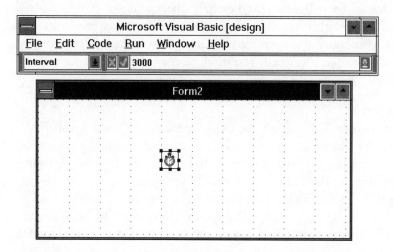

The CaptionOverwriteTimer_Timer Event Handler couldn't be simpler:

Figure 7-34: CaptionOverwriteTimer_Timer Event Handler

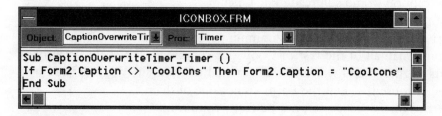

It uses the only-change-if-it's-different approach, too, to avoid flicker in the window's title. Now you can understand why the CoolCon_MouseMove Event Handler reset the clock on the CaptionOverwriteTimer: whenever the user runs the mouse over an icon, we want to wait *another three seconds* before the title gets overwritten. The easiest way to restart that three-second timer is to set this Control's Enabled Property to zero, then back to minus one: turning it off, then on again, starts the clock all over again.

Timers can be extremely powerful. Sometimes the logic to set them and reset them gets complex, but they're an indispensable part of your Visual Basic arsenal.

Hey, Hey, Hey, Do the Icon Shuffle

Did you notice how we glossed over the "resize and reposition" part of the Form_Load? Waved our hands and figured it would take care of itself? Well, it's come a-cropper.

Structured programming was supposed to let us bury stuff like that, so we could deal with the "minor implementation details" later on in a program's development cycle. While structured programming has its good points—we're using many structured techniques right here—it ain't got nuthin' on Event-Driven programming.

In the Form_Load Event Handler, we blithely reset the size and position of the IconBox Form and did absolutely nothing to move the icons around so they'd fit in the new box.

Not too surprisingly, resetting the size or shape of a Form triggers an Event—a Form_Resize Event. It's the same Event that's triggered when the user takes the mouse and drags around corners of a Form.

Our task in the Form_Resize Event Handler is really quite simple: we have to move the CoolCon icons around so they'll fit in the resized box.

We could try to build a fancy, complex routine that tries to minimize vacant space or some such. But users will get mad if we muck around much with the sequence of the icons: FileOpen comes before FileClose; if our routine sticks CheckSpelling between the two—no matter how good the physical "fit"—our users will be all up in arms.

So the CoolCons IconBox Form filler uses the simplest method you could imagine:

Figure 7-35: IconBox's Form_Resize Event Handler

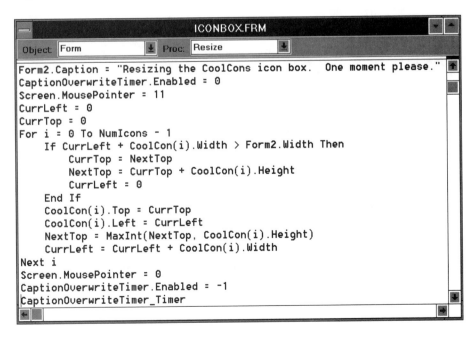

```
ICONBOX.FRM

Object: Form          Proc: Resize

Form2.Caption = "Resizing the CoolCons icon box.  One moment please."
CaptionOverwriteTimer.Enabled = 0
Screen.MousePointer = 11
CurrLeft = 0
CurrTop = 0
For i = 0 To NumIcons - 1
    If CurrLeft + CoolCon(i).Width > Form2.Width Then
        CurrTop = NextTop
        NextTop = CurrTop + CoolCon(i).Height
        CurrLeft = 0
    End If
    CoolCon(i).Top = CurrTop
    CoolCon(i).Left = CurrLeft
    NextTop = MaxInt(NextTop, CoolCon(i).Height)
    CurrLeft = CurrLeft + CoolCon(i).Width
Next i
Screen.MousePointer = 0
CaptionOverwriteTimer.Enabled = -1
CaptionOverwriteTimer_Timer
```

That wasn't so bad, was it?

The first line puts a new title on the window:

```
Form2.Caption = "Resizing the CoolCons icon box.  One moment please."
```

The second line disables the Timer (which would overwrite the title with "CoolCons"):

```
CaptionOverwriteTimer.Enabled = 0
```

The third line is a fun one:

```
Screen.MousePointer = 11
```

Visual Basic lets you get at the shape of the cursor. Setting this variable to eleven turns the cursor into an hourglass and keeps it an hourglass until you change it back. (You can also make the cursor look like a cross-hair pointer, an I-beam, a square-in-a-square, any of the sizing arrows, an up-arrow, or a "do not enter" sign.)

The next block of code does the icon shuffle:

```
CurrLeft = 0
CurrTop = 0
NextTop = 0
For i = 0 To NumIcons - 1
    If CurrLeft + CoolCon(i).Width > Form2.Width Then
        CurrTop = NextTop
        NextTop = CurrTop + CoolCon(i).Height
        CurrLeft = 0
    End If
    CoolCon(i).Top = CurrTop
    CoolCon(i).Left = CurrLeft
    NextTop = MaxInt(NextTop, CoolCon(i).Height)
    CurrLeft = CurrLeft + CoolCon(i).Width
Next i
```

You can dig into the code if you like, but basically it looks at each icon in turn and shoves the current icon immediately to the right of the previous icon—if it'll fit. If it won't fit, filling starts on the next line. The tallest icon in each row dictates how far down the next row goes.

We'll have to write another routine for the module/subroutine library, called MaxInt, that'll take two integers and return the larger. That should be easy.

Finally, the pointer is set back to normal (a value of zero), the CaptionOverwriteTimer is reenabled, and then "ticked" to get the "CoolCons" caption back up as the window title.

```
Screen.MousePointer = 0
CaptionOverwriteTimer.Enabled = -1
CaptionOverwriteTimer_Timer
```

What, twenty lines to rearrange the icons?

Everybody's Talking At Me

Well, we've worked all around it. Better get to it. Time to dig into the meat of the IconBox Form—the CoolCon_Click Event Handler.

Get ready for another 20 line behemoth:

Figure 7-36: The Hard Part

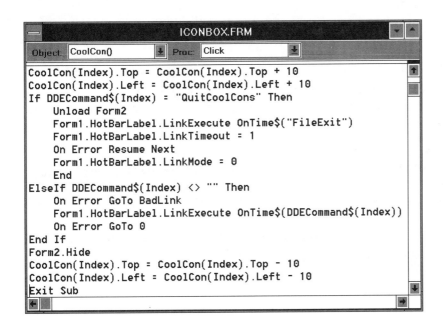

The first two lines

```
CoolCon(Index).Top = CoolCon(Index).Top + 10
CoolCon(Index).Left = CoolCon(Index).Left + 10
```

give the user visual feedback. By moving the icon just a little bit down and to the right (10 twips, not a whole lot), it "feels" like the icon has been clicked. Since it happens almost immediately after the mouse click, the user might even be tricked into thinking *the entire application* is quick.

It isn't, of course: DDE and Visual Basic both take their cuts on CPU cycles and there's not much we can do about it, but making something happen right away never hurts the all-important human perception.

The next block of code lets CoolCons die gracefully. Let's take the commands one at a time, as there are several tricks lurking just beneath the surface.

```
If DDECommand$(Index) = "QuitCoolCons" Then
```

That's something of an internal flag. The DDECommand$()s are set in the module/subroutine library's SetForm2 procedure. You can make them anything you like—and change Description$()s to go along with them. Most DDECommand$()s will look like "FileOpen" or "EditCut" or "FormatCharacter." But if you set a DDECommand$() to "QuitCoolCons," this Event Handler treats it as a signal to close down shop, kill off Word for Windows, close the DDE link, and shut down.

If the user chooses to quit CoolCons, the first thing we'll do is Unload that monstrous IconBox Form:

```
Unload Form2
```

Then we need to tell WinWord to die and break the DDE link.

This presents something of a quandary. And where there's a quandary, there's a trick!

Who Dies First? It's a chicken-and-egg problem.

If we break the DDE link first, there's no way to tell WinWord to stop.

Contrariwise, if we tell WinWord to shut down and then try to drop the DDE link, there won't be anybody at the other end of the phone, and the DDE gods will get angry!

In fact, if WinWord dies before the DDE link is severed, a big, ugly DDE Timeout Error Condition will be raised, and our graceful journey into that good night will transform into a bumpy ride down the road to DDE hell.

What to do?

■ **TIP**

Ignore the Error Condition! (And pray the gods don't get *real* mad!)

We'll start by sending WinWord the poison-pill command, the one that makes it disappear:

```
Form1.HotBarLabel.LinkExecute OnTime$("FileExit")
```

(OnTime$() is another one of those functions we'll have to write and put in the module/subroutine library. It turns a DDE Command—in this case "FileExit"—into the monstrous "[OnTime "Time$", "FileExit"]" command that DDE and WordBasic demand. For more details, see the section of Chapter 6 called "The DDE Execute Trick." If you don't remember the OnTime$ trick for DDE Execute, take a few minutes to refresh your memory: CoolCons won't work without it.)

Next we'll set the DDE Timeout just as short as we can—a tenth of a second:

```
Form1.HotBarLabel.LinkTimeout = 1
```

Then we'll ignore all errors—just long enough to hang up the DDE phone.

```
On Error Resume Next
```

. . . break the connection . . .

```
Form1.HotBarLabel.LinkMode = 0
```

. . . and real quick, before thunder and lightning threaten our very existence, duck heads and run for cover!

```
End
```

It's not nice to fool the DDE gods.

Yackety-Yak Most DDE commands, though, aren't quite so exciting. The typical DDECommand$() falls into this category:

```
ElseIf DDECommand$(Index) <> "" Then
    On Error GoTo BadLink
    Form1.HotBarLabel.LinkExecute OnTime$(DDECommand$(Index))
    On Error GoTo 0
End If
```

and are simply DDE Executed, using the OnTime$ machinations.

We've made a provision for null ("") DDE Commands, a sort of "do-nothing" option. It's convenient if you want to put an "OOPS! Turn off the icon box." option among your icons; we've done exactly that for the last icon.

The bypass on null DDE Commands also helps just in case somebody messes up when he or she works on the DDECommand$()s in the module/subroutine library. When you're playing with 50 different commands and 100 variables, it's easy to get a couple of subscripts switched around.

Duck Finally, in the spirit of keeping CoolCons out on the screen until the very last moment, the IconBox Form gets tucked away, and the clicked icon is returned to its original position.

```
Form2.Hide
CoolCon(Index).Top = CoolCon(Index).Top - 10
CoolCon(Index).Left = CoolCon(Index).Left - 10
Exit Sub
```

Here's what the error routine looks like:

```
BadLink:
Msg$ = "Word for Windows is not responding."
MsgBox Msg$, 16, "CoolCons"
Form2.Hide
Form1.SetFocusTimer.Enabled = -1
Resume Next
End
```

If the DDE Link times out, chances are pretty good WinWord is in the middle of something—a spell check may be in effect, for example, or there may be a dialog box awaiting user input. If that's the case, we don't want to do anything drastic.

The error handler merely pops a relatively benign message, hides the IconBox Form, then turns on the HotBar's SetFocusTimer. As you may recall, that timer waits about five milliseconds, then turns focus over to Word for Windows.

Finally the error handler uses a Resume Next to return to the command just after the one that caused the error, and CoolCons continues on its merry way.

Typing Pass-Through

Here's a little embellishment that demonstrates the KeyPress Event.

After working with CoolCons for quite some time, we hit a few odd situations. From time to time a user would swing the mouse up to the Hot Bar, suddenly decide he or she didn't want an icon, and start typing—rapidly, sometimes before the IconBox actually showed up on the screen.

Occasionally a user would get the IconBox Form on the screen and not realize that clicking on an icon could get rid of the box. That caused no end of confusion: "How do I get rid of the stupid thing?"

And—rarely—a user would plant the IconBox Form somewhere in the middle of the screen, a-la-Lotus SmartIcons, and expect it to stay there while they typed. As soon as the user clicked anywhere on the Word for Windows window, of course, the IconBox Form just disappeared underneath WinWord.

We played around with keeping the IconBox Form on top of the WinWord window, but ran flat up against the Lotus/Amí Pro SmartIcons problem: if the

IconBox Form is on top, you won't be able to see what's under it. Start typing, and when the typing goes under the Form, you can't see it. Move the Form automatically, and it can flip-flop all over the screen.

Thus, a compromise.

We decided to have CoolCons respond to typing by passing the keystroke on to WinWord and having the IconBox Form disappear. That isn't necessarily the best way; it's just the way we did it. And when you see how easy it is to change, well, have at it!

When the IconBox Form has focus and a key is pressed—you guessed it—an Event is triggered. This time it's a KeyPress event on the first CoolCon Control. The Event Handler is a two-liner:

Figure 3-37: Press a Key, Any Key

One of the items passed along to a KeyPress Event Handler is a variable called "KeyAscii," which is the ASCII number of the key that was pressed. Yes, you can get yourself into trouble with odd keys, but by and large the character pressed is just Chr$(KeyAscii).

After hiding Form2, Word for Windows gets focus, and the Visual Basic command SendKeys sends the indicated key to WinWord, just as if the user had typed it at the keyboard.

Global Module

Looking back over what we've done, there are only a few variables that need to go in the Global Module:

Figure 7-38: CoolConGlobal

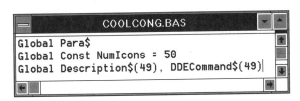

Para$, you will recall, started this section: it has to be assigned a value somewhere outside the Global Module.

The other three variables are just what you would expect. They have to be declared Global so they can be passed between the IconBox Form and the module/subroutine library.

That completes the coding for the IconBox Form. If you include all the multiple-line Messages, all the overhead, you're looking at maybe 75 lines of code.

Just try that in C.

Cool Module

The CoolCons module/subroutine library contains a handful of simple routines, plus one monster 100-line whale that initializes all the icon descriptions and DDE Commands.

Let's tackle the little guys first. If you have the Companion Disk, all of this is in the final program, COOLCONS.MAK.

Windows API Calls

We'll have to declare two Windows API functions, to be used in storing and retrieving the size and location of the IconBox Form. The declares go in the (general) (declarations) section of the COOLCONM.BAS Cool Module.

```
Declare Function GetPrivateProfileInt Lib "kernel" (ByVal\
  SectionName$, ByVal KeyName$, ByVal DefaultKeyValue As Integer,\
  ByVal FileName$) As Integer

Declare Function WritePrivateProfileString Lib "kernel" (ByVal\
  SectionName$, ByVal KeyName$, ByVal KeyValue$, ByVal FileName$)\
  As Integer
```

We've already worked with WritePrivateProfileString, in Chapter 5, where we stored the default WinLHA file names.

GetPrivateProfileInt is very similar to GetPrivateProfileString. It digs into the designated ".INI" file, searches for the section name (which is set off [in brackets]), then looks for the key name, and returns the value assigned to the key. All of that is identical to what we've come to expect from GetPrivateProfileString. What's different is how GetPrivateProfileInt interprets the data it finds.

GetPrivateProfileInt is only interested in integers. The rules are quite stringent:

▪ If the string starts with blanks, ignore them.

▪ If the first character is not a digit, plus sign, or minus sign, return zero.

- If the first character is a dash/minus sign, the number is negative; otherwise the number is positive.
- Gather all the digits (0 to 9) until reaching either the end of the string or a non-digit; that's the number.
- Return the value of the gathered number, positive or negative.

For example,

```
[Section Name]
KeyName=    -123ABC
```

returns a GetPrivateProfileInt value of -123.

These are the new rules for Windows 3.1. Windows 3.0 didn't work the same way.

WriteDefaultInt

WriteDefaultInt(Section$, Key$, Setting) takes the setting and writes it to COOLCONS.INI. Like this:

Figure 7-39: WriteDefaultInt

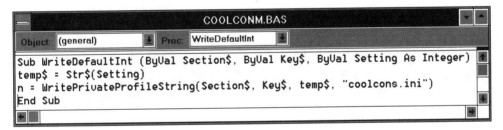

```
COOLCONM.BAS

Object: (general)          Proc: WriteDefaultInt

Sub WriteDefaultInt (ByVal Section$, ByVal Key$, ByVal Setting As Integer)
temp$ = Str$(Setting)
n = WritePrivateProfileString(Section$, Key$, temp$, "coolcons.ini")
End Sub
```

While the Windows 3.1 API includes a call for retrieving integers, there is no similar call for writing integers.

Thus, our WriteDefaultInt has to go through one additional step: converting the integer passed to the routine into a string. Couldn't be simpler. The resulting string is written to COOLCONS.INI as the value of the indicated Key in the indicated Section.

Nothing to it.

Did you notice how Windows API calls have become so humdrum that they hardly warrant a yawn? Do you remember the first time you tried one? Ah, life in the programming fast lane.

GetDefaultInt

Here's another tough one.

Figure 7-40: GetDefaultInt

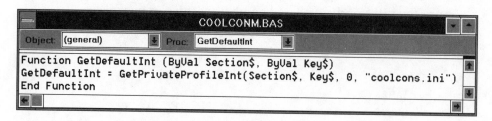

One line.

The only thing remotely remarkable is the "0." That's the value GetPrivate-ProfileInt will automatically assign to the Key if it can't find this particular Section/Key combination in COOLCONS.INI.

MaxInt

This one's so trivial, it's hard to imagine why Visual Basic doesn't include it as a built-in function.

Figure 7-41: Mad MaxInt Beyond Thunderdome

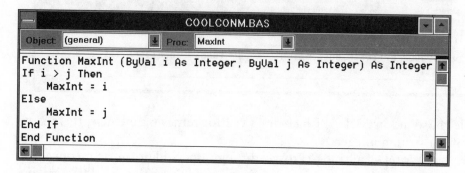

We had to use the term "MaxInt" because "Max" is a property of the Scroll Bar Control.

The OnTime(DDECommand$) Function

This is the function that takes a regular old DDE Execute command—like "FileOpen" or "ShowGroup" or "Collect DynaString$"—and turns it into that strange string that tricks the DDE gods. See Figure 7-42 on the following page.

Figure 7-42: OnTime$()

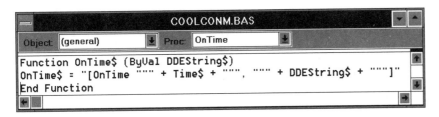

For example,

```
TrickString$=OnTime$("EditReplace")
```

when run at, oh, 6:00 a.m., returns this value:

```
[OnTime "06:00:00", "EditReplace"]
```

You can count the quotes if you want. Keep in mind that two quotes in a row come across the equal sign as one quote; three quotes in a row produce one quote and tell Visual Basic it's at the end of a string.

■ **T I P**

Fortunately, the Visual Basic Time$ function gives a "time" in precisely the correct format for WordBasic: WordBasic wants a 24-hour-clock time in the form "hh:mm:ss," and Time$ generates that exactly.

B U G

Perhaps not surprisingly, the WordBasic Time$() function does *not* produce a time in the correct format for the WordBasic OnTime function. *(Hard to believe, but true.)* In fact, WordBasic Time$() is formatted according to settings in the WIN.INI file, so it may change from "hh:mm:ss AM" to a 12-hour "hh:mm" format—and back again—at any moment! Creating an OnTime time for WordBasic from inside WordBasic is not an easy exercise.

■ **T I P**

This OnTime$() function produces a command valid for Word for Windows. If you try to modify CoolCons to work with other Windows apps, you'll have to pay special attention to this routine and make it churn out a string that will be recognized by the new app. For example, Amí Pro is looking for a string that says

```
[RunLater ("MacroName", 0.00)]
```

Thus, you need to replace that OnTime$ line with a line that says:

```
OnTime$ = "[RunLater (""" + DDEString$ + """, 0.00)]"
```

(Yes, we counted all the quotes for you. You're welcome.)

Since the OnTime DDE Execute trick works generally—with any DDE Server that supports some variant of an OnTime command—you should be able to hack this one-liner to work with almost any Windows application.

SetUpForm2

Here's the big one.

We have to set up all the icon Description$()s and all the DDEStatement$()s that correspond to the descriptions and the icons.

If you're working with the Companion Disk, you'll have our latest stab at a good set of Word for Windows icons, commands, and descriptions.

It'll be mighty disappointing if you don't change some of it! After all, that's the reason why CoolCons exists: so you can make it do what *you* want.

We recommend that you reserve one icon to leave CoolCons and WinWord—this example uses the first icon for that purpose. We also recommend that you have at least one "do-nothing" icon that will let the user get rid of the IconBox Form. We use the last icon, number 49, for that task.

If you're typing, this is but one possible combination of icons, macros, and descriptions. Look under "Quick Customizing Instructions" for a few ideas.

The macros marked [WOPR] are part of the Word for Windows Office POWER Pack. If you don't have WOPR, skip the macros so marked. *(WOPR is a big Word for Windows add-on discussed in Chapter 8).*

■ **T I P**

To avoid a wildly flickering IconBox Form, make sure none of the Description$()s are null—give each description at least one character, even if it's just a space.

```
Sub SetUpForm2 ()
DDECommand$(0) = "QuitCoolCons"
```

```
Description$(0) = "Exit Word for Windows and CoolCons"
Description$(1) = "Start a new document"
DDECommand$(1) = "FileNew"
Description$(2) = "Open a document"
DDECommand$(2) = "FileOpen"
Description$(3) = "Save the current document"
DDECommand$(3) = "FileSave"
Description$(4) = "Save As -- Save current document, giving it a new name"
DDECommand$(4) = "FileSaveAs"
Description$(5) = "Save all open documents, including NORMAL.DOT"
DDECommand$(5) = "FileSaveAll"
Description$(6) = "Close current document"
DDECommand$(6) = "FileClose"
Description$(7) = "Close all open documents [WOPR]"
DDECommand$(7) = "CloseAll"
Description$(8) = "Find a file"
DDECommand$(8) = "FileFind"
Description$(9) = "Delete current document [WOPR]"
DDECommand$(9) = "FileDelete"
Description$(10) = "Quick print, one copy"
DDECommand$(10) = "FilePrintDefault"
Description$(11) = "Print current document"
DDECommand$(11) = "FilePrint"
Description$(12) = "Print odd/even, duplex, booklet, 4-up [WOPR] "
DDECommand$(12) = "TwoByFour"
Description$(13) = "Print envelope with Enveloper 4 [WOPR]"
DDECommand$(13) = "Enveloper4"
Description$(14) = "Undo previous action if possible"
DDECommand$(14) = "EditUndo"
Description$(15) = "Repeat previous action if possible"
DDECommand$(15) = "EditRepeat"
Description$(16) = "Cut out selected text, place on clipboard"
DDECommand$(16) = "EditCut"
Description$(17) = "Copy selected text to clipboard"
DDECommand$(17) = "EditCopy"
Description$(18) = "Paste clipboard contents into document"
DDECommand$(18) = "EditPaste"
Description$(19) = "Select the entire document"
DDECommand$(19) = "EditSelectAll"
Description$(20) = "Find specific text or formatting"
DDECommand$(20) = "EditFind"
Description$(21) = "Replace text or formatting"
DDECommand$(21) = "EditReplace"
Description$(22) = "Go to a page or bookmark"
DDECommand$(22) = "EditGoto"
Description$(23) = "Zoom in or out"
DDECommand$(23) = "ViewZoom"
Description$(24) = "View characters - ANSI/ASCII codes [WOPR]"
DDECommand$(24) = "Viewer"
Description$(25) = "Count words in document or selection [WOPR]"
DDECommand$(25) = "WordCounter"
Description$(26) = "Insert page, column or section break"
DDECommand$(26) = "InsertBreak"
Description$(27) = "Insert a bookmark"
DDECommand$(27) = "InsertBookmark"
```

```
Description$(28) = "Insert date or time"
DDECommand$(28) = "InsertDateTime"
Description$(29) = "Insert symbol -© § » ñ á ¼ö and the like"
DDECommand$(29) = "InsertSymbol"
Description$(30) = "Insert page number, file name, author [WOPR]"
DDECommand$(30) = "InsertIt"
Description$(31) = "Insert a picture"
DDECommand$(31) = "InsertPicture"
Description$(32) = "Insert a frame, flow text around it"
DDECommand$(32) = "InsertFrame"
Description$(33) = "Insert an object - drawing, graph, equation, etc"
DDECommand$(33) = "InsertObject"
Description$(34) = "Insert a chart"
DDECommand$(34) = "InsertChart"
Description$(35) = "Format character - font, size, bold, italic, etc"
DDECommand$(35) = "FormatCharacter"
Description$(36) = "Make super/subscript [WOPR]"
DDECommand$(36) = "SuperSub"
Description$(37) = "Format paragraph - centering, spacing, indents, tabs"
DDECommand$(37) = "FormatParagraph"
Description$(38) = "Set border/shading for paragraphs"
DDECommand$(38) = "FormatBorder"
Description$(39) = "Spell check"
DDECommand$(39) = "ToolsSpelling"
Description$(40) = "Grammar check"
DDECommand$(40) = "ToolsGrammar"
Description$(41) = "Thesaurus look-up"
DDECommand$(41) = "ToolsThesaurus"
Description$(42) = "Make bulleted list out of selection"
DDECommand$(42) = "ToolsBulletListDefault"
Description$(43) = "Make numbered list out of selection"
DDECommand$(43) = "ToolsNumberListDefault"
Description$(44) = "Set options and defaults"
DDECommand$(44) = "ToolsOptions"
Description$(45) = "Indent selected paragraphs"
DDECommand$(45) = "Indent"
Description$(46) = "UnIndent selected paragraphs"
DDECommand$(46) = "UnIndent"
Description$(47) = "Insert a table"
DDECommand$(47) = "TableInsertTable"
Description$(48) = "Arrange all windows"
DDECommand$(48) = "WindowArrangeAll"
Description$(49) = "OOOPS! Get rid of this screen."
End Sub
```

That's All, Folks....

Is your Carpal Tunnel syndrome acting up? After typing in all that stuff, no wonder. *Ugh. Typing. Voice input won't come a minute too soon.*

Well, it's ready. Push F5 or click on "Run," then "Start," and CoolCons should be ready for a test drive.

Figure 7-43: Way Cool

Just a note on using CoolCons: we think it works best when you put the IconBox Form up as high on the screen as you can stand, and stretch it out the entire width of the screen.

But the whole point is: experiment! Find out what works best for you.

This next section will help you customize CoolCons. It's probably too elementary for you now—but it may be just right if you come back six months from now and want to change an icon.

If you feel this user documentation stuff is too simple for you at this stage of enlightenment, take a quick gander anyway. You might pick up some interesting ideas for your own docs.

Quick Customizing Instructions

As promised, we've gathered here all the tips you'll need to customize and recustomize CoolCons. If you're jumping in here without reading the other parts of Chapter 7, or the all-important DDE Chapter, number 6—in fact, if you're jumping in here never having read a bloody thing about Windows, Mortals, programming, or the wonders of Visual Basic and WordBasic—we'll try to step you through it anyway.

If we're very, very lucky, maybe this little excursion into Visual Basic will convince you to take the plunge and learn a bit about Windows programming! It really isn't all that hard. You'll have a great time. Really.

So much for the sales pitch.

We'll assume you know a bit about Windows. If you think Click and Drag is the name of a 42nd Street club, you need to brush up on Windows a touch before proceeding.

You'll need a copy of Visual Basic. Install it per the package instructions. It'll probably go into a subdirectory called "C:\VB" or some such. Don't bother with the tutorial—if you know a little bit about programming and want to learn Visual Basic, start with WinMortals!

You'll also need the CoolCons source code. Follow the instructions here in Appendix 3 to install the source; you'll probably put it in a directory called "C:\VB\COOLCONS" or something similar.

Finally, if you want to change the actions of any particular icon—as opposed to the picture or the size of the icon—you'll have to find the Word for Windows command that corresponds to the action.

For example, if you want to set up an icon to perform a Word for Windows Format / Section Layout, you need to know that the command for that is . . . uh . . . FormatSectionLayout.

■ T I P

If you ever screw things up beyond recognition, remember that you can always restore CoolCons to its original state by copying it from the Companion Disk.

Relax. Once you have Visual Basic installed and the Companion Disk decompressed, the hard part is over. Everything from here on is fun.

Opening up CoolCons

We're going to start at the very, very beginning.

Windows is running, and the Program Manager is in front of you. OK? Good. Now double-click on the Visual Basic icon:

Figure 7-44: Get Visual Basic Running

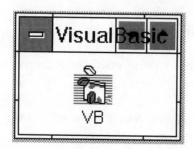

You'll be greeted by the Visual Basic design screen. It looks like Figure 7-45 on the following page.

Don't worry if your screen looks a little different from this one. Each of those four windows can be stretched and moved and slapped around any-which-way; their size and shape aren't important.

We're looking for the COOLCONS program. It's called COOLCONS.MAK.

Figure 7-45: Visual Basic Crawls Out

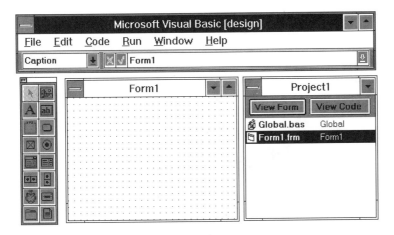

Click on "File," then "Open Project," and futz around with the directories and whatnot until you find COOLCONS.MAK. It should be in the subdirectory that contains the Companion Disk, probably "C:\VB\COOLCONS."

Like this:

Figure 7-46: Opening COOLCONS

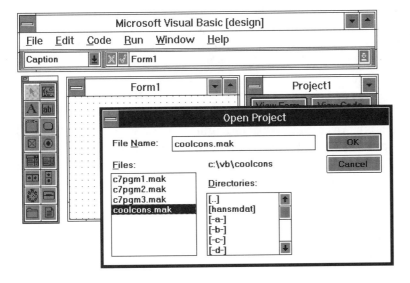

Click on "OK," and CoolCons will jump out at you.

Figure 7-47: One CoolCon, Coming Up

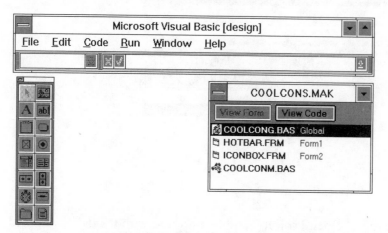

Kind of underwhelming, eh?

That window over there on the right lists the four parts of CoolCons: First, there's a Global Module that contains all the variables used across all the parts of the program. (CoolCong being a direct Fay Wray rip-off.) That second part, HotBar, is just the bar that displays up at the top of the screen. The third part, IconBox, holds the icons—that's the stuff we'll be working with. The fourth part, CoolConM, is what Visual Basic calls a "Module." It's just a library of subroutines used throughout the program. You may have to change part of one subroutine.

Not to worry. It's easy.

The IconBox

Double-click on the line over there on the right that says "ICONBOX.FRM Form2." You'll see something like Figure 7-48 on the following page.

Your version will have pictures in most (maybe all) of those blank squares. And the little clock you can see here may be obscured by a picture. No problem.

The window with the title "Form2," the window with all the icons plastered on it, is called a Form. Forms are Visual Basic's basic building blocks.

There are fifty icons—fifty pictures or blank spots—on this Form, and each one is at your disposal. Each has a number. *(Hey, we're talking computers. Everything has a number, right?)*

The numbers run from zero to forty-nine. The first icon, the Stop Sign in the upper left corner, is icon number zero. The icon just to the right of the Stop Sign is number one. The next one to the right of it is number two, and so on. The last icon, the Do Not Enter sign in the lower right corner, is icon number forty-nine.

So far, so good?

Figure 7-48: The Icon Treasure Trove

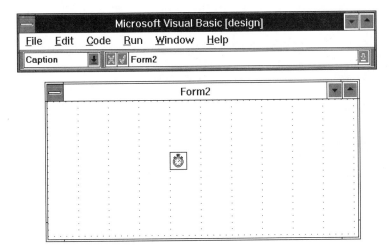

We generally recommend that you keep the first icon—that is, icon number zero—as the "Bail Out and Leave No Prisoners" icon. There's a certain safety in knowing that at least one icon will shut down Word for Windows and CoolCons and tidy everything up.

It's also nice to have the last icon—icon number forty-nine—as the "OOOPS! Get rid of this stupid screen" icon. It lets people extricate themselves from CoolCons before they panic. Those are just recommendations: there's nothing to prevent you from doing 'most anything you like. You can do quite a few things to each icon. Let's step through them one by one.

Changing the Picture on an Icon

Visual Basic lets you place any .ICO icon, .BMP bitmap or .WMF Windows Meta-file Format picture on the icons. You can also paste a picture from the Clipboard.

Here's how.

Pick the icon you want to adorn with a new picture. Doesn't matter if it already has a picture. Click once on the icon. The little boxes appear all around it, right?

If it helps any, you can move the icon wherever you like by clicking in the middle of it and dragging it any old place. You can even make the whole Form larger—just drag the edges or corners, like any other window—and plunk the icon down any place you want.

You may rearrange the icons if it'll make things easier, but keep one thing in mind: when it's running, CoolCons always rearranges the icons according to the original icon number. Icon zero will always show up in the upper left corner, icon forty-nine will always appear in the lower right, and numbers one to forty-eight will fall in from left to right.

Now, up in the "Microsoft Visual Basic [design]" window, see where the word "Code" is on the menu? Good. Underneath "Code" is a down-arrow. Click that down-arrow, and scroll down a bit. Here's what you should see:

Figure 7-49: CoolCon Properties

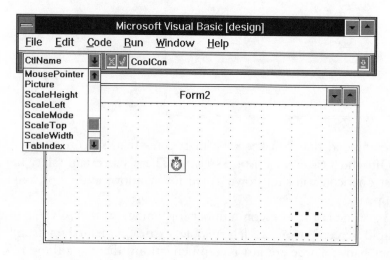

All of the things you can see in that list are called "Properties"—they're attributes of the icon you picked. We're after the Property called "Picture." Click on it.

Take a look to the right, over at the ellipses ("..."). Click on the ellipses. You should see Figure 7-50 on the following page.

Now all you have to do is decide which of the ten-million-plus icon, bitmap, or WMF files you have squirreled away belong on that particular icon. When you finally decide, double-click on the file name, and poof! the picture, shown in Figure 7-51 on the following page, suddenly appears.

Figure 7-50: Load Picture

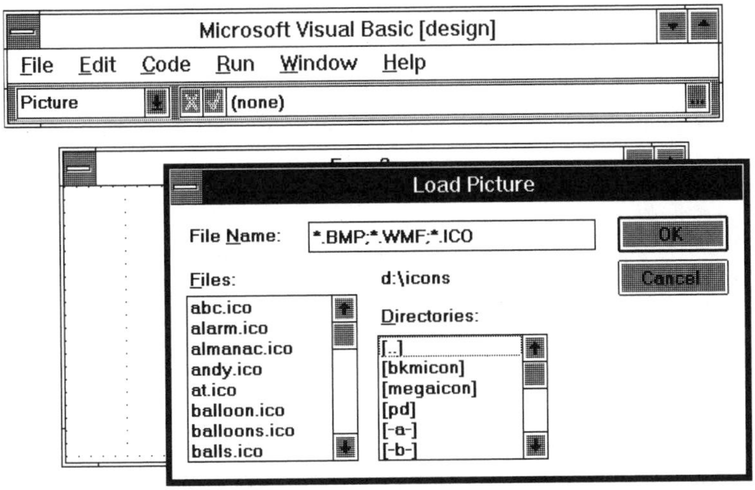

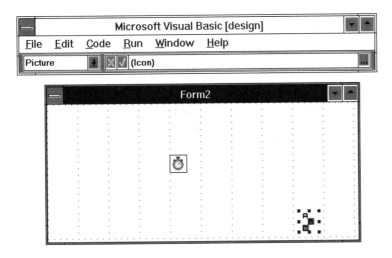

Figure 7-51: The "ABC" Icon

That's all it takes to put a new picture on an icon.

When CoolCons is running it automatically adjusts the box to fit your picture—so if your picture is a bit smaller than the box, don't worry.

Just in case you didn't know: Visual Basic comes with a few hundred icons, pretty good ones, too. Take a look in the "VB\ICONS" subdirectory and in the *Microsoft Visual Basic Programmer's Guide*, pp. 400 to 410.

From Clipboard to Icon The method for copying a picture from the Windows Clipboard to your icon is quite similar.

First, make sure the picture you want is already on the Clipboard. You can use Paintbrush or any other application that will put a picture on the Clipboard.

Second, pick the icon you want to change by clicking on it once.

Third, click on that down-arrow below "Code" and find the "Picture" Property. Click on "Picture."

Fourth, Click on "Edit," then "Paste."

Deleting a Picture Once in a blue moon you might want to delete a picture—wipe the face of an icon clean.

Normally you wouldn't bother: putting a new picture on the icon, using any of the previous methods, automatically deep-sixes the old picture.

Still, the occasion may arise. If it does:

- Pick the icon you want to change by clicking on it once.
- Click on that down-arrow below "Code" again, and look for the "Picture" Property. Click "Picture."
- Click on the box to the right of the one that says "Picture"—it says "(icon)" or something similar.
- Hit the Delete key.

There. It's gone.

The Icon Number

Once you have all the icons sized, with your preferred pictures on their faces, it's time to adjust the programming code that goes along with the pictures.

But before we leave, you may find it worthwhile to jot down which pictures correspond to what actions. Sometimes it's hard to remember just what you had in mind for a particular picture. (*Is that a fuzzy black bug for ViewCharacter? Or a black dingbat for InsertBullet? No, no, no. I remember now. It's an abstract characterization of angst for InsertKafkaesqueObject . . . Part of the Existential Menu.*)

Better to get it right now than change it later.

When you're writing out the descriptions, try to jot down the icon number. There's a little trick for finding an icon's number. It's the "Index" Property. Simply click once on the icon in question, click the down-arrow under "Code," and click Index. Like Figure 7-52 on the following page.

Armed with a list of icon numbers and what you want them to do, we're ready to go in and change the program.

Figure 7-52: Icon Forty-Nine, Please Sign In!

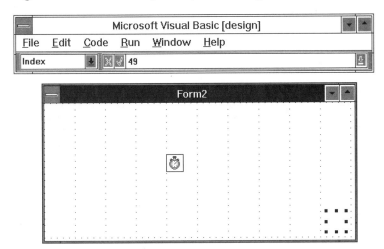

CoolConM

Double-click on the COOLCONM.BAS line over on the Project window:

Figure 7-53: CoolConM

You should get a Visual Basic program listing. Yeah, it looks pretty spiffy. Click on the right-most down-arrow, and click on SetUpForm2:

Figure 7-54: Real Basic Code

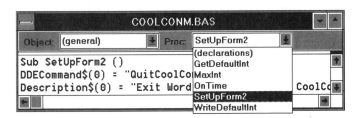

We need to change the SetUpForm2 Subroutine so its list of icons, descriptions, and commands matches yours.

You should be staring at a screen that looks more or less like this:

Figure 7-55: SetUpForm2 Code

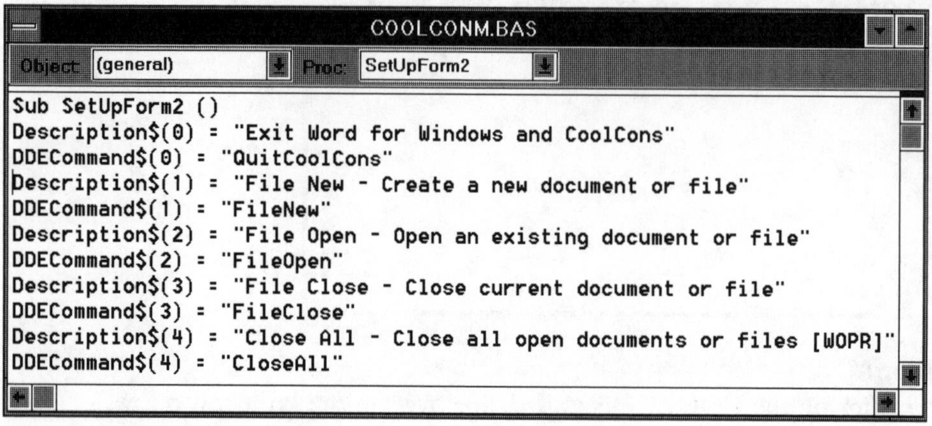

```
                          COOLCONM.BAS
Object: (general)          ▼   Proc:  SetUpForm2        ▼
Sub SetUpForm2 ()
Description$(0) = "Exit Word for Windows and CoolCons"
DDECommand$(0) = "QuitCoolCons"
Description$(1) = "File New - Create a new document or file"
DDECommand$(1) = "FileNew"
Description$(2) = "File Open - Open an existing document or file"
DDECommand$(2) = "FileOpen"
Description$(3) = "File Close - Close current document or file"
DDECommand$(3) = "FileClose"
Description$(4) = "Close All - Close all open documents or files [WOPR]"
DDECommand$(4) = "CloseAll"
```

There are two variables we'll be working with, DDECommand$() and Description$(). The subscripts on those variables correspond to the icon number: Description$(0), for example, is for icon number zero; DDECommand$(4) is for icon number four.

Description The Description$() is the text that flashes as the CoolCons window's title whenever you run your cursor over the icon. It can be any text you like, set between a pair of double-quotes.

If you want to include a double-quote, use two of them, like this:

```
Description$(33)="Description for ""Icon number 33"""
```

That line will give this description as the IconBox window title:

```
Description for "Icon number 33"
```

Keep in mind that long Description$()s may be cut off if the IconBox window is so narrow it can't hold all the text. Shorter is better.

Make sure you give every icon some Description$(), even if it's only a single space, even if the icon has no picture and you don't intend to use it. If you have a completely empty Description$()—what's called a null, or two quotes together with nothing in-between ("")—CoolCons takes you quite literally and displays no window title at all. The IconBox will start jumping all over the place, as its title rapidly appears and disappears.

On the other hand, if that's your idea of a good time, go right ahead.

DDECommand There's only one crucial part to all of this icon customizing stuff, and this is it.

When you click on an icon, CoolCons sends a command to Word for Windows. You have to get that command 100% absolutely right. If you're off by one letter—even a space—Word for Windows takes one look at the command, says *"Huh?,"* and ignores it completely . . . if you're lucky.

Typically a DDECommand$() will be a WordBasic command. You can see several examples in Figure 7-55.

In fact, though, you can use any command Word for Windows will recognize—which most emphatically includes any macros you may write for Word for Windows or macros others may have written that have been installed in your copy of Word for Windows. You can see one of those, too—CloseAll, a WOPR macro—in Figure 7-55. (WOPR, the Word for Windows Office POWER Pack, is a Word for Windows add-on; see Chapter 8. Thanks for asking.)

Where to find Word for Windows commands? Well, you can start right here in *WinMortals*, Chapter 4. We hit quite a few of them. For a definitive list, check *Using WordBasic*, a Microsoft publication.

Any valid Word for Windows command, i.e., any valid WordBasic statement *that doesn't contain quotation marks*, will work with CoolCons. Quotation marks inside commands are absolutely guaranteed to bring CoolCons crashing down around your ears.

If you need quotation marks in a particular command, you'll find it easier to write a custom one-line Word for Windows macro, that is,

```
FileOpen "Myfile.doc"
```

and then call that one-line macro from CoolCons.

So double- and triple-check your DDECommand$()s. If you start getting weird responses from Word for Windows (or no responses at all), double-check again.

There is one DDECommand$() that's used internally by CoolCons. It's "QuitCoolCons," and as you might imagine, it causes CoolCons to take out Word for Windows and then close itself down. For an example, see icon number zero.

A null Command$(), one that's set up like this,

```
DDECommand$(49)=""
```

with nothing between the quotes, is perfectly valid. (You can get the same thing by not having any "DDECommand$(49)=" line at all!) It tells CoolCons that you don't want to run any commands when this icon is clicked. That can be quite useful if you want to implement an "OOOPS! Get rid of this screen." icon, as we have done for icon number forty-nine.

Deleting Icons

Nobody's going to tell you that CoolCons sips at Free System Resources. Quite the contrary. It's a monster.

You can reduce the hit on System Resources by eliminating any icons that you don't need. Getting rid of icons is a little more complicated than changing an icon's command, for example, but not much more so.

Start by figuring out how many icons you can afford to lose. It may help to make a written list of which icons you want to keep and what they should do. Once an icon is deleted, it's very difficult to bring it back.

(Of course, if you screw everything up, you can always go back to the original CoolCons.

To physically delete an icon, start by double-clicking on the ICONBOX.FRM line in the Project window:

Figure 7-56: The Project Window

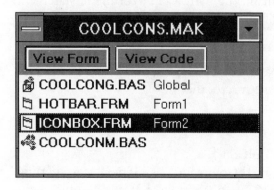

You should see the IconBox Form again. Click on the very last icon—icon number forty-nine—like this Figure 7-57 on the following page.

Now, simply, hit the Delete key. Voila! Icon number forty-nine is gone.

If you want to get rid of another icon, click on icon number forty-eight, which is immediately to the left of what used to be icon forty-nine. Hit Delete. It's gone.

Continue like that until you've knocked out all those little suckers that you can stand. But make sure, each time, you delete the *highest-numbered* icon. That's important.

Figure 7-57: The IconBox, Icon Forty-Nine Selected

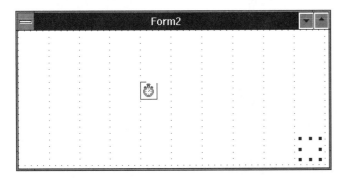

While you're here, go ahead and redo any icon pictures you'd like, and make sure you get a reliable list of icon numbers and what each icon is supposed to mean.

Knock Out Descriptions, Commands Next, double-click on COOLCONM.BAS in the Project Window. Click on the rightmost down-arrow, and click on SetUp-Form2. You'll get the SetUpForm2 code shown in Figure 7-55.

Scroll down to the end of the code, using the Scroll Bar over on the right. It'll look something like this:

Figure 7-58: The End of CoolConM

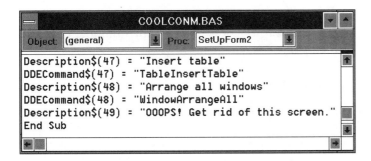

Get rid of any DDECommand$() and Description$() lines that don't apply any more. For example, if you deleted three icons, you should delete all the lines here that refer to DDECommand$(49), Description$(49), DDECommand$(48), Description$(48), DDECommand$(47), and Description$(47).

Make sure you don't delete "End Sub"!

While you're here, you can make any other changes that are appropriate: new descriptions and commands that correspond to any changes you've made to icons.

Edit the Global Kahuna   Finally, you'll have to go in and make a few changes to the Global Module, Cool Cong, rumored to be descended from the King Himself.

Over in the Project Window, double-click on COOLCONG.BAS. Here's what you'll find:

Figure 7-59: CoolConG

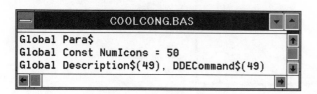

Not exactly what you were expecting, huh? Before you run away, here's a little tip: *all of Visual Basic is this easy!* Well, not all of it, but most of it, anyway. If you've ever used a programming language, macro language, batch language, almost any language, *you* can write Visual Basic programs. Real Event-Driven Windows programs. Really.

Just read the rest of this book.

Back to the changes. If you deleted any icons, you need to change three numbers here in the Global Module. First, NumIcons should be set to the number of icons. If you deleted three icons, you have forty-seven left, so:

```
Global Const NumIcons = 47
```

Next, you need to set the subscripts to one less than the total number of icons. Say, once again, you deleted three icons. Thus:

```
Global Description$(46), DDECommand$(46)
```

That's it. The Global Big Kahuna is ready for prime time.

VisualReality   Lest you think that we're pie-eyed about Visual Basic, blind to its faults (and there have been many accusations), here's a great example of how Visual Basic can be incredibly stupid. You would think that in this case, what with NumIcons being a declared Constant and all,

```
Global Description$(NumIcons-1)
```

would be valid. It isn't.

Visual Basic has many other shortcomings: try comparing the WordBasic editor to the Visual Basic editor; or, better, try printing a listing of a Visual Basic program!

Still, in the scheme of things, Visual Basic is one waycool programming language.

Saving It All

So you've changed the sizes of a couple icons, changed the pictures on some others, modified the actions associated with a few, and the descriptions of a few more. Might've deleted a couple of them, too, and you're ready to give it a try.

To go for a quick test drive, first *save your work*. We're playing around with Dynamic Data Exchange calls here, folks, and those are buried deep in the bowels of Windows. We're also taking a couple of hits directly at Windows, calling it from inside CoolCons. You never know when something might go *bump!* and take your labors along with it, so learn the first lesson of Windows programming: save early and often.

Saving your work is as simple as finding the Visual Basic [design] window, and clicking on "File," then "Save Project."

With everything stowed away, merely click on "Run," then "Start" (or if you. prefer, hit F5). CoolCons will spring into action. You can take it around the block a few times.

When you're ready to stop, you have two options: either use the Cool icon number zero Stop Sign, which brings everything to a grinding halt, or you can fish around on your desktop for the Visual Basic [design] window and click on "Run," then "Stop." (It's better using the Stop Sign, if you can, because Word for Windows can do some strange things if you leave it running while CoolCons takes a break. See the next section, "Some Improvements," for details.)

Is that how you wanted it to work? Good. We can turn it all into an .EXE file now.

First, save your work again!

Second, click on "File," then "Make .EXE File." Visual Basic tosses up a screen that looks like this:

Figure 7-60: Make EXE

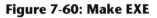

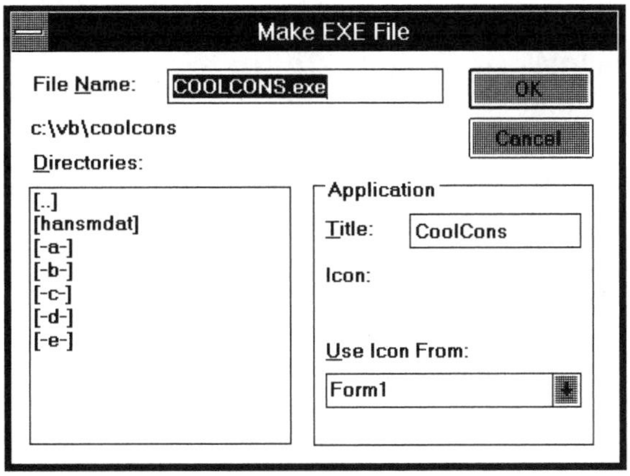

You may pick and choose the file name, its location, title, and icon. Click "OK," sit back for a few seconds, and you have a brand-spanking-new version of CoolCons, tailored to your every whim.

Finally, to leave Visual Basic, click on "File," then "Exit."

If you changed the name or location of the .EXE file, you may have to use Program Manager to find this new version of CoolCons. From inside Program Manager, click on the Word for Windows group, click "File," then "New," then "Browse," and go find COOLCONS.EXE wherever you put it.

And you're done.

Some Improvements

> There are Ways, but The Way is uncharted;
> There are Names, but not Nature in words:
> Nameless indeed is the source of creation
> But Things have a mother, and she has a Name.
>
> —Lao Tzu, *Tao Tê Ching*, ca. 550 BC

While many folks think CoolCons is better than those expensive big name icon boxes, there's still lots of room for improvement. The beauty of it all is that you can tinker to your heart's content, shape and reshape the program until it does precisely what *you* think it should do.

In this short section we'll take a look at some of the obvious ways to improve CoolCons and point you at a few potential problems and their solutions—where solutions exist.

Think of this as a list of existential exercises—a test of your programming mettle.

Exercise 1: Fix the "Cool Ends, WinWord Croaks" Oddity

CoolCons exhibits a few oddities from time to time; in most cases it's a reflection of how DDE handles things.

Probably the toughest problem we've seen arises when a user knocks out CoolCons using the Windows 3.1 Ctrl+Alt+Del three-finger salute. (Or when running CoolCons from the "Visual Basic [design]" window, ending the program by clicking on "Run," then "End.") When that happens, DDE—and in particular Word for Windows—gets very confused.

If the user kills CoolCons, the next time they try to exit WinWord, they'll have nothing but problems. WinWord apparently isn't willing to believe that the application on the other end of its open DDE link has died.

B U G

Confronted with a missing DDE partner, WinWord locks up the screen, the keyboard, the mouse, everything, for an enormous length of time— a minute or more—and you can't get Windows to do *anything*.

Having taken over your system for a ridiculously long period of time, WinWord then pops up a particularly uninformative box that says "The task is taking longer than expected. Do you want to continue waiting? Yes/No." We would've shown you an example of that box, except Windows gets locked up so tight there's no way to take a picture!

You can chuckle if this sounds like a Three Stooges routine.

The "task" in this case is hanging up the bloody phone—when there's nobody on the other end! Try explaining that to a neophyte Windows user, whose only offense was killing a DDE Client, then telling WinWord to File Exit.

It gets worse. If the user clicks on "No" when asked if he or she wants to continue waiting (as he or she should), WinWord leaves DDE all screwed up. Try restarting CoolCons after all that, and it'll die. The only solution is to leave and restart Windows!

T I P

There's a very scary element to all of this. Many C programmers test their DDE routines by bouncing them off of Microsoft applications, the logic being "Microsoft applications know how to DDE, so I can learn by talking to them." Wake up and smell the roses, folks. Microsoft apps aren't bug-immune.

That's the biggest problem we've found in CoolCons—so far, anyway—and there doesn't appear to be any easy way around it. If you decide to tackle this as a weekend project, well, you better plan on spending a long weekend.

Exercise 2: Modify for Other Cool Applications

The basic CoolCons structure and code may be used to control *any* Windows application that can act as a DDE Server. It helps—a lot!—if the application has an OnTime or RunLater capability: as we saw in Chapter 6 that's almost a prerequisite for getting DDE Executes to work properly.

Very little work is necessary to hack CoolCons for other DDE-Server-able applications. If you try, here are a few things you should check:

- HotBar's Form_Load: FindWindow has to be changed to point to the new application's ClassName$; the LinkTopic must be changed; and you'll have to find out what the new application needs to be fed to resize itself under the HotBar.

- IconBox's CoolCon_Click Event Handler: you'll have to replace the "FileExit" poison pill with whatever command the new application needs to make it quit.

- CoolConM's SetUpForm2: of course, you'll have to change the descriptions and commands associated with each icon.

- CoolConM's OnTime$: the hard part here is counting the bloody quotes! Use DDE Watch to make sure you got them right.

You should change messages that talk about "Word for Windows," natch. But that's about it. If you've worked through Chapters 6 and 7 here, you could change CoolCons to operate with another application in a day or two—maybe less, providing you have the icon pictures, descriptions, and commands down cold.

Remarkable, eh? Talk about reusable code!

Exercise 3: More Than One App

There's no reason why CoolCons has to be limited to one application at a time. If you have the HotBar's Form_Load procedure establish more than one link to more than one Server, and then figure out a way to mark the icons as belonging to Server "A" or Server "B" or Server "C," you could easily get CoolCons rigged to drive several applications all at once.

Fascinating. One IconBox Form could control Word for Windows, EXCEL, and DynaComm, and another Visual Basic application or two, *all at the same time!*

Probably wouldn't take more than a few days.

Exercise 4: Take Out the Path Restriction

In the HotBar's Form_Load procedure, we assumed that the user had WinWord on the DOS Path. It makes the code easier. And 90% of the time, it will be on the DOS Path.

It would be cleaner if CoolCons looked for WINWORD.EXE the same way WinLHA looked for LHA.EXE: have the user find it, then store the path in an .INI file.

Unfortunately, doing so requires an additional form and a couple dozen lines of code. We decided to leave it out because it didn't add anything to your understanding of Visual Basic—you already did the same thing, several times over, in Chapter 5.

Grafting the WinLHA code and Default Form onto CoolCons would be a great first exercise, if you're interested in such things. It's not trivial, but it's not too tough: probably less than a day.

Exercise 5: Better Description Display

If you happen to like your IconBox Form tall and skinny, you won't be able to read more than a word or two of the description: the window title box is too narrow.

We played with a floating description box—another headless Form, containing just one Label Control—moving the box with the cursor. Unfortunately, when the mouse moved from one icon to the next, the Form jumped, and the whole thing started acting like a speed freak hopping on one leg.

Can you find a better way to do descriptions? No time estimate; the problem is in the concept and design, not the implementation!

Big Exercise 6: Can the Picture Boxes

Unfortunately, CoolCons consumes enormous amounts of Free System Resources. The problem, simply, is the implementation. We used an Array of Picture Box Controls: they're easy, they're cool, they can be changed by a person who's never used Visual Basic, and they illustrate using Control Arrays. But they eat FSRs for lunch.

Here's a real challenge: implement CoolCons without all those Picture Box Controls. How? Well, you could start by looking at the possibility of making one Picture Box Control that covers the entire IconBox Form. The Control_Click Event Handler has access to the coordinates of the cursor when the mouse is clicked: a smart program would convert the location into something resembling an icon number.

There are several technical difficulties with that approach, though: resizing wouldn't be simple; customizing by a novice user would be nigh-on impossible; and a fast implementation would require use of the Windows BitBlt command to move pictures inside the Control.

If you take this on as an exercise, plan on spending a couple of weeks or more.

Exercise 7: Click-n-Drag Icons

Here's a project that's worthy of another week's work: implement click-and-drag icons in CoolCons, and make them work as well as Lotus's SmartIcons. Or better.

We played around with that for a few hours and finally gave up. If you think one IconBox Form eats up Free System Resources, just try putting two on the screen at the same time! Windows didn't like it one little bit.

If you'd like to try your hand at Click-n-Drag Icons, figure out how to get rid of the Picture Boxes first.

Exercise 8: Up-and-Down Icons

The very first rendition of CoolCons included two pictures for each icon: one was the "up" or unclicked picture, the other a "down" or clicked picture. If the user clicked on "Edit Cut," for example, the scissors in the picture actually sliced!

That kind of movement is not difficult to implement with the Visual Basic add-ons available these days. (See Chapter 9 for details.) Our challenge, though, is to get up-and-down pictures working in native Visual Basic.

There are several hurdles. First, of course is the ever-present Free System Resources problem. That shouldn't be surprising.

Just as important, though, is the interface: how do you put together a two-picture-per-icon Form in a way that a first-time Visual Basic user can understand? What about changing pictures? Deleting them?

Exercise 9: The Ultimate Icon Box

Turn CoolCons into a fully customizable beast: let the user pick pictures, descriptions, and commands—even specify the Windows application!—on-the-fly. Set up the customizing so it can be done without reverting to Visual Basic's design time. Keep everything that CoolCons knows in an .INI file.

Good luck!

CHAPTER ■ 8

More WordBasic, Visual Basic

Why didst thou leave the trodden paths of men
Too soon, and with weak hands though mighty heart
Dare the unpastured dragon in his den?

—Percy Bysshe Shelley, *Adonais*, 1821

As promised, we've followed a strange path to Windows Enlightenment. Instead of belaboring the intricacies of the Windows Basics' minutia—*how many different "If" statements are there, anyway?*—we've staked out the intellectual high ground, exploring Event-Driven programming, controls, Dynamic Data Exchange, and the Windows API. And we've done it by solving real problems with real Windows programs.

That's the good news.

The bad news: those sample programs, carefully crafted as they were, couldn't possibly cover all of the important capabilities of WordBasic or Visual Basic and, by implication, many capabilities of the other Windows macro languages.

This chapter attempts to ameliorate the more egregious oversights.

We are not going to try to cover all of the features of all the languages. By and large, you can look up the details whenever you need them. But there are a few key concepts you should examine before you try to build your own real applications.

While we're wrapping things up for Visual Basic and WordBasic, we'll introduce you to some of the more popular add-ons for those languages, which greatly expand your ability to build applications. We'll also look at the best sources of help and information.

WordBasic Dialog Boxes

Although there are several interesting parts of Word for Windows and WordBasic that we didn't cover, the most important by far is the use of custom dialog boxes.

WordBasic's capability for creating Forms doesn't hold a candle to Visual Basic. That shouldn't come as too great a surprise; after all, Forms are at the center of Visual Basic.

In WordBasic a custom Form is called a "User Dialog," a "custom dialog," or, simply a "dialog box." We'll use all those terms interchangeably.

If you have Word for Windows 2.0 there's a tool that will help you build and use dialog boxes. It's called a Dialog Box Editor. *You were expecting something more cool?*

The Dialog Box Editor lets you "paint" a dialog box and then translates what you've painted into the proper WordBasic commands. Using the regular Windows Clipboard and the standard Edit Copy / Edit Paste, you can move the WordBasic commands in and out of your program.

The Word for Windows 2.0 Working Model on the Companion Disk doesn't include the Dialog Box Editor, but that's okay. You should probably try building boxes once or twice by hand, just to get the hang of it, before entrusting your carefully crafted custom dialog boxes to an automated tool.

WinExplorer in a Box

Instead of discussing custom dialog boxes in the abstract, we're going to hack away at the target application of Chapter 4, WinExplorer.

We'll pull the most interesting parts of WinExplorer into a dialog box, so you can see at a glance what WinWord left out of the Help / About box—little things like Free System Resources. (The Free System Resources usually *are* little.)

If you're working from the Companion Disk, crank up WinWord, click on "File," then "Open," and open up the file C8PGM1.DOC. Click on "Edit," then "Select All." Click on "Edit," then "Copy." Click on "File Close" to get rid of C8PGM1.DOC. Then click on "Tools," then "Macro," and either type or select WinExplorer. Click "Edit." *<whew>* Now click again on "Edit," then "Select All," and hit the "Del" Delete key. Click "Edit," then "Paste."

If that sounds like a lot of work, well, typing it is a whole lot *more* work, guaranteed!

There's a listing of WinExplorer at the end of this section.

Begin Dialog

Before we take on the big, final, fancy dialog box, let's start with a very simple one.

WordBasic custom dialog boxes start with a line that looks like this:

```
Begin Dialog UserDialog 450, 200, "WinMortals -- Window Explorer"
```

The "Begin Dialog UserDialog" is boilerplate. You can't change it, so don't worry about it.

The next two numbers specify the width and height of the custom dialog box, respectively: in our case that's 450 and 200. You're no doubt wondering 450 and 200 *what* at this point—and the answer is . . . uh . . . *things*!

WordBasic isn't terribly precise in its definition of dialog box measurements. As a rule of thumb, though:

- If you take the width measurement and divide by eight, you'll get a rough approximation of how many characters will fit.
- If you take the height measurement and divide by twelve, you'll get a rough approximation of the number of lines that will fit.

Using those rules of thumb, this 450-by-200 dialog box will hold about 16 lines of text, with about 56 characters on each line, give or take a bit.

The "WinMortals -- WinExplorer" part of that Begin Dialog statement gives the dialog box a title.

OK?

The next command we'll need to construct a custom dialog box is an OK Button command. Every WordBasic dialog box has to have at least one button—whether it's an OK Button, a Cancel Button, or a custom Push Button.

An OK Button command looks like this:

```
OKButton 100, 170, 120, 21
```

Those numbers specify the x-location, y-location, width, and height using the inscrutable WinWord dialog box measurements.

In this case, we want the upper-left corner of the OK Button to appear 100 units from the left edge of the dialog box, and 170 units down from the top. The OK Button itself should be 120 units wide and 21 units tall.

Sounds confusing? Hang on. Once you see it, you'll understand.

End Dialog

Every custom dialog box declaration ends with

```
End Dialog
```

That's just a signal to WordBasic that you're through plotting out the dialog box and it's time to get on to some real code.

Don't Push That Button!

Two more lines are necessary to get a custom dialog box working. First, your program must reserve room for all the dialog box data. This simple dialog box doesn't hold much data—in fact, it will only report back that the OK Button has been pushed—but more complex dialog boxes can contain quite a bit of information.

Here's the command that sets up a variable to hold that data:

```
Dim ShowMortals As UserDialog
```

Yeah, it's the same "Dim" statement you've used to create arrays, pressed into service in a new way. This "Dim" statement tells WordBasic to reserve room for a custom dialog box, as just defined, and to call it "ShowMortals."

Finally, to bring up the dialog box, your program needs one out of these two statements:

```
Dialog ShowMortals
PushedButton = Dialog(ShowMortals)
```

That first command would just show the dialog box, the one set up as "ShowMortals." The second command shows the dialog box, but it also returns a number that will tell your program which Button the user pushed; in this case, the variable "PushedButton" contains that number.

Now that you're confused beyond all hope, let's play with it a bit. Much of the problem here is in boilerplate text that makes absolutely no sense to man or beast; the rest of the problem lies in the two conflicting methods of tossing a custom dialog box up on the screen.

The first method ("Dialog ShowMortals") is a throwback to the old days of WordBasic; it can lead to Error Conditions and all sorts of other mean, nasty, ugly things. We strongly recommend you avoid that method; we'll confine our examples to the second [("n=Dialog(ShowMortals)"] approach.

If you run this program

```
Sub MAIN
Begin Dialog UserDialog 450, 200, "WinMortals -- Window Explorer"
    OKButton 100, 170, 120, 21
End Dialog
Dim ShowMortals As UserDialog
PushedButton = Dialog(ShowMortals)
End Sub
```

you will get a custom dialog box that looks like this:

Figure 8-1: Custom Dialog Box OK

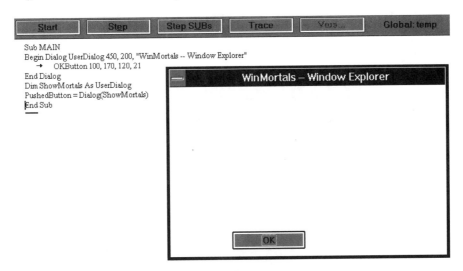

If the user clicks on "OK," the variable "PushedButton" will receive a value of True, or minus one. OK Buttons, when clicked, always return a value of minus one. If the user double-clicks on the hyphen-thing in the dialog box's upper left corner—effectively canceling the dialog—PushButton will get a value of zero. Canceling out of a dialog this way, or clicking on a Cancel Button, will always return a value of zero.

Now let's add just one statement to the pot:

```
Sub MAIN
Begin Dialog UserDialog 450, 200, "WinMortals -- Window Explorer"
    OKButton 100, 170, 120, 21
    PushButton 255, 170, 120, 21, "Print Report"
End Dialog
Dim ShowMortals As UserDialog
PushedButton = Dialog(ShowMortals)
End Sub
```

See how that PushButton should show up to the right of the OK Button? The first number is the one that determines the distance from the left edge of the dialog box; a larger number shoves the PushButton farther to the right.

Here's what happens:

Figure 8-2: Print Report PushButton

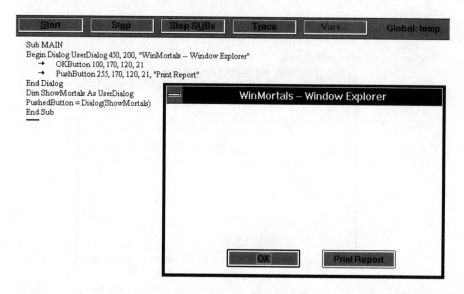

```
Sub MAIN
Begin Dialog UserDialog 450, 200, "WinMortals -- Window Explorer"
   →    OKButton 100, 170, 120, 21
   →    PushButton 255, 170, 120, 21, "Print Report"
End Dialog
Dim ShowMortals As UserDialog
PushedButton = Dialog(ShowMortals)
End Sub
```

And the PushButton was placed to the right of the OKButton, just as you would expect.

The variable "PushedButton" can now take on three values: zero if the dialog box is canceled; minus one if the user pushes the OK Button; and plus one if "PrintReport" is pushed.

You may have many PushButtons in a dialog box. WordBasic numbers them sequentially as it scans your UserDialog statements (starting at one!) and returns the sequential number of the pushed PushButton as the value of the dialog.

TextBox

Although WordBasic has quite a few Controls available for use in custom dialog boxes, we'll only be using PushButtons and TextBoxes.

Let's put in the first Text Box Control:

```
Begin Dialog UserDialog 450, 200, "WinMortals -- Window Explorer"
     OKButton 100, 170, 120, 21
     PushButton 255, 170, 120, 21, "Print Report"
     Text 10, 10, 440, 13,  "WinExplorer snapshot taken at " +\
 Time$() + " on " + Date$() + "."
End Dialog
Dim ShowMortals As UserDialog
PushedButton = Dialog(ShowMortals)
```

From the location of the Text Box Control—at 10, 10—you would expect it to be up in the upper left corner; distance to the left of the box is 10 units, distance from the top is another 10 units. The third number, 440, extends the Text Box all the way to the right edge of the dialog box (calculation: 10 starting position + 440 width = 450, which is the width of the entire dialog box). The fourth number, 13, says the Text Box Control should be just slightly taller than a typical line.

Run that and here's what you'll see:

Figure 8-3: First Text Box Control

See how the Time$() and Date$() functions can be added so easily to a Text Box Control? That's generally true of all WordBasic functions, and it makes writing custom dialog boxes comparatively easy.

WinExplorer Dialog Box

Let's put the entire dialog box together now. A few variables have to be retrieved from Windows; you've already seen how those go, by and large, so we'll skim over them. Here's the dialog box code:

```
Begin Dialog UserDialog 450, 200, "WinMortals -- Window Explorer"
     Text 10, 10, 440, 13,  "WinExplorer snapshot taken at " +\
  Time$() + " on " + Date$() + "."
     Text 10, 30, 440, 13, "Windows Version" + \
  Str$(MajorVersionNumber) + "." + Str$(MinorVersionNumber) + "   " +\
```

```
Mode$
    Text 10, 50, 440, 13, "Currently Available Memory (including "+\
"virtual): " + Str$(Round(AvailableMemory, 2)) + " MB"
    Text 10, 70, 440, 13, "Free System Resources:" +\
Str$(GetFreeSystemResources(0)) + "%"
    Text 10, 90, 440, 13, "Running an " + CPU$ + "."
    Text 10, 110, 440, 13, "Windows reports" + Str$(n) + " active "+\
"tasks."
    Text 10, 130, 440, 13, "Active Window Title: " + ActiveWindowTitle$
    Text 10, 150, 440, 13, "Active Window Handle: " + Str$(hWnd)
    OKButton 100, 170, 120, 21
    PushButton 255, 170, 120, 21, "Print Report"
End Dialog
Dim ShowMortals As UserDialog
PushedButton = Dialog(ShowMortals)
```

And here's what the resulting custom dialog box looks like:

Figure 8-4: WinExplorer Custom Dialog Box

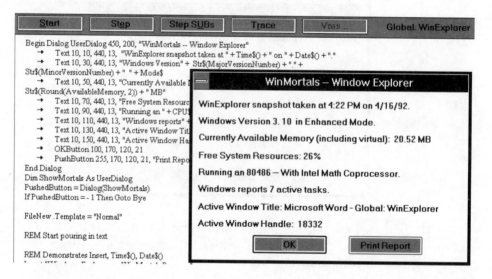

Pretty nifty, huh?

Back in Chapter 4 we displayed all that information by "Insert"ing it into a document; the user could scroll through the document at will, but the whole approach was clumsy. By extracting the most interesting information, boiling things down a bit, we're able to stick the "Top Ten" in a dialog box, then give the user the option of creating that long document.

Print PushButton

Finally, we want to print the WinExplorer report if the "Print Report" button is pushed.

Because pushing the OK Button returns a minus one, WinExplorer simply checks:

```
If PushedButton = - 1 Then Goto Bye
```

With the label "Bye:" sitting down at the bottom of the macro, that statement just bypasses all the printing if the OK Button was pushed.

Assuming that the user wants to print a report, WinExplorer starts up a new document:

```
FileNew .Template = "Normal"
```

and then dumps everything onto the printed page, prints it, deletes the new document, and quits.

That's it.

Assign to Menu

If you haven't already assigned WinExplorer to a Word for Windows menu, check the penultimate section of Chapter 4 for instructions. It's quite easy, really, and a worthwhile exercise in taming the intractable WinWord menu.

In fact, if you're feeling brave, you can even assign it to a CoolCons icon!

The Code

For the benefit of those who have lost the Companion Disk, here's the entirety of WinExplorer, in its final form:

```
Declare Function GetVersion Lib "Kernel"() As Integer
Declare Function GetWindowsDirectory Lib "Kernel"(DirPath$,\
 MaxChars As Integer) As Integer
Declare Function GetFreeSpace Lib "Kernel"(wFlags As Integer) As\
 Long

Declare Function GetProfileString Lib "Kernel"(AppName$,\
 KeyName$, Default$, ReturnedString$, MaxChars As Integer) As\
 Integer
Declare Function GetProfileInt Lib "Kernel"(AppName$, KeyName$,\
 nDefault As Integer) As Integer

Declare Function GetSystemMetrics Lib "user"(nIndex As Integer)\
 As Integer

Declare Function GetWinFlags Lib "Kernel" As Integer
```

```
Declare Function GetNumTasks Lib "Kernel" As Integer
Declare Function GetActiveWindow Lib "User" As Integer
Declare Function GetWindow Lib "User"(hWnd As Integer, wFlag As\
  Integer) As Integer
Declare Function GetNextWindow Lib "User"(hWnd As Integer, wFlag\
  As Integer) As Integer
Declare Function GetWindowText Lib "User"(hWnd As Integer,\
  CurrWindowText$, MaxChars As Integer) As Integer

Declare Function GetCurrentTime Lib "User" As Long
REM Or, Declare Function GetTickCount Lib "User" As Long
Declare Function GetFreeSystemResources Lib "user"(wflags As\
  Integer) As Integer

Declare Function GetDriveType(nDrive As Integer) Lib "Kernel" As\
  Integer

Declare Function GetDOSEnvironment Lib "kernel" As Long
Declare Function AnsiUpper$ Lib "user"(lpString As Long)

Sub MAIN

REM Get Windows version number, directory, free memory
REM Demonstrates simple arithmetic, Int, InsertPara, Str$
REM The version number is packed; decompress it thusly:
PackedVersionNumber = GetVersion
MinorVersionNumber = Int(PackedVersionNumber / 256)
MajorVersionNumber = PackedVersionNumber - 256 * MinorVersionNumber
AvailableMemory = GetFreeSpace(0) /(1024 * 1024)

REM More System info, this time from GetWinFlags
REM Demonstrates  ElseIf, and a (barely documented!) use of And
REM as a bitwise operator on
REM integers -- even though the integers are stored as reals.
WF_CPU086 = 64
WF_CPU186 = 128
WF_CPU286 = 2
WF_CPU386 = 4
WF_CPU486 = 8
WF_80x87 = 1024
WF_STANDARD = 16
WF_ENHANCED = 32


Flag = GetWinFlags
REM Find CPU type
If  (Flag And WF_CPU086) = WF_CPU086 Then
     CPU$ =  "8086"
ElseIf(Flag And WF_CPU186) = WF_CPU186 Then
     CPU$ =   "80186"
ElseIf(Flag And WF_CPU286) = WF_CPU286 Then
     CPU$ =  "80286"
ElseIf(Flag And WF_CPU386) = WF_CPU386 Then
     CPU$ =  "80386"
ElseIf(Flag And WF_CPU486) = WF_CPU486 Then
```

```
     CPU$ =  "80486"
Else
     CPU$ =  "Unidentified"
End If
If(Flag And WF_80x87) = WF_80x87 Then CPU$ = CPU$ + " -- With " +\
 "Intel Math Coprocessor"

If(Flag And WF_STANDARD) = WF_STANDARD Then
     Mode$ = "in Standard Mode."
ElseIf(Flag And WF_ENHANCED) = WF_ENHANCED Then
     Mode$ = "in Enhanced Mode."
Else
     Mode$ = "in Real Mode."
End If

REM List open windows
REM Demonstrates While/Wend
GW_HWNDFIRST = 0
GW_HWNDNEXT = 2
n = GetNumTasks
Dim WindowTitle$(50)
Dim Handle(50)
hWnd = GetActiveWindow
x = GetWindowText(hWnd, ActiveWindowTitle$, 200)

Begin Dialog UserDialog 450, 200, "WinMortals -- Window Explorer"
     Text 10, 10, 440, 13,  "WinExplorer snapshot taken at " +\
 Time$() + " on " + Date$() + "."
     Text 10, 30, 440, 13, "Windows Version" + \
 Str$(MajorVersionNumber) + "." + Str$(MinorVersionNumber) + "  "\
 + Mode$
     Text 10, 50, 440, 13, "Currently Available Memory (including" +\
 " virtual): " + Str$(Round(AvailableMemory, 2)) + " MB"
     Text 10, 70, 440, 13, "Free System Resources:" +\
 Str$(GetFreeSystemResources(0)) + "%"
     Text 10, 90, 440, 13, "Running an " + CPU$ + "."
     Text 10, 110, 440, 13, "Windows reports" + Str$(n) + " active" +\
 " tasks."
     Text 10, 130, 440, 13, "Active Window Title: " + ActiveWindowTitle$
     Text 10, 150, 440, 13, "Active Window Handle: " + Str$(hWnd)
     OKButton 100, 170, 120, 21
     PushButton 255, 170, 120, 21, "Print Report"
End Dialog
Dim ShowMortals As UserDialog
PushedButton = Dialog(ShowMortals)
If PushedButton = - 1 Then Goto Bye

FileNew .Template = "Normal"

REM Start pouring in text

REM Demonstrates Insert, Time$(), Date$()
Insert "Windows Explorer -- a WinMortals Program"
InsertPara
Insert "Run at " + Time$() + " on " + Date$()
```

```
InsertPara
InsertPara
Insert "Windows Version" +  Str$(MajorVersionNumber) + "." +\
 Str$(MinorVersionNumber)
InsertPara
LengthOfDirectory = GetWindowsDirectory(DirectoryPath$, 200)
Insert "Windows loaded from: " + DirectoryPath$
InsertPara
Insert "Currently Available Memory (including virtual): " +\
 Str$(Round(AvailableMemory, 2)) + " MB"
InsertPara
REM Settings from WIN.INI
REM Demonstrates GetProfileString, Instr()
InsertPara
Insert "Windows settings (from WIN.INI):"
InsertPara
LengthOfString = GetProfileString("windows", "load", " ",\
 LoadString$, 200)
Insert "Load= " + LoadString$
InsertPara
LengthOfString = GetProfileString("windows", "run", " ",\
 RunString$, 200)
Insert "Run= " + RunString$
InsertPara
LengthOfString = GetProfileString("windows", "device", " ",\
 DeviceString$, 200)
If LengthOfString = 0 Then
     Insert "No Default Printer"
Else
     FirstComma = InStr(1, DeviceString$, ",")
     Insert "Default Printer = " + Left$(DeviceString$, FirstComma -\
 1) + " on " + Right$(DeviceString$, 5)
End If
InsertPara
SSActive = GetProfileInt("windows", "ScreenSaveActive," 0)
If SSActive = 0 Then
     Insert "Windows Screen Save Is NOT Activated."
Else
     SSTimeOut = GetProfileInt("windows", "ScreenSaveTimeOut," 0)
     Insert "Windows Screen Save active;" + Str$(SSTimeOut) + \
 " seconds delay."
End If
InsertPara
REM A bunch of miscellaneous info from the GetSystemMetrics API
REM Demonstrates nested If/Then/Else stuff
InsertPara
Insert "System Metrics Information:"
InsertPara
SM_CXSCREEN = 0
SM_CYSCREEN = 1
SM_CXICON = 11
SM_CYICON = 12
SM_MOUSEPRESENT = 19
SM_DEBUG = 22
SM_SWAPBUTTON = 23
```

```
SM_PENWINDOWS = 41
Insert "Screen Width:" + Str$(GetSystemMetrics(SM_CXSCREEN)) + \
 ," Height:" + Str$(GetSystemMetrics(SM_CYSCREEN)) + " pixels."
InsertPara
Insert "Icon Width:" + Str$(GetSystemMetrics(SM_CXICON)) + \
 ," Height:" + Str$(GetSystemMetrics(SM_CYICON)) + " pixels."
InsertPara
If GetSystemMetrics(SM_MOUSEPRESENT) Then
     Insert "Mouse is present.  "
     If GetSystemMetrics(SM_SWAPBUTTON) Then Insert "Left and " +\
 "Right Mouse Buttons Swapped."
Else
     Insert "Mouse is NOT present.  "
End If
InsertPara
If GetSystemMetrics(SM_DEBUG) Then
     Insert "Running in DEBUG Mode. "
     InsertPara
EndIf
InsertPara
Insert "Running an " + CPU$ + "."
InsertPara
Insert "In " + Mode$
InsertPara
InsertPara
Insert "Windows reports" + Str$(n) + " active tasks."
hWnd = GetWindow(hWnd, GW_HWNDFIRST)
While hWnd <> 0 And i < 50
     i = i + 1
     x = GetWindowText(hWnd, WindowText$, 200)
     WindowTitle$(i) = WindowText$
     Handle(i) = hWnd
     hWnd = GetWindow(hWnd, GW_HWNDNEXT)
Wend
If i = 50 Then MsgBox "Overflow. More than 50 open windows."
InsertPara
PrintWindows:
For j = 1 To i
     Insert "Window #" + Str$(j)
     InsertPara
     Insert Chr$(9) + "Window Title: " + WindowTitle$(j)
     InsertPara
     Insert Chr$(9) + "Window Handle (hWnd):" + Str$(Handle(j))
     InsertPara
Next j

REM Get the Windows Time; the Windows API call returns milliseconds
REM Demonstrates more complex arithmetic
WinTime = GetCurrentTime
WinTimehr = Int(WinTime /(60 * 60 * 1000))
WinTimemin = Int((WinTime /(60 * 1000)) -(WinTimehr * 60))
InsertPara
Insert "Time since Windows was booted:" + Str$(WinTimehr) + \
 " Hours," + Str$(WinTimemin) + " Minutes  (" + Str$(WinTime) + \
 " milliseconds)."
```

```
InsertPara
REM Use a Windows 3.1-specific call to retrieve Free System Resources
Insert "Free System Resources:" + Str$(GetFreeSystemResources(0))\
  + "%"
InsertPara

REM Sort out the drives
REM Demonstrates Case statement
InsertPara
Insert "Drives available to Windows (RAMdrives are Fixed):"
InsertPara
REM Max 30 drives
For i = 0 To 30
type = GetDriveType(i)
Select Case type
Case 0      'Function can't determine drive type; skip
Case 1      'Drive does not exist; skip
Case 2      'Removeable drive
      Insert "Drive " + Chr$(65 + i) + ": Removeable"
      InsertPara
Case 3      'Fixed drive
      Insert "Drive " + Chr$(65 + i) + ": Fixed"
      InsertPara
Case 4      'Remote/Network drive
      Insert "Drive " + Chr$(65 + i) + ": Remote/Network"
      InsertPara
Case Else 'Skip
End Select
Next i

REM Here's a tough one -- parsing the DOS Environment string
REM Thanks to Jonathan Zuck for ... er ... pointing the way
Dim EnvironmentString$(50)
InsertPara
Insert "DOS Environment String:"
InsertPara
lpEnvString = GetDOSEnvironment
StringLength = 1
i = 0
While StringLength > 0 And i < 50
      EnvironmentString$(i) = AnsiUpper$(lpEnvString)
      StringLength = Len(EnvironmentString$(i))
      i = i + 1
      lpEnvString = lpEnvString + StringLength + 1
Wend
For j = 0 To i - 1
      Insert EnvironmentString$(j)
      InsertPara
Next j


FilePrint
DocClose 2
Bye:
End Sub
```

```
Function Round(Number, DecimalPlaces)
REM Rounds "Number" to "10 to the minus Int(DecimalPlaces)." Not
REM infallible, but usually reliable.
REM Round(1234.5,-2) returns 1200. Round(-4.5,0) returns -5.
REM Round(123.45,1.9) returns 123.5.
Base = 1
iDecimalPlaces = Int(DecimalPlaces)
Select Case iDecimalPlaces
Case Is > 0
     For i = 1 To DecimalPlaces
     Base = Base * 10
     Next i
Case Is < 0
     For i = - 1 To DecimalPlaces Step - 1
     Base = Base / 10
     Next i
Case Else
End Select
REM Strip out multiples of 32K to keep from blowing Int()'s
REM 32,768 overflow limit
On Error Goto Overflow
Over32KPart = Int((Number * Base) / 32767)
Under32KPart =(Number * Base) -(Over32KPart * 32767)
If Number >= 0 Then
     Round =(Over32KPart * 32767 + Int((Under32KPart) + 0.5)) / Base
Else
     Round =(Over32KPart * 32767 + Int((Under32KPart) - 0.5)) / Base
End If
Goto Bye
Overflow:
MsgBox "Calculation overflow in Roundoff routine. Returning a " +\
 "value of" + Str$(Number) + ". Errors may result.", "WinMortals "+\
 "Rounder", 16
Round = Number
Bye:
On Error Goto 0
End Function
```

So there you have it: a nifty little dialog box that pops up, producing all sorts of information about your system and how it's feeling; and a fancy, formatted report, ready at the push of a button.

While we've hardly scratched the surface of WordBasic, this is the last bit of *WinMortals* WordBasic code. But before we leave the topic entirely, let's take a look at what's out there to help you build dynamite WinWord programs.

WordBasic Add-Ons

Several developers have been struggling with WordBasic since its inception. As a result, there's a wide array of WordBasic add-on tools that most WordBasic developers will find invaluable.

We've gone to extreme lengths to keep these tools from appearing thus far in WinMortals, and (assuming we were successful!) it wasn't easy. The tools are simply pervasive; it's hard to imagine developing real WordBasic programs without them.

Doc-to-Help

> The gods help them that help themselves.
>
> —Aesop, *Fables*, ca. 550 BC

Windows 3.1 has one of the most advanced "Help Engines" ever constructed. You've seen it: push F1 and Help appears in its own window; you can browse help entries; jump between hypertext definitions; call up examples with just a click; trace your steps back whence you came; print this, browse that, hop to and fro.

No doubt you thought that constructing an on-line help facility like that for *your* programs would require months—maybe years—of hard work, that it was for the big guys who can afford to hire a couple of people dedicated to on-line help, help specialists who crack jokes in Rich Text Format.

The Equalizer That may have been true once upon a time, but it isn't any more. An extraordinary package, Doc-to-Help, takes a Word for Windows document and turns it into a cross-referenced and cross-linked on-line help system.

Here's how it works. The Windows 3.1 Help Engine is driven by a specially formatted file. Even though it's *possible* to create that file manually using Word for Windows, the mechanics are intimidating: text must appear in a certain way, with footnotes linking entries, paragraphs cross-referenced, and the whole saved in the Help Engine's file format.

Doc-to-Help takes care of all of the details. You need only construct a document—a user's manual, in effect—using Doc-to-Help. Click here, click there, and *boom!* Doc-to-Help converts the user's manual into a full on-line Windows Help package.

Doc-to-Help intelligently converts Word for Windows Table of Contents entries into the Help Engine's help topics; it turns WinWord Index items into Help keywords; it changes WinWord Glossary entries into Help pop-up definitions; and it links together WinWord chapter and high-level heading references with Help jumps.

In other words, Doc-to-Help can take a document with a Table of Contents that looks like this:

Figure 8-5: A Doc-to-Help Doc

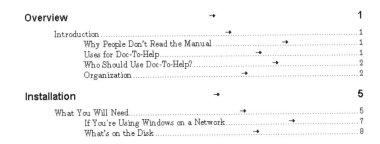

and with a few clicks turn it into on-line Help that looks like this:

Figure 8-6: Doc-to-Help Help

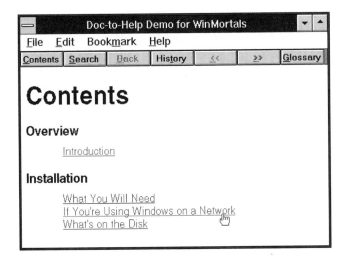

And the on-line help will be linked, with pop-up definitions, tables, search topics, the works.

Other Niceties Doc-to-Help has a few additional tricks up its sleeve, tricks that aren't important to a Windows programmer—unless you want to write a manual or instruction booklet to go along with your program!

The package includes several excellent templates, suitable for constructing short or long manuals, on 8 by 11 inch or 7 by 9 inch pages.

Long manuals may be broken into multiple files. Doc-to-Help keeps track of all the components using WinWord's "Referenced Document" or RD fields. The Table of Contents, Index, Glossary, and cross-linking are all managed, invisibly, as if you had never split the document.

Doc-to-Help also contains the most sophisticated Index generating program available for WinWord.

The Downside That's the good news.

Here's the first piece of bad news: it's $249. And it's not available as shareware.

Here's the second piece of bad news: once you get used to it, you won't be able to put it down. There's simply no better way to create Windows on-line help and no easier way to write a manual. That you can use Doc-to-Help to write the manual and *automatically turn the manual into on-line help* defies the imagination.

Doc-to-Help, $249, from Steve Wexler, Wextech Systems, 60 East 42nd Street #1733, New York, New York 10165. Voice 212-949-9595; Fax 212-949-4007.

There's a sample Doc-to-Help Help file on the Companion Disk. Take a look.

WOPR

No mention of WordBasic add-ons would be complete without WOPR 2.0, the Word for Windows Office POWER Pack, recently adapted to work with WinWord 2.0.

We cut our WordBasic teeth on WOPR (pronounced "whopper")—you may have already gathered that it's a Pinecliffe International product, and we're rather proud of it. *Skip the rest of this section if shameless self-promotion bothers you.*

In a nutshell, WOPR is the world's best-selling Word for Windows add-on. It concentrates on everyday office applications: organizing templates, printing envelopes, creating and customizing (color!) Toolbar icons, printing front-and-back "duplex" or "squished" four pages on every sheet of paper, the ubiquitous WOPRClock which takes no extra screen space to do its ticking, File Delete, Word Counter, SuperSub, Character Compose, and much more.

More to the point, WOPR also contains a large collection of WinWord macros. Here's a sampling:

- **Swap$(InString$,Old$,New$)** replaces all occurrences of Old$ with New$; **StripNonAlpha$(InString$)** strips all non-alphanumeric chars out of InString$; **LTrim$()**, **RTrim$()**, and just plain **Trim$()**.

Not that Microsoft's phone support is bad—it isn't. But the CompuServe route offers so much more.

CompuServe

> There are many who recite their writings in the middle
> of the forum; and who do it while bathing: the closeness
> of the place gives melody to the voice.
>
> —Horace, *Satires*, ca 30 B.C.

Yes, it takes a while to get used to on-line services. There are funny commands and temperamental comm software and accounts and passwords and phones that won't work and all sorts of excuses.

Still, the number-one source of information on WordBasic (and Visual Basic and Amí Pro and almost anything else you can think of) is CompuServe.

Microsoft maintains a Word for Windows forum on CompuServe, with (at last count) four employees devoted to fielding your every inquiry. Those employees have access to Microsoft's extensive databases, obscure documents, hot-shot problem solvers, even the WinWord development team—so when they tackle a problem, they have considerable firepower behind them.

In many cases a fellow CompuServe user will field your question, give advice, perhaps offer condolences. And once you get into the swing of things, you'll be able to eavesdrop (the official term is "lurk") on hundreds of conversations, see what problems other people encounter and how they solve them.

Several "legends" in the computer industry frequent the forum, as do most of the WordBasic heavies. It's a very egalitarian, friendly place. Kick off your shoes and stay a bit!

When you log on to CompuServe, start in the Practice forum: immediately after getting connected, type GO PRACTICE and hit Enter. When you're in the Practice forum, you can try almost anything—free.

To get to the WinWord forum, type GO MSAPP, hit enter, then type the number 12, and hit enter again. Sometimes the fora and section numbers change, so you may have to hunt and peck a bit (try GO MSWORD), but it's definitely worth the effort. As you gain more experience you'll learn how to reduce your CompuServe bill by using TAPCIS or one of the other CompuServe access programs. They make a big difference.

CompuServe, P.O. Box 20212, Columbus, OH 43220. For a sign-up kit check your local software store, or call USA 800-848-8990 or 614-457-8650; Germany (+49)(89) 66 55 0-222; UK 0800 289 458 or (+44)(272) 255111; Switzerland 155-3179. Rates in the USA: 1200 baud $12.80/hr; 9600 baud

$22.80/hr. Local call phone lines are available throughout most of the United States, or you may use the CompuServe 800 direct number for an additional $9/hr. Service is now available in Australia and many parts of Asia, and most of Europe. See you on-line!

Fireworks

Psssst. Have you seen the WinWord Fireworks?

Click on "Tools," then "Macro." Type in "Spiff" (no quotation marks). Click "Edit," then "Select All." Hit the Del delete key. Click "File Close." Yes, you want to save changes. Now click on "Help," then "About," then click the WinWord logo in the upper left corner.

Who says the WinWord developers don't have a sense of humor?

WordBasic Finis

That completes our journey into WordBasic.

It's hard leaving WordBasic without mentioning its position in the history of Windows programming.

Quite simply, WordBasic was the first *real* Windows macro language. Yes, there were earlier ones, but they couldn't hold a candle to WordBasic's power and flexibility.

In a very fundamental way, WordBasic blazed the trail—set the standard—for all other Windows macro languages. While Visual Basic, with its fancy controls and Event Driven capabilities, has taken over as king of the macro hill, and Amí Pro has started nipping at WordBasic's heels with a large number of fancy commands, WordBasic nonetheless ranks as a visionary product, first in what will be a long, long line of languages that will help Mere Mortals tame Windows. The term "seminal" doesn't do it justice.

The designers of WordBasic 1.0, and the folks who fought to get it into the very first version of Word for Windows, deserve a special place in annals of Windows history.

Yes, it's "just" a macro language. But what a language!

Next, we'll tie up a few loose ends in Visual Basic.

Visual Basic Menus

Visual Basic lets you create custom menus on each Form. You remember menus, don't you? They look like Figure 8-7 on the following page.

Figure 8-7: A File - Edit - Help Menu

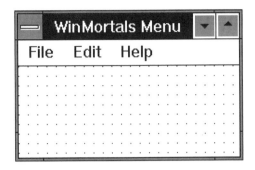

You might expect Visual Basic to support simple menus, like this Edit menu:

Figure 8-8: Simply Edit Paste

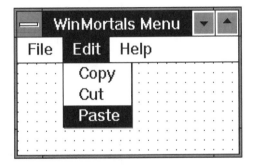

What may surprise you is that Visual Basic can take on a monster, multilevel menu, like this one:

Figure 8-9: File - Print - Special Formatting - Front and Back

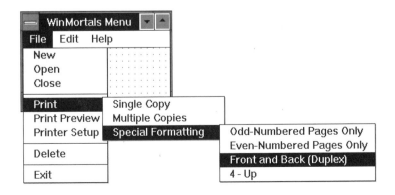

In this case "Print" is on the main menu, "Special Formatting" is on the first-level submenu, and "Front and Back (Duplex)" is on the second-level submenu. Visual Basic also support third-level and fourth-level submenus: more than enough to run across your entire screen!

Those horizontal bars are called separators. Visual Basic lets you put them between any menu items and, with a few restrictions, treats them as if they were "normal" menu items.

Finally, Visual Basic lets you put a check mark in front of any menu item, enable or disable an item (or "turn it gray"), make an item invisible, and change captions on-the-fly.

BUG

Well, that isn't entirely true. Once you change an item into a separator, you can't change it back. That's a bug.

Bug City

Each menu item, as you might guess, has a CtlName. And each CtlName can respond to one Event—the Click Event.

BUG

That isn't quite true, either. Any menu item that has a submenu actually generates a Click Event when the mouse button is pressed down; instead of waiting for the button to go down and back up again—the usual definition of a "click"—Visual Basic jumps the gun and raises a Click Event on mouse button down.

Want to drive your user nuts? Just set up a Click Event handler on a menu item with a submenu. They'll see the submenu flash by and won't be able to get to it.

TIP

And although you can write a separator Click Event Handler, there doesn't appear to be any way a user can trigger that Event; that is, there's no way to click on a separator. Visual Basic keeps tight control over Event handlers; its odd that you can create a handler for an event that never occurred.

B U G

No doubt a design feature: even though you can't write any sort of meaningful Event Handler for a menu item with a submenu attached to it, and you can't write a usable Event Handler for separators, you're still required to give each a CtlName, and you'll have to wade through all of those CtlNames when you're scrolling through your program code.

Now you know why we didn't play with menus earlier: of all the Visual Basic Controls, this may be the buggiest. At the very least, it's the most temperamental.

Menu Design Window

Forewarned and forearmed with just a peek at the menu flakiness, let's take a whirlwind tour through the Visual Basic menu construction set. No, this isn't on the Companion Disk. It's really pretty elementary. When it works right.

Crank up Visual Basic. Click on the Form you would like to endow with a menu. (Note that there can be only one menu per Form, and only one Form per menu.)

Click on "Window," then "Menu Design Window," like this:

Figure 8-10: Menu Design Window

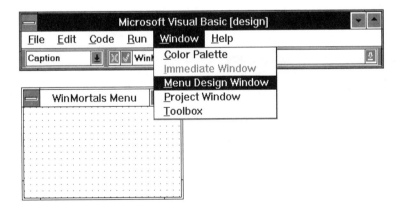

You'll be greeted with a rather strange fixed-size window—the Menu Design Window—which looks like Figure 8-11 on the following page.

Don't give up just yet. It isn't half as bad as it looks.

Figure 8-11: The Menu Design Window

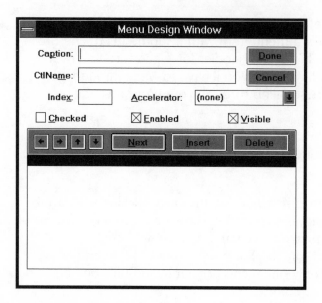

Menu Item File Start typing. Since the first menu item is usually "File," well, just type "File." Hit the tab, so you go over to the CtlName field, and type in a good Control Name . . . something clever like "File." Here's what you'll see:

Figure 8-12: File, File, File

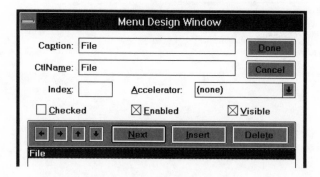

Don't nod off just yet. This gets better. A little bit, anyway.

Menu Item File New Now hit Enter. Then click that little right-arrow, the second in the group of little arrows. See it? When you click that little sucker, you're telling Visual Basic that you want to start a submenu. Visual Basic responds by tossing a few dots on the screen and indenting.

Let's see. What's the first thing you usually see under "File"? (We could dig through the official manual on such things—the IBM Common User Access specification, or CUA—but what a hassle! You're better off looking at the major applications and emulating them.) Here it is. First thing under "File" is usually "New."

Type "New," tab down to CtlName, and type a good Control Name. "FileNew" comes to mind. Here's what you should have:

Figure 8-13: File New

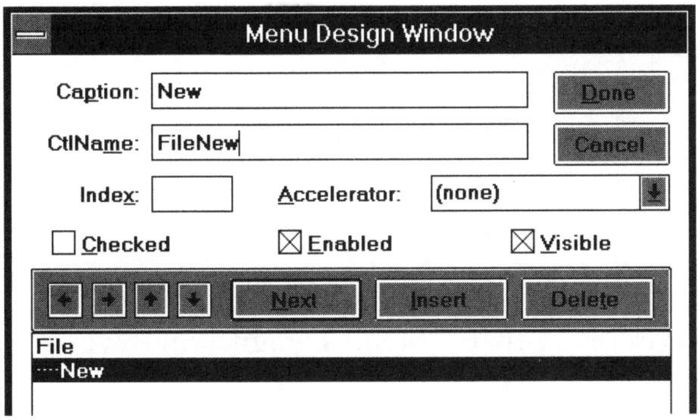

Menu Item File Open Now just so you get the hang of it, let's add one more. File Open . . . usually comes after File New, so hit Enter to start a new entry, type "Open," hit the tab key, and type "FileOpen." Here's what you should see:

Figure 8-14: FileOpen

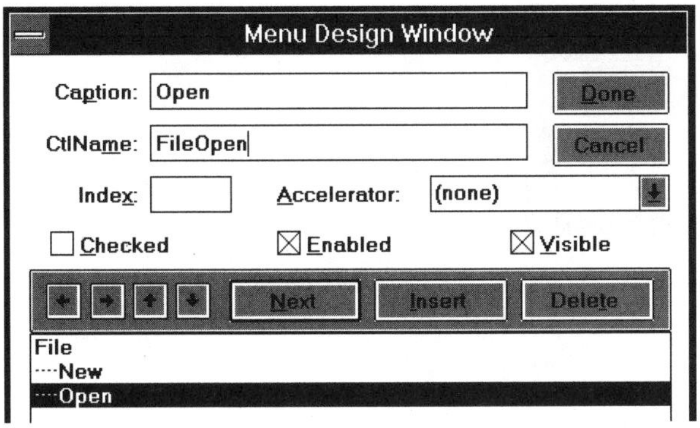

You get the idea.

Let's see what all this really does. Click on "Done"—the Menu Design Window won't go away otherwise. Bring up your Form. You don't even have to run

Visual Basic. The menu should be there, and if you click on "File," it should look like this:

Figure 8-15: Pass the Menu, Please

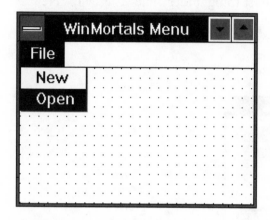

Separators Click once again on "Window," then "Menu Design Window," and fill in a few more blanks like this:

Figure 8-16: The Menu Takes Shape

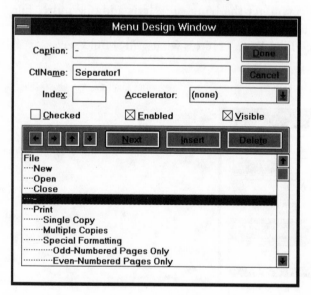

See how that separator goes in? You type a hyphen ("-") as the caption, and give it some bogus CtlName. (It's bogus because separators won't trigger a Click Event, and you can't change the Control's Caption, so the Control Name doesn't do much.) Each time you want to create a new submenu, click that little right-arrow. Visual Basic indents some more, and you're on your way:

Figure 8-17: Three Squirrel Burgers To Go, Please

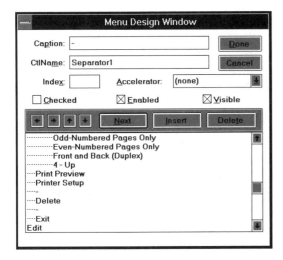

Not too surprisingly, when you're done with a submenu and want to go back to the original menu level, you click on the left arrow. That's what happened after "4-Up" and again after "Exit" here. Rounding out the demo:

Figure 8-18: Talk, Talk, Talk . . . When Do We Eat?

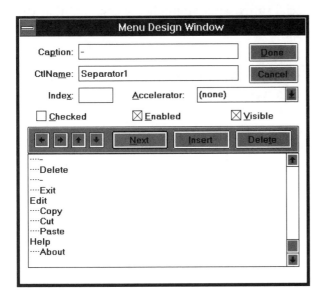

Go back to your Form (by clicking on "Done"), and you'll have the same menu structure you saw in Figure 8-9.

Design Considerations

Yes, it's nice to follow the CUA spec, constructing menus "by the book." But it's even more important to make your application as easy to use as possible, drawing on things your user may have learned from other Windows applications.

Don't feel that you *must* use a menu, that an application isn't a real Windows application without a menu bar. Sometimes menus just don't make sense; they hinder instead of help. The recent rush to icon bars carries an implicit realization that menus can be clumsy and confusing.

On the other hand, if your Form is starting to look like a patchwork quilt of Command Button Controls, with buttons tucked in every corner, it's time to move some of that functionality up to the menu.

Most important: if you use a menu, make sure you put things where they belong. "Exit" always goes under "File." "About" always goes under "Help." When in doubt, take a look at the classic Windows applications and follow their lead. There's nothing worse than having "Exit" stuck under "Misc."

Visual Basic Data Types

Throughout WinMortals we've used a very simplistic variable naming convention—the one used in WordBasic. Whenever we've used a string variable, the name of the variable ended in a "$" dollar sign. Whenever we've used a numeric variable, the name of the variable had no special suffix, and we implicitly assumed that the variable was real.

Diversity in Data

There's a whole universe of data types in the Windows world; WordBasic uses but a small subset of the most common data types. A few examples:

- Amí Pro only supports one data type—string. Amí Pro variables are always stored as strings and are converted only when necessary for certain operations.
- EXCEL has "numbers," string, Boolean, and error value data types.
- DynaComm has integers (whose names are preceded by "%," e.g., %MYINT), reals (starting with "!," e.g., !MYREAL), Booleans (#MYBOOL), and strings ($MYSTRING).

Visual Basic, on the other hand, runs quite a gamut.

The Elementary Types

Visual Basic variables come in six flavors:

- **Integers** are two-bytes long and run from -32,768 to +32,767.

- **Long Integers** (sometimes called, simply, "Long") are four bytes long and run from -2,147,483,648 to +2,147,483,647.

- **Reals** (sometimes called "Singles" or "Floating Point" or "Single Precision Floating Point") are four-byte floating-point numbers. Negative values range from -3.402823E+38 (where "E" means "times ten to the power of") to -1.401298E-45. Zero is stored as a zero. And positive values go from +1.401298E-45 to +3.402823E+38. Unless you do something to change them, Visual Basic variables are all Reals.

- **Doubles** (sometimes called "Double Precision Floating Point" or, confusingly, "Long Reals") are eight-byte floating-point numbers. Negative values go from -1.797693134862315D+308 to -4.94066D-324. Zero is stored as zero. And positive values range from +4.94066D-324 to +1.797693134862315D+308. *Some day you're gonna need these numbers, and you're going to wrack your brain trying to remember where to find them!*

- **Currency** is an eight-byte integer with four fixed decimal places. Values run from -922,337,203,675,477.5808 to +922,337,203,675, 477.5807.

- **String** variables can be either fixed or variable length. They're limited to roughly 65,535 characters in length. Fixed-length strings are established with the Dim xxx As String * n statement, like this:

```
Dim My50CharacterString As String * 50
```

Fixed-length strings are necessary for random access files.

Boolean (True/False) values are stored as Integers. A zero evaluates as False; anything else evaluates as True. Boolean operators—AND, OR, NOT, and the like—are applied bit-by-bit to the integer.

Controls and Forms may be passed as parameters to Visual Basic procedures. For that reason, you may see some references to "Control" and "Form" Data Types. That's stretching things a bit—there are no operators that apply to Controls or Forms; you can't add and subtract them, but they're presented as Data Types to make the lists complete.

The Quick and Dirty Declare

In WordBasic, any variable with a name ending in a "$" dollar sign is a string. Automatically. You don't have to do anything else to make it a string. It just so happens that the same holds true in Visual Basic.

In fact, Visual Basic lets you use this variable-naming convention for all elementary variable types: Integers end in "%" percent signs; Longs end in "&" ampersands; Reals end in "!"—or nothing at all; Doubles end in "#" pound signs; Currency end in "@" at-signs; and Strings, as mentioned, end in "$" dollar signs.

You might see Visual Basic code like this:

```
i%=i% + 1
PopulationOfChina&=1000000000
Pi#=3.141592653589793
NationalDebt@=3000000000
```

where i% is a simple, short Integer; PopulationOfChina&, at 1 billion, is too big for a regular Integer, and is thus stored as a Long; Pi# needs to be expressed with great accuracy, to 15 decimal places, and is therefore a Double; and NationalDebt@, at 3 billion, is too large for even a Long integer, but will fit as a Currency.

It's a lot easier to sort out variables when their names give you a hint as to their type.

Dim, Global, Static

Some people, though, insist upon using variable names without the telltale suffixes. They do it by using Dim, Global, or Static statements.

```
Dim i As Integer
Global Pi As Double
Static MyName As String
```

Dim, as you have seen, can be used within an Event Handler, for an entire Form (the general declarations section) or for a Subroutine Library/Module (also in the general declarations section).

You cannot use Dim in the Global Module; you must use Global.

Static refers to how long a variable's value hangs around. Usually, when a Form disappears its data goes along with it. If you declare a variable Static, though, Visual Basic goes to extra pains to make sure that the old value persists through a Form's various incarnations.

Yes, if you use regular short Integers you'll speed up some operations, and in some cases that may be important. By and large, though, unless you run monster

For-loops or extensive calculations, the data type doesn't make much difference in real-world execution speed.

Defxxx

Just to confuse things a bit, Visual Basic retains the old Basic "Defxxx" command. For example,

```
DefInt J
```

tells Visual Basic that variables with names starting with the letter "J" are to be Integers. For example, the variable "JUSTIN" would be an integer.

```
DefInt I-N
```

says that all variables with names starting with "I," "J," "K," "L," "M," or "N" will be Integers.

All of the data types may be "Def"d: DefInt for Integers; DefLng for Longs; DefSng for Single; DefDbl for Double; DefCur for Currency; and DefStr for Strings.

These commands, for example,

```
DefInt I-N
DefStr S
DefDbl Q
```

specify that variables starting in "I" through "N" are Integers, those starting in "S" are strings, and those starting in "Q" are Doubles.

If that sounds like a debugger's nightmare, it is!

Making life even more complex: the "Defxxx" statements are only valid for the Module or Form in which they are declared. For example, if you found this statement as the first line in a Global Module:

```
DefInt A-Z
```

you might expect that all the variables in the program would be Integers.

Ain't so.

In fact, that DefInt merely says, "Any variable that is explicitly declared in the Global Module—*and the Global Module alone*—will be an Integer."

Ready for the clincher? A Defxxx placed in a Form or a Module behaves in a rather different way. If you declare

```
DefInt A-Z
```

in, say, a Form's declaration section, all of the variables in all of the Form's procedures will be Integer. If you declare it in a Module's declaration section, all of the variables in that Module's subroutines and functions will be Integer.

■ **TIP**

Do yourself a favor. Use the explicit (suffix) data type declaration. Call an i% an i%. *Otherwise, you can bet your program will crash as soon as the boss sees it, and you'll spend most of a weekend trying to figure out which variables are integers, which are strings, and which are both—at different times, in different places.*

Structured Data

C calls them structures. Pascal calls them records. Visual Basic calls them User-Defined Types, but sometimes folks slip and call them data records. You've probably seen some variant of these critters in another programming language.

The idea isn't too tough: you want to keep a group of related data together, handle it as a unit. Maybe you want to keep track of American presidential candidates *(heaven knows why, but give it a shot)*.

Defining a Type   You could define a new data type, like this:

Figure 8-19: Type Candidate

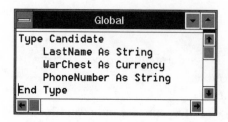

```
Type Candidate
     LastName As String
     WarChest As Currency
     PhoneNumber As String
End Type
```

That sets up the Candidate data type, which consists of three "fields" (think of them as fields in a record if that will help): a variable-length character string called LastName, a fixed-length currency field called WarChest, and another variable-length character string called PhoneNumber.

■ **TIP**

Note how you can have variable-length fields in Visual Basic Type definitions. Sometimes the variable-length fields conflict with DLL calls—particularly Windows API calls—so you have to be careful. Variable-length fields can also cause havoc if you use them in Visual Basic's random-access files.

Type declarations must go in the Global Module.

Using That Type Now say you want to keep track of 500 presidential candidates. This command in a Form's general declarations section:

Figure 8-20: 500 Prexy Candidates

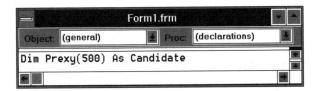

sets up an array called Prexy. Each item in that array is a Candidate—that is, each item consists of three fields, LastName, WarChest, and PhoneNumber.

Once the Type has been declared in a Global Module (but not in a Form), and once an array of that Type has been declared in a Form's general declarations section (but not in the Global Module or in any of the Form's procedures), you can work with it like this:

Figure 8-21: A Use for Prexies

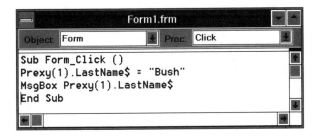

See how you use the variable name ("Prexy")—not the Type ("Candidate")? That makes sense. Take a look at how you specify the field in a record . . . er . . . user-defined data type: you use the ubiquitous "." dot to separate the variable name and the field. Finally, note how subscripts work. They go before the "." dot. That's the same naming convention as used with Properties of Control Arrays (remember them?), so it all looks familiar.

■ T I P

The "$" on the end of the "LastName" field is optional: Visual Basic doesn't care whether you include it or not. So include it. Some day you'll be glad you did.

Restrictions Just for the sake of your own sanity, you'll probably find yourself only using user-defined Types when they're absolutely necessary.

Some DLL calls absolutely, intractably demand that you use Types. A few Windows API calls are notorious for their reliance on Types.

And sometimes you'll find file input-output easier using custom Types. Take a look in the Visual Basic manual at the differences among the Input#, Input$, and Get# statements for an idea of how Types can make your life a little bit easier.

Objects, Properties, Methods, and Events

Good work, pilgrim. You're just about ready to take the Visual Basic tutorial and have it mean something. *That's a joke!*

Before you tackle Visual Basic, mano-a-mano, it'll help to get some terminology straight. You already know that Forms are just Windows that you can use; Controls are the things that live on the Forms; procedures attach themselves to the Form and its Controls; subroutine libraries are called Modules; and the Global Module is only useful for declaring global variables and simple constants.

Let's wade through some more VisualSpeak.

It's a Plane. No, it's a Train. No, it's an Object.

> An object in possession seldom retains the
> same charm that it had in pursuit.
>
> —Pliny the Younger, *Letters*, ca. 80 A.D.

In an apparent nod to the Object-Oriented School of Marketing, Visual Basic has the audacity to call certain things "objects." In Visual Basic land, all of these things are considered to be objects:

- Any Control—Check Box, Combo Box, Command Button, Directory List, Drive List, File List, Frame, Label, List Box, Option Button, Picture, Scroll Bar, Text Box, and Timer
- The Form itself and its Menu
- The Windows Clipboard
- The Printer
- The Debug Object, which is only used to print things to a particular window while debugging

- The Screen Object, which lets you write generic routines that apply to any Control or Form

Most Object-Oriented Programmers would croak if they saw a list like that—where's the encapsulation? the inheritance?—but Visual Basic uses the terminology, and you'll have to get used to it.

Think of it as a marketing Method.

Properties

Properties describe objects.

■ **TIP**

Well, some objects anyway; the Clipboard and Debug objects don't have any Properties. This is where the terminology starts breaking down.

We've hit many, many Properties, but there are still many more. Much of the work of creating Visual Basic programs lies in understanding and applying Properties. It's the kind of thing that only comes with experience—there are so many nooks and crannies that it's virtually impossible to keep them straight.

Methods

> "You know my methods, Watson."
>
> —Sir Arthur Conan Doyle,
> *The Memoirs of Sherlock Holmes*, 1894

Methods do things to objects.

■ **TIP**

Well, some objects anyway *(is this getting repetitious?)*: the Menu and Screen objects don't have Methods, and the Debug object only responds to the print Method.

We used two methods—AddItem and RemoveItem—back in the WinLHA file-selection routine, when adding and removing file names from a List Box. And we used four more while working with DDE.

Are you having a hard time keeping Methods and Properties straight? You aren't the only one.

- In DDE, the things that establish a link but don't change a Control are considered "Properties." LinkTopic (which looks for a Server and sets the Topic of conversation), LinkTimeout (which sets the DDE timeout stopwatch), LinkMode (which actually starts the conversation), and LinkItem (which picks a specific data item) are all Properties.

- Things in DDE that change the contents of a Control—or use the contents of a Control directly—are Methods: LinkRequest (which asks for data from the Server), LinkPoke (which sends data to the Server), and LinkSend (which also sends data to the Server) are all Methods.

- Ah, but here's the strange one. LinkExecute, which neither requires nor changes the contents of any Control, *is considered to be a Method!*

- The Show and Hide Methods act on a Form: they show and hide a form, respectively. But a Form.Show command is functionally identical to the command Form.Visible=-1—and *Visible is a Property!*

The Proverbial Bottom Line: don't get hung up on the difference between a Method and a Property. Somebody somewhere once had a good idea about the difference, but in the process of developing the language the line between Properties and Methods became blurred.

Now you know why we didn't make a big deal out of Properties vs. Methods.

Events

> I love to feel events overlapping each other,
> crawling over one another like wet crabs in a basket.
>
> —Laurence Durrell, *Balthazar*, 1958

Events happen to objects.

■ **T I P**

Well, some objects anyway: the Clipboard, Debug, Printer, and Screen objects don't have any associated Events.

Events lie at the heart of Visual Basic; they form the web from which Visual Basic is woven. A key is pressed, a mouse moved or clicked, a timer goes off, and there's an Event. Your program handles the Events, responds to them, maybe even generates a few Events of its own. Those Events in turn spawn other Events, and so it goes.

If you understand Events and the Event-Driven way of looking at things, you're ready to face Windows programming—*or at least the Visual Basic tutorial.*

That's it for Visual Basic programming. Let's take a look at what's available to make your hours before the screen more bearable.

Visual Basic Add-Ons

Perhaps the definitive sign of a vibrant language, the Visual Basic add-on market has been going gangbusters.

The designers of Visual Basic had the foresight to build a future into the language itself, primarily through published "hooks" for custom Controls.

Any C programmer *(there's the rub)* with the inclination and a few spare months can build a Control unlike any other. And you—or any other Visual Basic programmer—can use that Control as if it were one of the original, Microsoft-supplied kind.

As with WordBasic, we've gone to extreme lengths in WinMortals to try to present the plain, bone-stock Visual Basic product to you. It wasn't easy. The tools available right now span an enormous depth and breadth of function; the ones coming down the pike (which, regrettably, we can't discuss) are even more remarkable.

The Visual Basic add-on industry is changing rapidly, with the average lifetime of an add-on product approaching the lead-time for printing a book! We've chosen the MicroHelp and Desaware add-on products not only because of their value at this moment, but also because of the companies' commitment to producing more and better tools for us, the Mere Mortals.

VBTools

MicroHelp was one of the first to market with a Visual Basic add-on. MicroHelp—with its VBMuscle, VBComm, and VBTools—takes first place for variety and usefulness, at a patrician price.

The Muscle VBMuscle comprises an enormous collection of subroutines, many written in assembler and all readily accessible to mortal Visual Basic programmers.

Looking for an easier way to manipulate times or dates? VBMuscle has 20 different routines. Looking for fancier functions to twist and mangle strings? VBMuscle has 60 of those. Want to slug around larger arrays than Visual Basic can handle? VBMuscle will go to the ends of the earth—or at least the ends of your installed memory.

Perhaps most helpful of all, many of the most-common Windows API calls are easier to handle with VBMuscle: MicroHelp has written many interface routines that shield you from the vagaries of Windows. For example, with VBMuscle's assistance, you needn't ever set up a dummy empty string to feed into Windows' voracious maw. Your program merely calls a simple VBMuscle routine, and all the details are handled for you.

You might imagine that such extensive help doesn't come cheap. It doesn't. VBMuscle sells for $189, or half again as much as the street price of Visual Basic itself.

The Comm Visual Basic is not well adapted to communication. Writing to COM1 is a tad barbaric, even if it does work, some of the time.

VBComm, on the other hand, takes your program in hand and guides it through the maze of Windows communication arcana.

If you're thinking of writing any communication program in Visual Basic, consider writing it in the DynaComm script language and using Visual Basic as a front- or back-end. (Keep in mind that you'll have to buy a copy of DynaComm for each user.) As you've seen, DynaComm works well with DDE.

But if it simply must be done in Visual Basic, VBComm is the first place to look.

At $149, VBComm is only slightly less expensive than the full DynaComm package.

The Controls Here's the MicroHelp meat: VBTools 1.1 has ten custom Controls for Visual Basic. (VBTools 2.0, which wasn't available for review as we went to press, is said to contain 30 Controls.)

What to do with all those Controls?

Five of them are improvements on existing Visual Basic Controls. The other five are brand new. Let's look at the five "improved" controls first:

- The VBTools Scrollbar Control is a minor improvement over the built-in Visual Basic Scrollbar. It triggers a Change Event whenever the little box (the "thumb") is moved; the Visual Basic Scrollbar doesn't trigger a Change Event until the thumb is moved and released. It gives you a bit more control over the magnitude of changes and lets your program know if the area above or below the thumb was clicked. Not exactly earth-shattering—in fact, you may find the constantly triggered Change Event annoying if you tie it to a caption somewhere—but it's not bad.

- The "Tag" List Box lets your program work with more than one selected item in a List Box. Say you have a List Box with six items. The "Tag" List Box lets the user select any number of them; like Figure 8-22 on the following page.

Figure 8-22: Selected Items 2, 4, and 5

The "Tag" List Box has a few other capabilities: your program can clear all the items in the List Box with one command; you can load the List Box but turn off the screen update, so it doesn't flicker; and there's a built-in search capability. Unfortunately, though, the multiple selection method doesn't follow Windows standards—Ctrl+Click and Shift+Click don't work the same way as they do in most Windows programs.

- The VBTools Enhanced Text Box lets you set up real data entry Forms. Masked input. Defined data types (e.g., phone number, date). Insert and overstrike modes that change when the user hits the "Insert" key. Center- and right-alignment within the box. Even a built-in Edit / Undo. This is an industrial strength Control.
- An Enhanced Label Control adds 3D effects.
- The Enhanced PushButton lets you put your own pictures on an otherwise plain-vanilla Visual Basic Command Button Control. It also has provisions for left- or right-justifying text on a Command Button, and you can set it up so that "holding down the button" triggers repeated Events.

Here are the five "new" controls:

- The MhMulti Control is a first stab at a great idea. There are several variations on the theme, but basically this Control can appear on your Form as a stop light, a round "button," a flip-on-or-off light switch, or a happy face. Each click on the Control cycles through several predetermined settings: the stop light goes from red to yellow to green (*funny, most of the stop lights around here go the other way!*); the light switch cycles up-middle-down; and the happy face goes from a red frown to a yellow stoic to a green grin.

- The MhState Control lets you change the NumLock, CapsLock, Insert, and Scroll Lock state from your program. For example, you can set up a Control that, when clicked, will turn on NumLock.

- The Alarm Control is a horse of a very different color, indeed. The Control can look like an old-fashioned telephone, a wind-up alarm clock, or a wristwatch. Start the Control (by setting the Ring Property) and all of a sudden the Control starts beeping and the picture springs to life—the handset on the phone rocks off the hook; the wristwatch flashes; the alarm clock's bells clang back and forth. If these won't wake your user up, nothing will! You have control over the pitch and speed of the ring. You can even have this Control appear as your application's minimized icon—so your users will be greeted by a bleeping beeper, rocking back and forth on their Windows desktop. Neat stuff.

- The Gauge Control displays a slider-bar, thermometer-style bar, or a rotating-needle gas gauge-style needle superimposed on a picture of your choice. It's a very dramatic way to present analog data in a universally recognized way. Like this:

Figure 8-23: One Type of Gauge Control

Semi-circular gauge.

- Finally, the Playing Card Control looks like playing cards! Your Visual Basic program picks a suit and a face value and chooses from among a dozen card backs, and all the details are handled for you. If you're thinking about writing a Visual Basic card game, this Control alone will pay for the whole collection. Unfortunately, though, you can't use your own pictures as card backs.

The Sting VBTools is not cheap; at $189 it, too, is almost half again as much as the street price of Visual Basic itself. Buy VBTools, VBMuscle, and VBComm, and you'll find yourself suddenly $527 poorer. That's quite a hit for add-ons to a product that costs $125 on the street.

There are other problems: some users report difficulty getting the kind of telephone support they feel they deserve; there is no money-back guarantee; and the documentation can be hard to read.

Still, Mark Novisoff, founder of MicroHelp, maintains a most visible presence on CompuServe—and questions directed to him personally get quick, accurate, and helpful answers.

VBTools, $189; VBMuscle, $189; VBComm, $149. MicroHelp, 4636 Huntridge Drive, Roswell, Georgia 30075, 800-922-3383 or 404-552-0565.

Custom Control Factory

Another one of the first kids on the block, Desaware with its Custom Control Factory, achieves enormous virtuosity *with but one Control!*

Imagine a Picture Box Control with many pictures. Click on the Control, and it "plays" the pictures, in succession, just like an old-fashioned picture flip-book.

The standard flip-book sequence works much as you would expect: when the mouse button goes down, each picture is displayed in quick succession. Let go of the button, and the sequence plays backwards, returning to the original picture.

There are other sequences—play half the pictures when the mouse goes down, the other half when it comes up, for example. There's even a multistate capability that simply advances one picture each time the Control is clicked, like the VBTools MhMulti Control, but since you can use any picture you like, the CCF version is much more flexible.

And on top of it all, literally, you can place a caption. The CCF Control gives you lots of flexibility in setting and justifying the caption.

You can bring in pictures using the same facilities as Visual Basic—but you also have the option of bringing in *files* of pictures, dynamically, while the Control is running.

Finally, this extraordinary implementation manages to handle all those pictures without gobbling up copious quantities of Free System Resources. All of the pictures are handled by the Control itself, not by the normal Windows managers. The result: you can have hundreds, even thousands, of icons operating without bringing your system to its knees.

If you want to animate any part of your Visual Basic Form (and don't make the mistake of thinking that this is just for little 32-by-32 pixel icons; it'll work on any picture), CCF is a must.

Custom Control Factory, $49. Desaware, 5 Town & Country Village #790, San Jose, California 95128. 408-377-4770; Fax 408-371-3530.

Visual Basic Pro

As we were going to press, Microsoft was about to release a new product, code-named Rawhide, generally known as "Visual Basic Pro."

This product represents quite a departure for Microsoft. With a bit of luck it may be a harbinger of good things to come.

The ISV Dilemma All of the Microsoft Windows products are extensible, or at least malleable: that's the *raison d'etre* of macro languages, and it's led to quite an industry.

The quality of those extensions varies wildly, from so-so to excellent, and the add-ons themselves run the gamut from narrowly focused (say, spreadsheet macros for calculating fleet taxes) to wide ranging (say, word processing macros to print envelopes). They range in price from free-as-a-breeze to dear indeed.

Some of the capabilities pioneered in those add-ons have been "rolled in" to the Microsoft product itself, occasionally at the peril of the intrepid software vendor ("ISV"), the little company, that championed the idea.

Round 'em Up . . . Rawhide Happily, the Visual Basic folks at Microsoft have found a better way.

Instead of competing with ISVs—the little guys and gals who make Microsoft's products better, and thus help sell those products by the ton—the Rawhide approach is to gather the best of the add-on crop, tie them together in a single package, and make that package available to the world at large. It's a great deal, both for the ISV and for Microsoft.

All of the Controls we've described in this section—from the VBTools enhancements to existing Visual Basic Controls, to the fancy all-new VBTools Controls, to the astounding animator from Desaware—are in Visual Basic Pro.

In addition, Microsoft has developed an OLE Client Control and a Multimedia Control Interface (MCI) Control that begin to take advantage of Windows 3.1 enhancements.

Rawhide Features Here's a quick rundown of what awaits in Rawhide:

- **3-D Controls**—Check Box, Command Button, Frame, Option Button, "Panel" (a grown-up Frame Control, with a background color, rounded corners, etc.), and Group Push Button (like 3-D Command Buttons, except only one in a group can be "on" at any given time).

- **Animated Button**—the Desaware Custom Control Factory Control, described earlier. A must-have if you want to make your pictures move.

- **BEdit, HEdit**—for pen computing.

- **Gauge**—the VBTools Gauge Control, described earlier.

- **Graph**—an extraordinarily rich Control with direct links to the Bits Per Second Graphics Server. This Control puts EXCEL-quality graphing in the hands of Visual Basic programmers.

- **Grid**—sets up a spreadsheet-style grid of cells. *Hitch this to the Graph Control, and you can build your own EXCEL 5.0, in ten lines of code! Well. Maybe twenty.*

- **Instant Change Scroll Bars**—from VBTools, described earlier.

- **Key Status**—also from VBTools.

- **MDI Child**—uses the Windows Multiple Document Interface standard to set up windows that "belong to" other windows and can only exist inside the parent window. This Control isn't as powerful as it could be, because you must create all the unique Child windows at design time.

- **OLE Client Control**—quite probably the most far-reaching Control ever invented. Here's all it takes to set up an OLE link with Visual Basic as an OLE Client, the Microsoft Graph Applet (one of the little applications that ships with Word for Windows 2.0) as a Server, embedding the graph in Visual Basic:

Figure 8-24: An OLE Client Control

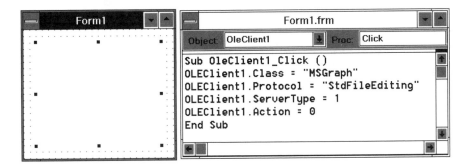

An OLEClient1.ServerType of one specifies embedding (linking leaves the data in the Server and is somewhat analogous to a hot DDE link; embedding actually pulls the data into the Client application and keeps it there). When the OLEClient1.Action Property is set to zero, Visual Basic initiates an OLE link and tells MSGraph to create a new embedded object.

Run that four-line program and click on the OLEClient Control, and MSGraph pops up, as shown in Figure 8-25 on the following page.

Figure 8-25: MSGraph as OLE Server

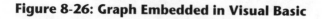

Once the user is through creating the graph—using the full services of the MSGraph Applet—he or she clicks on "File," then "Exit" and "Return," and OLE updates the contents of the OLEClient1 Control:

Figure 8-26: Graph Embedded in Visual Basic

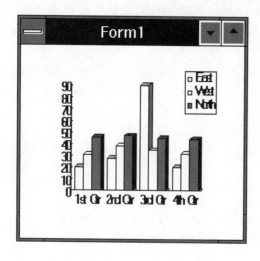

Yes, that's from a four-line program. All it takes is the right Control, and Rawhide has it.

- **Picture Clip**—the missing link for CoolCons. Picture Clip lets you store a large number of pictures and "clip" one of them off when you need it. The clipped picture can be pasted on a Picture Box Control or on a Form.
- **SpinButton**—have you ever wondered how to get one of those little up-and-down arrow thing? You know, the ones that aren't as big as real scroll bars. The SpinButton does it:

Figure 8-27: SpinButton Control

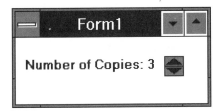

- **VBMCI Custom Control**—Multimedia being a topic in and of itself, we'll step lightly. Suffice it to say that this Control gives your Visual Basic program access to all the common MCI (Media Control Interface) commands: Play, Pause, Prev, Back, Step, Next, Stop, Record, and Eject.

On the whole, Rawhide speaks well of the ingenuity and talent of people—both inside and outside Microsoft—who are working to put stupendous capabilities into the hands of mere mortals.

Rawhide (Visual Basic Pro), price not set at press time. Microsoft Corporation, One Microsoft Way, Redmond, Washington 98052. 800-426-9400; outside the United States, contact your local Microsoft office.

By the way, MicroHelp/VBTools and Desaware/Custom Control Factory aren't resting on their (considerable!) laurels. Look for new products from both, probably by the time you read this. Visual Basic Pro is just a beginning.

How to Get Visual Basic Help

The world is full of Visual Basic books, consultants, and self-anointed experts. The tough part lies in separating wheat from chaff.

WinTech Journal

Another magazine? I can't read all the ones I get anyway!

Any magazine that launches its premiere issue with an article entitled "How Visual Basic Made Me A Better C Programmer," by none other than the immortal Charles Petzold, must ooze moxie. Such is the case with the *Windows Tech Journal*.

No, it isn't a startup from one of the big-name computer magazine empires, although it does have roots that go way back in the computer biz. It's just a little rag that tries to grab Windows by the tail and shake it a bit.

Mostly, *WinTech Journal* rates as a friendly gathering place for all of us who are going nuts trying to tame Windows.

The *Journal* has bitten off a big chunk: it will try to appeal to all Windows developers, from C ++ guri to mere mortals. So there's at least a small chance it'll head way out into hyper-tech orbit and leave the more Basically inclined staring, wondering where it will all end.

But if the first issues are any indication, editor J.D. Hildebrand seems to be doing a good job of mixing outer space and down-to-earth.

Windows Tech Journal, $29.95 for one year (12 issues). *Windows Tech Journal*, P.O. Box 70087, Eugene, Oregon 97401-9943. 800-234-0386; Fax 503-746-0071.

Be sure to tell J.D. what you want to see!

Undocumented Windows

Yes, if you're going to try your hand plumbing the depths of all those beckoning Windows API calls, you'll need the old stand-by: *Windows Programmer's Reference*, $39.95, Microsoft Press.

It contains (almost) all of the documented Windows stuff. Which is fine, far as it goes which isn't far enough, for some folks. To get the whole skinny on Windows, you'll have to hitch on the carabiners, reach for the pitons, and tackle the treacherous cliffs and rarefied atmosphere beyond mere documentation. Andrew Schulman and David Maxey's *Undocumented Windows*, $39.95, from Addison-Wesley—not coincidentally the flagship book in this series—points at the landmarks and then turns you loose.

CompuServe

The best source of Visual Basic information is on CompuServe.

While the Microsoft commitment to Visual Basic support on CompuServe isn't up to Word for Windows standards (WinWord has four employees working CompuServe; Visual Basic generally has one or two), it's still a great place to get your questions answered—often by one of the captains of the Visual Basic industry.

If you're just starting out on CompuServe, be sure to try your hand at the practice forum; simply type GO PRACTICE and you'll have a chance to try things without paying for connect time.

Once you're ready to dive in, type GO MSBASIC and look around for Section 5: that's the Visual Basic forum. (Fora change location from time to time, so you may have to hunt around a bit.)

There's one extremely important file maintained in the MSBASIC forum, called VB-TIPS. One forum denizen and Visual Basic guru, Nelson Ford, keeps on top of all the conversations. He periodically distills his findings into this document and makes the compilation available to one and all. VB-TIPS is a wonderful way to catch up on all that's happened; it's a wonderful testimony to the "Let's all help each other beat this sucker" spirit you'll find prevalent on CompuServe.

CompuServe, P.O. Box 20212, Columbus, OH 43220. See the WordBasic section earler in this chapter for complete details.

If you use VB-TIPS, drop Nelson a line and tell him how you like it.

Parting Shots

This ends the Basic part of the lecture, class.

Is Visual Basic a "toy language"? Are you prepared to throttle the next person who says, "It's just a macro"?

Have pity on people who say stuff like that. They probably don't understand that these mere macro languages have full access to the Windows API; they probably don't know that DDE in the macro languages is as simple as dialing a phone; they probably haven't seen how the macro languages can be tied together, each taking advantage of its own host application, to provide enormous power and flexibility; without doubt they've never tried to implement an OLE Client—and they've certainly never done it in four lines of code.

More important, they probably won't realize that *this is the future of Windows programming!* And the price of admission is learning (or relearning) humble, much-maligned Basic.

CHAPTER ■ 9

A Few Other Languages

This short chapter takes a look at several other Windows languages. Along the way, we'll also take a look at the connection between DOS and Windows, as it pertains to normal working folk.

Since the DOS connection relies so heavily on Windows' Enhanced Mode, we'll assume you're working with DOS 5 or later and that you're running Windows 3.1 in Enhanced Mode.

Talking DOS

Much has been made of Windows' seeming inability to "talk" to DOS applications.

Most Windows languages (including all the ones we've examined, except the WordPerfect macro language) have the ability to "Send Keys." Running the command:

```
SendKeys "abc{enter}"
```

is equivalent to—indeed, indistinguishable from—a user typing the letters "a," "b," then "c," and pushing the enter key.

Except.

Except it's impossible to "send keys" to a full-screen DOS application—that is, any application running in a DOS window where you can't see the window title.

You can "send" an Alt+Spacebar. That wakes up the system menu—the "hyphen" on the upper left corner of most windows—whether DOS is full-screen or not. Once the system menu is awake, you can send more keys, but they'll only go to the system menu. You're out of luck, however, sending keys straight into the DOS application.

For people who live, breathe, and eat Windows, that isn't such a big deal. But if you still have one or two (or ten or twenty) applications hanging around that aren't adapted to Windows, or if you have a DOS batch file that you want to run with Windows supplying the input, the lack of a Send Keys capability can get frustrating.

We're going to take a look at several of the most popular and least expensive Windows languages/programs and see what needs to be done to give them this DOS "key stuffing" capability. Then we'll take a look at Stackey, the premier DOS key stuffer, and see how it can be made to work. Finally, we'll hack together a little Visual Basic program that may (or may not) do the key-stuffing job for you.

The Challenge

We'll measure all of these languages and programs against The DOS Editor Standard, newly created for our testing purposes. The boiling question: How easy is it to launch the DOS Editor and start a File Open in the current directory with "*.BAT" files showing?

Successful programs will end with a screen that looks like this:

Figure 9-1: DOS Edit, File Open for *.BAT Files

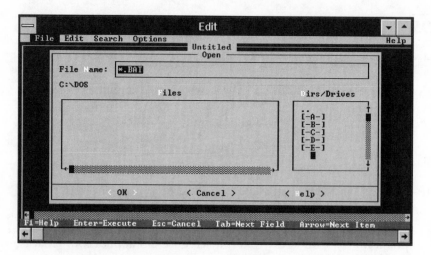

That isn't quite as simple as it looks. To get to this point, the language has to be able to start the DOS Editor, send an "escape" character to clear the initial Editor nonsense start-up screen, send an Alt+F key combination to select "File," send an O for "Open," then send *.BAT to select .BAT files, and finally send an Enter to display the .BAT files.

Not all languages are up to it.

Just to avoid the appearance of a one-horse race, while we're taking a look at these languages we'll linger a bit and go over how some of these products may save you time and gray hair. We'll also step—intentionally—into a few traps, giving you a feel for what's really in store.

Norton Desktop for Windows' Batch Builder

Even though Norton Desktop for Windows (NDW) has much to recommend it, Batch Builder/Batch Runner may be the most powerful part of the entire package.

Based on Morrie Wilson's WinBatch, Batch Builder/Runner let you program batch files—not unlike DOS batch files—that can be run under Windows.

The NDW Batch language has a distinctly DOS-batch ".BAT" file flavor to it. If you've slogged through hundreds of .BAT files you should be able to pick it up almost immediately; the more Basically inclined may need a refresher course in .BATspeak but shouldn't have too much problem translating.

Where It Lives

NDW Batch Builder resides in rather austere digs. Crank up the Builder and here's what you'll see:

Figure 9-2: NDW Batch Builder

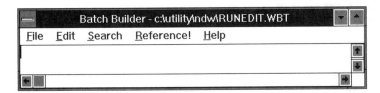

The Batch Builder is little more than a simple text editor and a non-context-sensitive help file, with one important kicker: the "Reference!" window.

Click on "Reference!" and a cut-and-paste window appears; like the one shown if Figure 9-3 on the following page.

Double-click on one of the commands there on the left, and it'll be inserted into your batch file. Nice touch.

Figure 9-3: Batch Builder's Crib Sheet

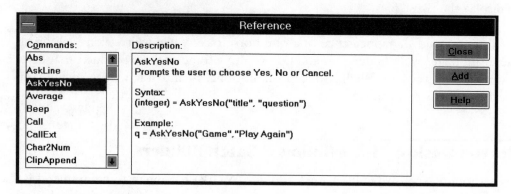

What It Does

WinMortals readers will find many of the NDW Batch commands familiar, although a bit watered down. The AskYesNo command shown in Figure 9-3, for example, tosses a simple Yes/No/Cancel dialog box with a question mark icon onto the screen.

Figure 9-4: NDW Batch Wants to Know

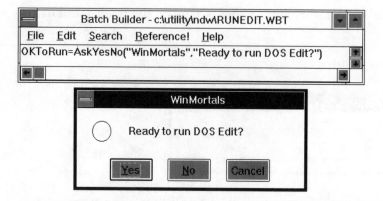

It's a handy enough dialog box, but you don't have any options: the question mark icon is a permanent fixture, as are the three buttons.

On the other hand, the NDW Batch language has a whole bunch of functions that would be useful in the Windows Basics—FileCopy, FileExist (returns "True" if the file exists), FileRename, DiskFree (returns the amount of free space on the current drive), and several others.

Remarkably, most of the window-related NDW Batch commands work on *partial* window titles, and there's a wealth of window-related commands. One simple example—if you want your NDW Batch file to wait until the user closes Word for Windows, all it takes is one line:

```
WinWaitClose("Microsoft Word")
```

The partial-window-title approach works wonders: your program doesn't have to be concerned with hWnds or exact title matches including file names, like "Microsoft Word - MYFILE.DOC." The NDW Batch language merely examines all windows' titles. Any that start with the characters "Microsoft Word" match.

NDW Batch has other tricks up its sleeve: your program can directly manipulate the Clipboard, using a ClipAppend command; access to the DOS environment string is as simple as an Environment() command; the language supports straightforward one-line access to WIN.INI or private INI files.

It's an amazingly powerful language.

How It Works

The odd .BAT-like syntax of the language poses a small hurdle for Windows Basic fans, but the operating environment will drive you nuts.

NDW Batch files are edited and run separately: there's no F5-run key or "Start" button. You have to independently start the .WBT batch file. That's why there's a distinction between "Batch Builder" and "Batch Runner."

Although Norton Desktop for Windows itself can be arranged to make the "launching" of .WBT files relatively painless—and the Windows 3.1 File Manager can do in a pinch—the edit/stop/run/edit/stop/run routine gets real old, real fast. Adding to the frustration: you have to explicitly save the batch file before running it; otherwise you'll just run whatever old version of your program happens to be hanging around.

There's a reasonably capable debug mode, initiated by adding

```
Debug (@ON)
```

to the program. It brings up a line-by-line debug box that shows the result of executing the current line of code; you can check the values of variables on-the-fly, but you have to remember the variable names—there's no list to jog your memory.

On the other hand, the SendKeys debugger works like a champ. Independently of the Debug mode, you can set up SendKeys Debug to construct a file of all keys that are sent during a batch file run. Think of SKDebug as a sort of DDEWatch, limited to keys sent from a specific NDW Batch file. If you're stuck using SendKeys, SKDebug provides a handy hardcopy post-mortem.

Finally, the NDW Batch approach to dialog boxes will make you yearn for simpler languages *like C and assembler*. The Byzantine "imbedded dialog template file called from a batch file" dialog box machinations leave much to be desired.

The Competition

So how hard is it to meet the DOS Edit challenge using the NDW Batch language?

If you read the NDW manual, *Using Batch Builder*, you'd think solving the DOS Edit challenge would be simple. There's an example on page 4-83 that appears to be tailor-made for our challenge. It looks like this (comment lines start with a semicolon):

```
;run DOS batch file to start the editor
Run ("edit.bat", "")
;wait 15 seconds for editor to load
Delay (15)
;send Alt+F N to the clipboard
ClipPut ("!FN")
;paste contents of clipboard to DOS window
SendKey ("!{SP}EP")
```

Sure looks like it should work, but it doesn't. There are two problems: one's easy to solve; the other appears to be insurmountable.

■ **T I P**

Note how the NDW Batch folks have hacked a brilliant work-around to the SendKeys problem. If Windows won't permit NDW Batch to send keys directly to a DOS window, well, that's all right. NDW Batch simply stuffs the keys into the Clipboard and then uses the Windows Control menu (the hyphen-thing in the upper left corner) to *Edit/Paste the keys into the document*. That's a great trick. We'll dig into the details here in a moment.

First, let's look at the code one line at a time.

To even the playing field, we'll have NDW Batch run the DOS Editor directly, so—assuming the DOS Editor is in "C:\DOS"—the above Run statement should read:

```
Run ("c:\dos\edit.com", "")
```

So far so good. Next we'll wait for a few seconds:

```
Delay (2)
```

The number inside the parenthesis is supposed to be the number of seconds' delay and can run from a minimum of 2 to a maximum of 15. On our 486, in this program anyway, Delay(2) actually waits for over 30 seconds. A real thumb-twiddler.

SendKeys Without Sending Keys

Next comes the brilliant part. The NDW Batch manual presents a great way to send keys to the DOS window, without actually using Send Keys. *(Remember, you can't send keys to the DOS box!)*

The first step is to put whatever key combination you want to use into the Windows Clipboard. The NDW Batch ClipPut command sticks stuff in the Clipboard. Visual Basic can do the same thing with Clipboard.SetText, Amí Pro with ClipboardWrite; WordBasic has to be kludged with an EditCopy. According to the NDW Batch manual, this puts an Alt+F and an O in the Clipboard:

```
ClipPut ("!FN")
```

The *piece de resistance:* a DOS window will recognize the send keys sequence that wakes up the Control menu—the hyphen-thing—whether you can actually see the window's Control menu hyphen or not. By sending an Alt+Spacebar, NDW Batch activates the DOS window's Control menu. Then an "E" selects Edit and a "P" selects Paste. The command

```
SendKey ("!{SP}EP")
```

where {SP} is the same as hitting the Spacebar, invokes the Control menu's Edit Paste function, like this:

Figure 9-5: Alt+Spacebar, E, P

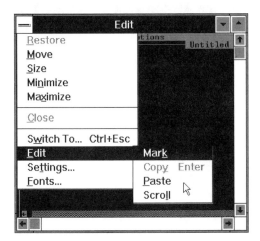

That's the trick.

If you stuff the keys you want to send into the Clipboard, then use Send Keys with the Alt+Spacebar, E, P sequence to perform an Edit Paste, the net result is very, very nearly the same as a send keys into the DOS window.

Back to the Competition

Now that you know the Send Keys trick, you'd think the rest would be easy: figure out which keys to send, stuff them in the Clipboard, and Alt+Spacebar, E, P them right into the DOS box. Unfortunately, we hit a slight problem right off the . . . uh . . . bat.

DOS Edit starts out with a nonsensical screen that looks like this:

Figure 9-6: MS-DOS Edit's Opening Screen

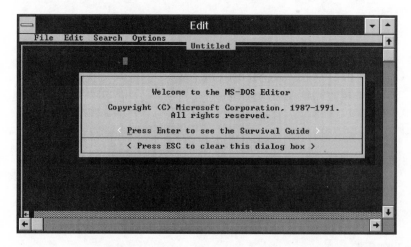

The only thing that will clear that screen is an "Esc" escape key press. You can't do a thing with the editor until the screen is cleared, and there's no way to start DOS Edit with a clean screen.

So, the simple Alt+F proposed by the NDW Batch manual won't work in this case. After you stare at it for a while, you'll see that we have to send something that looks like this:

```
{escape} Alt+F O *.BAT {enter}
```

where {escape} clears the screen, Alt+F selects "File," O is for "Open," *.BAT sets up .BAT files, and {enter} lists them.

Translated into NDW Batch-speak, it looks like this:

```
Para=StrCat(Num2Char(13),Num2Char(10))
ClipPut (StrCat (Num2Char(27),"!FO*.BAT",Para))
```

Note the two rather strange NDW Batch commands: StrCat() is rendered in most Basics as simply "+" (it concatenates strings); Num2Char is what most Basics call Chr$(), (i.e., it converts numbers into ANSI characters).

Putting it all together, this is the program that should solve our challenge:

Figure 9-7: Competition Killer

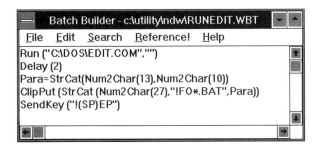

Run it, and here's what you get:

Figure 9-8: OOPS!

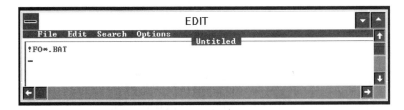

Guess what? The command recommended in the NDW Batch book doesn't work. This is supposed to put an Alt+F and an N into the Windows Clipboard:

```
ClipPut ("!FN")
```

It doesn't. In fact, it puts an exclamation point, followed by an F, and then an N into the Clipboard. (The exclamation point translates into an "Alt" key when running the NDW SendKey command; it don't translate into diddly-squat when placed on the Clipboard.)

And that's as far as we could get. Even the Norton techies couldn't come up with a way around the problem.

The NDW Batch language didn't meet the DOS Editor challenge.

Redux

Don't let the results of this one test sour you on the product, however. The NDW Batch Builder/Batch Runner is a powerful tool for Windows programming; it's also an easy language for .BAT-speaking Mortals to pick up and use. And it has more than a dozen commands that would be welcome additions to any Windows Basic.

NDW Batch Builder can meet the challenge, if one of the restrictions is eased. You'll see how when we discuss E'vent Manager.

Norton Desktop for Windows, $149, Symantec Corporation, Peter Norton Group, 10201 Torre Avenue, Cupertino, CA 95014; 800-441-7234; 408-253-9600.

hDC Power Launcher

Another prime contender in the Windows desktop wars, hDC Power Launcher, concentrates on starting—launching—programs. (Remember how we used the variable name "hWnd" to represent the handle to a Window? Well, an "hDC" is a handle to a device context—the way C programmers get at a printer, for example. The company's name is a pun. Get it?)

The hDC Enhanced Command language lies at the heart of hDC Power Launcher; it's a small but powerful language geared specifically to starting and controlling programs.

Where It Lives

Norton Desktop for Windows is designed to be used as a desktop, as a replacement for Program Manager. For most dedicated NDW users, the Windows Program Manager is banished to WinApp never-never land, permanently replaced by NDW.

hDC takes a different approach. You can make hDC your permanent desktop, but that isn't the normal way of doing things. Most hDC users get into the program by clicking on the hDC red-eye. When so instructed, hDC will change every window's Control menu hyphen-thing, which normally looks something like this:

Figure 9-9: Normal WinWord Control Menu

into a bright red hDC logo, like this:

Figure 9-10: hDC's Replacement Control Menu

(That "hDC" on the left shows up in red on most screens.)

Click on the hDC logo, and here's what you'll see:

Figure 9-11: Power Launcher Comes to Life

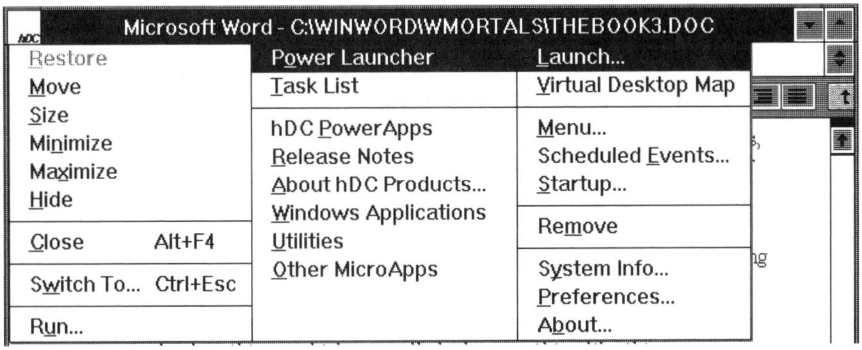

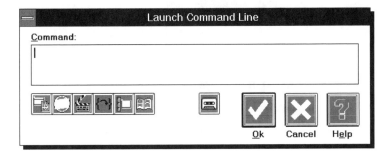

The first column—the first third of the Power Launcher menu—contains all of the traditional Control menu commands. The other columns, though, give you quick and easy access to all of the Power Launcher features.

Click on Power Launcher, then Launch, and you'll find yourself in the middle of the Power Launcher Command Central:

Figure 9-12: Where Power Launcher Lives

At this point you could type in the name of any executable file (or any file with an association defined in WIN.INI), click OK, and hDC Power Launcher would start it. That'd be something like writing a Visual Basic program to change directories: sure you can do it, but you'd be overlooking a few things.

What It Does

The real power of hDC Power Launcher is in those six little icons you can see at the bottom left of Figure 9-12.

We'll be using the first icon—the one that looks like a dog-eared sheet of paper on top of a window; the fourth icon—the one that looks like a quick rendition of Hurricane Hilda; and the sixth icon—which looks like a waterlogged open book.

Just in case you were wondering about the others:

- The second icon, which has an "M/A" in the middle, lets you get at hDC's Micro Apps. The built-in Micro Apps let you assign key combination "hot keys," mouse clicks, or icons to macros. One Micro-App is a screen saver.

- The third icon lets you pick from several dozen prebuilt "scripts" or macros. The scripts cover everything from printing the current document to minimizing the active icon to playing a little tune.

- The fifth icon gives you a hand at creating some Enhanced Commands. If you want to launch a program in a specific size window, pick a default directory, even run a DDE Execute command, this is where you'll find it.

So much for the buttons we won't use. Let's look at the first, fourth, and sixth.

The Applications & Documents Icon   Click on that first button and you'll find a typical File Troika. Well, by Jove, here's EDIT.COM. Click on it once:

Figure 9-13: EDIT.COM Unveiled

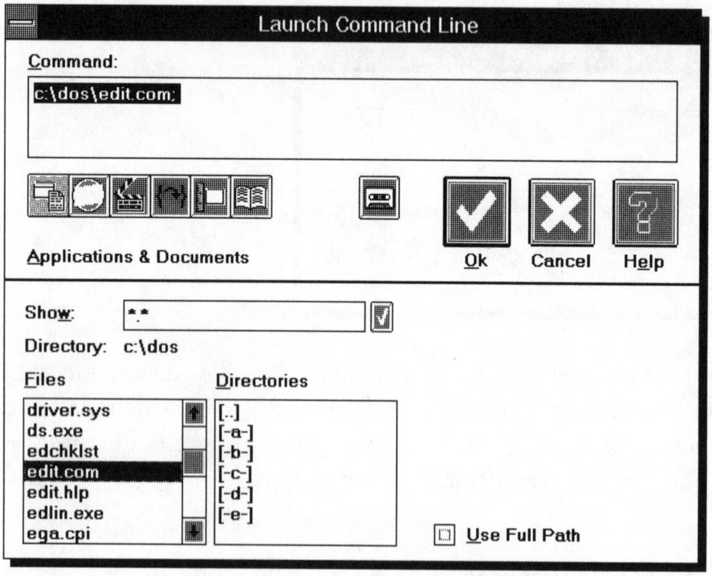

See how selecting EDIT.COM puts a command up on the "Command:" line? That's generally the first step in constructing an hDC Power Launcher Enhanced Command—picking the file or program that will be launched.

By clicking on EDIT.COM, we've set it up as the program to be launched. May as well set up the DOS Editor challenge while we're poking around.

Now let's see if we can send the right keys. Perhaps hDC Power Launcher can actually crack our little challenge.

Replacement Variables Icon If you click on the fourth icon—the one that looks like a meteorologist's hurricane symbol—you'll get hDC Power Launcher's fanciest option, somewhat cryptically called "replacement variables":

Figure 9-14: Replacement Variables

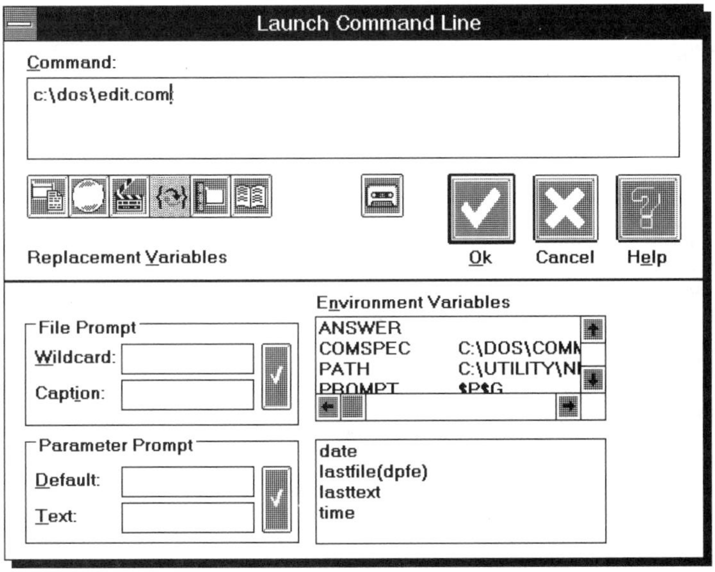

Don't get too worried about the strange terminology. This is where you build dialog boxes. They're very specific, predefined dialog boxes that pop up just before your application is launched. (Yes, you can change your DOS environment variables here, too, should the temptation ever arise.)

Departing a bit from our challenge here, let's see what it would take to have hDC Power Launcher (instead of the DOS Editor) display all the *.BAT files in the current directory, then launch the DOS Editor with our choice of .BAT file. (Norton Desktop for Windows can do this, too.)

Where it says "File Prompt Wildcard" we'll put in "*.BAT"—the files that we want to use in the challenge. Then we'll give the dialog box a Caption and click on that check mark. Here's how it looks:

Figure 9-15: One-Click Dialog Box

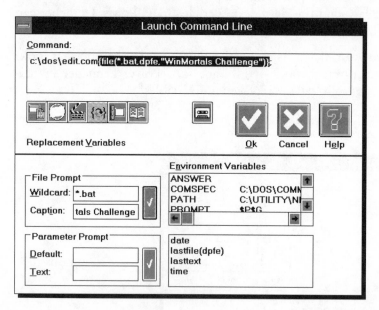

hDC Power Launcher has taken the file we picked—EDIT.COM—and the two parameters we entered—a DOS file wildcard specification and a dialog box title—and turned them into an hDC Enhanced Command that looks like this:

```
c:\dos\edit.com{file(*.bat,dpfe,"WinMortals Challenge")};
```

Pretty impressive, no?

In the hDC Enhanced Command language, that one line says: *Launch c:\dos\edit.com, but before you do, toss out a predefined dialog box, start it with "*.bat," and let the user choose which file to feed into the launched program.*

Which is very nearly what we wanted to solve the DOS Editor challenge. Yes, it's cheating a bit because searching for the file isn't under the control of the DOS Editor.

Click OK, and the standard hDC File Troika box appears.

Figure 9-16: hDC's Standard File Selection Box

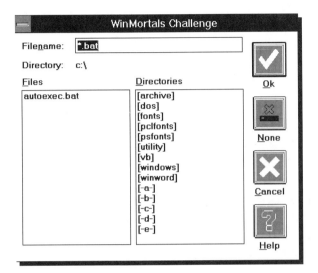

Everything looks great. Click once on autoexec.bat, click OK, and up pops the DOS Editor, with autoexec.bat loaded. Right?

Wrong.

Figure 9-17: Close, But No Cigar

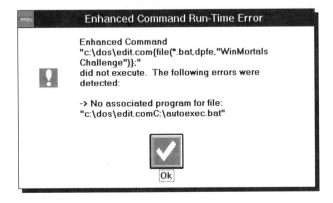

Guess what? We were led down the primrose path.

Given the cryptic "No associated program for file" error message, you could spend quite a bit of time trying to figure out what happened. (Hey, not to worry, it happened to us, too.) With a bit of luck, though, you'll find out sooner or later that there was a little problem in all that click-click-click automatic programming.

hDC forgot a space.

Yes. A stupid space. Instead of the program hDC generated:

```
c:\dos\edit.com{file(*.bat,dpfe,"WinMortals Challenge")};
```

what hDC really wanted was this:

```
c:\dos\edit.com {file(*.bat,dpfe,"WinMortals Challenge")};
```

The difference is a space after the ".com".

Enhanced Command History Button You might expect that, discovering the lack of a space, it would be time to grit your teeth, go back to the beginning, and rebuild the whole launch command piece-by-piece. But wait! There's hope!

Click on the Enhanced Command History icon—the one that looks like a paperback book sunk under four feet of water.

Here's what you'll find:

Figure 9-18: The History Lesson

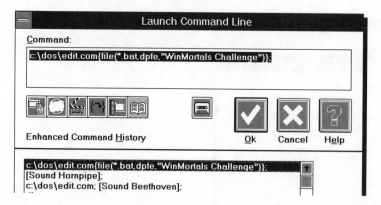

hDC Power Launcher has been keeping a list of all your commands. Retrieving the last one—the one that croaked for lack of a space—is as simple as clicking on it.

Nice.

Once you click on the last command, moving it up to the "Command:" box, all you have to do is put your cursor between ".com" and "{file," hit the spacebar, and click OK.

Figure 9-19: Victory!

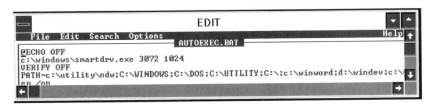

How about that. hDC Power Launcher cracked the DOS Editor challenge, albeit with the rules slightly bent.

The Competition

Alas, though, even the hDC gurus couldn't find a way to fulfill the original challenge. Selecting a .BAT file under the control of the DOS Editor remains an unattained goal. Feeding an Alt+key combination through the Windows Clipboard—the trick proposed in the NDW Batch manual, and one tricky way to meet the challenge—doesn't work for hDC either.

hDC Power Launcher and the Norton Desktop for Window Batch language will both meet the DOS Editor challenge with DOS running in a window—that's a trick we'll explore in the next section, on E'vent Manager—but neither can get at DOS running full-tilt-boogie maximized.

NDW has a Launcher, but it's nowhere near as sophisticated as the hDC flavor. NDW's Batch Builder language would permit you to construct a dialog box that asks you to pick a .BAT file, then cranks up the DOS Editor with the chosen file. That's exactly what we just did in hDC Power Launcher. Using the NDW Batch language would have taken considerably more time and effort; it's not a click-here fill-in-the-blanks-there whiz like hDC.

hDC Power Launcher has several other capabilities. There's a fairly rich set of Enhanced Commands that can be used to program a launch; the Enhanced Commands include DDE Execute and DLL calls; unfortunately, though, there's only a limited repertoire of dialog boxes. hDC Power Launcher also bundles a "Virtual Screen" capability that lets you putter with a screen 64 times the size of your real screen and snap back and forth between screens quickly. There's a scheduling capability. And a screen blanker.

hDC Power Launcher, $99.95, hDC Computer Corporation, 6742 185th Avenue NE, Redmond, Washington 98052, 206-885-5550, Fax 206-881-9770.

E'vent Manager

We've seen how two giants in the Windows biz have added all sorts of functionality to Windows. It's important to understand how they differ.

Norton Desktop for Windows, designed to take over your entire desktop, relies on a meager launcher and a powerful batch language. The NDW Batch language is a prototypical Windows batch language, the one against which all others will be measured.

hDC Power Launcher, which doesn't really hold such grandiose designs on your desktop, takes over the Control menu with the hDC red eye and delivers a high-powered launching capability. hDC Power Launcher, at this writing, is the most powerful launcher available.

Launching and batching are two different critters: yes, there's some overlap in function, but the concepts are quite different.

Lest you think launching and batching cover the entire universe of Windows add-on tricks, let us now take a look at a third approach, this one is from a smaller company.

A Given

E'vent Manager, unfortunately, cannot communicate with a DOS application running full-screen. The application must be running in a "real" window.

If you're going to try this at home, beware: E'vent Manager isn't terribly forgiving on that score. We had dire problems attempting to make E'vent Manager work with full-screen DOS boxes. So, before you try anything with E'vent Manager and DOS apps, make sure that your DOS application doesn't come up full-screen.

There are lots of ways to make sure DOS runs in a little box, but the simplest is to crank up the Windows PIF Editor. Click on File, then Open, and go look for the default Program Information File, otherwise known as _DEFAULT.PIF. Open it up, and make sure that the "Windowed" button is checked; like Figure 9-20 on the following page

That will make any DOS app without a PIF file pop up in a Window; if you don't like the setting in general, slog through the Windows manual and find out how to make a PIF file for EDIT.COM.

Or, if you're lazy, just change over to "Windowed" in _DEFAULT while you're playing along here, as shown in Figure 9-20. Just make sure you remember to change back to "Full Screen" when you're done.

If you want to make hDC Power Launcher or the Norton Desktop for Windows work with a "windowed" DOS Editor, this _DEFAULT.PIF approach is an easy way to ensure the Editor comes out of its corner in a little box.

Figure 9-20: DOS-in-a-Window

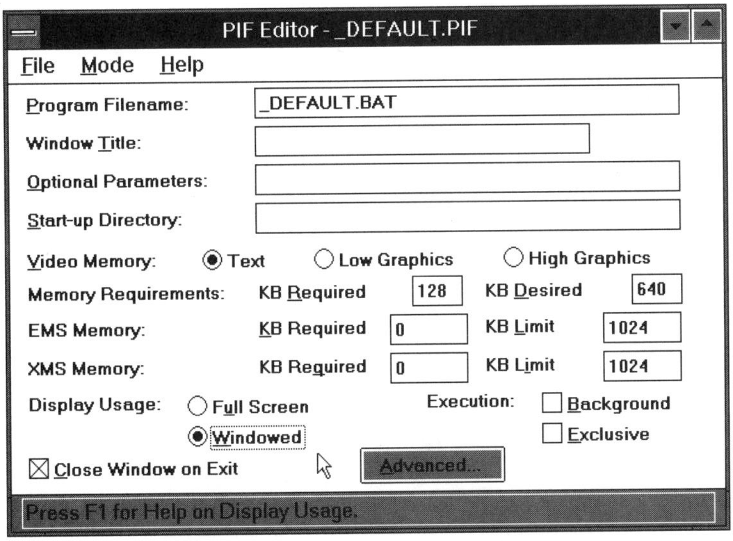

Shaken, Not Stirred

Merasoft's E'vent Manager is an "Agent."

Think of an Agent as a giant Event Handler, not unlike the Event Handlers we've written in Visual Basic. Where our earlier Event Handlers handled Events associated with Forms and Controls and the like, Agents handle (nearly) *all* Windows Events.

The E'vent Manager terminology is a little different, but the basic idea is quite familiar: once a certain Event (or set of Events) is triggered, E'vent Manager springs to life and runs a program. That program will typically do something to a window.

In E'vent Manager-speak, the Event or set of Events in question is called a "Condition." The program that runs is called a "Script." And the window that's affected by the Script is called the "Target."

It's actually a little more complicated than that: Scripts can act on multiple windows, multiple Targets. Specific Events may not trigger Conditions immediately, the way we're used to thinking of them; E'vent Manager scans everything once a second. There are other niggling details. By and large, though, an Event (Condition) triggers an Event Handler (Script) that operates on an object window (Target).

A Task, the basic unit of E'vent Manager activity, consists of a Condition (i.e., one set of Events), a Script (an Event Handler), and a Target (an object window).

We're going to build a Task that meets the DOS Editor challenge. Well, it almost meets the challenge: the DOS Editor can't run full screen. This same approach can be used in the Norton Desktop for Windows Batch language (with SendKey) and in hDC Power Launcher (with the appropriate instructions on the command line, after the semicolon following "c:\dos\edit.com").

Where E'vent Manager Lives

Once E'vent Manager is started, it lives everywhere.

Omnipresent E'vent Manager lurks in the Windows primordial ooze, waiting for the proper combination of Events, springing to life only when the right Events occur in the correct combination.

The easiest way to get in and program E'vent Manager is through the E'Bar. Unless you do something to change it, the E'Bar pops up every time you start E'vent Manager. It looks like this:

Figure 9-21: The E'Bar

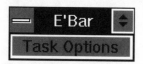

We want to write a new Task—a new set of Condition, Script, and Target, that will fulfill the DOS Editor challenge.

Click on Task Options, and here's what you'll see:

Figure 9-22: E'Bar's Options

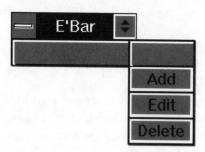

We want to Add a Task. ("Learn" is much like Add, except it relies on replicating your actions. Think of "Learn" as a macro recorder that will record and play back.)

Click on Add, and type in a good Task name, like, oh....

Figure 9-23: OK, Agent 007, Let's See Your Stuff

Figure 9-23: OK, Agent 007, Let's See Your Stuff

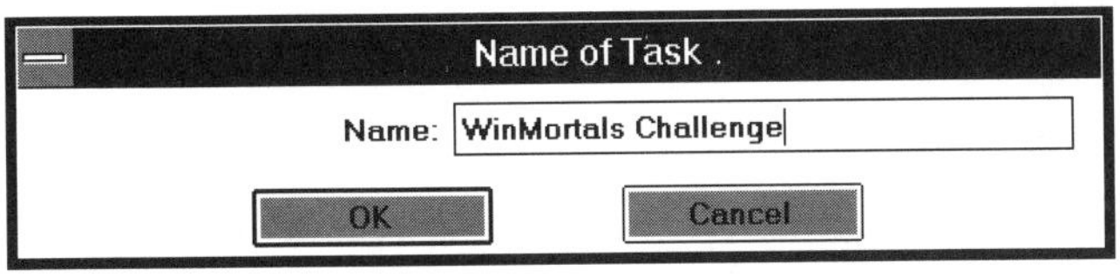

Click OK and you'll be greeted by the Task Editor:

Figure 9-24: Welcome Home, James

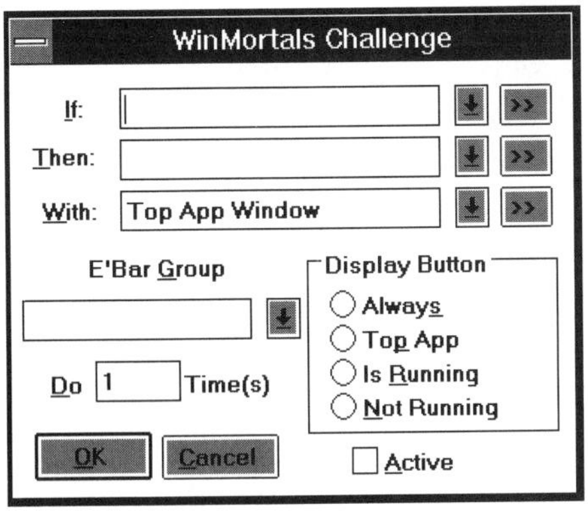

Although we've had to wade through quite a bit of obscure terminology to get this far, note how the Task boils down to three simple, easily identified components:

- If—the Condition, Event, or combination of Events that will trigger this Task
- Then—the Script or Event Handler or program that is to be run
- With—the Target or object window

Now it's starting to make some sense.

How It Works
Click the down-arrow next to "If." You'll see Figure 9-25 on the following page.

Figure 9-25: The Null Condition

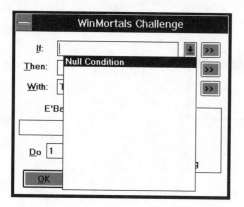

"Null Condition" sounds like some sort of college freshman's Existential Dilemma, but it's exactly what we need for the DOS Editor challenge. In English, the Null Condition is no condition at all: this Task shouldn't automatically respond to any Event; we don't want it assigned to a hot key or a mouse click combination or anything esoteric; it should simply sit and wait patiently until we start it.

Click on "Null Condition." Then click the ">>" box to the right of "Then". (That ">>" thingy is called a Goto button in E'vent-ese.) You'll be asked for a Script name. Try this:

Figure 9-26: Your Script, Mr. Connery

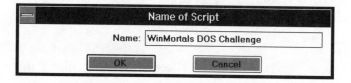

Click OK and you'll see the Script Editor. This is the place where you write the actual program, as shown in Figure 9-27 on the following page.

We'll step lightly through the actual Script. Suffice it to say there are many, many options—the E'vent Manager Script language is a full-fledged language in its own right.

Conceptually, you build your Script, one line at a time, by clicking through the "Options," occasionally typing in specific strings or values. The Options go many levels deep: clicking on one option brings up another set of options, which may in turn have additional options. The Script Editor keeps track of your location in all those options by posting a history in the "Path" box.

Figure 9-27: E'vent Script Editor

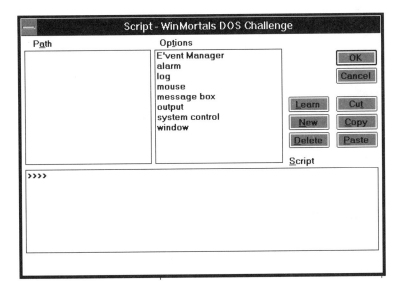

Once you've completed a line of code, it appears in the Script box, down where you can see the ">>>>." (That ">>>>" is effectively an insertion point in the Script; in E'vent-ese it's called an "Insertion Bar").

Complicated enough?

It gets easier when you use it. Let's build the DOS Editor challenge Script with the Script Editor.

Thank You, Miss Moneypenny

When E'vent Manager runs this script, it'll start by running the DOS Editor. We need to allow a few seconds for Windows, DOS, and the Editor stabilize. (No, you wouldn't know that in advance. It's one of those things you discover by playing with it for awhile.) So the very first thing we need to tell E'vent Manager is to wait a few seconds before sending keys to the DOS box.

If you rummage around in the E'vent Manager manual for a while, you'll discover that the Pause command is under "E'vent Manager / playback."

Click on "E'vent Manager." The Options box goes down one level, and the Path box reminds you where you've been, as shown in Figure 9-28 on the following page.

Figure 9-28: Let the Script Begin!

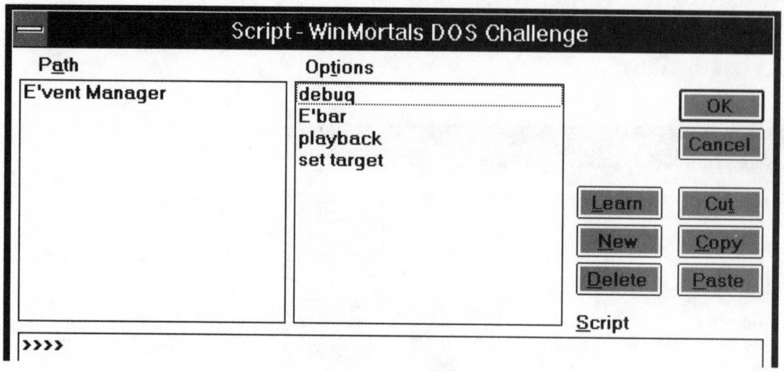

Next, click on playback:

Figure 9-29: Ready to Pause?

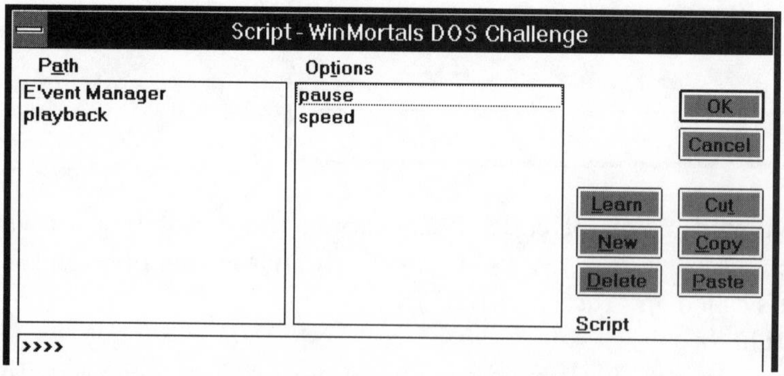

See how the Path box keeps track of where you've been? It can be a big help. Now, click on pause, and enter a reasonable number—say, three seconds. Like this:

Figure 9-30: The Pause

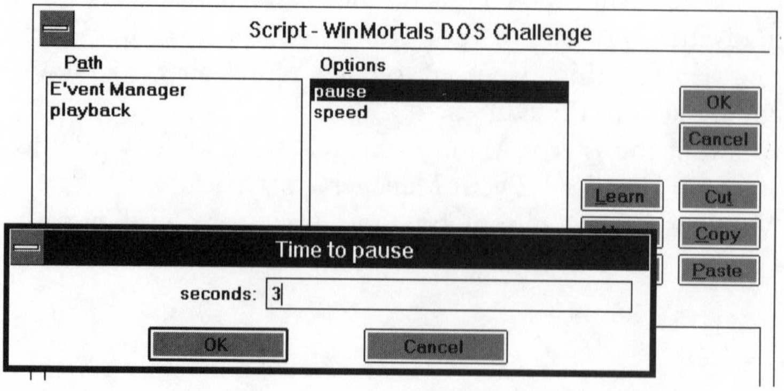

Finally, click on OK, and you'll see your very first E'vent Manager Script appear down in the Script box:

Figure 9-31: The Script Is Afoot

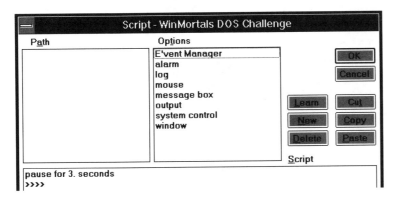

That was pretty easy, no?

Next we need to feed an "Escape" to the DOS Editor. The E'vent Manager manual will tell you that {esc} is the E'vent way of picking an escape. So click on output, then string, and type in {esc}:

Figure 9-32: The Great {esc}

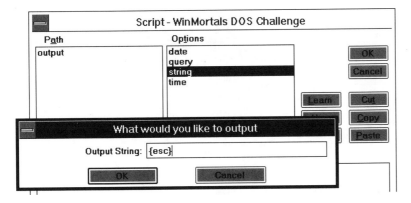

Click on OK, and the second line of the Script is done, as shown in Figure 9-33 on the following page.

Figure 9-33: Script Line Two

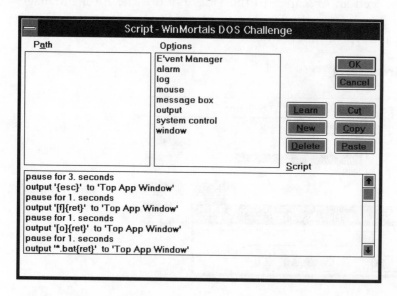

Now that you see how to do it, you shouldn't have any problem creating the remaining lines of the script. When you're done, it should look like this:

Figure 9-34: The Finished Script

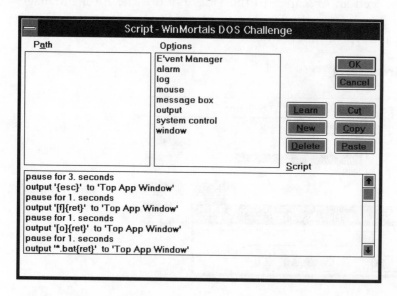

The only Greek here: [f] is the same as Alt+f, and {ret} stands for a carriage return. If you play with this a bit and tune it to your system, your script may differ from this one; in particular you may find some (even all!) of the pauses superfluous, and the [] brackets on the "o" may not be necessary.

Click OK and you're back at the Task Editor. All that's left is specifying the "With" Target window. Click on the ">>" to the right of With, and type in something meaningful like:

Figure 9-35: Pick a Target

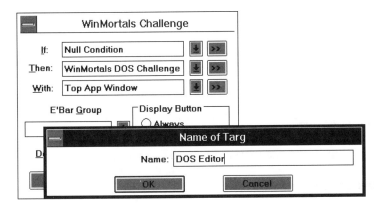

Click OK and flip around until you find the DOS Editor:

Figure 9-36: Nailing the Editor

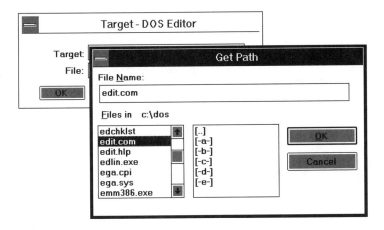

Click OK all the way back out, and we're ready to put this Task on the E'bar. Type a good name where it says "E'Bar Group," click the "Always" button, so this Task always appears on the E'bar, and check the "Active" box; like Figure 9-37 on the following page.

Figure 9-37: Ready to Run

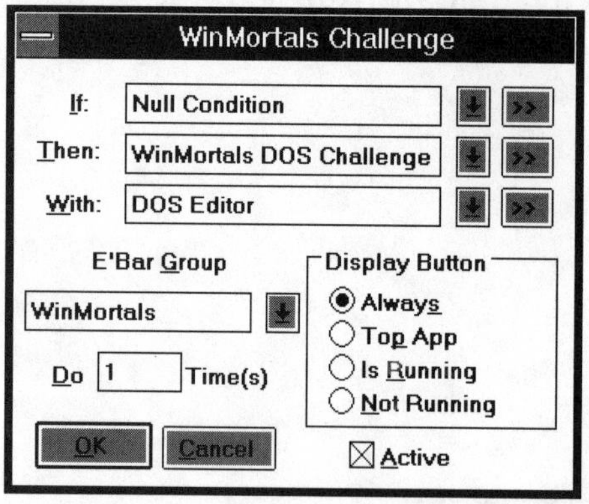

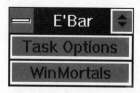

Click OK and your E'bar undergoes a marvelous transformation:

Figure 9-38: WinMortals on the Bar

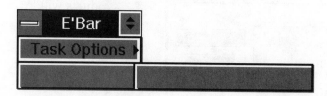

Click on WinMortals, and you're ready to launch:

Figure 9-39: Is It Up to the Challenge?

Click WinMortals Challenge—and sit back and watch while E'vent Manager meets the challenge, as shown in Figure 9-40 on the following page.

Figure 9-40: E'vent Manager vs. The Challenge

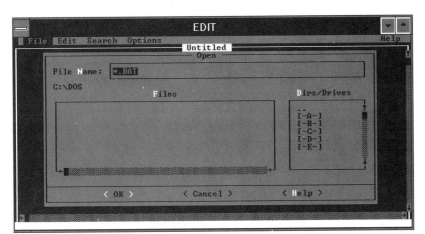

The Competition

Don't let this little demonstration fool you. Norton Desktop for Windows and hDC Power Launcher can both use the same trick—sending keys to a windowed DOS session—if you ensure that the DOS Editor comes up in a window, not full-screen.

Still, by floundering around a bit here, you can see how each of three approaches are so very different: NDW uses a batch language, hDC runs with a sophisticated Launcher, and E'vent Manager goes under cover as an Agent.

That begs the question: which is best? Alas, there's no simple answer.

It's entirely conceivable that you could use all three simultaneously!

With a bit of luck, though, our little excursion here will point you in the right direction. Each of these products has rough edges. Each of the products will lead you, initially, down blind alleys. Yet each of the products, in its own way, lets you tap into part of Windows, and do it with a minimum of fuss.

E'vent Manager for Windows, $179, Merasoft Corporation, 384 East 720 South, Suite 204, P.O. Box 1918, Orem, Utah 84059. 801-225-9951; FAX 801-225-9984.

Stackey

For fools rush in where angels fear to tread.

—Alexander Pope, *Essay on Criticism*, 1711

Stackey is one of the best-kept Windows secrets. This slick little DOS program doesn't claim to have any connection to Windows. Doesn't speak Windows. The Stackey manual doesn't even mention Windows.

But why should that hold us back?

Not so long ago, in Chapter 5, we figured out how to make Visual Basic drive a true-blue Windows-illiterate DOS program. All it took was a little .BAT file, and a Visual Basic Shell statement. Perhaps we can do the same with Stackey?

Stackey Shtick

As its name implies, Stackey stacks keys. You stuff keystrokes into Stackey, and Stackey obligingly plays them back. It's the kind of thing you'd think DOS itself would do, if it were a wee bit smarter.

Stackey runs off the DOS command line. Nothing fancy. If Stackey is anywhere on your DOS path, a command like this:

```
Stackey w36 "ABC" cr
```

starts Stackey, "w" waits for 36 clock ticks (about two seconds), sends the keys "A," "B," then "C" to the waiting DOS program, and then sends a "cr" carriage return.

That's too easy. Is it possible that humble Stackey could meet the DOS Editor challenge—and succeed where the big-name programs have failed?

Watch.

Visual Basic Front End

Crank up Visual Basic. We need one simple Form, flattened out. Double-click on the Command Button Control (the one that looks like an oval with a six o'clock shadow), and type in a Caption like this:

Figure 9-41: Push Here

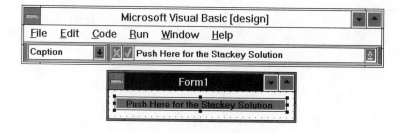

Now double-click on the Command Button Control, to bring up the Command1_Click Event Handler (hey, this is so simple we won't even change the Control Name). Type in this five-line program:

Figure 9-42: Stackey Solution

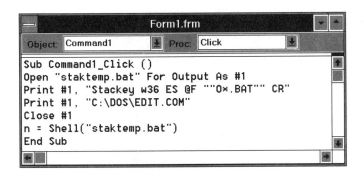

Some of that needs a bit of explanation. We're going to create a little .BAT file called "staktemp.bat." The first line of the .BAT file looks like this:

```
Stackey W36 ES @F "O*.BAT" CR
```

Rummage around the Stackey manual for a few minutes and you'll find that alphabet soup means "w" wait 36 clock ticks (about two seconds); then send an "ES" escape; then an "@F" Alt+F; then the character string "O*.BAT"; and finally a "CR" carriage return.

The first Print statement you can see in Figure 9-42 is complicated slightly by the double-quotes necessary to put single quotes in the .BAT file. Par for the course in Visual Basic.

The second line of the .BAT file created by this Event Handler is:

```
C:\DOS\EDIT.COM
```

Sounds familiar, eh? It just gets the DOS Editor going.

Finally, that little .BAT file is executed with

```
n = Shell("staktemp.bat")
```

and that's all she wrote.

Take it Away, Stackey

Click on F5 to run the Visual Basic program. Then click the Command Button to create and launch the .BAT file.

Figure 9-43: Challenge Met!

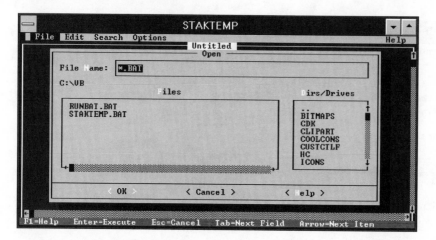

And there you have a complete, clean, easy solution to the DOS Editor challenge. It executes full-screen. There's no monkeying with SendKeys to a DOS window; no attempt to cram keystrokes into the Clipboard; no mind-numbing mental gymnastics.

The Sermon

There's a lesson in this, class.

In our single-minded pursuit of fancy solutions to complex Windows problems, sometimes we tend to overlook the easy, straightforward solutions *that exist in the DOS world.*

You'll save yourself a lot of headache if, while attacking a Windows problem, you sit back from time to time and think about whether the problem could be better approached from a completely different angle.

Even a *(shudder!)* DOS angle.

Sometimes that's the best way to go. Sometimes simpler really is better.

More Stackey Stuff

It doesn't seem fair to leave Stackey with such a cursory glance. Suffice it to say that Stackey can take care of an enormous breadth of DOS key-stuffing chores. Aside from the obvious ability to stuff any key or key combination known to your keyboard, Stackey can wait until certain characters appear, at certain places on the

DOS screen it'll even scan the entire screen, waiting for whatever cue you desire; it can beep, bop, and boop (within the confines of the PC speaker, anyway); it'll control screen colors; record key combinations; stuff dates and times, file names, and the like; speedup/slowdown; user input; and on and on.

If you use Windows to talk to the DOS world, Stackey will make the conversation much easier.

Stackey (and Batutil), $49 + $4 s/h, CTRALT Associates, Support Group Inc., Lake Technology Park, P.O. Box 130, McHenry, Maryland 21541. 800-872-4768 or 301-387-4500; FAX 301-387-7322.

Conclusions

Even though we haven't hit all of the Windows languages floating around—not by a long shot—you should have a pretty good feel now for some of the most popular ones and the varying approaches they take.

There are several Windows packages with macro languages that just don't cut the mustard: Crosstalk for Windows, 1-2-3 for Windows, dbFast for Windows, among others, come to mind immediately. You can be sure, though, that the purveyors of those macro languages will be catching up soon.

Other Windows languages are quite powerful, but they're sufficiently different that they would require a book of their own; many are also sufficiently expensive that digging into them requires quite an up-front commitment. Here's a partial list:

- GFA Basic for Windows, $295, GFA Software Technologies Inc., 27 Congress Street, Salem, Massachusetts 01970; 508-744-0201, FAX 508-744-8042. An industrial-strength Basic *sans* "Visual" front-end. Particularly interesting for those who must run the same program under both Windows and DOS.

- Object View, $899, Matesys Corporation; 900 Larkspur Landing Circle Suite 175, Larkspur, CA 94939; 800-777-0545, 415-925-9000; FAX 415-925-2909. Good "Visual" support; well suited for SQL and DB2 applications. Expensive.

- ObjectVision, $149.95, Borland International Inc., 1800 Green Hills Road, Scotts Valley, California 95067; 800-331-0877, 408-438-5300. ObjectVision fans cite its ease of use. Its detractors cite inflexibility and limited programming constructs. In rebuttal, ObjectVision doesn't really have a programming language; it's more a form design and data entry package—only more so. Like the Borland vs. Microsoft debates in general, much seems to depend on "religious" preferences. Good hooks into dBASE and Paradox databases. Very much Event-Driven.

- Realizer, $395, Within Technologies 8000 Midlantic Drive Suite 201, Mount Laurel, NJ 08054-5080; 609-273-9880. A heavyweight Basic without the "Visual" front-end. For a detailed description, see Michael Hyman's *Window's 3.0 for BASIC Programmers* (Addison-Wesley, 1991).

- Superbase, $695, Software Publishing Corp, P.O. Box 54983, 3165 Kifer Road, Santa Clara, CA 95056-0983; 408-986-8000; FAX 408-980-0279. Many people find the Superbase 4 macro language difficult to master.

That's just the beginning, of course. You might expect that most big software houses—and a fair percentage of little ones—will try to climb on the Windows Basic bandwagon. The next few years should bring an explosion in Windows languages, add-ons, tools, support systems, consultants, and books!

CHAPTER ■ 10

The Future—Say "OLE, Too!"

> "Would you tell me, please, which way I ought to go from here?"
> "That depends a good deal on where you want to get to," said the Cat.
>
> —Charles Lutwidge Dodgson, *Alice's Adventures in Wonderland*, 1865

What Hath Redmond Wrought?

In the six months it took to write and print this book—the six months immediately preceding the release of Windows 3.1—the world of Windows changed at a breakneck rate.

Never before in the history of computing has there been such a concentrated investment in time and money, such an onslaught of computer talent, such a wailing and gnashing of teeth!

With Windows at the epicenter of this maelstrom, the pace and fury of change must inevitably increase. Tools and techniques become obsolete within months—even weeks!—of their unveiling. Languages appear, mutate, and disappear with alarming frequency. Even *concepts* come and go, gaining their ordained fifteen minutes of fame, before being exposed as bloated façades, inflated by marketing hype and undeservedly lofty expectations.

A few stable points exist in this churning universe, strange attractors though they may be. One is the enduring popularity of simple, Basic-like languages. Another, the specialization offered by macros; no language can ring an application's chimes like that own application's macro language. Then there's the need for user interfaces that "feel" like Windows, and the ongoing battle to interact with the user without futzing around in the details of a specific hardware configuration.

By slogging through WinMortals, you've hoisted a leg up on the future of Windows programming. Yes, there will always be a need for hotshot C and Pascal programmers. But the future of Windows programming lies in normal folk—people like us—using these phenomenal tools to get the job done.

Event-Driven vs. Procedural: The Continuing Dichotomy

... a new theory, however special its range of application, is seldom or never just an increment to what is already known. Its assimilation requires the reconstruction of prior theory and the re-evaluation of prior fact, an intrinsically revolutionary process that is seldom completed by a single man and never overnight.

—Thomas Kuhn, *The Structure of Scientific Revolutions*, 1962

You can't put your finger on the most important thing you've hit in this book.

The exact syntax of Basic commands; the properties of Controls and how they can be used as building blocks of dialogs; the format of Windows API calls (indeed, DLL calls in general); the back-and-forth of DDE—all of these things are important. But they're not fundamental. You can look them up in a book—with a bit of luck, this one—and, give or take a twitch here and a bump there, get them working.

A Paradigm Shift

The fundamental part of this book, of course, is the Event-Driven way of looking at things. It's something you have to "get." If you had the luxury of stepping through WinMortals sequentially, the Event-Driven paradigm should've hit you over the head—the light bulb clicked on, the apple dropped from the tree, the *Aha!* slowly formed on your lips—somewhere between Chapter 4 and Chapter 9.

Event-Driven is *different*. It's not something you can look up in a dictionary, and walk away converted. Rather, like riding a bicycle or skiing down a slope, it's something you must try, over and over again, until you're comfortable with it. Like cycling and skiing, you don't really *feel* it until you've crashed and burned a few times, dusted yourself off, and given it another shot.

Event-Driven is a true paradigm shift in the computer industry, a revolution a-brewing, something that will shape the face of computing for years—perhaps decades—to come. While it may be a blip on the screen compared to Kuhn's revolutions (Galileo's theories, say, or Newton or Einstein), within our industry it may some day rate right up there with stored programs and compilers.

Back to Earth

Theories are nice, but it's hard to remember the niceties of Event Handlers and exotic Control Properties when the boss needs her report, like, yesterday.

Where is Windows programming headed? What can we do today to make sure our stuff isn't useless tomorrow? Where are the blind alleys?

Tough questions. But a few things seem pretty clear at this point.

- First, the macro languages are getting better. The big software companies are just starting to realize that a powerful macro language behind a Windows application can be a great marketing tool. As long as people want to customize an application, the macro is king. And since each application has its own quirks, strong and weak points, a flexible macro language will remain the best way to get into the innards of any application.

- Second, as the macro languages get better, we've seen very little effort to make them Event-Driven. That strategic blunder—if it is a blunder—makes it more difficult for us Mortals to build good, usable, complete custom programs within the macro languages.

- Third, ultimately, there must be a way to tie the macro languages together. There's too much riding on the macro languages to keep them stuffed into their own little boxes. The "Monster Basic from Hell" must include the capability of jumping back and forth from, say, the Amí Pro macro language to the EXCEL macro language, and then back again. Some day.

- Fourth, and most important: the distinction between "user" and "power user"—and the distinction between "power user" and "programmer"—is disappearing. While novices abound *(hey, we were all novices once or twice)*, they don't stay novices very long. People get excited when they see what they can do with their new Windows app. They want to change their environment, maybe toss a new item on the menu, or push around an icon, or write a little macro. They aren't content to take the bone-stock configuration lying down. As the number of Windows programmers—yeah, macro programmers—grows from the tens of thousands to the hundreds of thousands, and ultimately into the millions, the languages must grow with them.

That much seems clear.

But what conclusions can be drawn?

The Windows macro languages and various Windows Basics stand poised for explosive growth. You understand the Event-Driven paradigm. You can run Visual

Basic and 'most any other Windows Basic through its paces. You've seen how the pieces can be fit together to build real programs that solve real problems.

Even better, you have enough exposure to several different languages and programming environments that you should be able to pick up a new language in a week or two—and you should be able to tell a high-flyer from a turkey in a day or less. That's important because a plethora of important, advanced macro languages will see light of day in the next year.

Finally, you're in a position to choose. You and your company can help advance the cause of Windows programmability by simply voting with your pocketbook. If the Event-Driven paradigm is important to you, go out and buy Event-Driven products. If you're in the market for a word processor, a spreadsheet, a communications package, or a database package, make sure the package will fit into your Windows plans: do you need DDE? access to the Windows API? will that package prevent you from implementing an important application six months from now, because it doesn't have hooks into other Windows programs?

Food for thought.

Macro Manager and OLE 2

As we were going to press, Microsoft ever-so-slightly lifted the veil on an important new product.

It's called Macro Manager, and if initial hints are any indication, it'll be the first incarnation of The Monster Basic from Hell.

Where It Lives

It came from Hell . . . Really, it came from OLE 2, which is about a half-step removed from Hell. Or at least a quarter-step. You decide if it's up or down.

OLE, Object Linking and Embedding, teeters precariously atop Dynamic Data Exchange.

What It Does

The *Linking* part of OLE can be virtually indistinguishable from DDE: a Client picks up the phone, dials the Server, establishing a hot, warm, or cold link, transferring information. Sounds familiar, huh?

Object *Embedding*, on the other hand, is another kettle of fish altogether.

The idea behind Object Embedding comes through the technical wringer pretty easily: we want to take something from one application—a graph, say, or a spreadsheet, document, picture or an object—and stick it inside another application. They call that a "compound document." The OLE Client is in charge. The OLE Server does the Client's bidding, providing the object.

In OLE Linking, the Server keeps the data. In OLE Embedding, the Client holds onto the data, even if it's EXCEL data, say, inside a Word for Windows document. When the user requests an update of Linked data, a DDE-like conversation ensues, with the Server sending the new data back to the Client. When the user requests an update of Embedded data, on the other hand (typically by double-clicking on the data), the user is actually launched into the Server application, and has all the facilities of that application at hand. Returning to the Client application is as simple as leaving the Server program.

It's a great idea, when it works.

OLE support in the Windows Basics has been mighty Basic—virtually nonexistent, in fact, until Visual Basic's Professional Toolkit implemented a programmable OLE link. While you will find lip service in various macro languages directed toward OLE support, the actual implementation generally amounts to no more than triggering the application's built-in (and often woefully inadequate) canned OLE facilities. The Word for Windows 2.0 implementation of OLE, for example, both in the application itself and in WordBasic, amounts to little more than a comic book rendition of a great classic.

What It May Do

That was OLE 1.0. Even as you're reading this, Microsoft is coming up with OLE 2.0, and that's where Macro Manager comes in.

Much as OLE 1.0 lets users mix and match things from different applications—a document may include a spreadsheet from one application, a graph from another, and a piece of clip art from yet a third application—the OLE 2.0-based Macro Manager is supposed to allow macro programmers to pick and choose pieces of macros from various applications' macro languages.

Here's the real trick: Macro Manager apparently will implement the application-to-application hop by *diving inside OLE itself.* If you think of OLE 2.0 as a giant artifice of worm holes, the macro commands as individual worms, and Windows as the . . . uh . . . dirt that holds it all together, you get the idea.

While many, many details have not yet been set, at this writing it looks like Macro Manager will tie into Visual Basic; in fact, Visual Basic may be the driving force behind the whole kit-'n-kaboodle.

That's mighty good news for *WinMortals* readers.

If The Monster Basic from Hell emerges in Visual Basic clothing, tying together Basic-like languages and running on a DDE variant, you've already hit most of the key concepts. And much of the implementation. Right here on these pages.

Congratulations.

Now, *get back to work!*

APPENDIX ■ 1

Windows 3.1 API Calls in WordBasic

Here's a handy list of common API calls you may want to make from WordBasic. By all means, give them a try, but be forewarned: when you make an API call, you are messing directly with Windows. You may crash your system—repeatedly—trying to do what you want. So be careful, and back up thoroughly and often. Also, you should check to be sure that the particular API calls that interest you work the way you expect them to.

There's no way we can show you all the Windows 3.1 API calls that are accessible from WordBasic; the list would be lengthy, and not terribly useful. Instead, we've tried to show you some representative, useful, typical calls with a broad appeal. Think of them as a starting point for your own exploration of the intricacies of Windows.

Much of this material is derived from WOPR, the Word for Windows Office POWER Pack. WOPR is described more fully in Chapter 8. Some of this appendix repeats information found in Chapters 2 and 4; it's shown here in a highly condensed, cookbook form ready for your future reference. You may also find the material in Appendix 2 useful; generally a careful change of variable types (at least the ones that exist in WordBasic) will translate many Visual Basic calls to WordBasic.

For detailed explanations of the API calls, refer to the *Microsoft Windows Programmer's Reference* from Microsoft Press.

Talking To Windows

Change Window Title
This routine uses the Windows API call, SetWindowText, to temporarily change the Word for Windows window's title. *See* Chapter 2 for details.

```
Declare Function GetActiveWindow Lib "User" As Integer
Declare Sub SetWindowText Lib "User"(hWnd As Integer,\
 NewWindowText$)
Declare Function GetWindowText$ Lib "User"(hWnd As Integer,\
 CurrWindowText$, MaxChars As Integer) As Integer

Sub ChangeWindowTitle
REM Temporarily changes the title of the Word for Windows window
hWnd = GetActiveWindow
Length = GetWindowText$(hWnd, WindowText$, 255)
NewWindowText$ = InputBox$("Current window title is "  + Chr$(34)\
 + WindowText$  + Chr$(34) + ". Please enter a new title:", \
 "Window Title Blaster")
SetWindowText(hWnd, NewWindowText$)
End Sub
```

Get Windows Directory

This returns the directory from which Windows was loaded. See Chapter 4 for details.

```
Declare Function GetWindowsDirectory Lib "Kernel"(DirPath$,\
 MaxChars As Integer) As Integer

Function WinDir$
REM Returns the directory from which Windows was loaded
Length = GetWindowsDirectory(DirectoryPath$, 255)
WinDir$ = Left$(DirectoryPath$, Length)
End Function
```

Number of Tasks

Windows will tell you how many tasks—instances of programs—are running.

```
Declare Function GetNumTasks Lib "Kernel" As Integer

Function NumWinTasks
REM Returns the number of active tasks (programs or instances of\
REM programs)
NumWinTasks = GetNumTasks
End Function
```

Window Titles

Here's a very handy way to retrieve a tab-delimited list of Window titles and "hWnd" window handles. You might use the window titles in conjunction with the WordBasic command AppActivate, but beware of programs that may change the window title on-the-fly!

```
Declare Function GetActiveWindow Lib "User" As Integer
Declare Function GetWindow Lib "User"(hWnd As Integer, wFlag As\
 Integer) As Integer
Declare Function GetWindowText Lib "User"(hWnd As Integer,\
 CurrWindowText$, MaxChars As Integer) As Integer
```

```
Function WindowTitles$
REM Copyright © 1992 Pinecliffe International. All rights reserved.
REM Returns a tab-delimited list of Window Titles and hWnd Window\
REM Handles,
REM Including "blank" titles, e.g.,
REM "Microsoft Word<tab>12345<tab><tab>54321<tab>Srvr<tab>12789<tab>"
hWnd = GetActiveWindow
hWnd = GetWindow(hWnd, 0)
While hWnd <> 0
    x = GetWindowText(hWnd, WindowText$, 255)
    Temp$ = Temp$ + WindowText$ + Chr$(9) + LTrim$(Str$(hWnd)) +\
Chr$(9)
    hWnd = GetWindow(hWnd, 2)
Wend
WindowTitles$ = Temp$
End Function
```

Free System Resources

This is a Windows 3.1-specific command. If you run it under Windows 3.0, it will crash.

```
Declare Function GetFreeSystemResources Lib "user"(wflags As\
 Integer) As Integer

Function FreeSystemResources
REM Returns the FSR, between 0 and 100.
REM WARNING! Requires Windows 3.1
FreeSystemResources = GetFreeSystemResources(0)
End Function
```

The Outside World

Get Free Space

This returns currently available memory, including virtual memory, in megabytes. For a fancy rounding routine see Chapter 4. Contrast this to the WordBasic commands AppInfo$(9), (10), (11), and (12).

```
Declare Function GetFreeSpace Lib "Kernel"(wFlags As Integer) As\
 Long

Function AvailableMemory
AvailableMemory = GetFreeSpace(0) /(1024 * 1024)
End Function
```

System Metrics

Here's how to get at the System Metrics for screen height and width. For a more complete list of available System Metrics settings, see Chapter 4.

```
Declare Function GetSystemMetrics Lib "user"(nIndex As Integer)\
 As Integer

Function ScreenWidth
REM Returns the width of the screen in pixels
ScreenWidth = GetSystemMetrics(0)
End Function

Function ScreenHeight
REM Returns the height of the screen in pixels
ScreenHeight = GetSystemMetrics(1)
End Function
```

CPU Type

Windows will tell you the type of CPU running. Here's how to get at it.

```
Declare Function GetWinFlags Lib "Kernel" As Integer

Function ProcessorType$
REM Returns "8086", "80186", "80286", "80386", "80486", or null\
REM if processor isn't recognized
Flag = GetWinFlags
If  (Flag And 64) = 64 Then
     ProcessorType$ = "8086"
ElseIf(Flag And 128) = 128 Then
     ProcessorType$ = "80186"
ElseIf(Flag And 2) = 2 Then
     ProcessorType$ = "80286"
ElseIf(Flag And 4) = 4 Then
     ProcessorType$ = "80386"
ElseIf(Flag And 8) = 8 Then
     ProcessorType$ = "80486"
Else
     ProcessorType$ = ""
End If
End Function
```

Elapsed Time

This function is called "Windows Time"—it reports the number of milliseconds that have elapsed since Windows was started—but its primary use is as a stop watch. Call it before and after a loop or section of code you want to time, subtract the two numbers, and you'll get a rather accurate indication of how much time the loop or section of code took.

```
Declare Function GetCurrentTime Lib "User" As Long

Function WindowsTime
REM Returns the number of milliseconds elapsed since Windows was\
REM last started.
REM Accurate to +/- 55 milliseconds. Use to calculate time\
REM intervals.
WindowsTime = GetCurrentTime
End Function
```

DOS Environment String

Jonathan Zuck has a complete write-up on this function (using a slightly different approach that works around bugs in WinWord 1.x) in *Windows Tech Journal,* Volume 1, Number 1, pp 74-77. This version only works with WinWord 2.x. For more details, see Chapter 4.

```
Declare Function GetDOSEnvironment Lib "kernel" As Long
Declare Function AnsiUpper$ Lib "user"(lpString As Long)

Function Environment$
REM Returns the the DOS Environment string, all upper case, tab\
REM delimited, e.g.,
REM "COMSPEC=C:\DOS\COMMAND.COM<tab>FOO=BAR<tab>"
REM Thanks to Jonathan Zuck for ... pointing the way
lpEnvString = GetDOSEnvironment
StringLength = 1
While StringLength > 0
    EnvVar$ = AnsiUpper$(lpEnvString)
    Temp$ = Temp$ + EnvVar$ + Chr$(9)
    StringLength = Len(EnvVar$)
    lpEnvString = lpEnvString + StringLength + 1
Wend
Environment$ = Left$(Temp$, Len(Temp$) - 1)
End Function
```

Shelling to DOS

If everybody used the DOS command interpreter, reliably shelling to DOS would be quite simple:

```
Shell "command.com"
```

Unfortunately (or fortunately, depending on your perspective!), there are many DOS command interpreters out there. Here's how to find the right one and shell to it, using the Environment$ command above:

```
Sub Shell2DOS
REM Shells to the DOS command interpreter listed as "Comspec" in\
REM the Environment string
EnvString$ = Environment$
Starting = InStr(EnvString$, "COMSPEC")
Ending = InStr(Starting, EnvString$, Chr$(9))
Interpreter$ = Mid$(EnvString$, Starting + 8, Ending - Starting - 8)
Shell Interpreter$
End Sub
```

Global Variables in WordBasic

WordBasic lacks global variables, that is, variables that can be passed from one routine to another, or persist after a macro ends. WOPR implements global variables by using the Windows Private Profile String calls. These routines not only demonstrate how to use Private Profile Strings from within WordBasic, they also provide callable global variable commands.

Get/Set Private Profile String

Note how WritePrivateProfileString has been redefined to allow passing a null parameter to Windows.

```
Declare Function GetPrivateProfileString Lib "kernel"(AppName$,\
 KeyName$, Default$, ReturnedString$, MaxChars As Integer,\
 FName$)   As Integer
Declare Function GetPrivateProfileInt Lib "Kernel"(AppName$,\
 KeyName$, nDefault As Integer, FName$) As Integer
Declare Function WritePrivateProfileString Lib "kernel"(AppName$,\
 KeyName$, Value$, FName$)   As Integer
Declare Function WipeOutVar Lib "kernel"(AppName$, KeyName$,\
 WipeOut As Long, FName$)   As Integer Alias\
 "WritePrivateProfileString"

Sub WriteGlobalVar(VarName$, Value$)
REM ©1991-92 Pinecliffe International. All Rights Reserved
REM Stores global variable VarName$'s Value$ in WOPR.INI
REM Calling example: WOPR.WriteGlobalVar("MyVariable","abc")
n = WritePrivateProfileString("Global", VarName$, Value$,\
 "WOPR.INI")
End Sub


Function GetGlobalVar$(VarName$, Delete)
REM © 1991-92 Pinecliffe International. All Rights Reserved
REM Retrieves global variable VarName$'s value from WOPR.INI
REM If there is no global variable VarName$, returns a "" null.
REM If Delete is non-zero, GetGlobal retrieves the value,then
REM deletes the variable
REM Calling example:
REM MyVariable$=WOPR.GetGlobalVar$("MyVariable",-1)
n = GetPrivateProfileString("Global", VarName$, "", Temp$,255,\
 "WOPR.INI")
GetGlobalVar$ = Temp$
If Delete Then
     n = WipeOutVar("Global", VarName$, O, "WOPR.INI")
End If
End Function
```

Get Private Profile Int

There is no separate Windows API call to Write a Private Profile Integer, so WOPR does the necessary error checking.

```
Sub WriteGlobalInt(VarName$, n)
REM ©1991-92 Pinecliffe International. All Rights Reserved
REM Sets global variable VarName$'s value to Int(n), in WOPR.INI
REM If "n" is more than 32767, or less than -32767 stores zero
REM The value that is stored is returned to the calling program\
REM in "n"
REM Calling example: WOPR.WriteGlobalInt("MyVariable",123)
REM Note that Windows 3.0 will not retrieve negative integers,\
REM but Windows 3.1 will
If  n > 32767 Or n < - 32767 Then
    n = 0
    m = WritePrivateProfileString("Global", VarName$, "0", "WOPR.INI")
Else
    Value$ = Str$(Int(n))
    m = WritePrivateProfileString("Global", VarName$, Value$,\
 "WOPR.INI")
End If
End Sub

Function GetGlobalInt(VarName$, Delete)
REM © 1991-92 Pinecliffe International. All Rights Reserved
REM Retrieves global variable VarName$'s value from WOPR.INI
REM If the value is an integer, or an integer followed by\
REM nonnumeric characters,
REM then GetGlobalInt returns the integer.
REM If the value is not an integer, if VarName$ does not exist,
REM or if the value starts with a nonnumeric, GetGlobalInt\
REM returns a zero.
REM If Delete is non-zero, GetGlobalInt retrieves the value, then\
REM deletes the variable
REM Calling example: MyVariable=WOPR.GetGlobalInt("MyVariable",-1)
REM Note that Windows 3.0 will not retrieve negative integers;\
REM they come back as zero
GetGlobalInt = GetPrivateProfileInt("Global", VarName$, 0,\
 "WOPR.INI")
If Delete Then
    n = WipeOutVar("Global", VarName$, 0, "WOPR.INI")
End If
End Function
```

Dynamic Data Exchange

Chapter 6 gives lots of examples of DDE with WinWord. We won't repeat those examples here, mostly because you'll probably want to refer to the discussion along with the examples.

We hit one situation in WOPR, though, that may give you some idea of the raw power inherent in DDE. Instead of trying to graft it onto Chapter 6, we'll show it to you here. Think of it as just another sample of DDE with WordBasic as Client and EXCEL as Server. (There are *never* enough examples!)

Date and Time Functions in WordBasic

WordBasic has rudimentary Time and Date functions. Writing a WordBasic routine to subtract dates—"How many days from now until January 1, 1999?"—or add times—"Print the time 30 minutes from now"—for example, could take forever.

EXCEL has all those functions. We just needed to get to them from inside WordBasic. DDE provides a reliable (if slow) means to pull those functions into WordBasic. The WOPR Library implements all of the EXCEL Date and Time functions in WordBasic, using DDE. Here's a sample of the fundamental EXCEL call that retrieves the current time and date in serial format:

```
Declare Function GetModuleHandle Lib "kernel"(Name$) As Integer

Function wNow
REM © 1991-92 Pinecliffe International. All Rights Reserved
REM Uses EXCEL to return the serial number of the current date\
REM and time (8 decimal places)
REM See the EXCEL Function Reference for details
REM Since EXCEL and WinWord must run simultaneously, this is a\
REM memory hog!
REM Make sure you've done nothing to EXCEL to keep it from\
REM starting with Sheet1
REM EXCEL must be in your Path for the following Shell command to\
REM work
If GetModuleHandle("excel") = 0 Then
    Shell "excel", 0
    NewXL = - 1
End If
Channel = DDEInitiate("excel", "Sheet1")
DDEExecute Channel, "[Formula(" + Chr$(34) + "=FIXED(NOW(),8)" +\
 Chr$(34) + "," + Chr$(34) + "R1C1" + Chr$(34) + ")]"
Temp$ = DDERequest$(Channel, "R1C1")
wNow = Val(Swap$(Temp$, ",", ""))
On Error Resume Next
If NewXL Then DDEExecute Channel, "[ERROR(FALSE)][Quit()]"
DDETerminate Channel
End Function
```

Where the Swap$ function is an old standby:

```
Function Swap$(InputString$, OldString$, NewString$)
REM © 1990-92 Pinecliffe International. All Rights Reserved
REM Calling Example:  VarWithoutBs$=WOPR.Swap$(VarWithBs$,"B","")
Temp$ = InputString$
index = InStr(1, Temp$, OldString$)
While index <> 0
    Temp$ = Left$(Temp$, index - 1) + NewString$ + Right$(Temp$,\
 Len(Temp$) - Len(OldString$) - index + 1)
    index = InStr(index + Len(NewString$), Temp$, OldString$)
Wend
```

```
Swap$ = Temp$
End Function
```

WOPR has all the EXCEL time and date function calls set up similarly. This one returns the current date:

```
Function wToday
REM _ 1991-92 Pinecliffe International. All Rights Reserved
REM Uses EXCEL to return the serial number of the current date
If GetModuleHandle("excel") = 0 Then
     Shell "excel", 0
     NewXL = - 1
End If
Channel = DDEInitiate("excel", "Sheet1")
DDEExecute Channel, "[Formula(" + Chr$(34) + "=TODAY()" +\
 Chr$(34) + "," + Chr$(34) + "R1C1" + Chr$(34) + ")]"
Temp$ = DDERequest$(Channel, "R1C1")
wToday = Val(Swap$(Temp$, ",", ""))
On Error Resume Next
If NewXL Then DDEExecute Channel, "[ERROR(FALSE)][Quit()]"
DDETerminate Channel
End Function
```

Here are the ones that deal with date and time strings:

```
Function wDateValue(DateText$)
REM © 1991-92 Pinecliffe International. All Rights Reserved
REM Uses EXCEL to return the serial number of the DateText$ date
If GetModuleHandle("excel") = 0 Then
     Shell "excel", 0
     NewXL = - 1
End If
Channel = DDEInitiate("excel", "Sheet1")
DDEExecute Channel, "[Formula(" + Chr$(34) + "=DATEVALUE( " +\
 Chr$(34) +  Chr$(34) + DateText$ + Chr$(34) + Chr$(34) + ")" +\
 Chr$(34) + "," + Chr$(34) + "R1C1" + Chr$(34) + ")]"
Temp$ = DDERequest$(Channel, "R1C1")
wDateValue = Val(Temp$)
On Error Resume Next
If NewXL Then DDEExecute Channel, "[ERROR(FALSE)][Quit()]"
DDETerminate Channel
End Function

Function wTimeValue(TimeText$)
REM © 1991-92 Pinecliffe International. All Rights Reserved
REM Uses EXCEL to return the serial number of the TimeText$ time
If GetModuleHandle("excel") = 0 Then
     Shell "excel", 0
     NewXL = - 1
End If
Channel = DDEInitiate("excel", "Sheet1")
DDEExecute Channel, "[Formula(" + Chr$(34) + "=FIXED(TIMEVALUE( "\
 + Chr$(34) +  Chr$(34) + TimeText$ + Chr$(34) + Chr$(34) +\
```

```
  "),8)" + Chr$(34) + "," + Chr$(34) + "R1C1" + Chr$(34) + ")]"
Temp$ = DDERequest$(Channel, "R1C1")
wTimeValue = Val(Temp$)
On Error Resume Next
If NewXL Then DDEExecute Channel, "[ERROR(FALSE)][Quit()]"
DDETerminate Channel
End Function


Function wDate(Yr, Mo, Day)
REM © 1991-92 Pinecliffe International. All Rights Reserved
REM Uses EXCEL to return the serial number of the specified date
If GetModuleHandle("excel") = 0 Then
     Shell "excel", 0
     NewXL = - 1
End If
Channel = DDEInitiate("excel", "Sheet1")
DDEExecute Channel, "[Formula(" + Chr$(34) + "=DATE( " + Str$(Yr)\
 + "," + Str$(Mo) + "," + Str$(Day) + ")" + Chr$(34) + "," +\
 Chr$(34) + "R1C1" + Chr$(34) + ")]"
Temp$ = DDERequest$(Channel, "R1C1")
wDate = Val(Temp$)
On Error Resume Next
If NewXL Then DDEExecute Channel, "[ERROR(FALSE)][Quit()]"
DDETerminate Channel
End Function


Function wTime(Hour, Minute, Second)
REM © 1991-92 Pinecliffe International. All Rights Reserved
REM Uses EXCEL to return the serial number of the specified time
If GetModuleHandle("excel") = 0 Then
     Shell "excel", 0
     NewXL = - 1
End If
Channel = DDEInitiate("excel", "Sheet1")
DDEExecute Channel, "[Formula(" + Chr$(34) + "=TIME( " +\
 Str$(Hour) + "," + Str$(Minute) + "," + Str$(Second) + ")" +\
 Chr$(34) + "," + Chr$(34) + "R1C1" + Chr$(34) + ")]"
Temp$ = DDERequest$(Channel, "R1C1")
wTime = Val(Temp$)
On Error Resume Next
If NewXL Then DDEExecute Channel, "[ERROR(FALSE)][Quit()]"
DDETerminate Channel
End Function


Function tYear(DateText$)
REM © 1991-92 Pinecliffe International. All Rights Reserved
REM Uses EXCEL to return the year (1900-2078) of the DateText$ date
If GetModuleHandle("excel") = 0 Then
     Shell "excel", 0
     NewXL = - 1
End If
Channel = DDEInitiate("excel", "Sheet1")
DDEExecute Channel, "[Formula(" + Chr$(34) + "=YEAR( " + Chr$(34)\
 + Chr$(34) + DateText$ + Chr$(34) + Chr$(34) + ")" + Chr$(34) +\
 "," + Chr$(34) + "R1C1" + Chr$(34) + ")]"
```

```
Temp$ = DDERequest$(Channel, "R1C1")
tYear = Val(Temp$)
On Error Resume Next
If NewXL Then DDEExecute Channel, "[ERROR(FALSE)][Quit()]"
DDETerminate Channel
End Function

Function tMonth(DateText$)
REM © 1991-92 Pinecliffe International. All Rights Reserved
REM Uses EXCEL to return the Month (1-12) of the DateText$ date
If GetModuleHandle("excel") = 0 Then
     Shell "excel", 0
     NewXL = - 1
End If
Channel = DDEInitiate("excel", "Sheet1")
DDEExecute Channel, "[Formula(" + Chr$(34) + "=MONTH( " +\
 Chr$(34) +  Chr$(34) + DateText$ + Chr$(34) + Chr$(34) + ")" +\
 Chr$(34) + "," + Chr$(34) + "R1C1" + Chr$(34) + ")]"
Temp$ = DDERequest$(Channel, "R1C1")
tMonth = Val(Temp$)
On Error Resume Next
If NewXL Then DDEExecute Channel, "[ERROR(FALSE)][Quit()]"
DDETerminate Channel
End Function

Function tDay(DateText$)
REM © 1991-92 Pinecliffe International. All Rights Reserved
REM Uses EXCEL to return the Day (1-31) of the DateText$ date
If GetModuleHandle("excel") = 0 Then
     Shell "excel", 0
     NewXL = - 1
End If
Channel = DDEInitiate("excel", "Sheet1")
DDEExecute Channel, "[Formula(" + Chr$(34) + "=DAY( " + Chr$(34)\
 + Chr$(34) + DateText$ + Chr$(34) + Chr$(34) + ")" + Chr$(34) +\
 "," + Chr$(34) + "R1C1" + Chr$(34) + ")]"
Temp$ = DDERequest$(Channel, "R1C1")
tDay = Val(Temp$)
On Error Resume Next
If NewXL Then DDEExecute Channel, "[ERROR(FALSE)][Quit()]"
DDETerminate Channel
End Function

Function tWeekDay(DateText$)
REM © 1991-92 Pinecliffe International. All Rights Reserved
REM Returns the WeekDay (1-7, for Sun-Sat) of the DateText$ date
If GetModuleHandle("excel") = 0 Then
     Shell "excel", 0
     NewXL = - 1
End If
Channel = DDEInitiate("excel", "Sheet1")
DDEExecute Channel, "[Formula(" + Chr$(34) + "=WEEKDAY( " +\
 Chr$(34) +  Chr$(34) + DateText$ + Chr$(34) + Chr$(34) + ")" +\
 Chr$(34) + "," + Chr$(34) + "R1C1" + Chr$(34) + ")]"
Temp$ = DDERequest$(Channel, "R1C1")
```

```
tWeekDay = Val(Temp$)
On Error Resume Next
If NewXL Then DDEExecute Channel, "[ERROR(FALSE)][Quit()]"
DDETerminate Channel
End Function


Function tHour(TimeText$)
REM © 1991-92 Pinecliffe International. All Rights Reserved
REM Uses EXCEL to return the Hour (0-23) of the TimeText$ time
If GetModuleHandle("excel") = 0 Then
     Shell "excel", 0
     NewXL = - 1
End If
Channel = DDEInitiate("excel", "Sheet1")
DDEExecute Channel, "[Formula(" + Chr$(34) + "=HOUR( " + Chr$(34)\
 + Chr$(34) + TimeText$ + Chr$(34) + Chr$(34) + ")" + Chr$(34) +\
 "," + Chr$(34) + "R1C1" + Chr$(34) + ")]"
Temp$ = DDERequest$(Channel, "R1C1")
tHour = Val(Temp$)
On Error Resume Next
If NewXL Then DDEExecute Channel, "[ERROR(FALSE)][Quit()]"
DDETerminate Channel
End Function


Function tMinute(TimeText$)
REM © 1991-92 Pinecliffe International. All Rights Reserved
REM Uses EXCEL to return the Minute (0-59) of the TimeText$ time
If GetModuleHandle("excel") = 0 Then
     Shell "excel", 0
     NewXL = - 1
End If
Channel = DDEInitiate("excel", "Sheet1")
DDEExecute Channel, "[Formula(" + Chr$(34) + "=MINUTE( " +\
 Chr$(34) +  Chr$(34) + TimeText$ + Chr$(34) + Chr$(34) + ")" +\
 Chr$(34) + "," + Chr$(34) + "R1C1" + Chr$(34) + ")]"
Temp$ = DDERequest$(Channel, "R1C1")
tMinute = Val(Temp$)
On Error Resume Next
If NewXL Then DDEExecute Channel, "[ERROR(FALSE)][Quit()]"
DDETerminate Channel
End Function


Function tSecond(TimeText$)
REM © 1991-92 Pinecliffe International. All Rights Reserved
REM Uses EXCEL to return the Second (0-59) of the TimeText$ time
If GetModuleHandle("excel") = 0 Then
     Shell "excel", 0
     NewXL = - 1
End If
Channel = DDEInitiate("excel", "Sheet1")
DDEExecute Channel, "[Formula(" + Chr$(34) + "=SECOND( " +\
 Chr$(34) +  Chr$(34) + TimeText$ + Chr$(34) + Chr$(34) + ")" +\
 Chr$(34) + "," + Chr$(34) + "R1C1" + Chr$(34) + ")]"
Temp$ = DDERequest$(Channel, "R1C1")
tSecond = Val(Temp$)
```

```
On Error Resume Next
If NewXL Then DDEExecute Channel, "[ERROR(FALSE)][Quit()]"
DDETerminate Channel
End Function

Function tDays360(StartDateText$, EndDateText$)
REM © 1991-92 Pinecliffe International. All Rights Reserved
REM Uses EXCEL to return the number of days between\
REM StartDateText$ and EndDateText$
REM Based on a 360-day calendar. The number is negative if\
REM StartDate is after EndDate.
REM See the EXCEL Function Reference for details
If GetModuleHandle("excel") = 0 Then
     Shell "excel", 0
     NewXL = - 1
End If
Channel = DDEInitiate("excel", "Sheet1")
DDEExecute Channel, "[Formula(" + Chr$(34) + "=DAYS360( " +\
 Chr$(34) +  Chr$(34) + StartDateText$ + Chr$(34) + Chr$(34) +\
 "," + Chr$(34) + Chr$(34) + EndDateText$ + Chr$(34) + Chr$(34) +\
 ")" + Chr$(34) + "," + Chr$(34) + "R1C1" + Chr$(34) + ")]"
Temp$ = DDERequest$(Channel, "R1C1")
tDays360 = Val(Temp$)
On Error Resume Next
If NewXL Then DDEExecute Channel, "[ERROR(FALSE)][Quit()]"
DDETerminate Channel
End Function
```

For the analogous routines that use serial date and time numbers, take a look at the WOPR Library.

If you are making repeated calls to these routines, consider condensing the DDE calls so you aren't constantly making and breaking links. Loading EXCEL and establishing a DDE link consumes an enormous amount of time. You may be able to get away with loading EXCEL just once, and retrieving all the data over one DDE channel. That can save considerable time. The "R1C1"s are coded in here so you can use multiple spreadsheet cells without hassling the Chr$(34)s!

Windows 3.1 API Calls in Visual Basic

Here's a handy list of some common API calls you may want to make from Visual Basic. Give them a try, but be careful. Because, just like when you make a WordBasic API call, when you make a Visual Basic API call you are messing directly with Windows. You may crash your system—repeatedly—trying to do what you want. So be careful, and back up thoroughly and often.

This material is derived from a file called WINAPI.TXT, distributed and Copyright © 1991 by Microsoft Corporation. You will find a copy of the Windows 3.0 version of WINAPI.TXT on the WinMortals Companion Disk.

Visual Basic is structured differently from WordBasic. It also gives greater flexibility in accessing the Windows API. For these reasons, and a host of others, we've stuck to describing the most important Declare functions, and only included sample program snippets when they add something to the descriptions. This list of API calls is far from exhaustive: for that, you'll have to look at WINAPI.TXT. We're more interested here in presenting the most common API calls, grouped in a way that may jog your memory or help you solve a problem.

To make the code fit on a printed page, we've used the "\" backslash continuation character. In practice, you won't want the backslashes: they just indicate that you shouldn't end a line at that point.

We know of a small error in WINAPI.TXT. You might want to modify your copy of the file for future reference (we didn't want to change the copyrighted file, but there's nothing to keep you from doing so!). In WINAPI.TXT look for these four lines:

```
Global Const EM_GETMODIFY = WM_USER+7
Global Const EM_SETMODIFY = WM_USER+8
Global Const EM_GETLINECOUNT = WM_USER+9
Global Const EM_LINEINDEX = WM_USER+10
```

and change them to:

```
Global Const EM_GETMODIFY = WM_USER+8
Global Const EM_SETMODIFY = WM_USER+9
Global Const EM_GETLINECOUNT = WM_USER+10
Global Const EM_LINEINDEX = WM_USER+11
```

Note that there is no setting that corresponds to "WM_USER + 7".

For definition of the structured data Types (Visual Basic TYPE command) and variable values associated with various calls, the full story is contained on the WinMortals Companion disk, in WINAPI.TXT. For further detailed explanations of the API calls, refer to the *Microsoft Windows Programmer's Reference* from Microsoft Press.

Talking to Windows

Get Version Number

The Windows version number is packed. Unpack it as follows:

```
Declare Function GetVersion Lib "Kernel" () As Integer

PackedVersionNumber = GetVersion
MinorVersionNumber = Int(PackedVersionNumber / 256)
MajorVersionNumber = PackedVersionNumber - 256 * MinorVersionNumber
```

Focus

The call necessary to retrieve the hWnd of the active window is identical to WordBasic's:

```
Declare Function GetActiveWindow Lib "User" () As Integer
```

But the SetFocus Windows call has to be declared with an Alias. Why? Because, Microsoft built a command called "SetFocus" into Visual Basic itself; to avoid confusion, the Windows command of the same name must be given a different name. If both were called "SetFocus", everybody would get confused. So the Windows API command "SetFocus" is normally renamed "SetFocusAPI" in Visual Basic programs. You can call it anything you want, of course.

```
Declare Function SetFocusAPI Lib "User" Alias "SetFocus" (ByVal\
  hWnd As Integer) As Integer
Declare Function GetFocus Lib "User" () As Integer
```

When using all of the Windows API calls that return "hWnd" handles to windows, keep in mind that "hWnd" is a property name in Visual Basic; you won't be able to use "hWnd" as a variable name.

Module Handles

GetModuleUsage will tell you how many copies of a given program are running; GetModuleFileName returns the name of the executable file used to load the program. (Remember that backslashes ("\") are continuation characters; you won't want them in your program—they're here to show you that the lines *don't* end.)

```
Declare Function GetModuleHandle Lib "Kernel" (ByVal lpModuleName\
 As String) As Integer
Declare Function GetModuleUsage Lib "Kernel" (ByVal hModule As\
 Integer) As Integer
Declare Function GetModuleFileName Lib "Kernel" (ByVal hModule As\
 Integer, ByVal lpFilename As String, ByVal nSize As Integer) As\
 Integer
```

In Chapter 6 we looked at Class Names, and how they can be used to accomplish something similar:

```
Declare Function FindWindow Lib "User" (lpClassName As Any,\
 lpWindowName As Any) As Integer
```

Window Titles

These are very similar to the WordBasic functions:

```
Declare Sub SetWindowText Lib "User" (ByVal hWnd As Integer,\
 ByVal lpString As String)
Declare Function GetWindowText Lib "User" (ByVal hWnd As Integer,\
 ByVal lpString As String, ByVal aint As Integer) As Integer
Declare Function GetWindowTextLength Lib "User" (ByVal hWnd As\
 Integer) As Integer
```

Moving Around Windows

You can navigate through all the windows with this command. See Chapter 4 for a WordBasic example:

```
    GetWindow() Constants
Global Const GW_HWNDFIRST = 0
Global Const GW_HWNDLAST = 1
Global Const GW_HWNDNEXT = 2
Global Const GW_HWNDPREV = 3
Global Const GW_OWNER = 4
Global Const GW_CHILD = 5

Declare Function GetWindow Lib "User" (ByVal hWnd As Integer,\
 ByVal wCmd As Integer) As Integer
```

PeekMessage

If you want to look at Windows messages without Visual Basic's assistance, try this (definition of the MSG data structure is in WINAPI.TXT):

```
Declare Function PeekMessage Lib "User" (lpMsg As MSG, ByVal hWnd\
 As Integer, ByVal wMsgFilterMin As Integer, ByVal wMsgFilterMax\
 As Integer, ByVal wRemoveMsg As Integer) As Integer
'  PeekMessage() Options
Global Const PM_NOREMOVE = &H0
Global Const PM_REMOVE = &H1
Global Const PM_NOYIELD = &H2
```

Window Manipulation

Here are a few commands to get at window states:

```
Declare Function IsWindowVisible Lib "User" (ByVal hWnd As\
 Integer) As Integer
Declare Function IsIconic Lib "User" (ByVal hWnd As Integer) As\
 Integer
Declare Function AnyPopup Lib "User" () As Integer
Declare Sub BringWindowToTop Lib "User" (ByVal hWnd As Integer)
Declare Function IsZoomed Lib "User" (ByVal hWnd As Integer) As\
 Integer
```

The Outside World

Get Drive Type

Use an nDrive value of "0" for drive a:, "1" for drive b:, and so on.

```
Declare Function GetDriveType Lib "Kernel" (ByVal nDrive As\
 Integer) As Integer

'  GetDriveType return values
Global Const DRIVE_REMOVABLE = 2
Global Const DRIVE_FIXED = 3
Global Const DRIVE_REMOTE = 4
```

DOS Environment String

Visual Basic isn't nearly as picky about null terminators as WordBasic.

```
Declare Function GetDOSEnvironment Lib "Kernel" () As Long

Environ$=GetDOSEnvironment
```

Windows and System Directory

The Windows directory is the one from which Windows was launched. The System directory is the subdirectory under the Windows directory (usually called, simply, "\WINDOWS\SYSTEM") that includes all the Windows drivers and such.

```
Declare Function GetWindowsDirectory Lib "Kernel" (ByVal lpBuffer\
  As String, ByVal nSize As Integer) As Integer
Declare Function GetSystemDirectory Lib "Kernel" (ByVal lpBuffer\
  As String, ByVal nSize As Integer) As Integer
```

System Metrics

The Visual Basic call for System Metrics is almost identical to WordBasic's:

```
Declare Function GetSystemMetrics Lib "User" (ByVal nIndex As\
  Integer) As Integer
```
For a list of the valid SM_ "nIndex" values, see Chapter 4 or WINAPI.TXT.

Elapsed Time

As mentioned in Appendix 1, these are most useful for stop watch applications. Call them before and after a critical piece of code, then subtract the numbers to arrive at the number of milliseconds it took to run that piece of code.

```
Declare Function GetCurrentTime Lib "User" () As Long
Declare Function GetTickCount Lib "User" () As Long
```

Profile Strings

WIN.INI Settings

The Windows Profile String calls work with WIN.INI:

```
Declare Function GetProfileInt Lib "Kernel" (ByVal lpAppName As\
  String, ByVal lpKeyName As String, ByVal nDefault As Integer) As\
  Integer
Declare Function GetProfileString Lib "Kernel" (ByVal lpAppName\
  As String, ByVal lpKeyName As String, ByVal lpDefault As String,\
  ByVal lpReturnedString As String, ByVal nSize As Integer) As\
  Integer
Declare Function WriteProfileString Lib "Kernel" (ByVal\
  lpApplicationName As String, ByVal lpKeyName As String, ByVal\
  lpString As String) As Integer
```

Private Profile Strings

The Private Profile String calls let you set up your own .INI files:

```
Declare Function GetProfileInt Lib "Kernel" (ByVal lpAppName As\
```

```
   String, ByVal lpKeyName As String, ByVal nDefault As Integer) As\
   Integer
Declare Function GetProfileString Lib "Kernel" (ByVal lpAppName\
   As String, ByVal lpKeyName As String, ByVal lpDefault As String,\
   ByVal lpReturnedString As String, ByVal nSize As Integer) As\
   Integer
Declare Function WriteProfileString Lib "Kernel" (ByVal\
   lpApplicationName As String, ByVal lpKeyName As String, ByVal\
   lpString As String) As Integer
```

APPENDIX ▪ 3

The Companion Disk

Decompressing the Disk

All of the files stored on the Companion Disk are compressed in self-extracting archives. That lets us pack much more than two megabytes of data onto a 1.44 megabyte disk. Self-extracting archives are .EXE files that you run just like a program. The .EXE file unfolds into one or more files—in our case, mostly .DOC files.

If you've never (knowingly!) decompressed a file, not to worry. We'll take you through the steps right here.

Keep in mind, though, that you can't use the files on this disk directly; there's an extra step involved.

Before you start decompressing files, make a backup copy of the Companion Disk and work from the backup copy. File Manager or the DOS XCOPY command will do fine. Put the original Companion Disk in a safe place, where the cat or the kid can't get it.

Installing the Word for Windows Working Model

Microsoft has graciously permitted us to distribute a full Working Model of Word for Windows 2.0. The only significant restriction to the working model is on the size of documents you can save; in all other respects, it behaves precisely as WinWord 2.0 itself.

The Working Model gives you full access to WordBasic; in essence, you are getting a free copy of *the entire programming language* right here on the Companion Disk. More than that, the Working Model includes nearly all the features of WinWord 2.0 itself, as long as you don't try to save documents much over two pages long.

If you already have WinWord installed on your system, do *not* install the Working Model. There's nothing to gain, and there's a slight chance you could over-write your WinWord program file, WINWORD.EXE. If you do over-write WINWORD.EXE, you'll have to re-install WinWord itself from the original disks.

To install the WinWord Working Model, first make sure that you have Windows 3.1; the Working Model uses several DLLs not present in Windows 3.0.

You'll need about 2 MB of free disk space. Using the File Manager's File / Create Directory (or your favorite directory mangler), create a new directory call it, oh, WINWORD. Put the Companion Disk in one of your floppy drives. Use File Manager to copy the file WW2DEMO.EXE from the floppy to the new directory. Then from inside File Manager highlight the WW2DEMO.EXE on the hard disk, and double-click on it.

Sit back for a few minutes while the LHA self-extractor goes at it.

Finally, delete the copy of WW2DEMO.EXE you just placed on the hard disk.

You now have a full Working Model of WinWord 2.0, in that new directory. To get it working, you can double-click on WINWORD.EXE from inside File Manager, or you can go back out to the Program Manager and click on File, then Run, Browse, click your way down to the WINWORD directory, click on WINWORD.EXE, and click OK.

If you're feeling ambitious, you might set up an icon for WinWord: from inside Program Manager, click on the group you'd like to contain the new icon, then click File, then New, Browse, find the WINWORD directory and click on WINWORD.EXE, then click OK.

Take a few minutes to poke around WinWord, orient yourself a bit. Type some stuff and print it (click on File, then Print). Try an Edit Search or a Format Paragraph. You might even take the Tutorial, located under "Help". Don't be too surprised if you fall in love with it!

Ready-to-Use WordBasic Programs

All of the WordBasic macros mentioned in Chapters 2, 4 and 8 are in one self-extracting archive on the Companion Disk. The archive is called WBPGMS.EXE; it will unfold into these files: C2PGM1.DOC, C2PGM2.DOC, C4PGM1.DOC, C4PGM2.DOC, C4PGM3.DOC, C4PGM4.DOC, C4PGM5.DOC, C4PGM6.DOC, C4PGM7.DOC, C4PGM8.DOC, C4PGM9.DOC, and C8PGM1.DOC.

C2PGM2 is the WinWord Window Title Blaster; C8PGM1 is the final WinWord Windows Explorer. All the other files are intermediate steps in building those two "goal" programs.

To install all of those programs you'll need about 100K of free disk space.

Start by creating a new directory (in File Manager, click on File, then Create Directory) to hold the programs. If you call that directory "WMORTALS" and stick it under the "WINWORD" directory, you'll be able to follow the instructions in Chapters 2, 4, and 8 literally. If you're the independent type, you can stick 'em anywhere, just remember where you put 'em!

Stick the Companion Disk in a convenient drive. Using File Manager or whatever is handy, copy the file WBPGMS.EXE from the floppy into your new directory. Then run the extractor in File Manager, highlight the file WBPGMS.EXE in the new directory, and double-click on it. When LHA has done its thing, delete WBPGMS.EXE on the hard disk.

You'll need Word for Windows to look at any of those files. From inside WinWord, click on File, then Open, go out looking for the appropriate directory, and double-click on whichever file interests you. Detailed step-by-step instructions for breaking into these files and turning them into WordBasic macros are in Chapters 2, 4, and 8.

VBRUN100.DLL

If you don't have Visual Basic installed on your machine, well, you should seriously consider getting it!

For the benefit of those who don't have Visual Basic, we've included the Visual Basic Run Time Library on the 1.44 MB 3.5-inch Companion Disk that ships with the book.

What's a Run Time Library? Glad you asked . . .

Any program written in Visual Basic relies on this rather large collection of routines to make things work. Instead of putting all those routines in every program created by Visual Basic, the designers of Visual Basic decided to gather all of the support routines and stick 'em in one place.

That has advantages and disadvantages. The primary advantage is that programs generated by Visual Basic are fairly compact. All the overhead stuff got stuffed into the Run Time Library; there's very little duplication of code, swelling the size of each Visual Basic application. The primary disadvantage is that you have to get the Run Time Library somewhere before you can run *any* Visual Basic program. Not only is the Run Time Library fairly large, it's enormously difficult explaining to novices why they need this fat file to run a teensy-tiny program.

If you have Visual Basic on your system, you already have the Run Time Library; a file called VBRUN100.DLL. If you don't have Visual Basic on your system, the Companion Disk has a copy you can use. Here's how . . .

You'll need about 400K of free disk space to install VBRUN100.DLL.

We recommend that you install VBRUN100 in your Windows directory, providing your Windows directory is on your DOS PATH. (It probably is.) You can put it in any directory, though, that is on your PATH.

Put the Companion Disk in a drive. Using File Manager or something similar, copy the file VBRUN.EXE from the floppy to your Windows directory. Then run the new copy of VBRUN.EXE (in File Manager, click on VBRUN.EXE to select it, then double-click to run it). When LHA is done extracting VBRUN100.DLL, delete the copy of VBRUN.EXE on the hard disk.

You're now set up to run any Visual Basic program.

LHA213

The file LHA213.EXE contains the LHA file compression and decompression routines discussed in Chapter 5. At this writing, LHA version 2.13 is the most sophisticated file compression program available. LHA is a DOS program; it does not rely on Windows.

Decompressing LHA213.EXE is simplicity itself: create a subdirectory to hold it—put the subdirectory wherever you stick utility programs—then copy the file LHA213.EXE off the Companion Disk into that new subdirectory.

Run LHA213.EXE just like a program and you'll get the full LHA suite.

LHA is Copyright © 1991 by H. Yoshizaki. The copy of LHA on the *Windows Programming for Mere Mortals* Companion Disk contains all the LHA files, unmodified, and may be distributed without the author's permission providing you honor the distribution requirements noted in the documentation.

WinLHA

Chapter 5 builds a Visual Basic front-end for the LHA file compression program. We call it WinLHA.

Not surprisingly, WinLHA is the same program we used to compress all of the files on the Companion Disk when you decompress the files by running the .EXE self-extracting programs on the Companion Disk, you're actually running archive files produced by WinLHA.

You'll need about 100K of free disk space for WinLHA.

Start by creating a new directory, again using File Manager or whatever is handy. If you have Visual Basic installed on your machine, create a directory called

"WINLHA" under your "VB" Visual Basic directory. If you don't have Visual Basic, just create a directory called "WINLHA" anyplace that's convenient.

Stick the Companion Disk in a drive, and (using File Manager perhaps) copy the file LHAPGMS.EXE from the floppy into your new directory.

Run the new copy of LHAPGMS.EXE—from inside File Manager, select the file by clicking on it, then double-click to run it. You'll get 29 new files. Once LHA is done unfolding all those files, delete LHAPGMS.EXE.

If you have Visual Basic on your machine and want to step through the programs here in the book, you'll need all of those 29 files. If you don't have Visual Basic—and don't intend to get it—you may safely delete all of the files except two: WinLHA.EXE and WinLHAE.EXE.

Those two files are the working, final WinLHA programs. WinLHA.EXE does the compressing; WinLHAE.EXE expands. You might want to set them up in Program Manager: click on the group you want to hold the new programs, click on File, then New, Browse, and go looking for WinLHA.EXE. When you find it, click on it. Repeat those steps for WinLHAE.EXE, and you'll be all set.

If you don't have Visual Basic, you'll need VBRUN100.DLL (described above) to run WinLHA and WinLHAE.

CoolCons

Chapter 7 steps you through the construction of CoolCons, a fancy icon bar set up for Word for Windows, but modifiable to work with any program that supports Dynamic Data Exchange.

To install all the CoolCons files, you'll need about 150K of free disk space. If you want to copy over all those neat custom icons, you'll need an extra 100K.

If you have Visual Basic on your system, create a new directory under your "VB" Visual Basic directory, called "COOLCONS". If you don't have Visual Basic, make a "COOLCONS" directory anywhere you like.

Stick the Companion Disk in a drive, and copy the file COOLPGMS.EXE from the floppy into your new directory.

Run the new copy of COOLPGMS.EXE from inside File Manager, select the file by clicking on it, then double-click to run it. You'll get 14 new files. Once LHA is done decompressing those files, delete COOLPGMS.EXE.

If you want to step through all the book's examples, you'll need all of those 14 files. If you don't have Visual Basic, and don't intend to get it, delete all of the files except one: COOLCONS.EXE.

COOLCONS.EXE is the final, "goal" CoolCons program. You can set it up in Program Manager: click on the group you want to hold the new program, click on File, then New, Browse, and find COOLCONS.EXE.

If you don't have Visual Basic, you'll need VBRUN100.DLL (described above) to run CoolCons.

As a little lagniappe, we've included sixty icons you might want to use to customize CoolCons. These icons were all constructed from scratch, specifically for this book. They're designed to work together—the borders take into account the scrunching necessary to put many icons into a small space. These are a great starting point for building your own CoolCons.

Installing the icons takes about 100K of disk space.

Insert the Companion Disk into a drive. Copy the file ICONS.EXE into whatever directory you use for icons (or a new directory if you'd like to keep these guys separate from the run-of-the-mill). Run the new copy of ICONS.EXE. When LHA is done, delete that copy of ICONS.EXE.

Windows API Listing

Microsoft has developed a listing of Windows 3.0 API calls, translated into Visual Basic format. While that listing is free and freely distributed, it isn't distributed with Visual Basic, and it can be expensive to download from a bulletin board.

Ah, not to worry.

The file is called WINAPI.TXT, and it's set up so you can copy all those juicy Windows DECLARES directly from the document (using, say, Word for Windows), and into your waiting Visual Basic program.

It'll take about 150K of free disk space to decompress it.

Start by sticking the Companion Disk in a drive. Copy the file WINAPI.EXE into a reasonable subdirectory—perhaps your "VB" Visual Basic or "WINWORD" WinWord directory.

Run WINAPI.EXE (from File Manager, highlight the file, then double-click to run it). LHA will expand the file into WINAPI.TXT. When the expansion is over, delete the copy of WINAPI.EXE.

You'll notice that WINAPI.TXT isn't particularly well organized; for a somewhat less disjointed—but highly abridged—view of the DECLAREs, take a look at Appendix 2.

D2H Intro

If you have the 1.44 MB, 3.5-inch high density version of the Companion Disk—the one that is distributed with the book—there's one extra file we've tossed in.

It's a demo Help file from Doc-to-Help, the Word for Windows add-on that lets you make your own Help files.

No need to decompress the file. Simply insert the Companion Disk into a drive. Crank up "Help" from almost anywhere—in WinWord, click on Help, then Help Index; in Program Manager or Visual Basic, click on Help, then Index.

However you get into Help, click on File, and Open, then click on the drive containing the Companion Disk, and (finally!) click on D2HINTRO.HELP.

You'll find a simple example of the kind of on-line help that's so easy to create with Doc-to-Help. Though it has its shortcomings—no hot keys, for example–it is a far, far better way to help than has ever been created before.

For more info about Doc-to-Help, from WexTech Systems, look in Chapter 8.

The Windows Character Set

The current Windows character set for the "Helv" font looks like this:

Figure A4-1: The Windows Character Set

	0	1	2	3	4	5	6	7	8	9
30				!	"	#	$	%	&	'
40	(	)	*	+	,	-	.	/	0	1
50	2	3	4	5	6	7	8	9	:	;
60	<	=	>	?	@	A	B	C	D	E
70	F	G	H	I	J	K	L	M	N	O
80	P	Q	R	S	T	U	V	W	X	Y
90	Z	[	\	]	^	_	`	a	b	c
100	d	e	f	g	h	i	j	k	l	m
110	n	o	p	q	r	s	t	u	v	w
120	x	y	z	{	|	}	~	|	|	|
130	|	|	|	|	|	|	|	|	|	|
140	|	|	|	|	|	´	´	¨	¨	°
150	–	—	|	|	|	|	|	|	|	|
160		¡	¢	£	¤	¥	¦	§	¨	©
170	ª	«	¬	-	®	¯	°	±	²	³
180	´	µ	¶	·	¸	¹	º	»	¼	½
190	¾	¿	À	Á	Â	Ã	Ä	Å	Æ	Ç
200	È	É	Ê	Ë	Ì	Í	Î	Ï	Ð	Ñ
210	Ò	Ó	Ô	Õ	Ö	×	Ø	Ù	Ú	Û
220	Ü	Ý	Þ	ß	à	á	â	ã	ä	å
230	æ	ç	è	é	ê	ë	ì	í	î	ï
240	ð	ñ	ò	ó	ô	õ	ö	÷	ø	ù
250	ú	û	ü	ý	þ	ÿ				

Character numbers are listed down the left: character number 33 is the exclamation point; character number 255 is the lowercase "y" with umlaut.

Formal definition of the Windows character set is meant to be a standard, but the actual implementation varies from time to time. This is a good working example, taken from the Windows 3.1 font distributed by Microsoft.

Note that the collating sequence—the order of characters when sorted—does *not* correspond to the character numbers given above. Different Windows apps may collate differently; consult the appropriate application's documentation for details.

Glossary

Agent—A giant **Event Handler** that handles all (or almost all) Windows events. *See* Chapter 9.

API (Application Programming Interface)—A general description of how to call subroutines: the routines' names, their parameters, what they do, what they return.

Basic—A simple, powerful programming language. Often accused of spoiling a generation's grasp of computer concepts.

Boolean—describes a variable that can be true or false.

Bitwise—Done bit-by-bit.

Bug—(1) Something that doesn't work the way it should; (2) As used in *Windows Programming for Mere Mortals:* a very subjective classification of something that appears to be odd, unexpected, or worthy of note; (3) A design feature.

By Reference—A way of passing a **Parameter** to a **Subroutine** (or **Function**) that permits the subroutine to change the value of the parameter. Contrast with **By Value**.

By Value—The other way of passing a **Parameter** to a **Subroutine** (or **Function**). When a parameter is passed By Value, the subroutine is explicitly instructed to keep its hands off your variable; when the subroutine is done, your variable will come back to you with its original value, no matter how much mangling is done in the subroutine.

C—A complex, powerful programming language. C programmers deserve your respect. Just be glad *you* don't have to learn it!

Class Name—Every window is part of a class; every class has a name. *See* Chapter 6 for a discussion of why Class Names can be important.

Client—The **DDE** application that's in charge; the one that dials the phone.

Clipboard—In Windows, when you "copy", the stuff that's copied is put on the Clipboard. When you "paste", the stuff that's pasted comes from the Clipboard. To tell the truth, Clipboard isn't a place: the stuff isn't really stored anywhere in particular. The Clipboard is more a state of mind . . . but that's another story.

Cold Link—Describes a **DDE** conversation where the **Server** doesn't warn the **Client** at all when data changes. *See* **Hot Link**, **Warm Link**.

Compress—A method for taking all the redundant stuff out of a file. Good compression techniques can reduce the size of a file by 50% or more. Compressed files, when expanded, return to their original state, without any loss of data. *See* **Self-Extracting Archive**.

CompuServe—An on-line service used widely by mere mortals. *See* Chapter 8.

Control—Something you stick on a **Form**. When you create a window, everything you put on the window is a Control.

Control Array—A group of identical **Control**s, distinguishable by their subscripts. *See* Chapter 7 for a description.

CoolCons—A way cool, fully customizable **Icon box** built from scratch in Chapter 7. The version included on the Companion Disk is designed to work with Word for Windows, but it's rather easily modified to work with any app that supports **DDE**.

Custom Control Factory—A Visual Basic add-on from Desaware. *See* Chapter 8.

DDE (Dynamic Data Exchange)—A way for Windows programs to talk to each other. The **Client** application calls a **Server** application, and establishes a **Hot**, **Warm** or **Cold Link**. Most applications' macro languages support DDE. It is the subject of Chapter 6.

Design Time—When you're writing a Visual Basic program. You know you're in Design Time when the "Microsoft Visual Basic [design]" or "Microsoft Visual Basic [run]" windows are around. Once you've compiled a Visual Basic program by turning it into an .EXE file, you're out of Design Time: that file runs as a regular program.

DLL (Dynamic Link Library)—A collection of Windows subroutines that you can get at with most Windows macro languages. Windows *itself* is a DLL, a collection of subroutines.

Doc-to-Help—A WexTech Systems product that converts Word for Windows documents into Windows Help files. *See* Chapter 8.

Event—Something that happens in (or to!) Windows. That is, a mouse click, a keyboard keypress, a timer going off.

Event-Driven—A different way of looking at programs, programming ... in fact the entire computing universe. Instead of relying on input-process-output data streams, the traditional view of computing, the Event-Driven approach concentrates on identifying what can happen and how your program should react to what happens. It's a completely different concept. No, you won't understand it by reading these four sentences; it'll take most of the book.

Event Handler—A subroutine (Visual Basic calls it a "proc") that takes care of a certain event. A Visual Basic program is primarily a bunch of event handlers.

File Troika—A term pioneered in this book; refers to one of the most common Visual Basic constructs, where a Drive List Box Control, Directory List Box Control and File List Box Control are tied together with two lines of code. The resulting Troika lets a user choose a file.

Flag—When the official Windows documents aren't sure what to call a Windows **API Parameter**, they'll just call it a "Flag". Doesn't mean anything. Don't sweat it.

Free System Resources—A measure of how much room is left in two very confined areas of Windows, expressed as a percentage from 0 to (theoretically, at least) 100. When FSR approaches zero, applications may start behaving erratically. For a complete description, *See* Fran Finnegan's article in *PC Magazine* Vol. 10, No. 19 (November 12, 1991), page 449.

Focus—Refers to the window that's "hot". If you type at the keyboard, the keystrokes are sent to the window with focus.

Form—A window that you build.

Forum—A place on **CompuServe** where interested parties can exchange ideas.

Function—A routine (or program, if you prefer) that returns a value. Compare to **Subroutine**.

Global—In most languages, this refers to something applicable everywhere. Visual Basic is a little different, though; some things that are "Global" only apply to the Global Module.

Global Module—In Visual Basic, a place for you to stick certain kinds of constants, variable declarations, **DLL** declarations and the like. Unlike real **Modules**, the Global Module does not contain **Subroutines** or **Functions**.

Götterdämmerung—If you aren't into opera or German, no, it isn't what you think. Usually translated "Twilight of the Gods", but that doesn't quite do the term justice.

Hacker—One who seeks enlightenment at the helm of a computer. A term of respect, perverted in recent years by the popular press.

Handle—A number that identifies a window, module, etc. The number doesn't really *mean* anything to most folks, but if you're curious, consult *Undocumented Windows* (Addison-Wesley, 1992).

Hot Link—Describes a **DDE** conversation in which the **Server** constantly updates the **Client**. *See* **Warm Link**, **Cold Link**.

Hungarian Notation—A naming convention for variables, called "Hungarian" in honor of Charles Simonyi (who's considered by many to be the greatest programmer of all time). Traditionally, the convention involves a prefix to variable names that describe the data type: lpString is a long pointer to a String, nIndex is an integer Index, etc. More recently, extended to include prefixes like SM_ and WF_ to tie a variable to a specific Windows API call. The convention is often honored in the breach.

Icon Box—A generic term for a collection of pictures that do something when clicked. Almost every other phrase that includes the word "icon" has been trademarked.

Insertion Point *See* **Selection**.

Item—The piece of information of interest in a **DDE** conversation. Typically, an Item is a word processor bookmark or spreadsheet cell, but Visual Basic and other Windows applications will recognize any string as an Item.

Kahuna—A Hawaiian witch doctor.

Kludge—In Windows, a way of life.

Link Execute—A **DDE** command in which the **Client** tells the **Server** to execute a program.

Link Mode *See* **Hot**, **Warm**, and **Cold Links**.

Load—The action of pulling something off disk and sticking it in memory.

Logos—So you read the section headings, huh? Logos is a Greek term, the root of the English word "Logic." "In the beginning there was Logos," Genesis 1:1.

Macro—A program. Some people think a macro is a little program, one hardly worthy of your consideration, something recorded to automate trivial repetitive steps in an application. Well, some people think Beethoven's Ninth is repetitive, too.

Macro Manager—A product coming down the pike from Microsoft that may bring the **Monster Basic From Hell** to life. *See* Chapter 10.

Make File—The packing list maintained by Visual Basic that ties together the **Forms** and **Modules** in a **Project**. Each project has exactly one Make File.

Message Box—A type of **Form** that displays information and optionally asks the user to select from Yes/No, OK/Cancel or Abort/Retry/Ignore buttons.

Method—Does something to a **Control** or **Form**. The difference between a **Property** and a **Method** is somewhat arbitrary. *See* Chapter 8 for a discussion.

Menu—In most Windows applications, the list of functions up at the top of the window that usually starts with "File" and ends with "Help".

Modal—Describes a socially maladjusted window (that is, a dialog box) that takes control of your system and won't let go until you feed it what it wants; a psychopathic, oral-retentive window. *ant:* **Modeless**

Modeless—Describes a socially responsible, polite window that lets you continue your work until you are ready to get rid of it. *ant:* **Modal**

Module—In Visual Basic, a subroutine library.

Module Name—In Windows, a name for a program, established when a C programmer links the program. Often it's the same as the ".EXE" executable file name. *See* Chapter 6 for a thorough discussion.

Monster Basic From Hell—A term pioneered in this book, the MBfH will some day link all those Windows macro languages, including Visual Basic, so you can write programs that talk to different applications in their own languages.

NORMAL.DOT—the file that contains all the "global" WordBasic macros, as well as all the other WinWord global or default settings.

Null—Character number zero, often represented by two quotes together, that is, " ". It's the same as any other character, except in languages like WordBasic that use Nulls to terminate **String**s.

Null Terminator—A character number zero used to signify the end of a **String**. Some languages, like Visual Basic, keep track of the length of strings. Other languages, like WordBasic, don't explicitly keep track of the length, but instead plant a null terminator at the end of each string. There are advantages to each approach. *See* Chapter 4 for a discussion of some of the disadvantages.

Object—In Visual Basic, an Object is a **Control**, a **Form**, the Clipboard, Debug, Printer or Screen. If you don't get it, don't worry: it's all obfuscating terminology, with very little significance. *See* Chapter 8 for a discussion of how an "Object" is in the eye of the beholder.

Object Oriented Programming—At one time this phrase had some meaning; more than anything OOP involves bundling together data and the functions that operate on the data. But then the marketing types got a hold of the term and, in common parlance anyway, it's now essentially meaningless.

OLE (Object Linking and Embedding)—The next step in the DDE Evolutionary Chain (*'tho some would say in the DDE Food Chain*). Object Linking resembles DDE: it's a means of communicating between applications. Object Embedding actually buries the result of one application inside another. For example, a user might Embed an EXCEL spreadsheet inside a Word for Windows document. The spreadsheet may look like it came from EXCEL, but it behaves (in some respects anyway) as if it were part of WinWord. By double-clicking on the spreadsheet, the user is magically propelled into EXCEL, spreadsheet ready for editing; after leaving EXCEL, the spreadsheet is magically brought back into WinWord, and starts acting like its part of WinWord again. No, OLE isn't easy: Microsoft screwed up the first implementation of WinWord as an OLE Server. And if *they* blew it, you can't be expected to do too much better.

Overflow—What happens to a computer when you try to do arithmetic that involves numbers too large to handle.

Paradigm—A way of looking at things. The shift from sequential input-process-output programming to super-sequential **Event-Driven** programming represents a significant change in paradigm. *See* Chapter 10.

Parameter—A value or variable fed to a **Subroutine** or **Function**.

Pixel—One single dot on your screen. Yeah, there are fancier definitions, but that's the easiest one. Sometimes called a "pel", for no discernible reason.

Poke—A **DDE** command in which the **Client** sends data to the **Server**. Contrast with **Request**.

PRIME—A Plan B Consulting/Lee Hudspeth & Associates product that links Word for Windows to PackRat, using **DDE**. *See* Chapter 8.

Project—A Visual Basic program. That's all. Ignore the definitions in the Visual Basic manuals.

Property—A characteristic of a **Control** or **Form**. The difference between a **Property** and a **Method** is somewhat arbitrary. *See* Chapter 8 for a discussion.

Real—A variable with a value between, roughly, - 3.4 x 10^38 and +3.4 x 10^38. In WordBasic, all variables that are not **String**s are Reals.

Record Data Type—*See* **User-Defined Types**.

Request—A **DDE** command in which the **Client** asks for data from the **Server**. Contrast with **Poke**.

SDK (Software Development Kit)—The expensive, weighty, inscrutable collection of books and software from Microsoft that tells programmers how to get in and around Windows. While a handful of items in the SDK are useful for mere mortals, the main thrust of the package is to edify C programmers. If you're wondering whether you need the SDK, you don't. By the time you really need it, you'll know it. Not to be confused with the **WordBasic SDK**, which is cheap and useful to mere mortals.

Selection—Back in the not-so-good old days, we computer jocks had a cursor, that simple little blinking thing that moved across the screen from left to right, top to bottom, following along while we typed. With the advent of mice, things got a little more complicated. The old cursor can now extend across several characters (or sentences or cells or whatever). The stuff included in that new extended cursor is called the "selection". Typically you "select" something by highlighting it with the mouse, or by typing an arcane keystroke combination. Typically, you can see the selection because it's highlighted or turned black. If the selection is empty, the cursor is called an Insertion Point.

Self-Extracting Archive—A collection of **Compress**ed files that will expand when run like a program. All of the files on the *Windows Programming for Mere Mortals* Companion Disk are self-extracting archives. Follow the instructions in

Appendix 3 to expand the files on the Companion Disk and you'll get a good first-hand workout with self-extracting archives.

SendKeys—A command in most Windows Basics that simulates keyboard entry. SendKeys "a" (or a similar command) will behave as if the user had typed an "a" at the keyboard. Usually used as a last resort, when the macro language is inadequate for the task at hand. *See also* **Kludge**.

Server—A DDE application that does the Client's bidding; the one that answers the phone.

Strange Attractor—Can't do that one justice in under twenty pages; get a copy of *Chaos* by James Gleick.

String—A variable consisting of zero or more characters. In WordBasic, the names of all String variables end in a "$" dollar sign.

Structure—*See also* **User-Defined Types**.

Subroutine—A routine (or program, if you prefer) that does not return a value. Compare to **Function**.

System Topic—A special **Topic** in a **DDE** conversation, supported by most **Servers**, that lets the **Client** see certain information above the Server (typically, files that are open and available for a DDE link). *See* Chapter 6 for a discussion of common System Topic results.

Tesseract—Really, you shouldn't take the section headings so seriously. A tesseract is a four-dimensional cube; it's often used by science fiction writers to describe time travel.

TLA—Three letter acronyms. "TLA" is a TLA.

Topic—The subject of a **DDE** conversation. In Word for Windows, Amí Pro, EXCEL, and many other Windows applications, the Topic is often the name of a file. In Visual Basic and some other Windows applications, the Topic can be anything agreeable to both **Client** and **Server**. *See also* **System Topic**.

Troika—*See* **File Troika**.

Twip—The default measurement in Visual Basic. There are 1,440 twips to the inch.

User-Defined Types—In Visual Basic, a way of structuring data and assigning a name to the created construct. Similar to C's "Structures" and Pascal's "Records". *See* Chapter 8.

VBTools—A Visual Basic add-on from MicroHelp. *See* Chapter 8.

Visual Basic—(1) the macro language that lives inside Windows; (2) the best cookie jar ever invented.

Warm Link—Describes a **DDE** connection where the **Server** warns the **Client** every time data changes. If the Client wants the new data, it has to specifically reach out and get it. *See* **Hot Link**, **Cold Link**.

Windows—A collection of **DLLs**.

WIN.INI—A file used and maintained by Windows containing all sorts of settings for applications and for Windows itself.

WOPR—The Word for Windows Office POWER Pack, the world's best-selling WinWord add-on. *See* Chapter 8.

WordBasic—The programming language the lives inside Word for Windows. A revolutionary language that was, in many respects, the first real Windows Basic.

WordBasic SDK—The software development kit for WordBasic. *See* Chapter 8. Not to be confused with the (C) Windows **SDK**.

Index

D

G

M

W

Attention 5¼" disk drive users:

The disk to accompany *Windows Programming for Mere Mortals* is also available in a 5¼" high density format. Please return the coupon below with a check for $10.00 payable to Addison-Wesley to:

Addison-Wesley Publishing Company
Order Department
1 Jacob Way
Reading, MA 01867-9984

- -

Please send me the 5¼" disk (ISBN 0-201-63245-4) to accompany *Windows Programming for Mere Mortals* by Woody Leonhard. I am enclosing a check for $10.00.

Name_____

Address _____

City _____ State _____ Zip _____

Available wherever computer books are sold

Undocumented Windows™
A Programmer's Guide to Reserved Microsoft®
Windows API Functions
Andrew Schulman and David Maxey

This comprehensive book/disk package fully details all of Windows'
over 250 reserved functions and provides a set of utilities to explore
the Windows system, including MAPWIN (examines DLLs),
EXEMAP (produces a high level picture of Windows programs and
DLLs), RESDUMP (generates a list of all resources used by a
program), WISPY (the Windows version of Intrspy), CALLFUNC
(interpreter that uses run-time dynamic linking, VxD386 (the
Generic Virtual Device Driver), W3MAP (explores the
WIN386.EXE file), and Coroner (even better than Dr. Watson).

$39.95, book/disk package with 3.5" high-density IBM disk
640 pages, 0-201-60834-0
Coming in July 1992

Extending DOS, Second Edition
A Programmer's Guide to Protected-Mode DOS
Ray Duncan, Charles Petzold, Andrew Schulman,
M. Steven Baker, Ross P. Nelson, Stephen R. Davis,
Robert Moote

"Extending DOS *is a real winner.*" —PC Magazine

The definitive work on how to break the MS-DOS 640K barrier to
create powerful and versatile applications has been revised and
updated to cover all of the newest information on extending and
enhancing DOS, from 286 and 386 extenders to such programming
environments as DOS 5.0, Windows, and DESQview.

$26.95, paperback
544 pages, 0-201-56798-9

PC Interrupts
A Programmer's Reference to BIOS, DOS,
and Third-Party Calls
Ralf Brown and Jim Kyle

Covering over 25 major APIs (such as Windows 3, NetWare, and
DESQview), dozens of resident utilities, as well as BIOS and
MS-DOS services, *PC Interrupts* is the ultimate reference every
PC programmer must have. The book gives programmers concise,
essential information on each call and, for the very first time, reveals
potential conflicts between calls from different APIs. There is no
other PC programmers sourcebook as complete and authoritative.

$32.95, paperback
1024 pages, 0-201-57797-6

Undocumented DOS
A Programmer's Guide to Reserved MS-DOS®
Functions and Data Structures
Andrew Schulman, Raymond J. Michels, Jim Kyle,
Tim Paterson, David Maxey, and Ralf Brown

"The undocumented facets of MS-DOS have now been
documented...to a depth that should satisfy the programming
community for several years to come."—PC Magazine

"An essential book for a PC programmer"
— Dr. Dobb's Journal

This comprehensive reference provides concise information on
Microsoft's 100-plus reserved DOS functions, as well as offering
advice on when and how to use them. Two accompanying disks
include a hypertext pop-up database and several powerful utilities.

$44.95, book/disk package with two 5.25" IBM high-
density disks
720 pages, 0-201-57064-5